Same Dress Different Day

A Spiritual Memoir of Addiction and Redemption

Published by

OUR WRITTEN LIVES OF HOPE, LLC

Our Written Lives of Hope provides publishing services for authors in various educational, religious, and human services organizations. For information, visit ourwrittenlives.com.

Wedding Photos and Cover Design by Sarah K Asaftei, skaMEDIA Productions & Films, Inc.
www.skaMEDIAproductions.com | www.sarahKasaftei.com

Back Cover Author Photo by Hercules Images | HerculesImages.com
Interior Design by OWL of Hope | OWLofHope.com

Library of Congress Cataloging-in-Publication Data
Van Heerden, Juliet 1970
Same Dress, Different Day
Library of Congress Control Number: 2015908383
ISBN: 978-1-942923-06-0

Same Dress, Different Day

A Spiritual Memoir of Addiction and Redemption

Juliet Van Heerden

Dedication

For My Kinsman Redeemer

You author my life.

You calm my storms.

You redeem my losses.

I love You.

"'For your Maker is your husband—
the Lord Almighty is his name—
the Holy One of Israel is your Redeemer;
he is called the God of all the earth.
The Lord will call you back
as if you were a wife deserted and distressed in spirit—
a wife who married young,
only to be rejected,' says your God."
Isaiah 54:5-6 (NIV)

Author's Note

This is my story: prayerfully pieced together from memories, photographs and journals. Some details are recollections of loved ones who walked alongside me through the valleys. The dialogue here is not recorded perfectly, but is a combination of conversations resurrected from those hazy places in one's memory where only impressions remain after pain swallows the details. Although the wording may be imprecise, the gist of my private ramblings to God remains clear. Out of respect for the privacy of individuals and institutions, some names and places have been altered.

Contents

Preface

I didn't want to write this book. I've never been one to leave my diary lying open for prying eyes. It was only when my own eyes were opened to the ache in the hearts of women all around me, whose similar stories caused me to realize that our pews are full of addiction's aftermath: that I began to entertain the thought of sharing my own journey.

Why not let others know how what God has done for you?

The thought returned in different forms, constantly reminding me of the power of personal testimony and the healing that takes place with the realization that we are not alone, but that someone understands the wordless ache in our souls. So, I began to write. I wrote for myself. I wrote for my sisters who have not yet experienced the freedom that comes from fully trusting Jesus with their addicted loved one. And I wrote to give hope to those who feel like giving up.

May the power of this story bring glory to God, and to His Son Jesus, our "Kinsman Redeemer," Amen.

Part One

Chapter 1

Cigarettes and Crayons

"Why are you cast down, O my soul?
And why are you disquieted within me?
Hope in God; For I shall yet praise Him,
The help of my countenance and my God."
Psalm 42:11 NKJV

2000

Summer scorches Texans every single year. August of 2000 is no exception. Dripping sweat, waiting for the gas pump to click off at the Chevron station, I'm even scorched on the inside. Driving Jon to rehab isn't in my plans for this summer. I very much like for life to go as planned.

Glancing into the side mirror I catch a glimpse of him, squatting there next to another car, blasting cigarette smoke from one side of his mouth. During the five years and 363 days of our marriage, he's never let me see him smoke. Our eyes meet. He shrugs and flicks the butt into the parking lot. I remember the countless times I'd lectured my students about the dangers of smoking. They are first graders; the same age he was when he started.

I'm a planner. I guess that's the teacher in me. At seven, I knew my calling. Mother says I was *born* with a wristwatch and a clipboard in hand. In third grade, I forced my five-year-old sister, Annie, to listen to me read the complete *Little House on the Prairie* series. Night after night, we'd snuggled side by side in my trundle bed along with Laura, Mary, Ma and Pa, long after Mom had called, "Lights out little girls." I often created checklists for daily hygiene habits and begged my teachers to give me extra workbook pages so that I could "play school" at home. Always a lover of order, structure, and routine, I'd planned my whole life before my age reached double digits. Today, those childhood dreams seem impossibly far away.

Just breathe, I remind myself as he opens the passenger door. *Don't say anything. Don't think anything. Just drive and breathe.* As I breathe, I smell the lingering smoke. I am angry. That smell represents betrayal. Although cigarettes aren't the reason for this trip, they are the birthplace of a long journey leading to this day. No, this trip is about another, much more costly addiction, an addiction that is foiling my plans and destroying the good little life I was making for myself.

Why do I feel so irritated about that Marlboro, when I'm taking my husband to drug rehab for a cocaine addiction so deadly it could put him in the cemetery at any moment? My own emotions confuse me! Maybe I'm in denial, unable to process Jon's addiction to a substance I've never even seen and can't wrap my brain around. Whatever the reason, I'm focused on the cigarette and ignoring the "elephant" in the car with me.

We barely speak as the miles melt beneath my tires. Part of me longs to lecture about how nicotine exacerbates the desire for other drugs, but he'd already growled the "I can only do one thing at a time" warning. As usual, my expectations are too high. I just want to fix everything *right now*. I want our life back. I want my husband back.

As we arrive at Blue Sky, the detox/rehab facility, which did not appear to match its happy summer-camp-sounding name, an unusually cheerful staff member, Mayra, greets us. I receive information regarding visiting hours, phone calls and my role in my husband's recovery process. Basically, I am to leave him alone and let him "work the program." With a thick, stapled packet on cocaine addiction in my hands and an odd mixture of hope and despair in my heart, I hug my husband, shut *little-too-happy-hab's* door and face the Texas heat. That's it. I'll see him in two weeks when I return for a supervised visit.

I'm Juliet—also known as Julie, Jules, JuJu and a number of other variations of the Italian name my mother gave me after seeing Zeffirelli's 1968 rendering of Shakespeare's famous tragedy. Sometimes I wish I could be someone else, with another name altogether, someone whose life is more comedy than tragedy. The moments I relived while writing the above paragraphs marked a major turning point in the history of this regular churchgoing girl from Texas. Life never was quite the same after that. I wanted it to be. Tried to force it to be. But it just wasn't. Ever.

Opening my car door, I tossed the addiction information to the back and wilted into the driver's seat. With the click of the seatbelt, my internal dam burst. Anger and embarrassment poured from my soul as I drove and wept. Frustration and fear mingled with those tears as I howled to my heavenly Father. It was not the first time I'd taken the term "cry out to God" literally, but it was the first time in a long time that I cried out hoping life might improve.

"It has to get better, God. Isn't marriage supposed to bring joy? It's always been tough, but this past year and a half has been horrible! I didn't know he was using drugs! How could I be so blind? How do I face the people in my life with a truth I can no longer hide and can barely comprehend?"

I dreaded explaining to my church school colleagues why I'd be attending the teacher's convention alone.

No. He won't be coming with us. I'm sorry, Principal Steve. I guess it's just you and a bunch of females again this year.

I dreaded responding to well-intentioned inquiries about my husband's absence from church.

Yes, I'll tell him you missed him again today. Unfortunately we won't be able to host the Friday evening worship at our home this week.

I feared facing his boss, who served on the school board that hired me and whose children I'd taught to read.

He pawned your tools to buy drugs? Oh, I'm so sorry. I had no idea. How can we ever pay you back?
Trepidation trampled my tiny spark of hope as my tears dissolved into deep heaves.

"How do I do this, Lord? How will Jon's sudden 28-day disappearance affect our reputation in this church and this community? What will I say to my sister? You know she's been upset lately by Jon's strange behavior. Now I understand her probing questions. Oh, how will I hold my head up and keep it all together?"

School

I stacked colorful student workbooks neatly on my u-shaped teaching table. Small desks in pods of three filled the center of the room, while student activity stations lined the outside walls. I enjoy organizing and arranging my spacious classroom. I'd taught here for four years. This space feels like home to me. In fact, I think I spend more time within these walls than I do at our home. The structure. The routines. The little people who bring joy and life to this place and to my very soul, these are the things I can count on. These are just as sure as the familiar contents of my teacher desk, or the absolute of butterflies in tummies on the first day of school.

Tearing the "to buy" checklist from my yellow legal pad, I took a quick survey of the room before flicking off the light. *Everything is coming together. I want to be ready before teachers' convention. Just one more trip to Wal-Mart, and I'll be set.*

I love buying school supplies. Love pressing a bunch of super sharp Number 2 pencils against my palm, making them all even. Love the little scissors with rounded noses and the tiny, flat tips of brand new Crayola crayons. Something about loading up my shopping cart with washable markers and orange-topped Elmer's glue bottles makes me happy.

That day, I desperately wanted to be happy. I wanted to forget about the yesterday that had altered my world forever. Longing to get lost for a moment in the "Back to School" aisle, I stopped by Wal-Mart on the way to my empty home, numbing my pain by pawing through bins of markers and pens. On my way to the register I picked up a black and white composition book; you know, the ones with rounded corners and marbled cardboard covers with a line for your name right on the front? *Why not? They're on sale for only a quarter each.*

Recently, I rediscovered my stash of journals and composition books. Sifting through them was equally painful and cathartic. The neatly dated entry that fits into this narrative reads like this: *Tomorrow is Jon's and my six-year anniversary. Yesterday I took him to a drug detox and rehabilitation program. This is an incredibly difficult time, but I am hopeful Jon will submit to the treatment and allow himself to be helped. On August third, fourth, fifth and sixth he nearly overdosed on cocaine. On the fifth he realized he could die, and by the sixth he was ready to finally admit he has a problem bigger than he can beat alone.*

I am angry. He has used more than five thousand, five hundred dollars of our house money on cocaine! That money was supposed to go toward building our new home on the land we purchased last summer. I am shocked and surprised he is not dead. I feel angry, sad, discouraged and hopeful all at the same time. School starts in one week. I'm not ready. I have much to do and so many distractions. I am praying for Jon constantly. He has become such an incredible liar—a selfish, deceiving, conniving, thieving, angry, sick person.

The house is peaceful without him. I don't have to worry about him at night or anytime because he can't be doing bad stuff in rehab. Everyone has been so kind. I am thankful to God for Christian friends. Jon's employers, Larry and James, even promised to allow Jon to come back to work when he gets out.

I'm going to have to be firm about what I want, need and expect. I don't even know all of it, except no more drug use, or he is out of the house!

I needed the familiar comfort of a checklist, so I wrote:

- *No more drug use*
- *No more smoking*
- *Daily talking and prayer time*
- *Meet my emotional, physical, financial needs*
- *Everyone made right with and paid back*
- *I get full control of every penny*
- *Honesty in all dealings*

In hindsight, the rest of that sad little journal entry breaks my heart. I can see how bad things in my marriage really were and how much I wished for everything to be okay. At that time I didn't realize I could not mandate someone who was not okay to be okay. My seven-item checklist penciled into a twenty-five cent composition book from Wal-Mart didn't mean a hill of beans to my drug-addicted husband. I should have considered and questioned his habits long before he ever *became* my husband. But we were young then. I was naive. Isn't hindsight painfully 20/20?

I'm sure I slept better that night, having written my list and said my prayers. I know that God in Heaven witnessed my hurting heart. I remember the comforting presence of His sweet Spirit during that dark and lonely time. I wish I had known then the things I've come to learn. I suspect, though, I wouldn't be the me I am, and I wouldn't know the things I know, if it weren't for the catalyst of that dreadful Texas August day, the day I drove my husband to rehab for the first time.

Chapter 2

Broken Bones, Broken Dreams

*"O Lord my God, I cried out to You,
And You healed me."*
Psalm 30:2 NKJV

1992

I loved a boy once. He was much taller than me, and six years older. He made me laugh at silly jokes and got me hooked on bird watching. He was crazy about it. His whole family had the same disease. "Birding," they called it.

They'd phone the Birder's Hotline on a Sabbath afternoon, then dash to their minivan to chase the promise of a Snowy Owl in some field two counties away. It was exhilarating to join them on the adventure of discovering that proud lone owl, sitting right where we'd imagined him—on top of a giant, snow-covered hay roll in the middle of a Missouri farmer's field. That boy taught me to deeply appreciate the handiwork of my Creator. He gave me a gift that continues to bring joy whenever I lift binoculars to my eyes.

I hurt him—that bird-loving boy. Hurt his family. Hurt myself. That's what happens when a person expects another human to fulfill their unmet needs. Hurt people hurt people. I was a wounded girl, unaware that my deepest wounds were on the inside. I only knew of the ones on the outside; let me tell you about those first.

The Fall

Falling off the roof of our neighbor's barn was completely the result of my own stubborn selfishness. Contracting the job by myself and refusing help from any of my painting crew was simply foolish. I was trying to earn extra cash for my upcoming trip to Switzerland and didn't want to split the proceeds with anyone. *Selfish girl.*

Working atop a steeply gabled galvanized metal barn roof in the heat of summer is punishing, especially for a twenty-one-year-old female. I didn't care. I was super fit. I was also a semi-experienced painter who knew how to attach giant metal S-hooks to an extension ladder and stabilize it into a barn roof peak. The plan was to paint from the right-hand side of the extended ladder, top to bottom. Then I'd climb up and move the ladder to the left, continuing until the whole roof became shiny silver, the color of my favorite crayon in the Crayola specialty box.

My first mistake was not securing the ladder, or myself, with some kind of safety device. The second mistake was ignoring my sister Annie's plea to, "Just hurry up and finish already!" She, Mom and I had plans to go out for a special dinner that night to celebrate Mother's upcoming wedding and their move to Switzerland.

I'm so close to finishing this section. They can wait a few more minutes. Let me just finish this piece and then I'll go clean up. It's gonna take time to scrub this metallic paint off my skin. I look like the Tin Man from The Wizard of Oz. It wasn't the only time I've suffered the consequences of being headstrong and task-oriented, rather than humble and people-centered, but it was definitely one of the most painful.

Sis was still walking toward our home after delivering her curt message when she heard the spine-tingling scrape of metal on metal. Those huge S-hooks had come unhinged from the rooftop! Gravity immediately grabbed that fully extended ladder. It descended the steep roof at lightning speed, shooting across the lawn like an Olympic bobsled. I was not far behind, only I did not shoot across the lawn. First, I slid the full length of that barn roof on my shins and forearms, scrambling for a toehold; then free-fell twenty-two feet, landing in a crumpled heap on the concrete slab, next to a piece of fencing that could easily have impaled me.

"You pooped your pants." Annie's dry wit unearthed a smile as she leaned over the hospital bed-rail to kiss my forehead. My morphine-thoughts were derogatory. *What a great way to start the summer. I fall off a barn and poop my pants! Why didn't I just stop working when Sis called for me to quit? Why didn't I properly secure that ladder?*

Questions plagued me as I waited for surgery. *What if my spinal column is so damaged I end up stuck with that colostomy bag the doctor was talking about? How long will it take for my pelvis to heal? Have I ruined Mom's wedding plans? What was I thinking? I'm an idiot!*

"But, thank You God, at least I'm not dead."

That experience robbed me of many things, one of them being the innocence of my relationship with Bird Boy. He raced across several states in his red Trans Am to sit with me at the hospital. His initially comforting presence became uncomfortable for both of us. Our innocent romance wasn't ready for the "ugly" that recovery from a major accident brings. I definitely wasn't cute. I wasn't nice. I wasn't happy. I wasn't *me.*

For months afterward I was miserable and depressed. Feeling like a filleted fish, I refused to look at the scarlet scar running the length of my spine. The steel rods my surgeon had inserted made bending impossible. Additionally, I wore an ugly metal brace to keep everything aligned. Mirrors became enemies.

Although I could neither dress nor bathe myself in June, I stubbornly planned to return to college in August. My doctors, adamant I avoid prolonged sitting for at least a year, cautioned against it, but I insisted on graduating with my class. That was my goal, and it got me through physical therapy and well on the road to recovery.

The bird-loving boy stuck with me throughout that year. With Mom and Annie living in Switzerland with my new stepfather, Bird Boy and his binoculars were the constants in my life.

Our relationship survived my spring surgery to remove the steel rods and his futile attempts to help me find myself again. Although my hip and back had mostly healed, my spirit had not.

Weeks after doctors removed the rods, I still suffered nausea and hot flashes of pain each time I did anything requiring physical effort. I had to break the contract for my first teaching position because I was too weak to set up the classroom. My life seemed to be going nowhere.

Miserable inside and out, I began to fixate on the idea that marriage would solve my problems and secure my insecurities. *If Bird Boy would only propose, we could be together and I wouldn't feel like this. I want to be his wife, but he's just not that in to me anymore. Am I losing him? Even though we're together every day, I feel so alone. Maybe if we were married, things would be different. I wonder why he never mentions the future?*

For the entire summer, I moped around in a funk. In retrospect, I can see how God tried to woo me in myriad ways. He provided free housing within walking distance of the peaceful summer camp where my boyfriend worked. He gave me front row seats to His heart when I participated in the camp's lively worship experiences. He surrounded me with people who sincerely tried to reach out. I ignored God's attempts and chose to slip further into despair.

My blanket of darkness was so heavy that even now I can barely paint a word picture to describe my mental state. I think Crayola would call it "tar black." I remember surveying my mangled bedding and a summer's worth of mess in the darkened room where I slept. *Mom would kill me if she saw this! Have I ever even washed these sheets?* It was out of character and embarrassing for me to live that way, but I couldn't find the energy to do anything differently, or to do anything at all.

There is *one* thing I recall accomplishing that summer. I looked in the mirror. Not the regular mirror, face forward. Instead, I gazed into a tiny mirror, held slightly to one side of my face, with the big mirror behind me. I'd pulled my hair up so I could see the full length of my spine. *"Help me, Jesus. I think I'm going to be sick."* Sweat formed on my upper lip. With trembling hands I tilted the mirror to reflect the results of those two spinal surgeries.

"Oh, thank You! It's not as bad as I expected. He really did make the second cut right into the groove of the first incision. And he sewed it up straight. Although Crayola-salmon is not my favorite color, at least it's not crooked. My nurse promised the bright color will fade with time, but I'll always have this lengthy scar. Always."

By summer's end, Bird Boy needed a break from my moodiness and I was sorely missing my family. Everyone thought a flight to Switzerland seemed like a good idea, especially since I couldn't teach that fall and had no other plans.

I stayed for a month. It was a fabulous trip. My little American sister had morphed into an Italian-speaking supermodel. She enjoyed showing me off to her handsome friends as we shared laughter and pizza *margherita* and inhaled cool autumn air off the Alps.

Mother's newlywed bliss was contagious. I adored my new stepfather, whom we'd affectionately dubbed, "Mr. P." He adored my mother. They'd just celebrated their first anniversary. I loved their love. I missed *my* love. *Why doesn't he just ask me to marry him? We've been dating for two and a half years already. What is he waiting for?*

The day before I was to fly home, Annie and I took a fast train to Venice. She navigated those narrow streets as if she'd been born there. Weaving our way through shops and cafés, we stopped every so often to purchase pretty blown-glass candies from beckoning street vendors. "Ladies, ladies! Over here!" They called in sing-song English. It was a delightful day, forever etched on my memory's list of foreign favorites, despite the fact that our return train ride became a vomiting misery after we shared some olive-filled *foccacia*, which had baked too long in a sunny window display.

Isn't life just like that? Filled with wonderful highs, followed by lows that almost cancel the memory of the blessings? It's the enemy of God, scheming behind the scenes, who is never satisfied with letting something beautiful remain beautiful, but always looking for ways to steal, kill and destroy.

Thankfully we have a Savior, whose exclusive mission was to save us, once for all, by giving His very life for humanity on a crude wooden cross. He continues to rescue us from that evil enemy in countless ways. Some we see; some we don't. Those divine interventions we *are* aware of, certainly bear repeating. The miracle of the next few paragraphs deserves a retell, because if my Savior had not intervened, I would not be alive to share my story.

Exhausted and electrolyte-depleted, Annie and I silently sneaked into the P's apartment after arriving home late from our Venetian excursion. The four of us had planned to leave for the airport at dawn. I was going "home," although I wasn't certain where that was, or what I would do with myself once I got there.

I didn't have a car. I'd given up my university apartment after graduation. My stuff was packed in storage. Summer Camp was over, so my boyfriend would be going back to his parents' home in Missouri. We'd arranged for him to pick me up at the airport, but I really didn't have a plan after that. I didn't like not having a plan.

"God, I feel pretty good after this trip," I prayed. *"Maybe I will be able to get a job somewhere when I get home. I look better, too. Maybe Bird Boy will pay more attention to me. Maybe he will ask me to marry him. Then we could make a plan together. Start a life together. Have a home. Together."*

Dawn arrived way too soon. I was packed and ready to roll. Dragging myself from beneath the cozy duvet, I went to awaken Annie. "Sis," I whispered. *Why do we whisper when we are trying to wake someone up?* She didn't move. "Sister! Wake up. We've gotta go. It's a long way to Zurich. I can't miss my flight."

"I'm not going with you." Her muffled words escaped the covers.

"Why not?" I grilled. "You said you would go with us. I want you to come. It's our last time together. I don't know when I'll see you again. Come on. Pleeeeease."

"I can't go. I don't know why. I just can't." She refused to be convinced. I couldn't understand her sudden change of mind. I was hurt. *Why won't she just come along for the ride? It will be fun. I guess I'm not as important as her beauty sleep. Maybe she has plans with that Italian boyfriend of hers. Maybe it's just too hard to say goodbye.*

Humongous. Green. Exceptionally heavy. That pretty much describes my suitcase. It would fill the hatch of Mr. P's tiny Renault. Saying goodbye to Annie left my heart as heavy as that case. I could not fathom why she felt like she couldn't go with us.

"You know how she is," Mom had said in the elevator on the way down to the car. "Once she 'gets a feeling' about something, you cannot change her mind. At least now there will be more space in the back for you to rest. You girls barely slept last night, but I'm certain Venice was worth it! That's where Mr. P and I fell in love, you know." She beamed as she spoke that last sentence. They really did love each other. It was almost sickening. *Is it possible that my own mother is happier and more in love than I am? Isn't she too old for this kind of giddy?*

Fog enveloped the Alps as a light drizzle began. Mr. P guided his tiny gray car around curve after curve while Mom read to us from her daily devotional. Thirty minutes passed before I decided to lie down on the back seat. *All the more room for me since Sis isn't here. Maybe I can even sleep a little. We have nearly three hours to drive.*

The Accident

"Aiuto! Aiuto! Aiuuuuuuto!" It was more a wail designated for the ears of God than a plea for human help. Mr. P's voice in that moment is something time has never been able to erase from my memory. His anguished cry and flailing arms caught the attention of a passing motorist. From my perspective on the damp asphalt, I could see them frantically running back and forth from the trucker's lorry to the passenger side of the now upside-down and smoking Renault. My mother was still in there. Dangling, entrapped by her seatbelt.

"Are you dead?" I asked Mom after the "motorist" had severed the seatbelt with a knife from his truck, lugged her to my side of the road, then dragged both of us a safer distance from the seriously smoking vehicle. I placed the word motorist in quotes because he literally disappeared after rescuing Mom. We neither saw, nor heard him drive away. When Mr. P turned to thank him, he was gone.

Some may argue, but I choose to believe in a Creator God who created heavenly beings who willingly serve both Him, and those for whom He died. As I write these words, I thank God for orchestrating Mom's rescue and for sending the Holy Spirit to speak to my sister's heart and warn her not to go with us. Only He knows what would have happened if we'd both been in that Renault when "Mario Andretti" decided to pass us on a curve, clipping Mr. P's back bumper and sending us into an irrecoverable spin. When I later viewed photos of the vehicle's charred and flattened remains, I wept with the thought of two sisters sitting upright in that backseat and what might have been a much more tragic ending to that day.

"No, I'm not dead. Are you?" Mom's familiar voice sounded strange. I reached out to touch her hand.

"Me neither," I whispered.

We quietly lay side by side on the asphalt, holding hands and gazing into a gray Swiss sky. Suddenly the burning Renault exploded, sending bits of debris high into the air. Together we waited for the ambulance as ashes rained down on our upturned faces.

"Ring-a-round a rosie, A pocket full of posies, Ashes! Ashes! We all fall down." The silly-kiddy-nursery-rhyme ran through my head.

"Lord Jesus! I've already fallen down. Why am I down again? Oh, God. I cannot move my lower body. What if my back is re-injured? What if it's bad? What if it's really, really bad this time? What about Mom? Her head looks bloody. Ooohh! I can't look. Is she gonna be okay, God? Are we gonna be okay? Please Jesus. Please."

Another Hospital

"You pooped your pants again." She seemed to find humor in that fact. "They handed me a bag with your dirty clothes in it when I arrived at the hospital; just what I always wanted. Thanks a lot."

"Seriously Sis? I did not!"

How humiliating. How degrading. Why didn't they just throw that stuff away? I don't remember pooping. I don't remember anything. First I'm lying in the backseat on the way to Zurich Airport, and the next thing I know I'm sprawled in the middle of the motorway with the contents of my suitcase strewn around me like a badly organized yard sale. Nope, I definitely don't remember anything in between. Maybe that's a good thing.

"Did you know Mr. P remained conscious the whole time?" Mom directed the question to both of us. "He says it was like being inside a washing machine, tumbling around, then spinning and spinning on the rooftop. It's a wonder he walked away with only a bruised knee and some minor abrasions!"

Mother and I were in the same room, on the same hospital floor where Mr. P worked as a surgical nurse. She'd suffered a crushed right elbow, broken vertebrae, a fractured skull and yet-to-be determined injuries to her brain. Thankfully, I had not re-injured my spine, but I *had* broken my pelvis. Again. This time, much more severely than the original fracture. We were both bound for a lengthy and painful recovery process.

"Lord, I know I was unsure about my plans for this year, but this was definitely not what I had in mind. What, exactly could be Your purpose for all of this? Now Bird Boy will never ask me to marry him!"

My Swiss doctor had warned me, "Don't even think about having sex for at least a year. And you'll need to wait about five years before having a baby."

"I'll be so old by then. All my friends are getting married and starting their families. Why do I feel like I keep getting pulled backward?"

For six weeks God knit me together in that shared hospital room. It was tedious. Some days Mom and I simply lay there, ignoring the Italian TV shows that marked the passing of the hours. Sometimes we talked or prayed. Mostly, we just waited.

Mom wasn't herself. Something was definitely different. She was mellow. Quiet. Hurting. Mr. P came in and out to care for her. Sometimes he was officially on duty, sometimes not. But always, he was patient and kind, massaging her back, arranging pillows, administering her medications. I could see he was hurting, too, just in a different way.

The highlight of each day was when Annie would arrive, dressed to the nines and delivering treats. When she'd lean in to hug me, her signature fragrance, Jean Paul something-or-other, lingered. She brought Swiss chocolates or fresh pistachios, postcards and flowers. Once word of our accident reached friends and family back home in America, she'd deliver their letters and cards into our eager hands. With her French perfume and her Italian adventures, Sis brought life and laughter into our static space. In those weeks, I grew to know and love her as a person, not just as my little sister.

Toward the end of our hospital stay, I received a phone call from my birder boy. "I'm coming to get you," he said. "You can stay at my parents' house and finish recovering. We'll make a plan." *Finally!* I thought. *We can make a plan. I love plans.* I began working on my checklist. By the time he arrived, I'd mentally rehearsed our entire wedding, down to the style of the bridesmaids' shoes and the way the napkins would be folded on our reception tables.

When he walked into our hospital room, I could see that Bird Boy had somehow become Bird Man. My lanky, happy boy was gone. *When did that happen? How had I not noticed?* He looked at me with sad, man-eyes, their familiar sparkle squelched.

Instantly, I felt like a burden. Anticipation melted into apathy. I hated for him to see me like this. *Poor thing, he's come all this way and I can't even hug him with this contraption sticking out of my hips!* I had what medical people call an "external fixator," which was basically a crisscrossed metal frame, screwed directly into my pelvis through four puncture wounds in my skin. It was disgusting. I jokingly called it my towel rack and hung washcloths on it for effect. When Bird Man saw it, he averted his eyes.

"That's it. I'm doomed. There goes my sex life forever. He'll never want to marry me now. I wish he hadn't even come. Wish he'd never seen me like this, or like I was in that other hospital either. I wish we could just go back to our happy times; back to the good 'ole days of Mexican food-and-birding dates. Back to the times when he'd actually wanted to be seen with me. Oh, Lord. What are we going to do now?"

What we did was wait for the doctors to give me the okay to leave the hospital soon after my surgery to remove the external fixator. They disliked both the idea of me traveling so quickly after my release, and the fact that they could not follow up with my care.

My primary physician privately cautioned me on the fragility of my pelvis before releasing me from his custody. He began with a serious lecture about the dangers and repercussions of falling, sexual activity, and childbearing. Then he handed me a pair of crutches to support my prescribed daily walking until I could safely hobble on my own.

Not wanting to suffer further pain, I heard him full well. Two serious breaks within a fifteen-month time frame were enough. I was done with trauma. *I guess it's gonna be a while before I march down that aisle. These crutches wouldn't have looked good with my dress anyway, never mind the whole honeymoon thing . . .*

My final night in the hospital, I prayed a familiar whiny prayer that went something like this: *"I don't like this, Lord, not one bit. How can so many bad things happen to one person in such a short period of time? What did I ever do to deserve this? How will I ever get my life back? Why have You allowed me to suffer like this? Don't You love me? Don't You see me?"*

With those last two questions, my throat tightened. A few tears escaped through clenched eyelids, trickling into my ears. Once they began, it was difficult to control them. My chest heaved as I fought to weep quietly, so as not to disturb my fragile mother.

Finally, I surrendered myself to a deep, healing cry. It was the first time I'd been real with God; the first time I'd dared to mourn all that had happened since my fall from the barn. That night I released a year's worth of tears that had been suppressed by medication, angry fear, and doubt.

From childhood, I'd believed God *loved* me, but there was an aching honesty in my spirit that night as I questioned whether He really *saw* me. Did He see my unexpressed sorrow, the longing to be loved, and the uncertainty about my future that served great insecurity to my very soul? Did He see the *me* that looked in the mirror and felt ugly and marred? When all I'd wanted from life was to teach, marry, and have a massive family, did He recognize the fear of childbearing my doctor's warnings planted deep into my dreams for the future?

Of course He knew. I'd written it in my diary when I was eight. *"When I grow up, I want to be a teacher. And I want to get married to a nice husband and have lots and lots of kids."* It was written in smudgy left-handed pencil print, right there for Him to see. He knew. In theory, I *knew* that He knew. What I hadn't quite grasped was how truly deep, wide and vast is the love of our heavenly Father for each individual heart on this planet, mine included. I needed a deep, personal experience with Him. I needed to stop flinging prayers in His direction and expecting answers, when I was never mentally still or quiet long enough to hear His response. I needed to let Him be God in my life, but I didn't know how.

Though I was raised in a Christian home and attended Christian schools through college, something was missing. Despite my habit of praying the same basic prayers before meals and bed, there was a huge disconnect between my "God moments" and the rest of my life, when I mostly did my own thing, messed up, and expected Him to fix it. I had, and still have, a lot to learn, but I think the tiniest mustard seeds of my faith journey with Jesus began to sprout when I chose to reveal my deepest hurts to Him that night in the hospital.

Sometimes human beings don't want to hear what they already know. God is not like that. He knows it all, but He longs for us to trust Him enough to tell Him. I believe one of the reasons He invites us to verbalize our hurts is because it also helps us to identify them for ourselves. Putting a name to something that hurts us is a first step toward healing.

That night, I named fear and doubt. Like the boy's father in Mark 9:24 (NKJV) who said, "Lord, I believe; help my unbelief," I confessed with my mouth what I *did* believe: that He saw me, and that He had a purpose for my brokenness. Then I asked Him to help that faithless, willful part of me, the part that often drove me to make poor choices and place my trust in myself or other humans, rather than in the One who truly knows my heart and promises to meet its deepest desires.

Going Home

Kissing my family goodbye was tough, especially Mother. She was discharged from the hospital, but her healing had many facets, some of which would take decades. Her fairytale life with Mr. P would take a different turn, as he became her caregiver and advocate. I'm certain there are many details I will never know. What I do know is this: they have been married for twenty-four years and he still adores my mother.

Although the P's only experienced one blissful year together, they've had more than two decades of choosing to love one another through intense physical and emotional suffering. That example of unconditional love has healed deep wounds in our family. Theirs is a story for another book. Saying goodbye to them ends this chapter in mine.

Chapter 3

Gladiolas and Goodbyes

"She weeps bitterly in the night,
Her tears are on her cheeks;
Among all her lovers
She has none to comfort her.
All her friends have dealt treacherously with her;
They have become her enemies."
Lamentations 1:2 NKJV

1994

One hundred and forty-four gladiolas! I knew my Spanish was bad, but I thought I could handle placing a simple order for twelve long-stemmed tropical flowers. Apparently not, because they delivered twelve *dozen*! Gladiolas bloomed from every bathtub and toilet bowl in the villas booked by our wedding party, a gorgeous inconvenience for bridesmaids with full bladders at midnight.

As with all weddings, there were bloopers. And like most brides, I stressed about them. I also prayed. A lot. Costa Rican weather can be tricky in August. We'd planned a simple seaside ceremony in the middle of the rainy season! Most of my prayers surrounding the big day concerned the weather. Some of them referenced the "weightier" matters of how to keep my divorced parents apart during the event and whether or not to serve champagne at the reception. When families and cultures collide, there is plenty to pray about. In the rear view mirror of my life, I can easily see where I spent much bridal energy majoring in minors while ignoring some glaring "red flags" from my fiancé.

At the time, it didn't seem like a big deal that he kept disappearing whenever things got a little stressful, or that he always seemed to be forgetting "something" in the car. He partied so hard with his groomsmen the night before our wedding, that he forgot to pick up two of our out-of-country guests from the hotel and they missed the whole event. Somehow my radar didn't register concern when the people closest to me kept asking questions like, "Are you sure you're ready for this?" I attributed my tears and uneasiness to typical bridal nerves.

"Of course I'm ready," I'd reply. "I'm a planner." *Why do they keep asking me that? After all, I've known him almost a year and a half by now. We've been engaged for eight months. I've had plenty of time to be "ready for this."*

No one needed to know I'd planned this day to a tee while lying flat on my back in a foreign hospital. Okay, so a few individuals, including the groom, had been swapped from my original lineup, but some things really are best left unsaid, at least until someone writes a memoir.

At this point, you may be wondering what happened to Bird Man and how I ended up in Costa Rica with a totally different groom. Before wading further into wedding details, maybe I should explain. It hurts me deeply to recall this part of my story, but it must be told if I'm to show how gracious and patient God is with us, even when we take our lives into our own hands for a season. Please allow me to be transparent without judgment as I account for the irresponsible behavior that completely changed the course of my life and seriously affected the lives of our families. How often we bring our loved ones along on the rollercoaster rides of our relationships, never quite realizing the significant impact our choices have on each of them.

When Bird Man and I arrived from Switzerland, he loaded my crutches into his red Firebird and drove to his parents' home in Missouri. Winter had already descended upon the Midwest, making it difficult to keep up with my prescribed daily walking. Although everything around me was frozen, I was determined my twenty-two-year-old hips would *not* freeze! I walked through miserable cold, wind, and snow. When I wasn't walking, I was waiting: waiting for healing to take place, waiting for my boyfriend to propose. Although his parents were gracious, it wasn't long before we both grew restless in Missouri.

After several weeks, my bird-loving boyfriend came across an advertisement in *Birder's World* that brought an excited sparkle into his eyes as he told me about it. "Apparently," he said, "there is an American family, the Millers, operating two nature lodges in Costa Rica. They need a full-time birding guide for their guests."

Oh boy! Here comes reality. He's going to leave me here with his parents and go birding in Costa Rica. I know that look. It's the look he gets whenever he pages through his foreign field guides. It's a yearning expression he reserves for birds. I wish I had wings. I wish he'd look at me with that same longing.

It didn't take long for him to contact that family, convince them of his expertise as a guide, he really was a phenomenal birder, and purchase his plane ticket. Within days, he was gone. Just like that.

I was crushed. Did I reveal my disappointment? I can't remember, but on the inside I was not a happy girl. *"What am I supposed to do while he's off chasing his birding dreams? I feel awkward left here with his parents. Although they have been good to me, I need to get out of here. Something isn't right, Lord. Where are You? Where do I go now?"*

Soon afterward, I received an enthusiastic international phone call. "Guess what?" It was Bird Man, his usually calm voice animated. "Mr. Miller says you can stay here in exchange for helping in their nature lodge. Costa Rica is warm in December because it's the dry season. You can walk in sunshine every day. You will get better! What do you say?"

I said, "Yes." It wasn't exactly the proposal I'd had in mind, but it would do. I wonder what God would have said if I'd taken the time to sincerely inquire of Him and to wait for a reply? *Costa Rica! Yay! Sunshine! And my boyfriend! I need some binoculars. How will I afford a plane ticket? I don't know how to speak Spanish. What will Mom say? How soon can I go?* My mind raced. My heart pounded. My happy came back.

He met me at the airport. *Wow! Is that smile for me? His arms are so tanned. I've missed him.*

"See Lord, this was a good plan, wasn't it? If I can get well here, maybe he will love me like before. Thank You for healing me this much. Thank You that I didn't have to bring those ugly crutches. Thank You for the sunshine. This must be Your plan. It feels so good to be here and I only just got here."

Honestly, I don't know if the Lord's original plan was for me to go to Costa Rica or not. I believe God's intentions for each life are beautifully expressed in Jeremiah 29:11 (NIV): "For I know the plans I have for you," declares the Lord, "plans to prosper you and not to harm you, plans to give you hope and a future." I know He had a perfect plan for my life, but I inclined to do my own thing based on my feelings. I wasn't seeking godly counsel. I wasn't prayerfully soliciting God's will for my life. I assumed His will. I didn't seek Him with all my heart. I sought what made my heart *feel* happy. Feelings, as I would soon discover, can be very, very dangerous.

Costa Rica was intoxicating after Missouri's winter weather. Twelve hours of bone-warming sunshine every day! Lush green rainforests with walking trails that began just outside my window. Gorgeous iridescent hummingbirds greeting me like friendly good-morning faeries. I was enchanted with the beauty of my surroundings.

The people I'd be working for seemed nice enough. I only met one of them initially. He owned everything and didn't mind letting me know that. When Mr. Miller shook my hand, he crushed my knuckles. Hard. Secretly, I nicknamed him Dundee, because of his black hat with crocodile teeth on the band and the short machete strapped to his belt.

Dundee's smile was broad as he welcomed me into his family of employees with bold gestures and a generous offer. In exchange for room and board, I would help with early morning lunch-packing, shopping at the local market and making any non-birding visitors feel comfortable.

Bird Man and I initially enjoyed one another's company. He was in his absolute element as a guide. I had never seen him so alive as when he was excitedly pointing out some rare species to an avid guest.

Birders can be excessively driven souls. Some will travel across continents just to add a new bird to their "life list." They are also thoroughly competitive, so they usually vied for the guide's attention and expertise on the trails. Whenever I got to tag along, I ended up at the back of the pack, because *I* was not paying for his services. They were.

Most of the time, I didn't mind because I'd gotten quite good with my eighty dollar pawnshop binoculars. Often the experts would point out a particular species and I honed in on it from the back of the group. Sometimes I even got to see something the others had missed because they'd unknowingly rustled it up from the underbrush. I quickly examined the illustrations in my Stiles and Skutch field guide, seeking a match. What a rush! It was like a memory game on steroids.

My own life list lengthened daily. I was falling in love with birding! At the same time, I became intensely jealous of it because the whole lifestyle was consuming my boyfriend. I felt like he had a mistress. Her name was "Birding."

We barely communicated about anything else. From before dawn until late in the evenings, he'd either be birding from the balcony, birding on the trails, or going over the day's list of sightings with our eager guests. Sometimes, I was right there, participating in the excited buzz. Often, though, I had other responsibilities and I'd spend the day outside that circle of excitement. I began to feel disconnected from my boyfriend. Despite how I felt, I witnessed God's incredible handiwork in the bird world, each one a delicate work of art, a tiny reflection of its Creator. To this day, I have a deepened appreciation for *Him* because of those birds.

Have you ever felt "set up?" I mean have you ever looked back upon a grave wrong turn you made along life's journey and noticed the pieces were all in place for a major fall into the ditch? It has happened to me on more than one life-altering occasion. When I'm in close communion with God and spending quality time in His Word, I've often been able to recognize the setup and take appropriate action in order to avoid the ditch detour. Other times, I've been caught off guard and made one poor decision after another until I've ended up deep in a pit, wondering what happened. What occurred next falls into that second category. It's a prime example of the poor choices people make when we are emotionally or physically needy, vulnerable or disconnected from godly accountability.

Not long after my arrival in Costa Rica, Dundee introduced Bird Man and me to his son Jon. *Oh, he's kind of cute. Nice eyes. Too bad he smokes. That's unusual for a birder.* He'd come to help his parents with the business and to, "get his life together" after a divorce. *I wonder what happened to his marriage? He can't be much older than me, but that smoking has already etched deep lines along his mouth.*

Having another American around was fun. The three of us quickly became friends. *At least I have someone else to talk to when Bird Man is busy.* We often hung out together between tour groups, or after everyone else had settled down for the night.

While I'd love to tell you that nothing but a healthy friendship developed between Dundee's son and me, that would not be honest. I'm revealing the truth because there's healing in the telling. Secrets are some of the best weapons of the enemy of God. Since God can only heal what we allow Him to bring into the light, the enemy wraps our secrets in shame and convinces us to stuff them into the darkest closets of our souls.

My prayer is that my unveiled shame may be the key that frees some other soul from the bondage of flirting with the danger of forbidden fruit. I say bondage because flirting is the first link in a short chain that binds two hearts. Hearts once bound are tough to untangle. I believe that's why the Bible says, "guard your heart" (Proverbs 4:23 NIV). Our Father in Heaven longs to protect us from the pain of an unguarded heart.

It took a few weeks, but I began to trust the new guy. I also began to lose confidence in *my* guy. It had nothing to do with other girls. It was more of a distrust of his ability to see my heart and protect it. I feel silly for saying it, but I was jealous of birds!

Maybe you know what I'm talking about. It may not be birds that make you green with envy for the devotion your man gives to them, but it's something. It could be semi-innocent stuff like gaming, golf, or cars, or more costly addictions like gambling or pornography. If you've ever felt like you played second fiddle to *something*, you know how I was feeling. Now, I'm not implying that we shouldn't have passions and interests outside of our intimate relationships. What I am saying is that a partner will sense when something is out of balance. Sometimes we simply need reassurance that we're still at the top of their list.

I certainly did not feel like top-of-the-list material. I felt invisible. Although we were a couple, my boyfriend didn't appear to treat me any differently from other guests. Wanting to appear professional at all times, he did not like public displays of affection. So I just blended in with the crowd. More often than not, it was Jon who chatted with me, brought me a drink, held open a door or anticipated a need.

My heart was becoming hardened toward Bird Man. Hearts will do that in order to protect themselves. Like newborn baby feet, they start out tender and soft, but can eventually end up so calloused even a professional pedicure won't budge them. Unfortunately, it can take years, decades even, to soften a callused heart. By then, it's often too late for the relationship. Sometimes this even happens between us and God, but let's save that for another chapter.

One March afternoon, I became furious with Bird Man. It was a "last straw" kind of day. Here's my version. Picture a tall twenty-three-year-old girl, me, with a dark blonde French braid, dressed in skinny jeans and a striped T-shirt. I was feeling proud of myself for completing a lengthy and difficult hike with a group of foreign birders. Although the afternoon was early, we were all exhausted.

Jon and I packed everyone's lunches early that morning while Bird Man kept a group of guests busy on the balcony. Crack-of-dawn birding from the lodge's balcony was always fast and furious as dozens of species flocked to the fresh fruit and rice Bird Man had scattered on strategically placed feeders. After breakfast, we loaded our day packs into the lodge's two identical Toyota 4Runners and four-wheeled off the property. We spent a gorgeous morning birding the Rio Tuis valley.

The trail became quite narrow at times, forcing us into a single-file line. I brought up the rear, as usual. There was a particular older guest who continually lagged behind the group to chat with me in broken English. He was a giant redheaded German with thousands of birds on his life list. I'll call him Hans. For nearly a week Hans had closely followed Bird Man's every move, snatching up "lifers" left and right. A lifer is the name given to a bird when a birder positively identifies it in the wild for the first time. If a serious, red-bearded German birder could ever be giddy, it was Hans. After several days of Bird Man's expert guiding, Hans was soaring! Today was his final day with us. For some reason, he seemed to want to spend it with me, at the back of the pack of birders.

I was okay with that until the last leg of our downhill hike that afternoon, when we finally reached a footbridge that crossed the river near to where our 4Runners waited. Everyone had picked up speed, like horses heading back to the barn at the end of a working day, leaving Hans and me to cross the bridge alone. I could see Jon and Bird Man talking together ahead of the group.

Hans abruptly stood still and said, "Stop. I want to speak with you." I was caught off guard, but I stopped. He looked nervous. The next thing I know, Hans was proposing to me! Yes. PROPOSING. As in marriage. I cannot remember the exact wording. Something about a promise that I would never need to work. That I'd be supported. That we could go birding around the world together. Then he looked me square in the eyes and said, "If you will be my wife, I will take care of you. You will have a fantastic life." I was outraged.

Poor Hans. I was not angry at him. I'm sure he was a very nice man. I hope he eventually found a wife, nearer his own age, and that they are birding the world happily ever after. At that moment, though, I could feel my face turning scarlet as my ears began to burn. .

I do not recall what I said to Hans, but I do know what I said to Bird Man. It began with, "If a guest can spend an entire week with us oblivious to the fact that I am your girlfriend, then something is seriously wrong with our relationship!" And ended with, "How could you?" Sandwiched between those statements were some enlightening insights, including the fact that Hans had actually asked Bird Man if he could propose to me!

The supper table conversation was strangely subdued that evening. Maybe the other guests didn't notice that the air between Bird Man, Hans and myself was thick enough to slice into wedges, but Jon certainly did.

We talked about it afterward, Jon and I. I confessed that I felt betrayed by my boyfriend, and utterly vulnerable. "I've waited three years for a proposal from him, and he gives it away!" I howled. Jon agreed it was a terribly awkward thing to have happened, adamant that if it were *his* girlfriend, he'd never have allowed her to be put in that position. Those were just the words I needed to hear.

Isn't third-party sympathy such a soothing thing? I won't undermine the value of sympathy, but when the sympathizer is of the opposite sex and it's not your father, brother, or caring uncle, beware! The enemy uses situations like this to sow seeds of seduction among unsuspecting victims. Often the guilty parties in extramarital affairs will reflect upon the experience afterward and say things like, "I don't know why this happened. I wasn't looking to be unfaithful. We were just sort of crying on one another's shoulders. We never intended for it to ruin our marriages."

Wounded people of the opposite sex cannot "just be friends" without someone's *hunger* getting in the way. I experienced that piece of wisdom firsthand at twenty-three years old. It haunted me for the next fourteen years.

Shortly after the proposal incident, Bird Man decided to meet his father in Ecuador. "I will only be gone for three weeks," he explained. "Dad really needs me to guide with him on this trip. You know Ecuador is one of my absolute favorite places to bird." *Of course, I know. I also know that I wasn't invited to go with you. Thanks.* Anger underscored my silent sarcasm.

In all fairness, neither of us had the cash for another plane ticket. I still had the other half of the round trip ticket that brought me to Costa Rica. I needed it to go home, wherever that was, which I was secretly planning to do, just as quickly as I could.

April arrived while Bird Man was away. For teachers, April is hiring time. I finally felt ready to begin my career. All that hiking had done wonders for my physical health. Now I wanted to teach. Since my future with Bird Man appeared quite unpromising, I made arrangements to leave Costa Rica. The earliest flight I could get was a few days after he would return from Ecuador.

Jon was not thrilled with my plans to leave. He and I had become quite chummy in Bird Man's absence, spending our downtime discussing life and sharing our stories. Although we were both raised as Christians, our denominations and backgrounds differed significantly.

I came from an ultra-conservative, Jesus-loving, Sabbath-observing, vegetarian household and had little experience with worldly vices, apart from a few rebellious drinks in college and a short-lived smoking spree. I often felt cursed by my overactive conscience, which would never allow me to fully enjoy anything deemed blatantly "sinful."

These days I realize my conscience is the Holy Spirit's gentle whisper, "Danger ahead. Caution. Slow down. Pray." Now I am learning to listen and obey. Back then I was in the habit of ignoring or resenting the Spirit's soft prompts.

Jon's history included the fact that he was a twin, adopted at three days old along with his minutes-older brother, Roman, by Dundee and his wife. As a teenager, he had suffered a terrible car accident, which had badly smushed his face. We sympathized with one another on the common ground of long-term rehabilitation and permanent scarring.

One warm evening as we lounged on the balcony, Jon confided that his young wife had filed for divorce less than a year after their marriage. Without elaborating, he said, "One day she just decided to go home to her mother. I let her go."

He also volunteered that he had smoked for as long as he could remember. I recall casually telling him that smoking was a disgusting habit and that I would never marry a smoker. Hindsight observation: some words don't taste very good when you have to eat them.

On a guest-free morning, Jon and I took a quick trip into town to pick up some supplies. It was the first time we'd gone anywhere alone together. If I'd had proper boundaries in place at that time in my life, it would never have happened. After we completed our errands, Jon held the passenger door for me as I climbed into the 4Runner. Flashing a smile, he jumped behind the wheel.

Instead of driving toward the lodge, Jon turned off on a familiar side road near the river, suggesting a quick stop to see if we could spot a resident Sunbittern. I quickly agreed. Sunbitterns are elegant, elusive waders. Birders with time on their hands should never pass up an opportunity to document an uncommon sighting. *Great idea! I'm glad I've learned to never go anywhere without my binoculars. Bird Man would be proud!*

After several minutes of carefully scanning the water's edge, we gave up, disappointed. It was the wrong time of day for much bird activity, but usually we could spot *something* around the water. "Guess not today," sighed Jon as we slammed our doors in unison.

"Yeah, bummer. Maybe next . . ." His lips stopped my words as they pressed against mine. *Uh-oh. This is not good. This is not a good thing at all. What do I do? To kiss or not to kiss, that is the question . . .* We kissed. And kissed again.

Kissing complicates things. Girls in strange countries should not kiss boys they really don't know, especially when they have a boyfriend they haven't broken up with yet. Women in familiar workplaces should not kiss co-workers. Husbands should never kiss any woman to whom they are not married. Teenagers should pretty much avoid kissing altogether because they don't know what they are getting in to when they open those avenues. I can easily say all that now, twenty years later. Back then, I wasn't sure what to say. I was on dangerous ground.

Back in my room, I began to fret and pray. *"Oh, dear God. What was I thinking? What will I say to Bird Man? I just want to go home now. This is way too complicated. Jon really likes me. I don't know what I feel. I'm still angry with Bird Man. I am so over waiting on him. He doesn't really want to marry me. The whole Hans incident totally proved that! I'm wasting my time with him. I'm breaking up with him as soon as he gets back here. I* (choking back tears) *am* (sob) *going* (sob) *hooooome* (wail)*!"*

It was a mess. Bird Man returned from his trip with gifts and a smile. He'd had time to think, a heart-to-heart with his father, and a revelation of our future together. He'd decided that he really did love me after all and that we should talk about marriage. I would have none of it. Sometimes a girl takes a long time to be "done," but when she's done, she's done. Boy, was I DONE! A door that had been slowly closing inside of me had slammed shut with Jon's kiss. I was never going to be Bird Man's wife. No matter what he said or did, I was done betting on that dream.

Needing to get away, I asked Dundee if I could go stay at his coastal lodge until the day of my departure. He agreed and I left immediately for the other side of the country. Jon drove. On the way, he asked me where I'd be going in the U.S.A. I told him I'd be staying at my father's empty apartment in Tulsa, Oklahoma.

"My father and I don't communicate regularly. Not since I was five, when my parents divorced," I told him. "But when I decided to leave here, I contacted him and he's offered me his place until I find a teaching job."

Jon asked, "How would you like it if I came to visit you there? I'm also planning to move back to the States. I'll be staying near Dallas with one of my sisters. That's not too far from Tulsa."

"Okay," I agreed. I felt flattered. And guilty. My emotions were jumbled. On one hand, I was feeling low and confused about having said a permanent goodbye to a very bewildered Bird Man. On the other, my heart was doing fluttery things inside my chest whenever Jon flattered me. I could not hear anything from God. I had no one near enough to confide in.

One thing I have learned in the years since that confusing time is how practical God is when He reminds us that there is safety in a multitude of counselors (Proverbs 24:6 NKJV). When our senses are ambushed and our reserves low, those who know us well and desire our eternal good can help guide us out of the fog. One of life's greatest blessings is being accountable to someone who has witnessed the trend of our lives over time and will lovingly warn us when our choices are not reflective of who we really are.

I know all of that now, because I have been incredibly blessed by the influence and mentorship of godly men and women through the years. Back then I was a little too reserved, a little too tight-lipped and a *lot* isolated. I had put all of my eggs in one birder's basket and had no one else consistently speaking into my life. So when that basket tipped over, I did not have good council telling me what to do with the broken shells. I just began putting them in someone else's basket.

Bird Man was hospitalized a couple of days before I was scheduled to leave Costa Rica. Dundee broke the news. "Apparently he has been experiencing some abdominal pain," he announced from beneath the brim of his black hat. "He was on the trail with a group when the pain became excruciating. He had to be taken to the hospital in San Jose." I could tell he was watching me for a reaction. By this time he knew of his son's interest in me. I didn't know what to say.

This is awful! And awkward. I can't believe it! Poor thing. I know how it feels to be in a foreign hospital. I can guarantee that the hospitals in Switzerland are definitely less scary than the one in San Jose! What should I do? He stood by me when I was in the hospital.

"Lord, please give me some wisdom here."

I was conflicted. Bird Man had seen me through three hospital stays and my subsequent recoveries. Now he was the one hurting and I was leaving him. Alone. In a foreign country. I didn't feel great about that. I wanted to see him, wanted to know that he was going to be okay. My self-protective hardness toward him had disappeared with the news of his burst appendix, but my flight was already booked. In two days, I'd be gone. What would *you* have done?

I have to go and see him. I know it's going to be uncomfortable, especially since Jon is my only ride. But he's a friend too. Sort of. Does a real friend kiss his friend's girl? Never mind that. We're going. It's the only right thing to do.

The large, un-air-conditioned room was far from private. Thin white curtains separated the beds of a dozen or more patients who lay waiting. Bird Man was one of them. He was leaner than usual. In fact, the word gaunt would aptly describe his appearance—gaunt, green and happy to see me. I felt awful. My gut was a mixed tonic of guilt, sorrow and relief. Just hearing his familiar voice say, "I'm gonna be okay," brought a bit of comfort. Jon and I stood awkwardly at his bedside, casually chatting for ten or so minutes before saying goodbye. Jon held my hand in the parking lot on the way to the car.

The only other time I have felt like such a betrayer was when, as a fourth grader, I'd been part of a group of playground bullies making fun of a girl who chose to spend recess reading a book about Jesus. I loved Jesus. I don't know why I chose to deny Him that day. Deep down, I loved Bird Man too. I'm not sure why I abandoned him there, but I'd already chosen my path and was too proud and too enamored with Jon, to go back. So I walked away. I just said good-bye and walked away. It would be eighteen years before I again saw Bird Man's smile.

Chapter 4

Of Lace and Lies

"For nothing is secret that will not be revealed,
nor anything hidden that will not be known and come to light."
Luke 8:17 NKJV

1994–1995

Jon Miller gave me a diamond for Christmas. Soon after our engagement, I flew to Europe to share my delight with my mother, and to shop for lace with her in Italy. Although she still was not emotionally "herself," and her physical scars were permanent, she was more the mother I'd known before the accident than the person I'd said good-bye to when we were discharged from the hospital all those months before. From an American bridal magazine, I had chosen a gorgeous wedding dress by an Italian designer, knowing it was far beyond the reach of my budget. When I described it to Mom during a phone conversation, she excitedly spoke of a quaint Italian fabric shop she discovered, which sold real lace by the bolt. Since the mother of one of my students was a gifted seamstress, I could purchase my plane ticket *and* enough Italian lace to have my dream dress handmade for significantly less than the original cost of the designer version.

If I close my eyes for a moment, I can perfectly envision that narrow little shop. For at least a century, seamstresses had worn a pale path into dark wooden floorboards from the front door to the lengthy old-world counter, where bolts of fabric formed a colorful collage waiting to return to their proper pigeonholes along the back wall. A tiny, dark-haired woman greeted us as we stepped back in time. I'll call her Mrs. Italy.

"May I help you?" Her first question was fielded by our guide and translator, Mr. P. He explained the reason for our visit as I unfolded my bridal magazine page and smoothed it onto the countertop. After inspecting the exquisite lace bodice in the picture, Mrs. Italy nodded as her expression softened. I held my breath as her fingers searched the pigeonholes for a match. Pulling an ancient stepladder from behind the counter, she climbed toward a higher shelf and pulled down a bolt of lace that nearly weighed as much as she did. As she unrolled the bolt onto the counter, I fell in love! It was a *perfect* match. Elegant soft white flowers formed the intricate familiar pattern from my magazine dream. Not too modern, but not granny-ish either, just classy and timeless. I ran my fingers gently over one of the flowers as Mrs. Italy's heavy, black-handled scissors separated *my* lace from the rest of the bolt. Mother and I giddily hugged one another, as if we'd just discovered hidden treasure. We thanked the Lord for giving me this small desire of my heart. I viewed it as a sign that God was smiling on my plans.

I still wonder at the small miracles He performed in order for me to have the wedding of my dreams. I've never quite understood why He appeared to bless the mess I was about to make of my life. But, I have learned He loves our hearts, and He truly wants to give us the good things we long for, even if they seem as insignificant as a floral lace pattern that can only be found in an obscure shop on the other side of the world.

By the time my husband-to-be and I stood barefoot on our stretch of sunny beach, with Pacific Ocean waves creating picturesque whitecaps behind us, I felt ready to tie the proverbial knot. *"Thank You, Lord, for giving us perfect weather. Thank You for my gorgeous dress. I feel like a princess in this dress! I absolutely love it. I love You. Please help everything to be okay with our wedding, and with our marriage. I am a little nervous. But Jon did say that he wanted to have a godly wife and a Christian home. I think we really do want the same things."*

One hundred and forty-four colorful gladiola stems were carefully woven into the archway we'd walked beneath on our way down the makeshift aisle. Four barefoot groomsmen stood handsomely in long black shorts and silk shirts. My California-blonde groom made a striking contrast in a white linen suit. Two of his sisters, my sister Annie, and a pair of my longtime girlfriends, stood beside me, elegant in the sleek black dresses we'd ordered from the Victoria's Secret catalogue. Cookie and Vicki, my soon-to-be-nieces wore white dresses and shy smiles as they helped arrange my train. The whole scene was stunning, exactly as I'd imagined.

We'd written our own vows. They were detailed and lengthy. Watching the video years later, I marveled at how our siblings and friends remained still in the tropical sunshine for so long! Annie dabbed her forehead with the back of her hand a few times, but the rest of them stood like smiling statues for the whole ceremony. Only when I fast-forwarded, could I see everyone wiping perspiration and rocking back and forth as they shifted their weight from one bare foot to the other. Sometimes life is like that; real time observers view our sleek facades and think everything is so perfect, when in reality we are sweating bullets and slowly rocking on crumbling foundations.

Finally, we reached the traditionally worded oaths and I repeated these soul-binding words: "I, Juliet, take you Jon, to be my husband, to have and to hold from this day forward, for better or for worse, for richer, for poorer, in sickness and in health, to love and to cherish; from this day forward until death do us part." With his spoken promise mirroring mine, he lifted my veil and "kissed the bride." Everyone cheered. The groomsmen whistled. I blushed scarlet. Then we walked arm-in-arm back underneath that gladiola arch to the waiting hugs and kisses of our guests.

Those were magical moments. Our hired photographer captured them on film and printed them out on matte paper. For the next twelve years, my favorite photograph from that day stood framed on our dresser: a beaming bride and her blue-eyed groom, hand-in-hand beneath a colorful archway with sky marrying ocean on the horizon behind them. We were married for exactly three days when reality burst my bridal bubble.

Our honeymoon began in a quiet bed and breakfast. That first night, we sat head-to-head on the bed, watching the video of our wedding through my camcorder's mini viewfinder. I remember us howling with laughter each time the minister repeated the word "holy" as "holly" throughout the ceremony, and as the half-intoxicated marimba band played the same three notes over and over for every song.

Afterward, Jon wanted to take a walk outside, alone. I felt confused because I was ready to celebrate our first night together. Wanting to do things "right" in God's eyes, we had refrained from sexual intimacy for sixteen months since that first stolen kiss. I was proud of us for waiting, but I didn't want to wait any longer. By the time he returned, his exhausted bride was almost asleep.

Over the next couple of days, I thought we were having a wonderful time and didn't pay much attention when Jon regularly disappeared for a few minutes. Knowing he was an introvert and a bit of a loner, I was used to him "taking breaks from people." Since I was the only person around and we *were* on our honeymoon, I might have wondered why he needed so many breaks, but I didn't.

Even though we had dated for over a year, because we lived in different cities, we spent more time apart than together. Shortly after proposing, Jon returned to Costa Rica while I finished my school year in Texas. Communication between us was sparse. Phone service at the nature lodge where he worked was nonexistent. It didn't bother me much. I was extremely busy as a first-year teacher in a multi-age classroom, and I was *finally* getting married! *Thank You, Lord!* Teaching and planning our wedding kept me so busy I hardly had time to miss my fiancé.

They say, "What you don't know can't hurt you." That's a lie. Honestly, I only knew what Jon wanted me to know about him. He left many secrets unspoken. In hindsight, we simply had not spent sufficient face time to make thoroughly informed decisions regarding our compatibility as life partners. Quality time together puts major pressure on facades and good intentions.

Initially, I think Jon *did* have good intentions. He saw a girl who had many qualities he desired. He believed in marriage. He believed in God. Wanting to please his new girlfriend, he adapted to her way of life when he was in her presence. He even switched denominations and learned to wear a necktie to her conservative little church. Unfortunately, good intentions do not make good marriages. Honesty does.

I had believed Jon wholeheartedly when, months before our engagement he promised me he had given up cigarettes completely. I had no idea how naive it was for me to think that a twenty-year habit could simply be "given up" because one's girlfriend was so opposed to it she would never consider marriage. Loved ones are not God. He is the only one who can change a person's habits. As sinful beings, we must never expect that any person will be able to cease doing something that has habitually made him or her feel good just because we come into his or her life making demands. I learned *that* lesson on my honeymoon, thirty-six hours too late.

Most of us long to believe the best about those we love. That longing can blind us. The allure of romance can cloud some harsh realities lurking behind candlelit dinners and moon-kissed walks on the beach. The fact that our potential mate is "doing the right thing" in one area, doesn't guarantee that he or she is being completely honest in all areas. Before we take those life-altering wedding vows, we need to do our homework. As painful as it is to discover a "deal breaker" habit or character flaw in the person with whom you had planned to spend the rest of your life, *that* pain is minuscule compared to the heartache that happens when, years down the road, an entire family is devastated by divorce.

As a teacher, I was getting used to being on the *giving* end of homework, not the *doing* end, but I sure wish someone had given *me* an assignment or two while Jon and I were still dating. Before accepting an engagement ring, I wish I had at least asked basic questions about prior drug, tobacco and alcohol use. If I knew then what I know now, I would have grilled him about his previous marriage and why it failed. I'd also have questioned the absence of healthy male friendships and longstanding commitments.

I now know to advise a girl to speak with her potential mate's friends and family about his childhood and teen years. It may feel uncomfortable to ask him personal questions about pornography use, previous sexual partners or the possibility of sexually transmitted diseases, but it is vital. We think we are respecting someone's privacy by avoiding awkward conversations. In reality, we are providing a bigger favor by giving them an opportunity to be transparent and honest with someone who cares enough to ask.

If they start using smokescreens and diversion tactics in an attempt to avoid these kinds of conversations, beware. Proceed with extreme caution. How I ache for you to grasp the weight of my words in this paragraph. We all deserve to know what we are getting when we commit to someone for life. Don't *you* deserve that? I didn't know my rights. I cheated *myself* by not doing my homework.

Well aware of my own imperfections, I knew I had issues with abandonment because of the way things had played out with most men in my life. I carried a load of guilt for how I had treated Bird Man. My default for dealing with conflict was to internalize my feelings, pretending everything was fine, until I'd eventually implode or explode in some kind of a tantrum. There definitely were areas I needed to address and allow God to grow me through.

I understand that every human being on this planet has *something* that needs the healing touch of The Savior. I also know that not everyone is aware of or interested in dealing with their own "stuff." Some people choose to hide it on purpose. Those are the ones who are really risky. Before covenanting to another flawed human being, it's important to prayerfully seek healing for our self, and to observe that they, too, desire and seek wholeness. Otherwise, essential ingredients will be missing from the recipe for a happy marriage. Without these ingredients, your marriage, like mine, could turn into a nightmare.

After spending a couple of days alone, we decided to meet up with some of our family members who were sightseeing near Arenal, one of Central America's active volcanoes. My father, who had flown to Costa Rica to walk me down the aisle, was now cruising the country in his rental car.

Wanting to spend time with him and some of Jon's siblings before they left for the States, we all planned to spend a day together, picnicking and swimming in the volcano's natural hot springs.

Everything was dandy until I caught Jon smoking. I remember the moment distinctly. He was hanging out in the water with several members of his family, laughing and having a great time. I'd gone to check the spa prices at a nearby resort. The prices were exorbitant, so I hadn't lingered. My speedy return caught him off guard. As the group became aware of my approach, they grew strangely silent. Jon's movements were both subtle and lightning quick as he removed a lit cigarette from his lips and snuffed it underwater. My heart exploded in my chest as my brain processed what I'd just witnessed. Not knowing how to react, I did nothing. I said nothing. As the conversations resumed around me, I questioned whether I'd really seen what I'd just seen. Easing into the water, I eyed Jon as he continued talking as if nothing unusual had happened. My eyes searched the faces of my new family, looking for a clue that I was not crazy.

What I realized in that moment was this: when you marry into a family, you marry that family. They *will* stick together. You must earn the right to be trusted with their secrets. If some of their secrets are that they know things about your spouse that you will only learn in time, you must earn the right to hold a conversation about those things. I had earned no rights in this family yet. I was still an outsider, even though I legally carried their last name. It would be years before one of the sisters would speak to me about that day, years punctuated with similar subtle betrayals, embarrassments, and disappointments.

My heart was broken; the faith I placed in Jon shattered. I had accidentally glimpsed the other side of his double life. He unwittingly showed me he was bluffing. Everyone knew it except for me. I was a fool.

"*Oh God,*" I cried later, "*How could I have been so gullible, to have believed him when he said he quit? Why didn't I notice the signs? Now I understand why he avoids spontaneous kissing, why he goes for so many walks, why he's anxious and irritable on long car rides. Why didn't anyone tell me? What else is he hiding? Why did You let me marry a deceiver?*" I felt duped.

As we ate dinner with my father later that evening, I remember pretending that everything was newlywed wonderful. It wasn't. I imagined pouring my heart out to my dad and begging him to take me home. If we'd had a deeper relationship, I might have, but pride and reserve would not allow me to speak a word of my disappointment, not even to the disappointer himself.

It was early in our marriage when we began pretending in order to avoid potential conflict. As the years unraveled, those patterns of relating enmeshed themselves into the very fabric of our lives. We set ourselves up for failure, right from day three.

From my vantage point today, I better understand why I was so devastated by that honeymoon revelation. Some of you may be perplexed by my response and dub me a "drama queen." After all, it was only a cigarette, right? Wrong. It wasn't so much the cigarette that devastated me; it was a combination of the deception and the fact that others *knew* he had never quit, but that he was simply keeping it from *me*, that wounded me the most. I felt foolish on multiple fronts. For a proud, stubborn girl who has just sworn "holly" matrimony until death, realizing you have said, "I do" to a liar whose family will cover for him is quite a blow.

After the honeymoon dust had settled and my beautiful wedding gown was cleaned and packed away, I had a meltdown. Some unnamed thing inside of me had died. I buried it the day I zipped my dream dress into its Barbie-pink bag and pushed it to the back of our communal closet.

I remember threatening Jon, "For every cigarette you smoke, I am going to eat a donut." I was so frustrated with my husband I wanted to do something stupid in order to get his attention, to get even. It was severely flawed thinking, demonstrating that wounded humans, like wounded animals, will bite when they feel trapped.

One of the problems with this type of thinking is when we do self-destructive things in order to "get back" at someone who has hurt us, we are like the dog that bites his *own* leg, rather than the leg of the enemy. The Bible tells us who our enemy is. Surprisingly, it's not our spouse, our teenagers, or our co-workers. It is someone who uses these people as pawns, in order to create strife in all of our lives.

I was threatening to hurt my husband by hurting myself when I should have recognized our marriage was the target of a spiritual battle and I needed to be fighting on my knees, not by eating donuts!

The first year in any marriage can be tough. When two intrinsically selfish people suddenly become "one," there are bound to be problems, even if both of them are Christians. During those first formative months, it's imperative to establish healthy boundaries, to reciprocate respect, to lay a firm foundation of honesty and trust. Otherwise, that same enemy will come looking for any cracks in the "oneness" and will weasel his way into something God has ordained as sacred.

In my opinion, humility, humor, forgiveness and communication are four keys to unlocking the door to marital bliss. God holds the ring that binds those keys together and keeps them from getting lost in the chaos of life. We must continually go to the Keeper of the Keys in order to have the tools we need to make marriage work.

During our first year, Jon and I constantly lost our "keys." Although most days we read our Bibles and prayed together, we struggled to maintain a deep connection with God. Apart from one another, we did not have any godly accountability in our lives, no faith community.

We were both in need of spiritual mentoring. Neither of us grew up with consistent examples of someone to show us what healthy confrontation and communication looked like. Despite our good intentions, we defaulted to what we knew. It wasn't pretty.

Month after frustrating month, Jon's habit continued. Although he never smoked in my presence, by my calculations he consumed a pack of cigarettes each day. He did not want to talk about it, nor did he want to quit. I nagged and accused. He isolated. I sulked. He ignored me. The angrier I became, the more he avoided me. I began to feel alone in my marriage. "*Dear Lord, this is not at all what I thought marriage would be like. Please show me how to fix this,*" I pleaded.

God answered my simple prayer by giving me another "key." This key prevents us from being too inwardly focused and develops compassion and other-centeredness in our hearts. He opened my eyes to the needs of those around me. No, this key didn't "fix" my husband, but helping the needy in the rural areas surrounding our lodge definitely gave me an outlet and a purpose that kept me from eating donuts.

I began selling locally handmade items to our tourists and used the profits to purchase food and clothing for poverty-stricken families. A beautiful ministry evolved. It met my need to be a useful and active Christian in our community. When I began helping others, my anger at Jon and God (wasn't it *His* fault I married this guy?) began to subside, and the joy of the Lord returned to my wounded heart.

My husband didn't appear to be changing, but *my* attitude toward him was. Sometimes the best way to "get even" is to start serving people whose suffering is greater than our own. My Mamaw often repeated, "Two wrongs don't make a right." She was correct. If I'd started eating twenty donuts a day, rather than looking for a wholesome outlet, I would have ended up obese and unhealthy, but no less bitter or angry.

I'm thankful God diverted me from a potential donut addiction, but that wasn't the only time the enemy has tempted me with self-destructive thinking. As months turned into years, my husband's other skeletons began creeping out of our closet. I was often confronted with the choice to numb my own pain in unhealthy ways, or to go to the Keeper of the Keys and ask for humility, humor, forgiveness, or an assignment to help someone whose problems appeared worse than mine. Sometimes I made the right decision, sometimes not; however, I believe that the times I chose wisely kept me sane and allowed our marriage many opportunities to thrive, or at least to survive for as long as it did.

Chapter 5

Wrestling and Rehab

"For we do not wrestle against flesh and blood,
but against principalities, against powers,
against the rulers of the darkness of this age,
against spiritual hosts of wickedness in the heavenly places."
Ephesians 6:12 NKJV

2000

My heart felt as empty as the place on the padded pew next to me. Church was one of the canvases upon which we painted the facade of our lives. I'd loved church. Not because it was a place to be fake, but because church felt familiar and safe. It was a place to be fed. It was where I sought God's assurance all would be well. Seeing the happy families sitting like well-dressed ducks in a row gave me hope that one day I, too, would have what they had.

For four years, Jon and I had stepped out of our car with Bibles and smiles and walked through the doors of this church. We shook hands at the door, hugged the friends we'd made, and participated in a lively discussion class. Ryan, the group's leader, and his talented wife, Meredith, had become dear friends who eventually knew what was really going on behind our Sabbath smiles. They were just two, of a handful of people, who were aware of the rollercoaster we'd been riding. Most members were oblivious, and that's the way we wanted it.

Our silence was rooted in pride and fear. Worried about what people would think or say about us, I was reluctant to admit which part of the addictive cycle was ruling our lives during any given moment. While I was teaching the "3 R's" to children at school, my husband cycled through the 3 R's of Relapse, Rehab and Recovery.

A surge of loneliness crept over me as I glanced around our half-filled sanctuary that second week after driving Jon to rehab. *We've been attending church with these people for years, but I can't disclose the truth about Jon's absence.* When the few folks who asked about him last week approached me, the same lame excuses made their way past an obnoxious lump in my throat and escaped into their sanctified ears. I don't know why it was so difficult for me to voice our reality to my well-meaning church family, but it was. I just could *not* do it.

Even though there were people outside our small circle who suspected my husband's drug use, they never directly approached me. Their indirect inquiries were a hybrid of curiosity and compassion. Church can be a lonely place, especially if you believe yours is the only family battling addiction. It's even more lonely when the few people you have been transparent with aren't sure what to do with the information. Disclosing a family secret like drug addiction can quickly become fodder for gossip if a church body is unhealthy or unequipped to handle it. I didn't trust most people in my church to be able to handle our truth, or trust that they would be able to help.

There *was* one man, a gift from the Lord in our time of need, whose counsel I trusted. His name was Leon. I'd become acquainted with him because his wife, Elaine, was a colleague. Leon, a former pastor, was the chaplain at our local hospital. He was also a licensed chemical dependency counselor who understood addiction, both from a Christian and a clinical perspective.

Some people have the ability to pick up on pain, and the courage to gently pry the lid off of another person's private pressure cooker. Leon is one of them. I remember the day he dropped by our school to bring lunch to Elaine. I could not escape his radar. You know how it is, when your heart is breaking and you don't want anyone to hear it? Every morning you pull on your "big girl panties" and set your face like flint, hoping no one will notice what's beneath your facade. I was good at hiding my hurt, especially in front of children, but I couldn't keep it from Leon. Before I knew it, the whole story was out, right there in the schoolyard, with my students laughing and climbing up and down the monkey bars.

Leon immediately offered to counsel both Jon and me in his office at the hospital one evening a week. He promised, for no fee, to help us navigate the rough waters we were facing and to be a friend and mentor to both of us. Relief melted my facade as I tearfully took his business card and accepted his warm embrace.

That was Leon. As far as the rest of the church, well, they just didn't know. Our pastor was unprepared for the gravity of our situation. Addiction wasn't something I'd ever heard a sermon on. We didn't have a "12 Step" group in our church. Nor did we know of anyone else who struggled with this issue.

Fear knocked upon my hollow heart as I focused on our problems. Sinking lower in our pew, I allowed the enemy to steal my peace. I was afraid of the future. I was afraid of gossip. I was afraid of losing my job if the school board, comprised of church members, discovered that Jon was in a treatment facility for drug addiction. Fear nearly suffocated me as I sat alone in a church full of people.

I'm really gonna lose it if anyone else approaches me with questions. I've got to get out of here. Standing up quickly, I raced back down the aisle and out the door to the isolated safety of my car.

My plan had been to attend church, then drive an hour and a half to the rehab for family visitation. It was week two of Jon's program, and the first time family members were allowed to see him. *I'll just go early,* I thought as I slipped into my oven on wheels, flipping the A/C to cold and the fan to high.

My Pontiac Fiero didn't cool down fast enough to prevent drops of sweat from mixing with my tears as I exited the church parking lot, heading for the highway. I had ninety minutes to pray through my fears and prepare myself for whatever the visit would hold. I did not know what to expect, or what I even wanted. All I knew was that visiting hours were from two to five and I was expected to go.

The two weeks without Jon had been both peaceful and painful. Part of me was thankful to have the house to myself and to experience relief from the drama. Part of me missed the dysfunction that had begun to feel normal. The overwhelming emptiness I'd felt at church was the result of a slow leak that began on our honeymoon, with that too-late discovery of deception.

Over the six years of our marriage, my heart had been neglected and my girlish dreams dashed. I had become more of a parent than partner. Afraid of the truth, I lived in denial of the fact that my husband avoided intimacy and related to me like a mother, rather than a wife. Oh, he liked to put on a show for others by pretending to be crazy about me, but the reality was that I went to bed alone nearly every night while Jon stayed up watching TV in another room, waiting until I fell asleep before going outside to have the day's final cigarette. I had grown increasingly lonely in my marriage. This desolate feeling wasn't new, it was just finally being acknowledged for what it was. I was not well-loved.

When a spouse is chemically dependent, it is actually impossible for them to properly love us, but I didn't know that at the time. My expectations, those of any normal young wife, were consistently met with rejection. My husband lived from high to high virtually unable to relate on any level of intimacy. Some relationships survive on love without much sex. Some survive on sex, without much love. Ours had little of either, only facades of both.

I contemplated our marriage for several miles as my car finally began to cool down. *"Facades are difficult to keep up, Lord. Help me find my authenticity and identity in You."*

A few months before Jon went to rehab, hopelessness and depression crept up on me. I repeatedly battled suicidal thoughts. One particularly gruesome image of slicing my wrists haunted me until the night I expressed it to Jon in the form of a question. "What if you came home one day to find me dead in a bathtub full of bloody water?"

Pausing at the bedroom door, he queried, "Why would you even say something like that?" Then he took our dogs out back so they could romp while he had a cigarette.

That moment confirmed in my mind how very little Jon valued me. The dogs' need for exercise and Jon's need for nicotine trumped my urgent need for compassion and understanding. That realization, combined with the confession I'd just made, left me feeling limp and vulnerable. I realized that without divine intervention, I would end up punishing Jon for his neglect by making him clean up an ugly, bloody mess. I quickly grabbed my Bible from the nightstand.

A worn photograph of Mr. P standing grimly in front of his burnt-up Renault marked the place in Ephesians where I had last read. That image reminded me of the miraculous ways God preserved my life in the past.

If I kill myself now, all those miracles would have been in vain. It would be like spitting in God's face. No matter how I feel, I cannot do that to Him. He loves me. Then came the pitiful question I'd asked from my Swiss hospital bed, *"You do love me, right, God? Jon doesn't, but You do."* How I coveted an audible affirmation that night, as my thoughts were drawn down dark alleyways that only ended in death.

I began reading my way through Ephesians. By chapter six, the TV was humming in the other room. I could picture Jon lying there with one dog on his belly and the other perched on the back of the futon with her little pug tail curled into a donut roll. Verse twelve reminded me I was not wrestling against "flesh and blood" (my husband), "but against principalities, against powers, against the rulers of the darkness of this age," and "against spiritual hosts of wickedness in the heavenly places" (NKJV).

My upbringing had fundamentally prepared me for the battle I was in. I just needed a mighty reminder from God's Word that my fight wasn't against the flesh and blood in the other room.

The battle for our minds is always a spiritual battle. I needed to change my tactics from those of a wounded woman to those of a warrior woman. Lying across my bed that night, I got dressed for my husband, no, not in lacy little lingerie, but head-to-toe in Ephesians 6 armor. I used my tiny shield of faith to stop those suicidal thoughts by saying aloud, "In the name of my Savior, Jesus Christ, and by His blood, I bind and rebuke all evil spirits of suicide and despair! I command you to leave my mind. Leave this house, never to return! I choose to put on the helmet of salvation and to allow God complete access to and reign over my thoughts." Then I prayed, "*Please, God, give me the mind of Christ that I may choose life—no matter what Jon chooses.*"

That night dawned the dismal realization that I did not have a husband who was capable of empathy or compassion for me. I knew that until a miracle took place in Jon, God would have to be my husband. It would take many more experiences of choosing God and using His Word to fight my unseen enemy, but eventually I came to realize God *is* enough.

His grace is sufficient to carry me through deep emotional valleys. The name of Jesus is powerful enough to pull down any stronghold—from suicidal thoughts to extensive root systems of bitterness and anger. I only had to be willing to ally myself very closely with my Savior. That became easier to do when Jon's choices eventually removed him from our home and placed him in Blue Sky rehab center.

The most painful consequence of having Jon gone was financial. Although he'd been snorting much of his paycheck each week, our budget was still built around two incomes. Jon's admission into rehab brought his income to a screeching halt, but our monthly bills didn't get the memo. The day I ducked out of church early, thoughts of how I could keep everything afloat financially plagued my already-anxious brain.

We were in a monetary mess. In addition to our basic bills, we were in the process of building a new home. We also owned a small café with my sister, Annie. Buona Notte Café had been an investment my mom and I had made with some of our settlement money from that horrible Swiss car accident. Annie, Jon and I were partners.

Each of us had specific roles. Jon's job had been to handle the accounting. Annie worked full time as manager, chief cook and baker. I did all the shopping for the business, as well as some baking and dish-washing before and after school. Mom, who still lived in Switzerland, was a not-so-silent partner who had bargained on getting at least her initial investment back. It was a hectic life for all of us, but we were excited our city voted us "Best Café" both years we had been open.

I prayed about our business as I drove. *"Lord, I'm embarrassed about what our teenage employees confided to Annie—that Jon buys his drugs from the same dealer their friends use.*

"I am also struggling to believe what Sis says about the financial problems at the café. She blames Jon for us not being able to make payroll or pay our taxes. She says he has been stealing cash from the till and the bank deposits. I know she has been unable to pay herself, although she works six days a week. We have plenty of business, so what other explanation is there for why we aren't making it?

"How could he do that to us? Financially cripple something we've all worked so hard for? Why can't I believe my sane and sober sister, whom I've trusted for my lifetime, yet I defend the husband who has deceived and lied to me ever since we married?" Pounding the steering wheel for emphasis, I pleaded, *"I need to know the TRUTH! Please help me to see and believe the truth in front of me, rather than the lies I seem to so easily swallow."*

Then I fired off a bulleted list of questions:

- *Why do I believe him when he lies to my face?*
- *Why do I give him the benefit of the doubt, even when it affects my relationship with my family?*
- *Why do I defend him?*
- *Why do I allow what I allow in our marriage?*
- *What is wrong with me, Lord?*

"Only You truly know what it's like for me. You know how much I try to make a happy home. You see me, God. Every night, when I pray by myself, You see me."

Mile after mile, I hosted my own emotional wrestling match. My heart wanted the rehab program to change Jon, but my brain was skeptical. I knew nothing about substance abuse. It was a whole new language. I needed to decide whether or not I *wanted* to learn that language, whether or not I was going to continue to fight for this marriage. Part of me yearned to run away. There wasn't much within the actual marriage to keep me. Truthfully, I hadn't left already more out of obligation, stubbornness and pride rather than love, commitment and devotion. I felt a spiritual responsibility to keep my vow, "for better or for worse." Believing physical infidelity was my only Biblical "out," I felt obliged to stay. At the time, the principle behind fidelity—that provides for a wife's needs on many levels, was foreign to me. I did not yet realize unfaithfulness can be so much more than a sexual encounter.

Stubbornness pulses through my veins. Mom says I get it from both sides of the family. All I know is I am part pit bull. Once I sink my teeth into an idea or a project, I don't easily release. Early in life, I determined that any marriage of mine would defy statistics and never end in divorce like my parents' marriages. So, when I chose to marry Jon, it was for life, no matter what. I just had no idea what the "what" was, nor could I imagine that our relationship would become more of a project than a marriage.

I was also proud, too proud, of the life we were making for ourselves. When we decided to relocate to Texas after two years in Costa Rica, all we had was what was left of my settlement from the car accident. With that, we purchased a used Honda Accord and rented one side of a tiny duplex in a not-so-nice neighborhood close to my school. Within four years we'd been able to move to a better part of town, build a business, and buy some property for our future dream home.

It all sounded nice, but now we made payments on two vehicles, a larger house, our café rental space, four credit cards, and the home loan we had taken out to begin building on our property. Why I was proud of all those payments, I don't know. Somehow, they all added up to what I felt was a lifestyle comparable to my friends'. I wanted to keep it that way. If things fell apart with Jon and me, everything else would also collapse. I needed him to make it, so that the image we had worked so hard to create wouldn't crumble.

Writing these words thirteen years later, I feel sad and embarrassed for my younger self. She wanted the appearance of normalcy so much she was willing to believe lies, become immune to deception, live in a loveless marriage, and fake her way through her middle-class, Bible-Belt, American life. Poor, poor girl. No wonder her heart felt empty. Her life, *my* life, was a facade!

Obligation, stubbornness and pride are not buoyant enough to keep a marriage afloat. There must be some love in the mix somewhere. I had been so hurt and angry when my denial bubble finally burst just before Jon went to rehab, that I forgot about love. The shocking truth of his habit, his stealing, his pawning and lying, completely numbed my heart to love. When those flash-in-the-pan emotions subsided, there was only hollowness where love once lived. It was the same hollowness I carried inside of me to family visitation day at Blue Sky Rehabilitation Center that second Saturday in August.

He met me on the front porch, with bright blue eyes. I could not remember when Jon's face had been more peaceful. We briefly embraced before he guided me toward a group of picnic tables alongside the building, stopping here and there to introduce me to a few of the other Blue Sky residents.

That is when I saw her again, short, square, smiling, and oozing compassion as she wove her way among the residents and their families. "Remember Mayra?" Jon motioned as we moved toward the group gathered around her, "She's amazing!"

Observing her from across the lawn, I felt as if I were watching Jesus himself move among the people as life-hardened faces softened and haunted eyes made contact with hers. Gaunt, tattooed addicts and alcoholics of all ages appeared to hang onto Mayra's every word.

Soon we were standing directly in front of her. Holding my gaze, she spoke as if I were the only person on the property. She wore scrubs. A red headband framed her round, brown face. There was nothing physically attractive about her appearance, but Mayra was beautiful. It was the love radiating from her whole being that made her so. She obviously loved her work, loved the people she was hired to help.

"We're proud of your husband." Mayra smiled, shaking my hand. "He's made great strides in these two weeks." Glancing sideways at him, I observed he appeared to grow taller with her compliment. *I hope so.* I almost spewed the words, but I swallowed them instead.

"God, I only hope so," I prayed silently.

"We'll talk more after the group meeting," Mayra promised as she moved toward a couple of parents who had come to visit their teenage daughter.

Turning toward my husband, I was amazed by the change in him. Jon's whole countenance was different. He appeared confident, hopeful even. Over the next half hour, person after person told me what a blessing and an inspiration he was. Guys were thanking him for Scriptures he'd shared, and several who were going home that day asked for his number so they could keep in contact. *"What's going on here, Lord? Is it possible that these people see something in Jon I've been missing?"*

After lunch, we attended a mandatory family meeting. My eyes searched the faces of other second-hand victims of drugs and alcohol. Reflected there were hope and despair, anger and resignation. For some, like me, this was, as we say in Texas, their "first rodeo." Others, like the pretty wife with three young children, had a disheartened déjà vu expression. Her husband had not had a drink for fifteen years until the day he gave in to temptation and went out after work with his "friends" rather than going home to his family. Over and over I heard similar versions of, "It only took one . . . " One shot, one snort, one puff, one hit. Whatever the "drug of choice," it only took one use to either hook a person for the first time, or spiral them into relapse.

Some of the family members were parents, clinging to hope that the teenager they would take home would be dramatically different from the one they had deposited at Blue Sky. My heart ached for all of them, the disappointed wives, the desperate parents, the confused children. My heart ached for me.

Sitting on a metal fold-up chair next to Jon, listening to Mayra explain what happens inside the brain of an addict, I began to feel a kernel of compassion well up inside my self-protected soul. She unpacked the cycle of addiction, explaining the "triggers" and "red flags" that send addicts and alcoholics into a panic, and how family members get caught up in the whirlwind.

She also mentioned that certain drugs, like cocaine, physically forge pathways in the brain, altering the landscape of the frontal lobe. "That portion of a person's brain," explained Mayra, "is the emotional and personality control center. Cocaine also destroys the brain's ability to make dopamine and endorphins, which produce feelings of well-being within the body."

It was an a-ha moment for me. *No wonder he has been unable to show empathy toward me! No wonder his personality has changed so drastically over the past few months!* She went on to state that once a person ceases using, cocaine remains in their system for up to three years.

My eyes opened to the seriousness of Jon's situation and the possibility of his addiction being even more devastating than I had fathomed. I had just wanted him to stop using, to come home and be "normal." According to Mayra, recovery could be, "just a little more complicated than that." After the initial detox at a rehab center, it involved "working the program," attending weekly

Narcotics Anonymous meetings, being accountable to someone, and eventually helping others along their path to sobriety. Blue Sky was not guaranteed to be a quick or permanent "fix."

Mayra described recovery as a process. "And," she went on to say, as she looked squarely at each of us who had come to visit our loved one that day, "everyone in the addict's life will be affected by the process. With understanding comes responsibility. You are here because you are committed to seeing your family member succeed. They will only succeed if they daily choose recovery for themselves. If you try to choose it for them, they will fail. If you enable them, they will fail. If you are codependent with them, they will fail. If you love them unconditionally with an understanding of what they are experiencing, and set the healthy boundaries and consistency they need to work their program, they will have a better chance for success."

After that meeting, I definitely had an increase in understanding. What I needed to decide was whether I *wanted* the responsibility. I had to choose if I was in this for the long haul or not, especially if it was going to be three years before my husband's frontal lobe would be able to function on a pre-cocaine level. I knew that if I wanted to run, now would be a good time to do so. Otherwise, I would be committing to the lengthy processes and unknown language of a lifestyle called "recovery." I wasn't sure I was ready for that. *"God, please show me what You want me to do here. I don't know if I can take this much longer."*

A little while later, while observing Jon participating in the optional-for-family, mandatory-for-residents group session, I was again surprised by his confidence and openness within the group. I felt like an outsider, as if I were watching a movie. For some of the residents, this was their final meeting before launching back into "real life," so they were sharing words of wisdom and accepting encouragement and support from their peers.

Jon had been deeply impacted by a poem one of the counselors had shared with him upon his arrival at Blue Sky. He was asked to read it aloud at the close of the meeting. Pulling a creased photocopy from the back pocket of his Levi 501's, he quietly addressed the group. "When you feel like you aren't worth much, and the bad things you've done seem to overshadow any good, always remember that in the hands of the Master, you are valuable." Then he began to read an unknown author's poem, "Twas battered and scarred, and the auctioneer thought it scarcely worth his while." A simple, beautiful rhyme that ends with the auctioneer increasing the price of a dirty old violin by a thousand times, because, in the hands of the Master Violinist, a useless, castaway instrument became something precious and valuable, something worth saving.

Emotion cracked Jon's voice as the last lines came out almost in a whisper. "But the Master comes, and the foolish crowd never can quite understand, the worth of a soul and the change that is wrought, by the touch of the Master's hand."

The room was quiet except for a few sniffs. For a moment the only movement was the backs of several hands whisking away silent tears. Then applause, and hugs all around as the group gathered into a tight circle to repeat The Serenity Prayer.

Everyone participated. Even me. It was my first time. Right foot forward, arms looped around the shoulders of those on either side, I mumbled along as the others repeated Reinhold Niebuhr's now-familiar petition, "God, grant me the serenity to accept the things I cannot change; courage to change the things I can; and wisdom to know the difference."

Niebuhr's timeless words pierced my heart, becoming *my* prayer. In that moment, with eyes closed and arms encircling a group of total strangers, I chose to stay. Instinctively I knew I needed tremendous wisdom from the Master Violinist. I needed Him to pour His love into me, so that it could flow out to others, especially to the husband who was too broken to reciprocate.

Years before, I had read in a book by Gary Smalley that, "love is a decision." If our future was based on feelings, there was not much to work with. But that day, I made the decision to love my husband. Then I asked God for the feelings to go with my choice. That simple decision changed the way I would live my life.

Visitation was over. As Jon hugged me goodbye, he whispered a few final words in my ear, "Please leave some money on my account so I can buy cigarettes." My body instinctively stiffened. By way of explanation he mumbled, "I'm giving up so much right now. That's not a battle I'm ready to fight yet."

Oooooh! I did not want to do that, but neither did I want to argue about it. Leaving funds for "sundries" made me feel as if I were contributing to one of the habits killing my husband. I wanted to control him AND his nasty habit by walking straight past the reception desk and out to my car. I didn't. Nodding my consent instead, I left twenty dollars with the receptionist and quickly left the building.

It would be years into my own recovery before I found an escape from my tendency toward codependent control and indulgent enabling. Setting healthy boundaries was something our friend Leon was instrumental in helping me with. I had no clue where to begin.

On the drive home, I thought about Leon. I wanted to call and tell him of my decision to choose love. I needed to share the details of the visit and to thank him for using his connections to get Jon immediately admitted into Blue Sky.

Without Leon's intervention, I believe it may have been *me* who one day arrived home to a dead spouse. Maybe the mess would not have been as ugly as the one I was tempted to create by ending my life with a knife, but death is never pretty, no matter how glamorous Romeo and Juliet made it appear. *"Thank You, God, for sending Leon to our home three weeks ago on the very day I feared for Jon's life after his dangerous weekend binge."*

I recalled the scene. Leon leaned toward Jon as they sat side-by-side on our sofa. He asked, "Where is your stash?" Jon appeared surprised.

"Huh?" He replied.

"No, not, 'huh?' Where?" Leon quickly responded. "Please go and bring me all the cocaine you have stashed so you can dump it down the drain." Shockingly Jon stood up and walked into our garage. Two minutes later he returned with a powder-filled baggie. That was my first real-life sighting of the drug that ruled our world.

Kindly but firmly, Leon convinced Jon to choose rehab as an option to the certain death that awaited him were he to continue his downward spiral. He invited Jon to dump his drugs down the kitchen sink and to apologize to me for bringing an illegal substance into our home.

In my eyes, Leon was our best human ally. From that moment, I have loved him like a hero! I could not wait to tell him the good news that the rehab center appeared to be helping Jon. Since that was before I owned a cell phone, I would have to wait until I got home. In the meantime, I had another ally, One whom I could access any time, day or night. One who had given His very life for mine. For Jon's. The rest of the drive home, I told Him everything He already knew, asking Him again to give me His love where I had very little of my own.

My journal chronicles my own emotional rollercoaster during that month, as I waited and prayed for God to work a miracle in Jon's life. On August 9, our wedding anniversary, I wrote: *I feel very depressed today. Sad. I hope there is hope. I feel stupid for believing such a liar. The things he did to cover his problem! I hope God will teach me to forgive regardless of whether or not he is sorry.*

Annie reminded me today of how kind and thoughtful Jon used to be. Always looking out for others, anticipating their needs or doing little things to help them out. That is why I fell in love with him. He treated people kindly. I don't want him to come home yet, even though I miss him terribly.

Two days later, I wrote: *Jon sounds like his old self on the telephone. I'm pleased that he is so upbeat and positive. He's sharing Scriptures each day with the others there. I'm proud of him for that. I can't wait for him to come home.*

August 12: *I visited today. Felt very sad—had to weep in my car. Jon is better. I can see it in his face. Praise God! He is working hard to do what he must do. He said, "sorry" to me and shared a poem. I have faith he is going to make it.*

August 14: *I watched a movie tonight called "28 Days." It said only three out of ten patients in rehab do not relapse. I pray Jon doesn't relapse. I don't know what we'd do. I asked God to keep him from harm and prayed he'll be willing to get continual help through counseling, reading, praying, and studying. Only by God's grace will we get through this thing with our health, sanity and marriage intact. "I can do all things through Christ who strengthens me" (Philippians 4:13 NKJV).*

August 15, Tuesday: *Jon called. He sounded so upbeat, so positive. I hope he isn't overconfident. He said he's never going back. That he will make it.*

After he told me he loved me several times, I said, "Show me the money." He cried. I just meant, "Show me you love me; don't just tell me." I feel bad. I wasn't trying to hurt his feelings. Not a good way to end our conversation.

August 17, Thursday: *Talked to Mom. She sounds awful. Head seizures again. Will my poor mother ever stop suffering? After the severe head trauma she sustained in our accident, she can't handle the stress of all this. She wants me to be very cautious of Jon. She fears this will take a long time to get over. I know it will, but I am in it for the long haul. I just hope I don't get taken for a fool again.*

August 18, Friday: *Even though I want him to come home and earn money, I really want him to get well. I'm starting to believe he wants to be well. God is in control. I'm willing to do what He needs me to. I just wish I knew what that was. I wish I knew how to help Jon. Guess I have to give it to God, because there's not much I can really do. Pray and forgive. That's all I know.*

August 19, Sabbath: *Spent the afternoon with Jon. His countenance is peaceful. He told me he's praying a lot and that God has lifted the guilt and shame. He asked me to forgive him. He said he's, "come to terms" with his smoking.*

I'm so pleased with the progress I see. I thank the Lord for His goodness, mercy, forgiveness and promise that He will carry all of these burdens. My prayer tonight is that we'll trust in God and not trust ourselves at all.

August 20, Sunday: *I cut off the end of my finger with a peeler at the Café today. I felt totally sick. Talked with Jon tonight. He told me he loves me a whole bunch of times. I want to believe that so much, but I need to see evidence.*

August 21, Monday: *Today was a good day at school. I feel tired and depressed. My strength feels gone and I just want to bawl. I feel like I can barely do anything tonight. Even talking to Jon did not lift my spirits.*

August 22, Tuesday: *Woke up with tears—going to sleep with tears. I think the shock and numbness is wearing off and real anger, fear and depression is coming. I must rebuke it for "God has not given us a spirit of fear, but of power and love and a sound mind," 2 Timothy 1:7 (NKJV). I want a sound mind. I feel so overwhelmed with everything—the bills, the questions and looks from people, no money, all of it. I don't know exactly how to cope with how I'm feeling. What is reality?*

August 24, Thursday: *Cleaned up the house and prepared for Jon's return tomorrow. "God, am I ready for him to come home?"*

Part Two

Chapter 6

Living "Clean"

"Even the sparrow has found a home,
And the swallow a nest for herself,
Where she may lay her young—
Even Your altars, O Lord of hosts,
My King and my God."
Psalm 84:3 NKJV

2000—2001

Life is different when lived from a place of one's own choosing, rather than as a victim of circumstance. Once I chose to begin practicing a lifestyle of love and forgiveness within my marriage, regardless of reciprocation, the Lord began to give me feelings to accompany my decision. Just a short while before, I had felt anger, fear, and utter disgust with Jon. Toward the end of his stay at the drug rehabilitation center, I began experiencing feelings of compassion, forgiveness, love and hope for my broken spouse.

Leon warned me about a "honeymoon period" following rehab. He also shared that the relapse rate for cocaine addicts is acutely high; statistically they had less than a ten percent success rate of recovery. My faith in God's power to heal was stronger than statistics, which I knew nothing about, but I also knew Jon needed his own deep connection with Christ in order for him to stay clean once he came home. There were some concessions he would have to make regarding his freedom. I allowed his counselors and Leon to explain that to him. I did not want to be Jon's mother. I yearned to be his wife.

In the meantime, Annie and I made arrangements at the café so Jon no longer had access to the finances. I would continue taking care of our finances at home and he would need to be accountable for anything he purchased on our Chevron gas card. If Jon would deposit his weekly paycheck into our household budget and agree to operate within the boundaries of a reasonable allowance, we would eventually get back on our financial feet.

One of the most difficult parts would be letting our lenders, Bob and Aubrey, dear Christian friends whom we had known since before our marriage, know that Jon had spent a large portion of our building money on cocaine. Since our home was only partially complete, and Jon and his employer were doing the work, we needed an additional loan in order to finish the project. Because we had not given them prior indication of Jon's drug problem, the conversation would be awkward. I dreaded it.

Speaking with my mother would also be challenging, because she and Mr. P had poured several thousand dollars into our business in order to keep it afloat when we were struggling so badly back in the winter. The P's loved Jon and had always been kind to him, but Annie's repeated tearful phone calls to Europe brought out the "mama bear" in our mother. She was quite displeased with her son-in-law.

I was emotionally torn. I wanted to pay my family back and make things right financially as soon as possible. I too was angered by Jon's abuse of our loved ones' generosity. Only Mother and I fully comprehended the depth of suffering we had experienced in order to obtain that accident settlement money in the first place. For him to carelessly and selfishly squander it on his own pleasure was beyond my comprehension.

Because I did not realized what Jon had been doing until just a short time before he went to Blue Sky, it was difficult to answer Mother's questions. I didn't have all the details. I only knew I was miserable, and felt too ashamed to let on how hurt I really was.

If a person is trying to salvage a marriage, they must be particularly careful what they say to family members about their spouse. A mother's wrath regarding how her son-in-law treats her daughter lingers long after the daughter has forgiven and forgotten. I didn't want my family or friends to loathe my husband if we were going to stay together and fix our broken marriage. I was guarded about what I shared with anyone.

The one person who knew the most truth about what we were going through was Leon. I do not know how I ever would have managed without his counsel. He and Elaine became two of the most precious people in my world. I believe God reveals His heart to us through certain human beings who allow God to use them. Through Leon's ministry, I experienced some aspects of God's character I had no prior understanding of.

I learned unconditional love does not mean passively allowing another person to use you. I learned forgiveness is a choice, not a feeling. Slowly, I began to learn how to find joy in life, apart from any choices Jon made. My joy did not have to depend upon another's decisions.

Merriam-Webster.com defines codependency as "a psychological condition in which someone is in an unhappy and unhealthy relationship that involves living with and providing care for another person (such as a drug addict or an alcoholic)." Because of Leon, I began taking my first steps away from unhealthy codependent patterns in my relationships, toward the freedom of living with healthy boundaries.

At the time of Jon's release from Blue Sky, I was only beginning to understand some of the basic principles of recovery. Jon and I were both products of brokenness passed down to us in various forms by our family members who were also emotionally or relationally damaged. God used Leon to equip us with several tools missing from our mental health tool belts.

A week before Jon came home, I decided to buy him a truck for his upcoming birthday. His old truck was disgusting. The very sight of it upset me. It had been baking in our driveway for weeks before I bravely rolled down the windows to air it out. I do not know exactly what he'd done in there, but my Mamaw would've said it "smelled like the devil."

I knew Jon's truck had carried some shady characters to and from the worst places in our town. From what I had learned about a drug-user's "triggers," sitting behind the wheel of that blue Dodge Dakota could trigger Jon right back down the same road, which dragged him so far off course that he'd almost not made it home.

On the way back from visitation day, I saw a dealership advertising trade-ins. I got their number and made an appointment to bring Jon's old truck in for an estimate. They didn't seem to mind the stench and offered to take it off my hands. Jon's birthday would be the weekend of his release, so I arranged to trade his old truck for a much newer, full-sized Dodge Ram.

The Ram was green and shiny with a cattle guard grille and a seat so high I had to use the sidebar step and the grab handle to get up into it. When I filled out the paperwork, it seemed like a good deal. The payment would be only a few dollars more per month than we were already paying. Mr. Used Car Salesman took my picture standing next to Jon's new truck and turned the photo into a key ring and a calendar for Jon. Driving it off the lot, I felt like a true Texan.

"He's gonna love this. I know he's just gonna love this truck! I cannot wait to see his face when I give him the keys. Thank You, Lord for getting me a good deal on this thing!"

Knowing I would be taking Jon's new truck to pick him up at the end of his stay at Blue Sky heightened the anticipation of his homecoming. I thought it would be a delightful birthday gift and a symbol of new beginnings. In the meantime, school started and I had many last minute, beginning-of-the-year details to attend to, so the week passed swiftly. Before I felt ready, the first of thirty-six weeks in our school year was behind us and I was on my way to Blue Sky in a giant Texas truck to retrieve my remodeled husband.

Going through goodbyes and discharge details was tedious. Mayra met with the two of us to make an action plan for long-term recovery. She informed Jon that attending weekly Narcotics Anonymous meetings was a fundamental part of his recovery process, and gave him the locations of groups that met in our "neck of the woods." Then she told me what warning signs to look for as indicators that Jon might be headed for relapse. She encouraged us to stay in counseling with Leon in order work on the underlying roots of Jon's addiction issues.

When I pulled her aside to whisper that I had purchased a new truck for Jon's birthday, Mayra appeared unimpressed. She simply cautioned me to be careful.

When we finally left the building, I twirled my wrists in a "ta-da" motion and cheered, "Happy Birthday Jon!" as, "Vanna-style," I handed him the fancy photo key ring with two keys to his almost new truck. We stood on the sidewalk directly in front of the truck's cattle guard grille. Jon's knees buckled. In a millisecond he was kneeling next to the truck with tears streaming down his cheeks. To say he was overjoyed would be an understatement. He was incredulous! Back he raced back into the rehab center, instantly returning with several residents and employees, including Mayra, in tow.

"Look what my wife has given me for my birthday!" He proudly exclaimed. "I've been redeemed!" He opened the door and hopped into the cab, tossing his leather duffel bag onto the back seat with one smooth motion. Then he got out and opened the passenger door for me before jumping back into the driver's seat. With one hand he waved goodbye and with the other he started the engine. As soon as we were out of the parking lot, he pulled over to give me a hug and a kiss. "Thank you for believing in me," he cried, "even when I wasn't sure if I believed in myself."

On the drive home, Jon offered to fill-in many gaps about what I knew of his life story. He answered several haunting questions. I learned he had experimented with alcohol in grade school, done some serious drugs in high school, and had partied a lot during his first marriage. He shared he began using cocaine again about a year and a half prior to his admission into Blue Sky. That eighteen-month binge began, he said, when he went to visit a recently discovered sister, who was also addicted to cocaine. The story was complicated.

I blamed myself for two things. First, for not realizing how deeply Jon was affected by the news of his birth mother's death, even though I knew it was his lifelong desire to meet her, and second for not going with him to meet his "new" sisters in Florida. "So," I questioned as he stopped talking for a moment. "When Roman called you two years ago to tell you he found your birth mother, that was the beginning of this nightmare?"

"Pretty much," he replied. "When Roman told me we had three other siblings, I was ecstatic. I guess I wasn't prepared for what he said next." Roman shared with Jon that he had spoken with one of their biological sisters and she revealed the heartbreaking story of how their mother died unexpectedly three years earlier from complications during a routine surgical procedure.

I remembered the anguish following the phone call. It was one of those things a wife doesn't easily forget; one of those frozen moments when you feel so small in the shadow of overwhelming bad news and you don't know how anything you can do or say will ease the blow. After receiving that information, Jon had coiled into a fetal position in our queen-sized bed and sobbed like a small child for what seemed like hours.

Subsequently, he seemed obsessed with contacting those other siblings. Two of the sisters responded. Immediately they invited us to come visit them in Florida. Jon wanted to go right away, rather than wait for a holiday when I would be off from school. The timing was difficult and I didn't feel comfortable leaving Annie alone with all of the responsibility of our newly opened café. Regrettably, we decided Jon should go to Florida alone.

As he shared the story of how his newfound sister laid a line of cocaine out on her coffee table as she told him all about the mother he had never known, I envisioned the scene in my mind. Can't you see how that whole situation was a setup from the enemy's camp? Satan always takes advantage of moments of vulnerability. That is why it is important to recognize when we are weak, and surround ourselves with people who can pray us through the valleys. Unfortunately, Jon was on dangerous ground and his helpmate, who missed the warning signals, was several states away. Unbeknownst to me, my husband came home from that trip with a powdery white mistress. She would compete with me for years for his affection, but for now there was hope.

Our journey home was notably different from the one we had taken to Blue Sky Rehab just a few weeks earlier. Our conversation was animated and intimate, including a heartfelt apology from Jon. "I'm sorry for lying to you, and for shutting you out of my pain. I didn't want you to be disappointed in me. I didn't mean to hurt you. I will do my best to make it up to you. Will you please forgive me?"

"Yes," I said. "I am choosing forgiveness. I cannot go through life angry anymore. You must promise to be honest with me, Jon. That includes not hiding your smoking. Don't you want to quit? You know what Mayra said about caffeine and nicotine being gateway substances that can create cravings for other drugs."

"Yeah, yeah. I know. You just don't understand. Cigarettes are like a mother to me. Whenever I was little, and my parents would fight, or things went wrong and I became upset, I'd go hide in the shed and smoke. It's not easy to give up the one comfort you've had for almost your whole life."

"But where does a child get cigarettes?" I asked.

"With teenage sisters and their boyfriends around, there was always plenty of alcohol, marijuana and tobacco. They thought it was cute to bring Roman and me to their parties and let us try stuff. I think I was seven years old the first time I got drunk. I started smoking way before that," he explained.

"All I'm saying is keep me in the loop," I said. "Don't avoid kissing me because you're afraid I'll smell cigarettes. Don't let everyone but me see you smoking. Of course I don't want you smoking in the house or our vehicles, but until you quit, I'd appreciate if you would treat me like anyone else, and excuse yourself for a smoke, rather than sneak around. It's not like I don't know what you are doing anyway."

"I'll work on it," he promised, changing the subject. "How are the girls?"

"They've missed you, but they're good," I answered, knowing he had put the brakes on *that* part of our conversation.

The "girls" were our two dogs, Snuffles and Whipper Snapper. I've mentioned them before, but let me tell you a bit more about them. Snuffles, a fat fawn-colored Chinese pug with a slight under-bite, was my baby. Jon gave her to me for my birthday the first year we moved to Texas. Little Snuffs was lonely at home while we both worked long hours, so when she was a year old, we added an energetic Boston terrier runt to our family.

At first, the stubborn pug refused to even acknowledge her new "sister." Turning her back, she escaped to the yard and jumped up onto our picnic table, where Whipper could not reach her. From there, she complained by making whiny, grumbling yaps every few minutes so the humans would know just how unhappy she was. Insistent that they become friends, I forced them to sleep together in the same doggie bed on the floor beside ours. It wasn't long before Snuffles' heart melted and the girls became inseparable.

The dogs kept our lives on a routine and gave some semblance of normalcy to our home before Jon succumbed to rehab. When he returned, we re-established our routines and again became a couple who played, prayed and worshiped together. Like me, our friends and family members accepted Jon's apologies and moved forward with life as we all knew it. His employers even took him back to work. Before long they resumed building our little house in the country.

On August 26, my journal says: *I have a lot of hope for the future as long as we both stay in Christ. Jon admitted demons had taken control of his life and mind. I hope he will not allow the devil any type of foothold ever again. I want us to grow as Christians. I know Jon is sincere and that he will do what it takes. He has even quit smoking. I praise God for that! Now I can weep tears of relief.*

Annie was the person who had the most difficulty believing in Jon's transformation. She learned not to trust him. It wasn't until he approached her at church to make amends during a special service that she accepted his sacrifice of repentance and in turn offered her forgiveness. As they tearfully prayed together, I whispered, "Thank You, God, for the power of Your Spirit to bring reconciliation. I had no idea how You would orchestrate this moment, but I am so grateful for what I am witnessing. Praise You!"

That rift in our family was hurting me. I constantly felt forced to choose sides, even though I knew the only side a wife should choose is her husband's—if she plans on keeping him. My decision to stand by Jon didn't help dissolve the disapproval hanging in the air every time the three of us were together.

A week after Jon returned home, we began attending Narcotics Anonymous meetings. I didn't have to go. I went because I didn't trust him going out alone at night. I also wanted to see what they were doing that was so vital to Jon's recovery.

Those meetings, in addition to our weekly counseling sessions with Leon became the hub of our lives. As introverts, we were both exhausted by the combination of meeting and greeting unknown people and putting ourselves "out there" emotionally. We were committed to "doing this right," and Mayra said Jon would not make it if he did not attend weekly recovery meetings.

I had never participated in a 12 Step program before and found myself dreading the words my husband had to repeat every Tuesday night at 7 p.m. "Hi, I'm Jon and I'm an addict," did not seem redemptive to me. *Is he going to recite this week after week until Jesus comes?* I thought one evening as I searched the faces in our circle as they choroused, "Hi, Jon!" with somewhat forced enthusiasm. *What about 2 Corinthians 5:17, which says, "If anyone is in Christ he is a new creation?" Where in the Bible do we find that we must continually make our sin our identity? I just don't get it. This seems like a self-fulfilling prophecy to me"* (NKJV).

Conflicted thoughts flooded my brain as I listened to tale after tale of ruined relationships, failed job or educational opportunities and attempted overdose suicides. Most of the participants were in their teens and twenties, slumped and grungy young men with hollow, hopeless eyes. The meetings unveiled a grim picture of life I had never viewed before. It broke my heart, especially the part where my rugged blonde thirty-three-year-old husband, fresh out of rehab, shared how he had become so entangled in the web of lies he had created by trying to live two lives, that he had felt like ending life altogether.

How does the enemy bring two Christian people to the brink of suicide without anyone noticing? Thank God for Leon. He has saved our lives.

On the way home one evening a few weeks after Jon's confession, he asserted, "I want to start coming to Narcotics Anonymous alone."

"Why?" I questioned. "I don't think I feel good about that."

"I just need to start doing this by myself," he snapped. "I don't need you to hold my hand all the time."

I did not understand his reasoning. Nor did I like it, but I conceded. What could I do? If he didn't want me there, he didn't want me.

Months slipped by and we settled into what felt like normal life. On the January 18, I wrote in my journal: *I think Jon has been smoking again. He's not telling me anything about himself; says he's not really tempted.*

"Please God, help him to be honest. Show me the right questions to ask. Help me see through the facades. Give me wisdom to work through the anger I have about our finances, Jon's dishonest nature, everything. I need help to be like You, Jesus. I need the Holy Spirit to give me those special fruits: love, joy, peace, patience . . ."

By the following spring, phase one of our house was almost complete. Our plan was to build a double garage with an apartment above and live in that until we had saved enough money to add the main house. We weren't sure how long that might be, so the apartment was designed to comfortably accommodate us. We thought perhaps one day, the P's might end up living there. In the meantime, I made it my own.

I absolutely loved it! The ceiling was cathedral-high and tall windows made the small space seem light and airy. I did all interior painting myself, including the cream-colored custom kitchen cabinets and my cheerful yellow laundry room. An added bonus was that our friends Ryan and Meredith lived just down the street; Ryan had drawn the plans for our home. We had all become tight since Jon's release from rehab.

Ryan and Meredith supported us with practical godly counsel. Their marriage was proof of what God could do with two broken people committed fully to Him. Their lives demonstrated the results of daily abiding with Christ and the positive effects of journaling one's conversations with God. It was Ryan who introduced Jon to the works of Neil Anderson, encouraging him to allow God to be The Bondage Breaker in his life. I was excited about being their neighbors so we could spend even more time under their wings.

Just prior to moving in that May, we received two surprises: the first from the enemy, the second from Annie. We were spending long hours at our new property putting final touches on the home and erecting a fence for the girls. Jon even built a tiny stucco doghouse just for them. With our move-in date breathing down our necks, Jon and I were working late. Sometimes we did not get home until well after dark, exhausted, but excited about the progress we were making. Our friends, and lenders, Bob and Aubrey came for a few days to help install the heating and air conditioning. After that, everything moved quickly.

One evening, we arrived home at dusk to discover our front door ajar. *I'm sure I shut this door when I left today. What in the world?* Upon entering the house, I noticed the contents of my overnight case strewn across the living room floor. *We've been robbed!*

"Jon! We've been robbed!" I shakily followed a trail of discarded panty liners to the master bedroom. "Whoever was here was obviously in a great hurry."

"Looks like they dumped your case and filled it with stuff they really wanted," Jon said. "Jerks! They got all our electronics."

"And my coin collection," I moaned. "They totally trashed our closet. That was the only thing of value I had in here though."

We carefully combed the house, looking for missing items. They didn't get much. Most everything could be replaced, except for those coins, which I had collected for years. Mr. P had contributed a large portion of that collection, treasures gathered from a lifetime of travel. It was a huge loss, but not the worst.

For me, the greatest loss was my baby book. In it my mother lovingly wrote sweet details of my first months and years of life. There were letters and photographs of my parents from when they were first married, and keepsakes from special events. It was absolutely irreplaceable. I could not fathom why anyone else in the world would want it. As a deeply sentimental person and a keeper of scrapbooks and mementos, that was a heavy loss for me. I felt like a part of myself had been stolen.

Annie's surprise was more joyful, but not without its own sprinkling of loss. Eddie, a handsome young captain from the army base stopped by our café for more than breakfast bagels each morning. He captured my sister's heart and now they were planning a wedding. This news affected everyone involved with the business. Without Annie, there was no Buona Notte Café. We had to devise a plan, because in six months she would leave us.

At first, we decided to try to sell the business "as-is" to anyone interested in keeping it running as Buona Notte Café. Embarrassingly, any time a potential buyer asked to see our books, we immediately lost their interest. Although we had a line of customers from our counter to the door almost every day, we did not look good on paper. It was difficult not to point blaming fingers at Jon as we struggled to salvage our investment.

Eventually we simply sold the contents of our beloved café to a stranger who would rearrange them in another space. Annie and I deeply mourned the loss, so did many of our loyal clientele. Our final day of business was an emotional one. It was July 14th, my sister's birthday, exactly three years after we opened our doors. Many of our customers and employees brought flowers and laid them at the entrance, as if creating a memorial for someone who had died. I suppose in a way, it was a death. It was the death of our dream.

The death of one dream often creates room for another. For me, closing our café created chunks of unoccupied time in my life. Since Jon appeared to be doing so well and we no longer spent every waking hour engaged in work of some kind, my suppressed maternal longings began to awaken.

There is something that awakens within a woman when she is making a nest. With the move into our new home, nesting was exactly what I was doing. I cannot easily explain it, but it is a motherly kind of fluffing that takes place. As I chose window treatments and bedding for our new home, I could feel it stirring within me. Unpacking kitchen boxes, and placing treasured blue and yellow dishes in the plate rack suspended over our shiny granite countertop, I felt as if I were also unpacking my faded fragile dreams of a cheerful home filled with love and children. I savored those dreams as they surfaced, mulling them over as I contentedly arranged furniture, fluffed pillows and watered the cheery red geraniums in my yellow window boxes.

That summer was a happy one as Jon and I nestled into our cozy loft apartment. We enjoyed being out of the city, having a space to call our own. Often we would grab our binoculars, watching from our balcony as wild turkeys foraged in the neighbor's field. A family of white-tailed deer made a trail through our lawn, their frisky twins growing up before our eyes. We celebrated several stunning full moons and Sandhill Cranes making their way to Mexico.

Slowly a thread of trust began to weave its way into our marriage. The combination of our new rural surroundings, more evenings together, and Leon's wise counsel, brought us closer than we had ever been. God's love was building a bridge between us. I could feel it. *One day soon I will share my deepest dreams with him,* I thought one evening as we sat quietly together on our balcony. *For now, I will simply enjoy this time we have together. I will trust in the Lord for his timing in all things. Doesn't Hebrews 13:5 (NKJV) say, ". . . be content with such things as you have?" After all, it's been barely a year since Jon has been "clean." According to Leon, we are still on our honeymoon.*

And we lived and loved like honeymooners for seven months.

Chapter 7

Baby Love

"For this child I prayed . . ."
1 Samuel 1:27 NKJV

2002

Annie and Eddie married in October and moved to Fort Leonard Wood, Missouri. I mourned her leaving. After slaving for three years under great stress, building the café business and watching my marriage nearly buckle, Sis needed to get away and make her own life. My acknowledgment of those truths did nothing to alleviate the aching void she left behind. Still to this day, we have not lived so closely entwined as we did before Annie married. Nostalgia often pulls me back to the days of chopping celery and chatting together while mixing our famous veggie chicken salad in the café's tiny kitchen. She was my closest ally, my eyes when I was blind, my best, best friend.

February surprised Jon and me by delivering an unexpected gift into our lives. It's a lengthy, painful story. I wrote the chapters before and after this one with relative ease, but skipped Chapter 7 because I knew birthing it without anesthesia would be excruciating. Yet my story would be incomplete without it. Irony has it that "Chapter 7" is also a common abbreviation for "Chapter 7 Bankruptcy." That describes exactly what happened to my heart during the course of this chapter of life. My heart became bankrupt.

"Okay, Lord Jesus, here I go. This is going to be hard. The lump is already right here in my throat. I can feel it rising up to cut off my breath. Breathe, girl. Breathe and pray. You can do this.

"Oh, and God, thank You for giving me this serene place to write. I know that only You could have orchestrated my life in such a way that I could take an uninterrupted week to focus on this pour-out-your-soul kind of work. Thank You for the hospitality and prayer-covering of my sweet friend, Nancy, and for the lovely orange grove and lake front views from her picture window. Thank You for the peace coming over me as I key these words into my laptop. Thank You that I can do all things through You, and that this testimony will connect me with other mothers who understand the searing pain of loss. Amen."

It was February. The day after Valentine's Day to be exact. My first and second graders were busily tidying up our classroom when Priscilla's dad, Phillip, walked in wearing his Army uniform. Sometimes he picked Priscilla up from school on his way home from the base. After motioning me to the door, he surveyed the classroom and waved Priscilla away from the pencil sharpener toward the backpack on her desk. "Do you want to drop by on your way home this afternoon?"

He asked me as his daughter grumpily stopped sharpening and snatched up her backpack. "Carrie has something she wants to show you."

"Okay," I responded as I intercepted two boys playing tag between the desks. "I should be finished here around 4:30, then I'll head your way. Looks like I'll be seeing *you* a little later!" I said to Priscilla as she tugged her dad out the door toward the parking lot. "Tell your daddy how you did on your spelling test today. He will be so proud!"

Priscilla's mom and I had become friends over the course of that school year. Carrie was an inspirational, generous woman with a huge heart for kids. She and Phillip were foster parents to several small children in addition to Carrie's three daughters from her previous marriage. They were expecting their first child together any day now. I figured she had some new baby item she wanted to show me after school that day.

"Hey everybody! How's it going?" I cheerfully greeted Priscilla and four younger siblings who answered my knock at the door. Grabbing me by the hands, they led me into the semi-dark living room where a very pregnant Carrie sat quietly on the sofa holding a squalling newborn swaddled in a pink blanket.

Looking up, she motioned for me to sit down beside her and said, "Hi, I wanted you to meet Kiki. She's just arrived."

"By the looks of you, she didn't come in a conventional manner," I joked as I peered into the scrunched up face of an adorable bundle of frustration and pointed to Carrie's overripe belly.

"Not exactly," she smiled. "Her mama left her in the hospital. Just got up and walked out after delivery. Cocaine. Hospital called Child Protective Services. CPS picked Kiki up, but couldn't find anyone to take her, so they called me. I explained that I'm about to go into labor and cannot take in a newborn at this time, but they brought her anyway, promising they'll soon find another foster family."

"She's adorable. What's all this fussing about? Is she hungry? She looks mad," I quizzed, wondering how something so small could be so angry. Or so loud!

"No, she's not hungry. She's detoxing. Wanna hold her?"

"Okay. Poor little honey. Maybe I can calm her down." Reaching for that tiny bundle, I pulled her close to my heart and began whispering soft little things to her.

"Do you want her?" The question came quiet, but direct.

"What do you mean?" I responded raising my eyes to meet Carrie's.

"I mean do you want to adopt her?" She replied. "She needs a loving home. You would be a wonderful mother. You don't have any children. We would take her, but we already have eight and one on the way. I think you should consider it. Go home and ask your husband if he wants to adopt this baby."

"God, is she serious? Why would she joke about something like this? I know she's a praying woman, but how could she know the deepest desire of my heart? Did You tell her?"

I had a few frank conversations with God about my desire to be a mom without hospitals and the possible trauma that pregnancy could inflict on my weakened pelvis. I loathed the smells and memories of being a patient. My aversion to hospitals was so strong I became faint and nauseous the moment I walked through the doors to visit a sick friend or family member. Only He knew my secret wish for a stork to drop a baby on my doorstep. That's why Carrie's question caught me by surprise.

"What would we have to do?" The words were out before I had time to edit them. In two seconds, my rapidly beating heart was "on my sleeve" for all to see. I was hooked.

Carrie excitedly explained the foster-to-adopt program. "In Texas," she said, "there is a program that makes it easy for foster parents to adopt. Once they jump through the basic hoops of background checks, parenting classes, and infant CPR, the rest should go smoothly. As her foster parents, the state will pay you to care for her until the adoption goes through. Call me immediately when you and Jon make a decision on this. We can be references for you since we already participate in the program. Kiki can stay with us until you finish all of the classes. It should only take a few months before she is permanently placed in your home."

Kiki fell asleep while we talked. Now I could examine her without all the wailing. *Poor little thing. Her doesn't have a mama. No wonder she hollers. She knows this world is so big and so scary without a mama. How could her mother walk out on her like that? I cannot imagine.*

I think of Kiki's birth mother as I write these words, wonder if she is still alive, if she ever got clean, if she dreams of her baby girl, or celebrates the day of her birth on the twelfth of each February.

I thought of the tiny little one in my arms. Her dark curls and olive skin contrasted against my pale chest. While she slept, I curled her long fingers around mine, inspecting each perfect pink fingernail.

She is so cute. Just a tiny doll. She certainly does not look like either of us. But I don't care one whit about that.

I don't know about you, but when something tiny and helpless is placed in my arms, I instinctively want to care for it. When that tiny, helpless thing is a living, breathing child—a real person made in the image of God, but damaged by a sinful world, one tends to be even more compassionate. In the past, I prayed for a child of my own, but the drugs my husband used had thwarted those dreams because I feared the drama of bringing a little one into that uncertainty. Yet here I was, presented with a ready-made baby, albeit an adorably angry one. Who could resist?

"I'll speak with Jon about it," I said handing the three-day-old bundle back to my friend. "I can't make any promises, but we'll talk. I'll call you later." The little ones unglued themselves from *Sesame Street* to escort me to the door. I hugged them all and waved goodbye to Carrie. She winked at me and nodded.

"Bye Mama," she prophesied.

"Oh, Father. What will Jon say? How shall I approach him with this? I am excited and nervous. Is this Your will? Are we ready for a baby? Are we ready for a "crack baby"? How ironic is that, after what we have been through? Is this how You redeem an addict? By giving them a detoxing baby? Please, Lord,

don't let me get wounded here. I have been through enough, haven't I?" The drive home was filled with pleading prayer as I begged my heavenly Father for answers.

"How would you like to adopt a baby girl?" I launched the question from across the bedroom that evening. Without pausing for a response, I showered him with the rest of the information. "She's only three days old. Her mother was on cocaine and left her in the hospital. Carrie and Phillip have her now, but their baby is going to be born any second. They are looking for a family to take her. She is adorable and addicted. You aren't opposed to having a racially mixed child, are you? I don't mind. She's a little person in need of a family. What do you think, Jon?"

By the following Sabbath, we had talked to our families and counseled with Leon and Elaine about the possibility of becoming foster parents to an addicted baby girl. Jon quickly agreed to "give it a try." As an adoptee, his heart held a soft place for rejected babies. We immediately put my Fiero up for sale so I could invest in a car with a back seat.

In my journal that day I wrote: *A lot has happened since finding out about baby Kiki. I've had two people interested in my car. Mom has given her "OK" and Leon and Elaine think we can do it. I have mixed feelings. One moment I'm scared and the next excited. I don't want to make a grand mistake. Yet, this could be an incredible opportunity to love and minister to another human being. "What, Lord, can we lay out as a fleece? How can we know Your will?"*

I claimed the Scripture inscribed on my journal page for that day, "You will show me the path of life" (Psalm 16:11 NKJV).

My next journal entry is dated *March 8, 2002: I feel in my heart that the timing just isn't right for us to take this baby. I don't know what, exactly, has caused me to feel this way. It just doesn't feel right.*

On the opposite page I had written this list (me and my lists…) of obstacles:

1. *House plans – no space*
   (We hadn't planned enough space for a baby or child.)
2. *Classes in timely manner for both*
   (There was A LOT of paperwork and classwork we would have to accomplish between our full time jobs.)
3. *Time management – Sitter?*
   (I had no idea how we would afford a babysitter or manage our busy lives with a baby.)
4. *Financial obligations*
   (How often is anyone financially ready to have a child?)
5. *Car – no backseat*
   (I already started working on this issue.)

Somehow, neither my gut feeling, nor that list of obstacles deterred us from moving forward. By April we abandoned ourselves to unconditional love and had named "our baby" Chloé Faith. She wasn't exactly ours yet, but we had begun the process. On my birthday, April 9, I wrote: *Today I turned thirty-two. I feel God is in control of my life. He is leading me to be like Him. Chloé is my constant prayer.*

"May God bless her and keep her and heal her. Amen."

Ever since we made the decision to become Chloe's parents, Carrie was gracious enough to allow me to spend as much time as possible with her. I began stopping by almost every day so Chloé and I could bond. (They never knew we named her "Chloé." In their presence we continued to call her Kiki, as she'd been introduced to them.) Phillip and Carrie's baby, Frankie was born just a week after Kiki arrived at their house. I often watched in amazement as they juggled both babies and the rest of their brood. Although she was never allowed to spend the night in our home, we began daytime visits as soon as we completed the basic fostering classes. I prayed over Chloé, asking God to take all traces of drugs out of her system, as I worked to get her to make eye contact with me.

Three days later, on the twelfth of May, I wrote this journal entry: *Chloé came "home" for the first time. She stayed from about 5:30 – 9:00 p.m. Jon gave her a bottle. He had tears in his eyes when he was looking at her. He said he never expected this to happen, but that it was a good thing. I feel blessed to have known and loved her, even if we cannot keep her. I pray we can. I learned more about her biological family history today. She has two siblings. One is six years old and the other ten. Her mother began using drugs after the six-year-old was born.*

The following day, I excitedly wrote: *She recognizes my voice! Oh, I love her. Her sweet little baby smell and round brown eyes. What a precious, precious gift from God!*

I felt a kindred spirit with Chloé whenever I loved on her and lured her to make eye contact with me. She and I had both been affected by cocaine. We were both healing, and helping one another in the process.

Was it a coincidence Chloé's birth mother was caught in the same addiction that nearly destroyed our family? Knowing we both had experienced abandonment by someone who should have loved us best, yet chose substance abuse instead gave me a fierce and bottomless love for that child. Her little body and soul did not deserve the pain or rejection she had experienced. I lived to love her to wholeness.

How I celebrated our first eye-to-eye moment! What joy I felt the first time she genuinely smiled at me in recognition when I went to pick her up. How my heart broke on those nights when, after bath and story and prayers, I would buckle her into the car seat for the drive to Carrie and Phillip's for bed. She would whimper all the way, recognizing this was goodbye for another day.

Once the school year finished, I began picking her up in the mornings and keeping her all day. I'd sing to her on those nighttime drives and whisper, "Mama's going to be back tomorrow. Just sleep now. Before you know it, I'll be there. We'll spend another happy day together. Just a few more weeks until we finish all our adoption classes. Then you'll be able to sleep in your crib at our house. Just hold on now, shhhhhh. Mama's coming back. Don't cry. I promise."

I shed my own tears on the way home, counting the days until she would come home to stay. I had never experienced such unabashed love for another human being. Neither had Jon. The odd thing was we both knew it, yet neither of us was jealous of the other's love for Chloé.

I cannot wait until this fine-toothed-combing is done. I silently pleaded to God one August evening on my way back home from dropping Chloé off with Carrie and Phillip. *"How much more information does this agency need? I am exhausted with the waiting. Please move things along so we can get her settled with us before another school year begins."* I whispered many such pleas heavenward regarding our paperwork. Fervently, I prayed the agency would not discover it had only been a year since my husband's release from drug rehab.

Jon convinced me to leave the rehab information off our personal history inventory. His pride would not allow him to check the "Yes" box" next to the question, "Have you ever used illegal drugs?"

"No one needs to dig up old bones and use them against me," he said. "What's in the past is the past."

He was persuaded that if God and his wife forgave him, no one else needed to know of his sins. He forbade me to include any of his drug history on our paperwork. I felt like I had to make a choice between being loyal to him or loyal to God and telling the truth. I chose poorly.

At the time, I felt like Achan's wife in Joshua chapter 7, silently participating in a hidden sin. Like she may have done, I tried to convince my husband that hiding things is never a good idea. In the end, manly pride and persuasion won over common sense and conscience. Like Achan and his wife, we ultimately ended up being punished. It was a lesson I'll take to my grave.

When we become aware of hidden sin in our family, we cannot afford to turn a blind eye or a deaf ear. We cannot afford to cover that sin, or shove it under the proverbial rug. We cannot protect the sinner for the sake of the family, for the sake of the marriage, or the sake of the relationship. The Bible is very clear, "The wages of sin is death . . . " (Romans 6:23 KJV). When someone who is in our bed, under our roof, or under our authority is opening doors to the enemy with our silent consent, we place our entire household on dangerous ground. Achan's family quietly slept in their tent over the buried, stolen wedge of gold, the two hundred shekels of silver, and the fancy garment. In the end, they were all found guilty by association. How could they have avoided the consequences? How could I?

It is a tricky thing to bring hidden sin to light. It is painfully difficult to speak the truth in love. It goes against the softness of our feminine nature to stand our ground when everything within us wants to protect (a.k.a. enable) the sinner, wants to bail them out, wants to help them, wants to believe their promises and even their lies. Sometimes we see sin with our own eyes, yet they can convince us it did not really happen. Then we question *our* vision!

The rest of Romans 6:23 says, "…but the gift of God is eternal life." Eternal life is a gift from God. We cannot be another person's salvation. We can actually contribute to their prolonged separation from God by allowing them to continue uninterrupted on a path leading to destruction. The path may appear as narrow as a checkmark in a box that says, "Do you have a history with drug use?" but deception of any kind is a highway to unhappiness. I know what I'm talking about. I did it for years. Living with an addict or an abuser will do that to you. Your senses become dulled. You begin to distrust even yourself.

As Chloé's move-in date drew near, Phillip and Carrie basically released her to us during the daytime. She came to church with us, attended several Christian concerts in our arms, and just lived life with us that summer. I have a clear mental image of Chloé wearing a lime green jumper on the fourth of July, contentedly sitting on Jon's lap as he chatted with a group of friends around a backyard bonfire. Everyone adored her, especially Jon.

I remember the day he almost injured her. Of course it was an accident, but terrifying! We were only a couple of weeks away from moving her in. Our home had definitely taken on a new, kid-friendly look. Her crib and sliding rocker waited in our bedroom. The Pack 'n Play took up considerable space in our living room, and her car seat doubled as a high chair. We wanted her to be with us, but we didn't have anywhere else for her to sit while we ate dinner. Often we would place her, eye level, in the center of the table, where she could feel like part of the family.

The one thing we didn't have was area rugs. Ceramic tiles are beautiful, but brutal. I had already dropped a couple of dishes. Humpty Dumpty had it easy compared to my plates and glasses!

The accident happened just before we sat down to supper. Chloé was waiting in her car seat on the floor next to the table while I ferried food from the kitchen to the dining area with the phone tucked between my shoulder and ear as I chatted with my father's wife, Janet, a registered nurse. Snuffles followed me back and forth as usual, hoping for a dropped morsel, while Whipper lay quietly at Chloé's feet. They both skittered across the tile toward the door when they heard Jon's footsteps in the stairwell.

He came in and made a beeline for the baby, not even acknowledging the girls or removing his shoes.

"Hey little one," he cooed squatting down beside her. "How's my girl? What are you doing way down here? Don't you want to come sit up at the table with Mommy and Daddy?"

With that last question, Jon jerked the car seat up toward the table with one swift motion. I didn't have time to tell him she was not buckled in, that I had just placed her there to sit for a few moments while I answered the phone.

At six months old, Chloé was heavy. The force of Jon's movement pitched her forward and propelled her head first toward the tile floor. Lightning-quick, Jon extended his right foot, buffering her fall with his tennis shoe. We both froze momentarily as Chloé inhaled sharply, suspending her cry in mid-air like kids do when it's going to be a giant howl. "Oh, God! What have I done?" Jon flung the car seat and bent down to gently roll her over as she let out an ungodly guttural wail.

"Janet, I've got to go!" I screamed into the phone. Something terrible has happened."

"Please, Jesus let her be okay! Don't let anything be wrong with her. I cannot believe how quickly Jon put out his foot and prevented her face from pounding that floor. You did that, God. You saved her from a direct hit! What if her neck is injured? What if something else is wrong? Help us, please."

Janet called back and calmly talked us through a basic body check. "Look at her eyes for signs of blood or abnormal pupils," she instructed. "Can you gently move her limbs without obvious discomfort? Check her body for visible signs of swelling or bruising."

Kindly and carefully we looked her over. We noticed nothing abnormal. Nothing. Janet advised us to immediately contact Phillip and Carrie and "go from there." Since they were her legal guardians, we could not take the baby to the hospital without them. When we got off the phone with Janet, Chloé seemed her usual happy self. Jon and I were still shaky and tearful.

I remember making the call to Carrie. "Hi Carrie. I'm sorry to bother you, but we have a possible emergency here." I explained what had happened as Carrie quietly listened.

"Bring her to us," she instructed. "We're not home right now, but Phillip will tell you how to get here." Within minutes, we had Chloé safely buckled into her car seat in the back of my newly purchased four-door Mercury. Jon drove. I sat in the back with the baby. We were silent and scared.

When we arrived at their church ten minutes later, Phillip took one look at us and said, "You two look way worse off than the baby!" Carrie thoroughly inspected her. "She seems alert and content. I don't see anything wrong," she reassured us. "We will continue to monitor her and take her to the emergency room if anything changes. I'll call you if we decide to do that. Don't beat yourselves up. Accidents happen. We can just thank God that Jon has quick reflexes!"

The ride home was quiet as we reflected on what had happened. As we walked into our house two confused dogs greeted us. Brushing them off, Jon and I sat side by side on the sofa. Our dinner was cold on the table, but it didn't matter—neither of us had an appetite. We were anguished by conflicting emotions as we struggled with the fact that we were not Chloé's parents, and could not be with her right then. Neither of us could explain the strong bonds of parental love that pulled us toward her. It hurt to know we had placed her in danger.

Jon, traumatized and angry with himself, stomped downstairs for a cigarette. I remained limp on the sofa, thanking God for His mercy, as Whipper incessantly licked the back of my hand. She always tried to comfort people by nearly licking the hide off any exposed body part; only quitting if she knew you felt better, or you yelled at her to stop.

That stressful day somehow bonded us. We were a family. Chloé never went to the emergency room or had any complications from the fall. Jon and I never discussed it again, but we always made sure her car seat was buckled securely—even when we weren't driving.

Finally . . . finally, after six months of being mommy by day and returning Chloé to Phillip and Carrie each night, the day arrived for our final home inspection. Everything was in place. We had spent hundreds of hours, and dollars, in preparation for that day. Once we passed the inspection, Chloé would be allowed to come home to stay. After that, everything we did as foster parents would simply be a formality until we signed the final adoption papers. We did not plan on taking in any more children.

Our petite young social worker met us in the driveway. "Good afternoon Mr. and Mrs. Miller." We shook hands formally. She seemed more serious than usual, but I only acknowledged that observation in hindsight.

We excitedly gave her the grand tour of our miniature home. She liked the layout, didn't mind that the crib was in our bedroom, but was concerned about the steepness of the stairs to the loft. "We promise to place a baby gate there, once Chloé begins to crawl," I rushed to explain.

"Well, it looks like you have everything in order," she affirmed as the three of us sat down in the living room. She then uncomfortably looked from Jon to me, and back to Jon before announcing, "We received some disturbing information from an anonymous phone call to our office today, which could prevent you from being able to continue to work with our agency."

My throat instantly tightened and my body went limp. I knew what was coming. "Yes," she continued, "someone phoned this morning to inquire whether we were aware of Mr. Miller's drug use and recent stay in a treatment facility. Since it was just an anonymous tip, I need to ask you face-to-face whether or not that information was valid. Of course we will have to do an investigation if you deny the allegations, because drug use and lying automatically disqualify individuals from our program."

I do not remember the conversation that followed, except that I asked if there was an appeals process. "Yes, there is," she replied. "You must to do that through our central office. I'm sorry," she said softly as she stood up to leave.

Chapter 8

Relapse

"When you pass through the waters, I will be with you;
And through the rivers, they shall not overflow you.
When you walk through the fire, you shall not be burned,
Nor shall the flame scorch you."
Isaiah 43:2 NKJV

2002–2003

Yellow-orange light crept across the sky just as I finished typing. From my seat in our loft, I saw the sun rising red through the round window overlooking our scrubby three acres. I had been up all night, pouring my heart into words as I wrote a letter to the adoption placement agency. My words became paragraphs, then pages of explanations, apologies and pleas for mercy. In a desperate attempt to appeal to the head director, I wrote our unabridged story, including the part about how we loved Kiki as if she were our own flesh and blood, promising we would never do anything to intentionally cause her pain.

"If you do not trust my husband's ability to refrain from relapse," I wrote, "I am willing to adopt her myself, apart from Jon. I promise to care for her on my own should anything ever happen between Jon and me."

We had a meeting with the director scheduled for 9 a.m.

"*Please Lord God,*" I prayed as the printer spit out page after page, "*Please let him have compassion on us.*"

I wore a navy blue pantsuit and twisted my hair into a French roll. Jon wore the saddest eyes I've seen. We rode quietly together in his truck. My spirit was heavy, but I clung to a scrap of hope, believing if the director would only read my letter he might understand and be willing to work with us.

Jon and I waited in the reception area for less than two minutes before the director escorted us into his office. I can neither remember his name, nor any detail about him. I only know that he looked straight at my husband and quizzed, "How long have you been clean?"

"One year."

"Do you still go to meetings?"

"No."

"You must not be very serious about staying clean. I'd almost guarantee that you end up back in rehab."

Then, including me in his gaze, he continued, "If people are dishonest on their paperwork, they are automatically disqualified from adopting any child from our agency. We also share that information with the other agencies in the state of Texas."

In addition to blackballing us, he also refused my letter of appeal, saying as he stood with a dismissive gesture, "There really is no point in reading all of this. It won't do you any good. I'm sorry for your disappointment, but we believe it's in the child's best interest to be adopted by the foster family she's been with all along."

I felt small enough to wither into one of the cracks in the linoleum flooring. I walked toward the door, still clutching those desperate unread words in my manila envelope. I remember Jon slamming his fist onto the dashboard of the truck, angry curses spewing from his lips as his foot hit the gas and he sped us home at a frightening speed.

When we arrived, he wordlessly went upstairs to change into work clothes. I was motionless on the sofa when he left. We were two souls in such agony there was no comfort to be found in each other. From that day on, Jon sought the numbing comfort of his snowy white mistress, Cocaine. The arms of my Savior became my only refuge.

I rarely cry. When I do, I howl like a trapped hyena. It is not cute. Growing up, my family teased me, thinking it hilarious to hear a person emit such a sound. Fortunately no human ears had to hear my cries that day. There was nothing funny about them. My sense of loss was so great I could not express it in words, only howls. When my tears were all used up they were followed by heaves and hiccups. Then silence.

I lay on our bed, staring at her barren crib. Knowing she was alive and well and just down the road waiting for me was almost worse than the permanency of death. Jon did not come home to console me. My family felt far-removed with Annie now living Missouri with her new husband and expecting a baby of her own. Even cuddling with Snuffles and Whipper brought no comfort. Only my heavenly Father felt near enough to minister to my aching soul.

As evening came, the silence was suffocating. I made my way down the stairs and down the street toward Ryan and Meredith's place. They must've sensed me coming, because they met me on their Southern front porch with open arms. Fresh tears wet Ryan's shoulder as I wept there for a moment before he passed me to his wife. The creak-creak of Meredith's porch swing chains continued long into the night as we rocked together, back and forth, back and forth. When I returned home, Jon was asleep on the futon upstairs in the loft, the television blaring.

In the morning I asked, "Jon, do you want to go with me to see the baby?" He didn't. I quietly gathered her favorite books and toys from our home and drove across town to say goodbye.

Chloé rested in my arms while I slowly inhaled her soft smell and spilled my side of the story to her foster parents. They were already informed we'd been removed from the adoption list and were no longer allowed to take her for unsupervised visits. A warm blanket of shame spread over me as we sat speaking together. I choked back tears as I awaited their response.

Graciously Carrie invited me to be Chloé's godmother promising, "You can still visit her any time."

"Thank you. That means so much." I looked up from Chloé's sweet sleeping face, her limp body heavy in my arms. Although they ached with her weight, I refused to put her down.

"I *will* be her godmother. I need to wean myself from her, though. It hurts too much right now . . . to be with her, knowing she is no longer mine."

My gut told me if we continued spending time together, the bond between us would hurt us both. My thoughts were confirmed a little while later as Chloé cried for me when I was preparing to leave. Instinctively, an awful protective barrier erected itself around my heart as I turned my back on my baby's extended arms and told her mother I would stop by after school sometimes to visit. It would be weeks before I could do it. In the meantime, I tried to function as normal as possible when in public. In private, I crumbled.

I can recall several ways God reached for me during that storm. One was through the music of a brother and sister group called Selah. After their ministry in our church a few weeks earlier, I'd held Chloé on my hip while waiting for them to sign their new CD, "Be Still My Soul." The powerful words of those resurrected hymns became salve to my broken heart, each song a prayer. *"Be still, my soul: the Lord is on thy side. Bear patiently the cross of grief or pain. Leave to thy God to order and provide; in every change, He faithful will remain . . ."* I played the music relentlessly to keep the calling darkness at bay.

I'd managed to start another school year, but have no recollection of the details. Teaching was my second skin. I depended on its rhythms to hold me together. My class that year was particularly precious. One gap-toothed first grader was a boy named Ian. His intuitive mother picked up on my pain and handed me Beth Moore's best-selling hardback, *Praying God's Word,* along with a 3x5 index card with a Scripture prayer printed neatly in pencil. That book became another tool God placed in my hands along with Selah's music. I carried it with me everywhere. Praying the Scriptures from the chapter entitled "Overcoming Despair Resulting From Loss" became a crucial part of my survival.

Although a few people attempted to reach out to me through my months of darkness, I doubt any human fathomed the depth of my loss. In my mind, Chloé was my one hope of ever becoming a mother. Adoption was now out of the question, and Jon's relapse-response to our disappointment severed any dreams he and I might have a child together. I felt like a wounded animal, caught in a trap.

Because of the time I'd spent in counseling with Leon and the things I'd heard in Jon's 12 Step meetings, I began to recognize he was not the only person in our family with issues. Reading Beth Moore's book made me painfully aware of some specific strongholds the enemy had in my life. My own patterns of relating were far from healthy. I was not dealing well with my losses.

Knowing I would be going home to a deserted house, I chose to work longer and longer hours at school. Any elementary school teacher knows the work is never finished; one just has to decide what time to go home. I would stay until I was too hungry or too tired to do anything else.

No matter what time I got home, my poor dogs raced from their doghouse to joyfully greet me at the gate, bless their little hearts. They never held a grudge, even when I didn't come home for six weeks. Let me tell you how that happened. But first, I must tell you where I am as I write this chapter.

I've been lying all afternoon in the warm September sun as it creeps across a tiled balcony in the quaint seaside town of Novigrad, Croatia. When I stand to stretch, I can see the harbor with its rows of tiny fishing boats. From this vantage point, the darkness of the past appears very black indeed. Because I know the rest of the story, I can ink line after line in my college-ruled spiral notebook with hope and joy, knowing I serve a Savior who redeems the dreams we think are lost. Hang with me, and you will see what I'm talking about. Hang with Him, and you will experience it in your own life. Now, back to those six weeks . . .

"You need to set a boundary with him," Leon counseled. "He's taking advantage of the fact that you will pay the bills and put food in the refrigerator."

"But what am I supposed to do?" I whined. "I don't want our credit to be ruined. *My* good name is on everything too."

I was complaining to Leon about Jon charging more than five hundred dollars on the credit card *and* spending most of his paycheck on cocaine, again. Leon suggested I put him out of the house, "until he is ready to get help."

"I don't feel safe there alone since we got robbed. I'm just not sure that's what I want to do," I resisted.

"Well, is there anywhere you *would* feel comfortable staying for a while?

"Maybe. But I don't think it's fair that *I'm* the one who has to leave *my* home because of what *he's* doing! I think it's *his* fault we've been robbed again. Why would someone come to our home and pound the door down with a shovel?"

Leon heard my frustration and offered some Dr. Dobson-inspired "tough love" solutions. I was fed up with Jon's downward spiral since we lost Chloé. He was out of control, and I was trying to keep everything together in the midst of compounded grief. On top of it all, our home was invaded again.

It was a sunny, September afternoon when Jon called the school, leaving a message for me to come home immediately because we had been robbed. "Robbed" was an understatement. Our house was *ransacked!*

In the process of beating our metal door in with a shovel, thieves overturned several potted plants that lined the tiled stairwell from the garage to our inner front door. They tracked rich black potting soil into the house, grinding it into our cream-colored Berber carpet as they trekked up and down the loft stairs with our television, our sound system, and nearly everything with an electric plug. Every sofa cushion stood precariously on end. Our mattress was lifted and shifted cattywampus on the bed frame. My orderly home looked like an earthquake casualty. The thieves even violated our teetotal-refrigerator, leaving a half-empty Budweiser to mock me from the top shelf.

Already infuriated by the upheaval of our walk-in closet, I truly lost it when I discovered even my undergarment drawer was defiled. Utterly defeated, I threw myself across our disheveled bed, wailing about my missing perfume as police officers traipsed through the disaster, taking notes for their report. I was beyond talking. Jon handled everything.

Later that evening, Ryan and Meredith dropped off a loaner TV. They were strangely quiet as they helped us order our home. A few minutes later, some other friends showed up with supper—soup, I think. The gesture was touching. Kindness in a time of crisis is remembered, even when details aren't. When Jon finally got the front door fixed, we fell exhausted into our freshly made bed.

"Who do you owe?" I boldly accused. Doesn't anger have a way of trumping exhaustion? I blamed Jon's drug activity for the crime and I wanted answers. "Why would anybody know where we live?"

"I don't owe anyone anything. I promise. All I can think," he answered slowly, "is that they got our address from my license."

"From your license!" I screeched. Zero to sixty decibels in 2.2 seconds—the ugly clamor of a wife's unresolved grief and anger. "Why would anyone have your driver's license?"

"Because you have to leave it with someone when you go in to get your stuff."

"YOU LEAVE YOUR LICENSE WITH DRUG DEALERS? HAVE YOU LOST YOUR MIND?" I screamed the words as fresh tears appeared. They continued soaking my pillow long after Jon had retreated upstairs to the loft. His withdrawal confused the dogs. First they pattered after him, but soon returned to their own bed.

Those high emotions remained fresh as I conversed with Leon about boundaries and tough love. Within weeks my happy country home became my own private hell. I was afraid to sleep there alone, and afraid to sleep with my spouse who had once more become a stranger. I needed wisdom that was not my own, to know how to deal with my reality.

The following Friday, Jon did not come home from work. On Saturday morning, I went to church as usual, a sickening feeling curdling in the pit of my stomach. Afraid to be home alone when the bad news came, I arranged to spend the night with Principle Steve and his wife Renée who had been my classroom aide for six years. After working together for so long, we were more like family than colleagues.. I didn't know what the bad news was, but I felt restless . . . uneasy. Rushing home after church, I cared for Snuffles and Whipper, left a here's-where-you-can-reach-me note and raced back out the door.

Late Saturday night, the call came through to my new cell phone. Since I was already asleep on Steve and Renée's well-loved sofa, voicemail picked it up. "I'm okay. I'm home." That was it. Those four words triggered both relief and anger. I played them repeatedly as Sunday morning sunlight filtered through the windows, spilling patterns onto my makeshift bed. I was relieved he wasn't in a ditch somewhere, but furious he'd disappeared again without warning. Nights like that one were torture.

Those few hours, as I discovered later, cost him his paycheck. That angered me, but I was even more distraught about having no idea who my husband had spent the weekend with. I knew nothing about the drug culture, and was terrified of what I didn't know, terrified of what I couldn't monitor or control, of what I didn't trust.

After that, I did not want to go home. A couple of phone calls created temporary accommodations with another couple from church. They had strong German roots and a great studio loft not far from my school. "You can stay for as long as you need to," they kindly offered. "We're just sorry there isn't a kitchen up there."

"Dear God in Heaven," I prayed one rainy, October morning as I arrived at school early so I could heat my breakfast-corndog in the microwave and have a moment of silence before anyone arrived. *"Why am I the one suffering the consequences of Jon's choices? Why must I eat frozen corndogs and Ramen noodles from a Styrofoam cup when I have a gorgeous kitchen at home? I miss cooking. I miss my girls. I miss my own bed and bathtub."*

Right there in my classroom, I began to wail as I continued my plea. *"Am I doing the right thing by staying awaaaay? Does Jon even care that I am gooooone? Please show me what to dooooo."*

Ding! Breakfast was ready. Before my wailing got out of hand, I stifled it with a hot corny-dog.

It was hard to leave the girls behind, but no pets were allowed in the studio. Besides, being responsible for them increased the odds of Jon of going home each night. I asked Ryan and Meredith to drive by each evening, to see if he'd made it home to care for them. I didn't want my girls to suffer.

Turns out, they were fine. I was the one suffering.

I'd left a brief note on the fridge the day I packed my suitcase.

"Dear Jon, I no longer feel safe here. I will come home when you decide to get some help." Encrypted between those lines was the heart-cry of every maiden to her prince: *Do you love me? Am I worth rescuing? Will you come for me?*

Unfortunately for my heart, after six weeks he had neither responded, nor come for me. I'd sneak home every few days to water my plants and play with the dogs. They seemed okay, always overjoyed to see me. The house, however, had morphed into a man cave: messy kitchen, moldy linens, and mountains of junk food. The leftovers littering the loft indicated Jon spent his at-home time in front of the newly replaced large-screen TV.

Ever since we lost Chloé, I had zero tolerance for television's din. Instead of false hilarity and distorted reality TV, I discovered treasured sources of sanity in times of silent solitude, in the Scriptures and in prayer. Despite the fact Jon had almost gone bachelor in my absence, and knowing that the battle for quiet was one I would have to fight, shortly after that corn-dog-morning I felt it was time to return home.

Leon agreed. He could see we weren't getting the expected results of our one-sided experiment and Jon was enjoying his freedom a little too much. Missing his wife appeared to be the last thing on his mind. It was time for a reality check.

We both got one when we were robbed again a few weeks later. We had just completed our Christmas shopping. Several wrapped gifts sparkled under the extra-tall, pre-lit pine Jon charged to our Lowe's card during a drug-enhanced shopping spree. I came home from school one afternoon to another unwanted surprise. The thieves opened our gifts, taking only the items they wanted. In addition, they stole every newly replaced electronic, and Jon's new Nikes, which had only been worn once or twice.

None of that devastated me like the disappearance of my cedar hope chest. The burglars had lifted it from its place at the foot of the bed, and lugged it out the door, probably thinking they were making a haul! That chest contained nothing worth pawning, but much worth shedding tears over. A quilt, handmade by my Mamaw, scrapbooks, photos, and keepsakes from my travels – all irreplaceable.

Also missing was a gift from my mother, a unique hand puppet named Ursli, whom she had purchased in a tiny Swiss village where they still speak the unusual Romansh language and treasure the art of storytelling and craftsmanship. I had often used the puppet and its companion book, *A Bell for Ursli*, when teaching my students about Switzerland. Ursli was special.

Nothing in my hope chest was worth diddly-squat to anyone outside my family, but it was a tremendous blow to know someone carried it out of my home in broad daylight.

"Father, I cannot fathom what thieves would want with my personal things. I am sick of being robbed! My home no longer feels like a place I want to be. God, please get me out of here."

In another side note: Today I'm writing from a raised canopy daybed on the Croatian seaside. Sitting here under blue sky, gazing periodically at the sparkling Adriatic, with the breeze gently swaying the gauzy white canopy, it's easy to forget how dark those days were. I want to remember. I'm praying to remember, because I want my story to bring hope to those facing similar darkness. I long to share my valley experiences because another woman may see her reflection in the girl in this story. She may choose to handle her own life differently because of something I share, or she may have greater compassion for someone in her circle who lives a similar nightmare.

"Father, as I offer this story, this testimony of Your goodness, Your faithfulness, and Your providence, I pray my readers will not become discouraged as they wade through the valleys and the losses I've experienced. Please give them hope that there are blue-sky-and-sunshine days ahead. Guide them through the storms of their own lives. Amen."

God answered my *get-me-out-of-here* prayer, but before He moved me He sustained me through the rest of a tough school year. Maintaining my professional commitments was challenging because I was so distracted by the craziness of my home life. Despite the crazy, God used me to share His love with the mother of "the new kid."

Shane was one of those tapping drumming wiggling jiggling talking humming kinds of kids, a challenge to teach. He'd transferred, mid-year, to our Christian school because he just wasn't making it in the county school system. Somehow, I managed to get through the wiggle and jiggle and teach him to read. I tried to gently redirect his behaviors rather than shout. He was accustomed to shouting. Once I did blast him; I felt terrible about it afterward, and apologized. He looked at me in shock and then wrapped his arms around me like a twist tie around a loaf of bread. I took that as forgiveness.

Shane wasn't from a Christian family, but his parents desperately placed him in a Christ-centered school to see if it would help. God only knows how He gave me patience for that particular child, that particular school year. He did, though. He also gave me a love for the boy that caused his mother to want to know the Lord.

The best way to remember and experience God's love for us is to share Him with others. Right in the middle of my emotional mess, with a heart shattered by the loss of my baby, and a husband strung out on cocaine, God asked me to share His love with Shane's mother. I could not have possibly pawned that responsibility off on anyone else because she came to me personally, asking if I'd study the Bible with her. How could I say no?

That's how God worked to turn my focus from *my* self, *my* losses and *my* pain to *His* love and *His* gift to humanity through His son, Jesus Christ. Week after week, as I prayed with Shane's mother and opened God's Word with her, I felt the Lord reassuring me that He saw me, that He loved me, and that He would heal my hurting heart.

My part of accepting God's promised healing was allowing Him to use me, even when I was broken. God invited me to be a clean vessel for His love to flow through, as long as I refused to be consumed by bitterness and blame. It was a daily battle, but I did not want anger or an unforgiving heart to block the channels of God's goodness in me. I believe He handed me Shane's family for my benefit as much as theirs.

The months crawled. Much of that year remains foggy. Chloé turned one in February, only she was now officially named Alexandra since Carrie and Phillip had legally adopted her. In my mind, she'll always be Chloé, because that's the name I love her by and that's the name I use when I pray for her.

They invited Jon and me to attend her birthday party. We went together. Before the cake was served, we were both emotional wrecks. Chloé was slightly shy with Jon, but reached straight for me. Every blessed time I had gathered enough courage to see her in the past months, I had hyena-howled in my car on the way home. It was an agony that never got easier. This party did not absolve my pain.

It didn't help that Phillip and Carrie had pulled us aside to share their caseworker's theory that one of the strikes against us was that we were not "black enough" to be Chloé's parents. Chloé didn't seem to realize that because she clung to me like the skin on a banana as I was trying to say goodbye. Kids don't care about skin color. They know what's in your heart.

I could never decide which was worse, seeing her, or not seeing her. I tried to refrain from too much contact after Carrie explained she was having difficulty bonding with her after we were denied the right to adopt. Their mother-daughter relationship was important. I faltered between not wanting to interfere and not wanting to desert her, since many adopted children struggle with abandonment issues.

Only much later did I understand spiritual soul ties and the influence they can have over relationships. That is when I severed our bond in the spiritual realm so she would be released to love and receive love from her adoptive mother. After that, I distinctly remember Carrie sharing that their relationship significantly improved. My prolonged absence may also have had something to do their bonding, as Chloé was no longer bonding with me.

About the time spring bluebonnets began to paint the Texas Hill Country with an ocean of color, I finalized my plans to move away. Living with the perpetual dread of being robbed, and the gossip circulating about Jon made me want to leave. Fear for Jon's life was catalyst enough for me to call a meeting with his boss, Larry.

"Please just fire him," I begged as we sat on a picnic table in the park next to my school one April afternoon. "He cannot continue to have access to money. He'll end up killing himself. He's high all the time, snorting on the job and at home." I had never witnessed him using, but his behavior, his purplish-red face and his chronic post-nasal drip gave his secret away.

"I'd been suspicious for a long time." Larry averted his eyes. "Even one of our homeowners approached me about Jon's erratic behavior awhile back. When my tools started disappearing and his on-the-job injuries increased, I was positive he was using again. I just cannot bring myself to fire him. I like the guy. He's a good worker when he's working."

Frustrated, I left the conversation and hiked up the hill to the school.

"God, I cannot understand why Larry would keep employing him after all the stuff he has stolen and pawned! He's a danger on the job. It's a wonder he didn't kill himself when he fell off the roof and broke his arm. And what about that time he shot himself through the hand with the nail gun? I just don't get it. If Larry really liked Jon, he would fire him, wouldn't he? That might even save his life! I'm worn out with it all. Please give me some wisdom."

Later that week, I called Bob and Aubrey about selling our house. I sought their counsel first, because I had to let them know Jon wrote so many personal checks from the building funds that we owed more money than the place was worth. Because I am a naturally private person, and because you never want your lender to think you may not be in a position to pay them, I hadn't shared with them the fact that Jon had gone off the deep end again and was spending about a thousand dollars a week on cocaine. We were in major debt, with not a lot to show for it, except a very large Christmas tree, and a yellow stucco home on three country acres.

The compassion and love that wrapped our friends' response was relieving. I poured my heart out to them, telling them everything, seeking their advice. They offered an interesting solution.

Bob suggested we get a real estate agent and put the house on the market, asking for ten thousand dollars more than we owed. He also offered to take Jon immediately to work with him in his heating and air conditioning business. Aubrey agreed, saying, "Jon can stay in our home for a while, so he can detox. He needs to get away from his current environment."

"It's true," Bob chimed in. "He's welcome here, but he has to be willing to agree to stay away from drugs."

I thought it sounded like a good plan.

"Bob and Aubrey live in a rural area about five driving hours north of us. That's too far for a drug run," I told Leon during our next counseling session. Surprisingly, Jon was again going with me to see Leon. I think he realized he was headed for death or prison. He was also humbled because, although Larry had not fired him, he *had* confronted him about stealing and using on the job.

Leon had been tough lately. He rebuked Jon for not having a sponsor or attending regular Narcotics Anonymous meetings. Jon made lame excuses like, "I don't have enough time for meetings," and "They're too far away." Leon didn't buy his lies.

"You have plenty of time to find drugs and to get high. That's no excuse. What do you really want from your life, Jon?"

"I don't know."

Leon looked him square in the face. "Do you want to live?"

"Yes."

"Do you think you'll live if you stay in this city?"

Lowering his eyes, Jon shook his head and mumbled, "No."

We each knew it was true. Jon's face was gaunt and hollow. He often experienced serious heart pain, and the cocaine had literally burned a hole through his septum.

Leon promptly agreed that moving away was a brilliant idea. He had already warned us, "Addicts greatly improve their chances of staying clean if they start fresh in a new environment upon release from rehab."

Jon's response was delayed, but in alignment with his expression of wanting to live.

"I'll go," he finally consented.

We left Leon's office with an intervention plan to keep Jon alive by sending him to live in North Texas with Bob and Aubrey. I would stay behind to sell our home and finish the school year. My relief was immediate. Having a plan felt good.

I'd resigned myself to the fact that I could easily become a widow at age 32. I know it sounds terrible, but sometimes I just wished that Jon would hurry up and get it over with so I could stop worrying about him. It was becoming exceedingly difficult to have enough emotional energy for a classroom full of first graders when I'd been awake all night worrying whether Jon was dead or alive. I was exhausted from the months of grieving, compounded by Jon's rejection and addiction, the debt and the robberies. I could barely wait for the school year to end. It was only my Jesus who sustained me through April and May.

Life immediately improved after Jon left. I rested easier, knowing that he was living with my praying friend Aubrey, and wouldn't be sneaking into our bed in the middle of the night after returning from a binge. I also knew that Bob had asked him to park his truck and relinquish the keys. That meant no running around. They'd ride to jobs together in Bob's service van and eat the healthy lunches Aubrey packed. Those few weeks gave me time to think and pray about what to do next. Although I was getting similar counsel from several sources, I was torn between that counsel and my feelings.

Leon had suggested a legal separation when I complained about the financial mess Jon's habit had created. "There are different types of abuse that can take place in a marriage," he explained. "Financial abuse is one of them."

Then he asked pointedly, "How long has it been since you and Jon have been intimate with one another?" I couldn't remember, but I completely identified with Leon's explanation of the vulnerability created in a marriage when there is not a healthy sex life. He took a step closer to my pain with his follow-up question "Do you still want to have children?"

"Yes. But not with Jon like he is. I couldn't do this to a child."

"Do you want to continue to do this to yourself?" Ouch. Leon knew just how to force me to face my reality. His next question was no less forthright. "Can you envision things improving in your marriage?"

"I don't know. It's difficult right now for me to picture the future. I just see blackness. But, I don't want to give up on Jon if things can get better. God never gives up on us, right?"

"That's true. But you are not Jon's savior. He has a Savior in Jesus Christ. You cannot choose freedom for him. You cannot continue to rescue him from himself. You need to begin thinking about you, because your husband is certainly not looking out for you. Let's pray about it, but I'm not convinced he wants to stay clean or stay married. When only one person is doing all the work, that person can easily lose sight of themselves and their purpose. I see that happening to you."

I knew Leon was right. I could feel myself being swallowed up by codependency and control, my default mechanisms when life felt out of hand. We prayed together, asking for wisdom about what I should do. I continued to pray for myself in the following weeks, asking God to help me listen to His counsel above all. Part of me wanted to let Jon go. Part of me pleaded for a miracle in our marriage.

I was learning to walk closely with my heavenly Father. My daily sanity and strength depended upon my connection with Him. I had to stay tapped into His power because I was also battling some kind of resident evil. Whatever agreements with the enemy Jon had made on our property had invited the presence of some dark spirits. Just because he had gone didn't mean they had gone.

There was a heavy presence around the house, especially downstairs in the garage and guest bedroom. Unfortunately I had to go down there to get to the laundry room. I couldn't pinpoint the problem, but there definitely was one. Years later, my sister shared that she had seen and rebuked an apparition in the guest room once, when she had visited.

Since then, I've learned more about spiritual warfare and the "doorways" that evil spirits use to gain access to a person's life. Drug use is definitely one. I had enough knowledge back then to remove anything from our home that I thought might be an invitation to the dark side.

A few months earlier, when I was battling depression, I'd felt impressed to remove Chloé's crib from our bedroom and to release anything else that would idolize her or constantly remind me she wasn't coming home. That helped dispel the darkness.

Now that Jon was gone, I searched for anything he may have left behind. In our closet, I found a tin can with part of a McDonald's straw in it. (Ever notice how the straws from McDonald's are larger in diameter than other straws?) Immediately I knew *that* straw had been used to snort cocaine. Into the trash it went. I found little else of his, but I prayerfully purged my music collection and tossed some pretty whiskey and wine bottles I'd collected over the years. I didn't want anything in my house representing a lifestyle that did not bring honor to God. Even with all of my eradications, there was still an evil presence. I couldn't always sense it, but sometimes it was quite strong.

"For God has not given us a spirit of fear, but of power and of love and of a sound mind." Standing at the bathroom sink, I repeated 2 Timothy 1:7 (NKJV) through a mouthful of toothpaste. *"I've been fearful a lot in this house, haven't I, God? - Afraid of being robbed, afraid of finding Jon dead, afraid when he didn't come home, afraid when he did come home. I am afraid of what people are saying about us, afraid of losing Chloé, afraid of going bankrupt, afraid, afraid, afraid!"*

Maybe it was spirits of fear lurking around. Maybe they were there by my invitation and not Jon's. Maybe my own lack of trust had invited them to taunt me. Whatever the spirits or their reasons for being there, I had enough of their foolishness.

One night I locked myself out of the main part of the house. Arriving home from a weekend with Jon, I groggily realized I'd left my key at Bob and Aubrey's. It was too late to call our real estate agent. My garage door opener got me into the bottom floor. I decided to sleep in the downstairs guest room and contact our agent in the morning to get a copy of her key. Exhausted by an emotional visit and the long drive home, I fell asleep instantly.

Have you ever had that disconcerting feeling of knowing someone is watching you while you sleep? Well, sometime in the wee hours, I had that eerie sensation. I knew I had locked both the garage and the bedroom doors. I'd heard no noise, but fear was closing my throat. I felt its dark, heavy presence.

"In the name of Jesus Christ of Nazareth," I commanded from underneath my covers, "Get out of this house! You have no right to be here! I reclaim this territory for God and I renounce any unholy activities that have taken place in this room or on this property. Now, Go!" By then I was sitting up, shouting, "And do not come back!" Immediately the oppressive darkness disappeared.

"Thank You, Jesus, for the power in Your name and for Your shed blood, which has already saved me from all powers of darkness and given me authority over them because of the eternal victory You won on the cross."

I lay down and slept peacefully until morning. From that night until I moved out completely, I never again felt afraid in that house. In obedience to Jesus and in relationship with Jesus, there is power and protection from the enemy. That experience provided one more tool for my spiritual tool belt - holy boldness in the face of fear.

After Jon left town, opinions fell like rain, some unsolicited, some quite welcome. I tried keeping an open mind because I had big decisions to make.

Bob and Aubrey kept me up-to-date on Jon's detoxification program. It was simple: "Work so hard all day long in the heat that you don't have one ounce of energy left to even think about drugs. Then get up and do it again tomorrow." According to them, it seemed to be working.

"The only thing is," Aubrey confided into the phone one evening, "he will not quit smoking. He's respectful enough to go away from us when he's doing it, but he doesn't appear to want to stop."

"Well, where's he getting cigarettes if he can't go anywhere?"

"He bums or buys them from other workers on job sites, or he'll run into the gas station when Bob fills up the van."

"He can live without me, but he can't live without his mother," I muttered.

"What?" Aubrey sounded confused.

"Oh, never mind. I guess we can only cross one bridge at a time."

Bob and Aubrey thought I should move north and start fresh with Jon. They said they had some friends who helped many people find freedom from drugs and all sorts of bondage through their prayer and deliverance ministry. They thought Jon might benefit from something like that. "He's already so much better. Maybe you should give him another chance," Bob encouraged.

Other friends had different opinions. Ryan deemed Jon's behavior immensely selfish and thought he'd treated me badly without much remorse. Meredith agreed, adding, "I'll support your decision, but honestly Julie, I think you'll just get more of the same." They encouraged me to think long and hard about moving to another part of the state to be with a husband who didn't appear to care about me.

My family was angry about the robberies, Jon's relapse, and the deep disappointment I'd experienced that year. Mom and Annie remained sore from our Buona Notte Café losses. They were weary with the hurt and disappointment in my voice, though I rarely revealed much of what was happening. Sometimes those closest to us know things without being told with words.

By spring break I had decided to lay out a Gideon-style "fleece" to God. I would apply for a teaching position near Jon. If I got hired, I would take that as a sign I should move there and reconcile with my husband.

By the time I started interviewing, Jon was much more himself. He had apologized to me several times and agreed to do "whatever it takes" to stay clean and to be a better husband. I needed to believe him.

"I found a house!" He'd declared excitedly during one phone conversation. "It's a rental on one acre. Not too far from Bob and Aubrey." I could tell he wanted me to be happy about it. "The owner will let me fix it up in exchange for a couple months rent. Why don't you plan to come up during spring break? We can paint the inside together." Against Leon's counsel, I agreed to go.

By April's end I had a freshly painted yellow kitchen in a creaky old house on a one-acre lot. I had also secured a new position teaching first grade in a local public school.

"I guess I'm moving to North Texas," I informed my realtor as we completed the final paperwork on our house sale. After she took her cut and Bob and Aubrey were paid off, we would have enough cash to settle the property taxes and bank five thousand dollars. Unfortunately, that was only a fraction of our credit card debt. Nonetheless, I was thrilled with the outcome of the sale. I wasn't as positive about moving north. I consoled myself with the thought that I'd be close to my friend Aubrey.

"This isn't just me trying to force things to work, is it? You did answer my fleece prayer, right God?"

Leon remained unconvinced. He again mentioned long-term separation during one of our counseling sessions, maintaining that Jon wasn't taking active measures to deal with his issues.

"He is just masking them for now by working hard and living in a semi-controlled environment. This is not something sustainable unless he is actively engaged in a deep-level healing process. Yes, God can restore Jon. But Jon needs to seek that restoration. Otherwise he can easily end up right back where he started. Have you seen any evidence of this on your visits? Is he attending a recovery group or seeking counseling on his own?"

Those were difficult questions. I knew the answer was no. "But," I reasoned, "do I leave my husband because he is broken and refuses to get fixed?"

I erroneously equated "separation" with "divorce," which I could *not* justify. I had made a promise till death. I meant it. I vowed not to perpetuate the pattern of divorce in my family.

"I am choosing to give him the benefit of the doubt," I said to Leon during our last session before leaving town. "If I'm erring, I'm erring on the side of forgiveness and compassion. I don't want any regrets."

"I'm always here for you guys if you need me," he promised. "I'm just a phone call away. Anytime, day or night. I love you both and I really do want the best for you. I mean that."

"Thank you Leon. I don't know how I would have survived this without you. You've been a life saver." He hugged me goodbye.

Leon was an angel. I probably should have listened to him. Some of us insist on making our own mistakes. Unfortunately, I fit *that* bill. Besides, I had my fleece.

Saying goodbye to Chloé was rough. She grew so quickly I'd already missed a lot in-between visits. Now I had to say goodbye for an indefinite period of time. It would be months, maybe years before I would hold her again. The ache in my heart ripped deep and long as I kissed the top of her curly brown head before closing Carrie's front door. Goodbye had never become easier. It never would.

Jon returned home for the last bit of packing and cleaning. Our church threw us a great going-away party. We'd been part of their family for seven years. It was hard to leave friends who had walked through life's ups and downs with us. God had truly loved me through some of those precious people. I would carry them with me in my heart.

Years later we would catch up on Facebook, but at the time, it was a huge loss to walk away from a community that felt like home, believing I'd lose touch with most everyone.

Our closest friends came out to help load the U-Haul on Sunday morning. I cherish the mental image of our circle of friends, holding and praying over us before we drove away. At this point, I wish I could write, "And they all lived happily ever after. The end." But that's not quite the way things turned out. I felt both a twinge of sadness and a spark of hope when I caught a glimpse of our precious stone and stucco home in my rear view mirror as I rounded the corner into the future.

Chapter 9

A Fresh Start

"Why, my soul, are you downcast?
Why so disturbed within me?
Put your hope in God,
for I will yet praise him,
my Savior and my God."
Psalm 42:11 NIV

2003-2004

"Oh Aubrey, I'm glad you answered," I cried. "I can't reach Jon and I've wrecked my car. I think I'm okay though."

"I'll be right there," Aubrey gasped. "Where exactly are you?"

I knew she would come. Aubrey and I have history together. She's come to my rescue on many occasions. While I waited, I replayed her greatest rescue in my head.

It was 1993. I had convinced the school board of a tiny Christian academy I could handle the position they offered: full-time teacher, grades Kindergarten, first, second, third, fifth, sixth and eighth. Even though there would only be twelve students, an assignment like that was a challenge for a first-timer. Aubrey, a retired teacher herself, was on the board that hired me.

It was the summer after I deleted Bird Man from my life. After Costa Rica, I moved to Texas seeking interviews for any teaching job hiring rookies. Jon relocated from Costa Rica to stay with his sister Laurel in Dallas, which was about fifty miles away. I didn't realize my physical and emotional fragility as I entered that school year.

Aubrey showed up one August day to help me organize and inventory the classroom. Because of her helpfulness, my year began with a well-ordered workspace. She also took me to lunch a couple of times, which made me feel like I had a friend in a city where I knew no one. I had no idea what a blessed friend she would turn out to be.

I had done my practicum in a multi-age classroom, learning how to balance direct instruction with independent practice and how to use peer tutoring to everyone's advantage. That experience helped me know how to structure the school days. Some flowed remarkably well. My students were sweet and helpful. I struggled, though, to know what to do with two active Kindergarteners with limited English. "Si Maestra," they giggled each time I redirected their innocent antics toward more appropriate classroom behavior.

95

Every classroom moment was a juggling act. The real work, though, took place after school and on weekends as I handled teacher manuals for several subjects across seven grades. After checking papers and developing lesson plans, my evenings and weekends shriveled to a few hours of sleep and worship, with little time for anything else. I even recruited Jon to grade math papers when he came to visit.

By the time the October rains arrived, I knew I would not make it to May. I felt I was doing a disservice to those children, but could not find time to implement necessary changes. My sixty-hour workweeks were physically draining. I was often tearful. I remember driving over a bridge one morning with the thought: *I could just run my car off this bridge, then I would at least be able to rest.* In that moment of desperation I decided to quit.

The decision hurt because the word quit was not part of my vocabulary. I was a go-getter, not a quitter, but after only two and a half months as a teacher, I was burned out. Finishing the year was not an option.

When the school board chairman received my resignation letter, he called an emergency meeting. Scanning the faces around that table, I found only compassion. "I know just a few months ago I convinced all of you I could do this." My voice trembled. "I really thought I could. But I can't. I'm not going to make it through this year. I'm very sorry. I don't know what else to say." I bowed my head in shame.

Silence. Then Aubrey spoke up. "What if you had some help?"

"You mean, like an assistant?" I asked.

"Yes, but what if that person took the lower grades, so you could concentrate on providing the older students with what they need."

"That would definitely help," I sighed. "The little ones demand so much attention."

Aubrey then addressed the board. "I have spoken with Bob, and we are in agreement if the educational superintendent and the board think it would be a workable situation." She paused. "What if I were to teach grades K through two, four days a week while Ms. Julie teaches the others? On Fridays, she would have all of the students, but the day could be structured with assessments and special projects."

The board agreed unanimously, recommending the superintendent accept Aubrey's written proposal. I was rescued!

The unselfish sacrifice Aubrey and Bob made that year for a floundering young teacher was huge. You see, they lived an hour's drive from the school, and rather than spending two hours a day driving, Aubrey came to town on Monday mornings and went home on Thursday evenings. She stayed with the board chairman and his wife three nights a week for eight months! I become emotional, remembering how she redeemed my career with her sacrificial love. When I was ready to walk away, thinking I chose the wrong profession, Aubrey rescued me.

"Thank You, Lord God, for sending her to rescue me then, and now. She has been a wonderful friend."

Back to the situation at hand, it was exactly thirteen miles of winding country road from where we lived to my new school. Before the accident, I was on my way to orientation. An early rain wet the road just enough to bring oil to the surface. I braked on a curve, instantly losing control of my Mercury Sedan. Hydroplaning into a spin, I simultaneously called on Jesus, took my foot off the brake and clung to the steering wheel. My car reeled off the road and smacked hard into a large oak, bringing me to a sudden stop, facing the opposite direction from the way I'd been traveling. My sandal caught under the gas pedal twisting my right foot with the impact.

"I'm okay. I'm okay. I think I'm okay," I'd half-cried, unhooking my seatbelt and opening the door. As I stood up, pain shot through my foot. I tried walking on it. It seemed fine. My car was definitely not fine.

Aubrey arrived in twenty minutes. I began sobbing as soon as she hugged me. After inspecting my foot, she agreed I probably didn't need an ambulance. We did call the police and tow truck for my poor car. Aubrey took me to school and one of my new colleagues brought me home that afternoon.

Later that week I went to the wrecking yard to retrieve my belongings. When I saw what that tree did to my car, I was thankful I'd only needed some Neosporin and a good chiropractor. It could have been much worse! According to the insurance report, the car was totaled.

Aubrey recommended a chiropractor from our new church. "He's very good. And he's a nice Christian man."

"I don't know if I feel comfortable going to someone from church."

"It's up to you," she replied. "He's the best in town."

I went. It was the beginning of a relationship that would enhance my life on many levels. Dr. Alan, and Darcy, his fun-loving wife, became fast friends with Jon and me. God used them to bless us with much more than chiropractic care.

I was cautious at first. Making friends was difficult for me as a child and teen. Between moving a lot and being a natural introvert, I found it tough to break into the existing social groups at school or church. The friendships I had formed, I kept for life.

Adulthood hasn't made it easier. Women can sometimes be quite cruel to one another, even ones who call themselves Christians. I learned to be a bit wary, especially since Jon and I had secrets. Gossip destroys relationships. I knew I didn't need any gossiping girlfriends. I had Aubrey as my friend, and I wasn't sure I wanted to be close to anyone else in my new town.

Darcy's exuberant personality and genuine interest broke down my barriers and brought me into her circle. I quickly learned I could trust her with my secrets. She and Dr. Alan were active members in our new church. They included us in everything! If Jon and I were going to make it, we needed good Christian friends. We needed to plug in to the body of Christ, so we could begin to heal by reaching out to others rather than self-medicating with drugs or work.

The Texas summer heat kept Bob and Jon hopping with air-conditioning work. Hard work was good for Jon, both financially and physically. He'd developed a layer of muscle and picked up a few healthy pounds. With a little bit of suntan and four months without drugs, Jon looked much better. He had also begun acting more like a husband and less like a roommate. We both thanked God for giving us a new beginning.

Following Leon's counsel, we began attending a Christian recovery group called Celebrate Recovery in a larger city twenty-some miles away. I appreciated the fact that, unlike the Narcotics Anonymous meetings, Jon no longer had to introduce himself by saying, "Hi, I'm Jon and I'm an addict." I never agreed with the premise that an alcoholic or addict should repeat that week after week, year after year, no matter how long they had been clean. In a way, it seemed like a self-proclaiming curse.

The more I came to understand the gospel and to believe that in Christ a person really can be a new creation as 2 Corinthians 5:17 (NKJV) says the less helpful it seemed to continue making statements about always being an addict. I began to believe knowing our identity is in Christ is vital to long-term recovery. The Bible is clear; after accepting Jesus Christ and His sacrifice, a person is able to live in victory by faith in Him. Galatians 2:20 (KJV) says, ". . . the life which I now live in the flesh I live by faith in the Son of God . . ." I was happy to join a new recovery group where Jon could say, "Hi, I'm Jon and I'm a believer in Jesus Christ. I struggle with a life-threatening cocaine habit."

As I continued to learn about addiction and recovery, I began to realize we are all addicts, with sin as our common addiction. Our sin may be socially acceptable, like gluttony or an unhealthy dependence on prescription medication or television to numb our pain and get us through a day. Or it may be the kind of sin that is frowned upon in churches and polite society, like illegal drugs, illicit relationships, or a proclivity to pornographic material. Whatever it is, any person, activity, or thing we consistently turn to in order to make ourselves feel better, or not feel at all, is our addiction. Whether or not it is viewed as "normal" in our society is beside the point.

The great news, as we were learning in our new recovery group and from our young pastor's sermons, is that we all have a Savior "who was in all points tempted as we are, yet was without sin" (Hebrews 4:15 NKJV).

It is because of His victory we can be victorious too. Our faith in Jesus Christ, who dwells in the hearts of His followers through His Spirit, squashes every addiction and gives a believer something very exciting and powerful to share with those who do not know Him. This is The Good News, the gospel, in street clothes. We can truly begin living the joyful, abundant lives Jesus meant for us to live. Right here! Right now! I began to be, and still am, very excited about this! I began to ask for the joy of the Lord on a daily basis. I wanted abundant life for myself and for Jon.

There were times when Jon wanted it, too. Those were the times of spiritual breakthrough and growth. The leaders in our lives placed some beautiful tools in Jon's hands while we lived in that small town. He was always a reader, but his previously preferred genres hadn't helped him spiritually. Suddenly he was devouring books like C.S. Lewis' *Mere Christianity* and Watchman Nee's classic, *Sit, Walk, Stand*. For his birthday, Ryan sent him *Wild at Heart* by John Eldredge. Through the influence of these works, and the godly example of men like Bob and Dr. Alan, Jon began to grow up in the Lord.

Probably the most important message God poured into Jon's life through every possible channel was his new identity in Christ. That beautiful theme was repeated over and over in books, sermons, Bible studies and conversations with friends.

It is vital for all of us to understand our identity isn't who our parents are or aren't. It's not what we have done, or what we haven't done. It's not our work or where we go to school or church. Our identity as sons and daughters of the King of the Universe gives us authority over the enemy and his evil angels (Luke 10:19 NKJV). It gives us an eternal inheritance that begins right now, because, as Ephesians 2:6 (NIV) states, "We are seated [with Jesus] in the heavenly places." Romans 8:16-17 (NIV) says it this way, ". . . we are heirs—heirs of God and co-heirs with Christ."

For Jon, this truth was transformational, giving him a whole new image when he looked in the mirror. Instead of being a little baby, rejected by his birth mother, he was a treasured child of The King. It was no longer necessary for him to count his Christmas presents to see if he'd been slighted, because he was an individual worth dying for. Rather than being hyper-critical or puffing himself up with false pride, he could encourage others in their walk because he believed that only "through Christ" could he do "all things" (Philippians 4:13 NKJV). No longer a hopeless drug addict, Jon was victorious moment by moment as he walked with Jesus and put on the breastplate of His righteousness each morning before leaving the house.

As Jon allowed this message to seep deeply into him, it began transforming his life from the inside. This was different from anything that happened in the past. This was not a formula, a program or a mindless repeated prayer. This was not Jon trying harder, doing better, or using more willpower. This was a relationship. This was sonship. This was a prodigal finally accepting the fact his Father wasn't just pretending when He ran out to meet him and gave him a royal robe, special ring and party that shook the heavens!

When Jon began understanding and accepting how much he was loved, how much he mattered to God; when he began to embrace his true sonship and his real identity, then he began to be able to serve God by serving others. That's when he started to serve in our local church.

Jon was ordained as a deacon one Sabbath afternoon in a memorable service. He said, "It's the first time I've ever felt worthy to serve in church." It was a big deal. He even invited his family from Dallas to attend the ceremony. I was thrilled, because through the years, those sisters and I prayed many prayers together. I wanted Mona and Laurel to see the positive changes for themselves.

Jon wore a suit. That was almost unheard of for a man who usually wore black button fly Levis and cowboy boots to church. His tie matched his eyes. He looked sharp. I snapped a stunning photo of him sporting that suit. It was a benchmark picture. Frame worthy.

His smile is what I remember best from the day. "There is joy in his smile!" I whispered to Mona, who sat next to me on the cushioned pew. True joy in Jon was rare. Most often, his face muscles made the motions of a smile, but there was no emotion behind the movement. It was like a plastic mask that a mime might hold up in a play.

On Jon's ordination day, however, his emotions were authentic. He shed tears as he shared a few words with the group. He smiled and laughed at the celebratory meal afterward, thanking everyone for coming and for supporting him in his fresh walk with God, as he began to serve our church in an official capacity. The day marked a milestone in both of our lives.

I recall feeling immensely proud of Jon, but even more proud of God for working a transformation in my husband. He was still far from perfect, but I could see the "goodness of God leading him to repentance," as Romans 2:4 (NKJV) promises. That was something guilt, fear or shame had never done. When Jon, without warning suggested, "weaning off of cigarettes," I *knew* a transformation was taking place. I tried hiding my excitement while my insides did the hallelujah dance!

Soon after Jon became a deacon, I took the Community Services Director position in our church. Apart from wanting a happy home and marriage, I dreamed of us being a team who worked together to serve people. It was an answer to prayer when Jon and I began to serve not only our church family, but also the poor in our community. My position as a public school teacher gave me an inside track to some of the neediest families in our area. I was burdened to do something to help. God provided in remarkable ways to meet those needs.

Our church members were completely willing to participate in our community service adventures. Together we delivered food and clothing, paid overdue utility bills, and visited lonely shut-ins and hungry illegal aliens. The people even pulled together to purchase a new set of teeth for a woman.

We hosted a holiday food drive. Jon's truck came in handy for delivering all those boxes. He even went caroling with us in December and helped a grandmother hang her Christmas lights while our church friends delivered bicycles for each of her grandchildren. Jon was a huge part of our ministry that first year as we began to be known in our community as a church that helps people.

Working together to show God's love in a tangible way gave us a common goal. Because of Jon's addictions we developed some bad habits in our marriage. One of them was doing things independently of one another. Our new life and ministry gave us a reason to communicate more and spend productive time together. This, in addition to the other plusses, made the move to North Texas worth it. I could see Jon was growing in the Lord. That was the best reason of all. I banked on him making it.

Jon wasn't the only one blooming. Because of my own suffering I became much more intuitive about the suffering of others and began to notice when other women were hurting. God used my experience to continually connect me with people I may never have had compassion for otherwise. He truly works all things together for the good of people who love Him (Romans 8:28). I was beginning to believe that.

Our first year in North Texas vanished without incident. Summer was soon scorching all of us and providing Bob and Jon with plenty of work. Apparently Jon was excelling because he got a significant raise, and a promotion! There was even talk of making him a partner when Bob retired and merged his heating and air conditioning business with his brother's. Jon loved coming home waving a big, fat Friday paycheck. Everything was great. Until the Friday Jon didn't come home.

"Oh God. Oh no. Oh, please no . . ."

A sickening, sinking feeling overwhelmed me as I pulled into our circular drive with a trunk full of groceries. It was later than I intended; I'd been sidetracked in the grocery store by curious students and a church member wanting to chat. By the time I got home with my groceries the sun was hanging low over the pasture behind our house. Jon's truck was not in its usual spot next to the carport.

Bob, like us, was a Sabbath keeper who observed a twenty-four hour day of rest from sundown Friday to sundown Saturday. He only worked late on Fridays if it was an emergency, and he always let Aubrey and me know. My phone remained silent. I quickly called Jon's number. It went straight to voicemail.

Whipper leapt at the backyard fence as I pulled into the carport. She was a sure sign Jon was not yet there. Our first move upon arriving home from anywhere was to open the gate and allow the girls to come into the house with us. They happily trotted back and forth with me as I unloaded groceries.

As the golden rays of sunshine disappeared, I stood at our kitchen window scraping mint chocolate chip Blue Bell ice cream from the gold-rimmed lid. It was a weekly tradition I looked forward to. If the trunk was particularly hot, the ice cream would be semi-melted along the container's sides and I would spoon along the edges until I'd eaten all the soft parts. That was the only time I ate Blue Bell ice cream. The rest went into the freezer for Jon to enjoy as he wound down in the evenings after working all day in the heat.

Standing in a pool of plastic Wal-Mart bags in my cheery yellow kitchen, I swallowed spoonful after spoonful of Blue Bell mint chocolate chip. It was so cool and refreshing, with tiny square chunks of chocolate that lingered on my tongue after each bite of ice cream was gone. Over and over as if in slow motion I dipped my spoon into that round half-gallon container, scraping along the sides where the melty part was. Soon, all that was left was a lopsided little green mountain in the middle, and I was feeling much better about things.

Maybe they are working out of cell phone range I thought, pressing the lid over the mountain and shoving it into the freezer along with two bags of frozen Brussels sprouts and a Totinos pizza. *Maybe his phone battery died and that's why my calls are going to voicemail.* I opened the pantry door and began neatly stacking cans of black and pinto beans, labels facing front.

My phone rang just as I finished putting away the last of the produce. *"Oh, good! Thank You, Lord!"* It was Aubrey.

"Hi!" She was cheery as usual. "I hope I'm not interrupting your supper. We have just finished ours. Bob and I have invited some friends over for a light meal tomorrow evening. I'm sorry I didn't call you earlier, but you are welcome to join us if you don't already have plans."

My brain was scrambled eggs.

If they just finished supper that means Bob is home and she's assuming Jon is here with me. But he isn't, so that means he is somewhere else, which, historically has not been a good thing on pay day. What shall I say? Should I let on that he's not here? What if it's not what I think it is? I don't want to plant seeds of doubt in Bob or Aubrey's minds if it's nothing. Neither do I want to commit us to an evening at their home tomorrow if it's something.

"Uh. Thank you for thinking of us," I replied after an uncomfortable delay.

Think! Think quickly. I can't lie. What can I say? "Help me, Jesus."

"That sounds like fun, but we may have to take a rain check," I answered. "Thank you, though, for thinking of us."

"Perfect. Thank You!" Why didn't I think of that?

"Oh, I understand. You two are always doing something. I should have caught you earlier in the week. Well, have a good night."

"Thank you, Aubrey. You too. Bye."

I burst into tears as I laid the phone on the arm of the sofa. Immediately both dogs came near to comfort me. Poor things. They heard me cry more than any human had. They did not appreciate the howling part. It had been a while since I had howled, but I'm certain they had not forgotten. Whipper was particularly sensitive to tension or grief. Her whole black and white body would tremble and her ears worked back and forth in a gesture of worry. Snuffs usually tried to get up on my lap. If I ignored them, they would curl up together in their bed, waiting for the storm to pass.

Knowing in my heart that particular storm had just begun, I did something out of the ordinary. Something only reserved for special occasions or moments of great weakness. Making my way to our bedroom, I crawled into bed and patted the mattress twice. Immediately Whipper leapt across the room, landing on the bed and diving under the covers to her favorite spot near my feet. Not nearly as agile and weighing a third as much, Snuffles could only stand on her back legs, wagging her tail and waiting for me to lift her. She never went to the bottom of the bed, but rather found an unoccupied pillow and parked herself as close to my head as possible.

That's exactly how we spent the evening, cuddled up together on the bed, waiting for Jon to come home. If I dozed off I knew they would hear him long before I would and alert me to his presence in the house.

Though my tears ended, my prayers continued long into the night. I remember repeatedly using the word *why* as I rebuked the lurking spirits of fear and anger and prayed for God's protection over my husband.

"Please, Lord God, send Your angels to protect him and guide him safely home. Please don't allow anything harmful to happen to him. Why oh why is he doing this again?"

I prayed until I could no longer stay awake.

The girls heard his key click in the lock. Before I was fully aware, they perched on the edge of the bed, ready to jump off and skid across the hardwood to meet him. I wasn't quite as enthusiastic. An oil and water mixture of relief and anger welled up inside of me, each emotion vying for top position. While they excitedly circled his legs, I sat up in bed, silent.

From past experience I knew a 4 a.m. confrontation with someone just coming off a binge was a bad idea. But as his strange rank odor reached my nostrils I could not resist two words. "You stink," I spat as he unbuttoned his 501's, dropped them to the floor and crawled into bed.

The girls came to my side, standing on their hind legs, waiting for an invitation to join the party. "No!" I shouted them down. "Go get in your bed!" They obeyed without a fuss, slinking into their bed beside ours. I could feel them staring at me. Turning my head I saw their large eyes reflecting starlight from the window. My poor girls. It wasn't the first time they were recipients of my misdirected emotions.

Tears threaten at the corners of my eyes as I pen this chapter in my green spiral notebook. I'm on a fast train from Venice to Milan. The scene I just described seems surreal in comparison to my present surroundings. I take a breather, staring out the window at picturesque Italian countryside.

"God, You most surely redeem the things I thought were lost."

With thankful heart, and courage to continue, I return to my story.

Jon's steady breathing soon told me he was sleeping. He *did* stink. It was an unfamiliar combination of stale sweat, cheap cigarettes, and something else I couldn't quite identify. Whatever it was, I hated it. I hated all of it. Hated him.

"Hate the sin, love the sinner." The Christian cliché bounced through my brain as I struggled to find sleep.

"I cannot do it, God. You'll have to do it through me. This is just too much. Too stinkin' much."

Only much later was a tiny nugget of truth about that night revealed. Although I have never understood the "why" of Jon's relapse, I did learn that after work he went to the city where we attended Celebrate Recovery. Rather than looking for a meeting, he hunted for cocaine. When he couldn't find any of the "good stuff" he was used to, he accepted a dealer's offer of a less expensive, more easily attainable substance called "crack."

The unusual odor that night was the residual smell of crack cocaine permeating Jon's clothing and skin. Highly addictive, immensely dangerous to one's health, and easily attainable from shady sources, Crack was Jon's new lover. The night he opened the doorway to crack cocaine forever altered our future. Recovering from that blow to our new beginning felt impossible. I clamped down tight on Jon's freedom and resources. He didn't like it. In fact, he rebelled. Very quickly Jon morphed into the sallow, surly, deceitful soul he was before he went to Blue Sky Rehab Center.

I reached out to Leon and discovered he and Elaine moved to a city just two hours from us. He invited Jon and me to come for a counseling session as soon as we could. Surprisingly, Jon agreed to go.

"I'd like to meet with Jon privately first, if you don't mind," Leon said after greeting us both with a compassionate embrace.

"Sure. I'll just wait out here in the lobby," I said. Desperate for *someone* to get inside Jon's head, I was happy to leave Jon alone with Leon. Since they already had a good relationship and he knew Jon's history, I figured if anyone could make a difference, it would be Leon.

"Thank You, God, for Leon," I prayed as I sat in the plush lobby just opposite an overpriced gift shop. Leon had transferred to chaplain a much larger hospital. Although his new workload was heavy and his schedule tight, he once more availed himself to us free of charge.

"If he will see us, even once a month, it would be such a blessing. He knows us. He knows our history. Please God, give Leon wisdom right now as he speaks with Jon. Please touch Jon's heart and soften it.

"Forgive me for hating Jon. Forgive the angry words I have spoken. I want to be like Jesus. I do not want to give the devil a place in my life by harboring ungodly thoughts toward my husband. I know I promised to love, honor and cherish him in sickness and in health. This addiction is sickness. Please, Lord, pour Your love into me that I may love him appropriately right now. Because—if I am honest—I just feel angry and hopeless."

I continued praying as an hour passed before Leon opened his office door to motion me inside. Jon was angry. The muscles in his jaw clenched and unclenched as he sat stiffly on the chair nearest the door. Leon explained the conversation was difficult, but that Jon knew what he needed to do if he wanted help.

"What would *you* like to do?" Leon directed the question at me. "Are you prepared to continue this journey with Jon?"

"Yes," I said. "If he will be honest with me. And if he will continue to get help." I quickly added, "He also needs to allow me to be in charge of our finances without fighting me. I'm trying to dig us out of a hole. He keeps digging the hole deeper."

"Jon, are you willing to do that?"

"Yes."

"Good," affirmed Leon. "You can call me any time. If you have a red flag, call me. We can work through it. Get back into your weekly support group. You can do this. Let's pray together." Leon pulled us into a tight circle for prayer. When Leon prayed, I felt as if everything was going to be okay.

I was glad he hadn't said, "I told you so." He didn't have to. I'd already said it to myself. *He told me so.*

The ride home was tense. At first Jon, still miffed with Leon's straightforward approach, remained silent. Jon was used to flying under the radar with people, coming across as a nice, quiet guy. He managed to keep folks at arms-length. Apart from me, no one was asking him hard questions or holding him accountable.

Bob was a non-confrontational person. He wasn't going to ask Jon if he was using again. He was also Jon's employer, so their relationship was primarily about work. Given our history with Bob and Aubrey, I wanted them to know what was going on, even if it risked Jon's job. I wanted Jon's weekly paychecks to be made out to both of us, so there was no skimming off the top for drugs, but Jon did not want Bob to know about the relapse. He definitely opposed having my name on his paycheck.

"But Jon," I pleaded, "there are no checks and balances. You know cash is a trigger. Let's just do it for a little while. At least until you have more time clean. It's not fair you can blow your whole check and I still have to pay the bills with mine. I want to prevent that from happening again. I cannot carry us. Not with all the residual credit card debt!" My voice rose with every sentence.

"I know. I'm sorry, okay! I don't know what happened. It won't happen again," he growled. "Nobody needs to know our business."

Words like that build walls of isolation between couples who have problems and the people who can help them. Finding the balance between healthy accountability and maintaining boundaries that protect the privacy and dignity of a marriage can be difficult when one spouse is a substance abuser, or an abuser of any kind. When things began to spin out of control I wanted to take charge, clamp down, fix, organize, and guarantee the crazy wouldn't overtake our lives. The more I clamped, the more Jon resisted. And so, our cycle of addiction, isolation and codependent control continued.

Chapter 10

Warfare on Drugs

"The weapons we fight with are not the weapons of the world.
On the contrary, they have divine power to demolish strongholds."
2 Corinthians 10:4 NIV

December 2004–July 2005

In 2004, we spent the holidays in Kentucky with Annie and Eddie. It was our first Christmas together since cancer had stolen Grandma 'Dessa, my maternal grandmother. Mom, Annie and I were tearfully nostalgic. It was a year of tough changes. Eddie came home from serving in the Iraqi War, having lost his innocence and sense of idealism. We lost Gram. Jon lost his mind. We each needed a fresh start and were looking forward to a kinder 2005.

Back in August, Eddie accepted a civilian job in Lexington, where he and Annie promptly purchased a three-story home. By Christmastime, baby Lucas was almost two, and Sis was pregnant again. Between Eddie's charming sister, Jill, the P's, and us, their nest was full that holiday.

My spirits soared as Jon and I loaded food, gifts and dogs into his trusty green Dodge. Jon was experiencing his own kind of high that day. Despite his antics, I was determined to spend time with my family. The hours and miles could not pass fast enough. Well, actually, they went by a little too fast. Jon was speeding. Although I felt unsafe, Jon refused to relinquish the wheel.

"Dear Lord, please protect us from ourselves. Protect others from us," I prayed as we flew down the nighttime highway, fueled by high-octane cocaine.

With outside temperatures in the teens, Snuffles and Whipper remained hunkered down between us. I forced them to get out at the rest areas. Although he tried to hide it, Jon used those opportunities to have a snort and a smoke so he could hurl us another hundred miles toward our holiday destination. When high, which turned out to be most of the time for the next six months, he became the Energizer Bunny on steroids.

By springtime, I was desperate. Jon's addiction was full-blown.

"God, I'm worn out. I cannot do this any more. The hiding, the secrets, the pretending. It's killing me. He's really starting to scare me now. I don't want to be near him when those dark moods take him over. Something has got to change!"

I was once again keeping up appearances to the point of exhaustion, afraid our tiny community would discover Jon's secret. I didn't share Jon's problem with Aubrey because it could jeopardize his job. We couldn't afford that. I was ashamed to tell my teacher friends, and I suffered silently at church, especially on the Sabbaths Jon was too strung-out to make an appearance. I didn't want to tell my family. They had enough of his nonsense.

Annie was still fuming from Christmas, when Jon flirted with Eddie's sister. "Just get away from him," Sis begged after Jill indignantly relayed the incident to her brother. That was my first inkling of Jon's potential for infidelity. I knew he was no longer interested in me, but I thought it was just the drugs making him lose all desire. Unfaithfulness was not his modus operandi.

Jon's drug use escalated throughout the winter. We didn't tell Bob and Aubrey. We didn't have to. As with most addictions, Jon's couldn't be kept a secret forever. Eventually it began to rear its ugly head in the workplace. Bob noticed the changes: first attitude, then behavior. Aubrey came to me with open arms and an "I-already-know" expression on her face. I let her hold me as I sobbed.

As we prayed together, I thanked God for the comfort of a friend who didn't keep me at arms-length even though I tried to keep her and everyone else out of my own private pity-party. Sometimes we need to let our guard down so someone safe can love on us when the one who is supposed to love us has let us down. Sometimes we need to be like Aubrey and prayerfully approach a walled-up friend with open arms and an invitation to solace, even though they've appeared to withdraw or reject our previous attempts. It doesn't hurt to gently point out the "elephant in the room" and to offer the simple comfort of nonjudgmental acknowledgment. It was a rare occasion during those years to have someone approach me and say, "I can see you are hurting. Would you like to talk about it?"

That's why church often felt lonely even though the programs were nice and the people, friendly enough. In all fairness it wasn't the church folks' fault I was an expert at hiding behind busyness and serving with a shiny smile. Back then "putting on a happy face" was just as much part of my morning routine as brushing my teeth.

Fortunately, God consistently placed people in my life who could and would hold me accountable. Apart from my family, I had support from friends like Bob and Aubrey, Leon, Ryan and Meredith, and our new friends, Dr. Alan and Darcy. These people didn't allow me to slip through the cracks. They listened when God's Spirit prompted them to keep me on their radar.

One Friday in March, Jon never came home from work. I blasted his cell phone dozens of times. I always got his recorded voicemail: "This is Jon. Leave a message." I wanted to call Aubrey to ask if Jon and Bob were working late, but my gut already knew the answer. Nights like that were agonizing. I hated the not knowing, the infinite waiting, the sick part of myself that pressed redial over and over and over, desperately hoping he would respond to my call.

The Biblical invitation to pray without ceasing took on new meaning during those incessant hours. I prayed for his safety. I prayed he would be arrested. I prayed he wouldn't kill anyone while driving high. Sometimes I prayed he would die.

Then I prayed for sanity, for peace, for a spirit of forgiveness. I used Scripture as ammo against my unseen enemy, and to soothe myself. Those nights exhausted me. I was torn between compassion and repulsion. I pleaded for him to be okay, while in the same breath I begged God to just take him so I could get on with my life.

Before going to sleep, I anointed every door and window with oil and invited holy angels to war with any dark spirits that tried to come home with him. I prayed most of the night. God answered by giving me a fierce compassion for Jon. I had a renewed desire to see him free again.

Jon slipped into our bed sometime near dawn, smelling like the devil's den. I felt the battle as soon as he arrived in the house. The air was heavy, the dogs restless. Jon's countenance was black.

Despite the long night, I decided to attend church the following morning. Sometimes forcing myself to be fake was too exhausting after nights like that, but that Sabbath I felt motivated to go. Isn't church where people go when evil appears to be winning the war for the souls of their family?

A Cry for Help

That was one rare Sabbath, when I dared to show up without my mask. Doesn't desperation tend to produce transparency? When the pastor and elder greeted me at the door, their friendly "Hello!" was followed by, "Where's Jon this morning?"

"He's at home in bed, recovering from a drug binge," I blurted.

"Are you sure?" Pastor Josh questioned incredulously after a moment of stunned silence. He and Elder Scott quickly guided me to his study where we could speak privately.

"Of course I'm sure. Jon opened himself up to darkness and now he is taken over. It's complicated. We probably should have told you before, but we moved here two years ago to start fresh when he badly relapsed after going through drug rehab. I know Jon gave himself to God and became a deacon in this church, but now he is full of the devil. There is a heavy battle going on in our home. We need help. Maybe you can come over this afternoon and do something." My monologue left them speechless. By the time they found their bearings, it was time for the service to begin.

Pastor Josh, his wife Kyra, and their two youngsters *did* come over after church. Jon was bathed, clothed and appeared to be in his right mind as he sat chatting with them on our floral sofa. When Kyra excused herself to play outside with the kids, I hid in the kitchen while Josh spoke with Jon.

Moments later, Pastor Josh stepped outside; our picture window perfectly framing his family as he stood speaking with Kyra while the kids clambered up our oak tree. *I wonder what they are saying? They probably don't believe me, since Jon is putting on this grand act of sanity. I wish they could have seen him a few hours ago.*

When Pastor Josh again stepped through the kitchen door, he approached the sink where I stood rigid with anticipation. "Kyra is more familiar with stuff like this than I am," he whispered. "She says she didn't feel any evil spirits when she came in here. She thinks Jon's just in need of a good detox and some counseling."

I was stunned. Of course he needed detox and counseling, but what I had described earlier was a battle in the spiritual realm. I experienced enough evil in our home to know what I was talking about. There were times when Jon literally ran out of the house if I read the Bible aloud. Times when he could not pray, or allow me to pray over him. Times when the oppression was so heavy I felt as if I were swimming through molasses as I moved from room to room. I knew what manifested in Jon the night before. It was ugly and scary. It was *not* my husband.

Unfortunately that was not the first, nor the last time a pastor let us down when we sought help in the spiritual realm. Sadly, there are ministers who manage to complete seminary with sparse practical knowledge of how to help people with demonic strongholds. Somehow, the myth prevails that evil spirits live only in foreign lands.

Just as we gathered in the living room to pray, Dr. Alan and Darcy arrived. I had briefed them at church and invited them to come over to "do battle." They joined our prayer circle and we each took a turn praying for Jon, who stood sandwiched between Dr. Alan and me, his calloused hands limp in ours. Pastor Josh led us in a sincere, but perfunctory final prayer. Then everyone left.

Only later did Darcy inform me she and Dr. Alan had taken my cry for help so seriously; they went home after church to pray, prepare for warfare and grab some spiritual resources to share with Jon. They had come ready to see God "clean house." After the prayer circle, though, they realized we were not all on the same page, and that Jon was denying his need of help. Both Darcy and Alan sensed a resistant spirit and chose not to force the issue.

After they left, I stared at Jon in disbelief. "Don't you even *want* help?" I hissed. "Why didn't you tell them what was really going on?"

"Why did you invite them here in the first place?" He snapped. "You know I don't feel like company today!"

"They aren't company. They are our friends. Josh is our pastor! Why don't you let somebody help you?" I cried.

"Nobody can help me," he muttered. "Just leave me the hell alone."

Retreating to the kitchen, I brewed a cup of chamomile, knowing it was pointless to argue with that mindset.

"*What now, Lord?*" I added a drop of honey to my tea, stirring my way to the table. "*What do I do after I've already done everything I know to do? Unless he wants help, what else can be done? I am so disappointed! I'm disappointed in Pastor Josh for not understanding spiritual warfare. I'm disappointed in Kyra for making a judgment call without knowing what I've been through. I'm disappointed in Jon for pretending everything is okay when it's not. I'm sorry I said anything at church. What good did it do anyway?*"

Three days later, Pastor Josh showed up at school during my car line duty.

"Can I speak with you a minute please?" He asked as I slid open the door of a maroon minivan and waved a kid off the wall where the first graders waited like a row of lizards. Springtime sunshine warmed the bricks of our building and the waiting car riders backed up to the wall trying to draw some of that heat into their bodies.

"Of course. Do you mind waiting until I get these munchkins loaded into their vehicles?" I replied as a yellow Jeep roared up to the pillar where we stood waiting. Soon the last kid was clipped into his seatbelt. I closed the door carefully and waved him out of the parking lot.

"Thank you for waiting." I spoke cautiously to my pastor, realizing this was more than a casual visit. "What's going on?"

I wonder if he regrets how things turned out at the house last Sabbath. I'm surprised I haven't heard from him before now. He probably thinks I'm the one who's nuts and needs counseling.

"How are things with Jon?" His approach was direct. "Has he decided he wants help? We realize he stiff-armed all of us the other day. He didn't want to own up to anything being out of the ordinary. But we know you wouldn't have said those things and invited us over unless something was wrong."

"Things are about the same," I said. "He may be inching out of denial. When I called our former therapist and made an appointment, Jon agreed to go. We drove four hours round trip. I know that sounds crazy, but Leon has been through some deep stuff with us. He knows Jon. I think he broke through the evil and got to Jon's heart," I explained. "Do you want to come inside? This wind is getting to me, and I need to put my students' chairs up so the custodian can vacuum."

"Sure. I can't stay long, but I wanted to share a thought with you. Are you familiar with The Rehab, a residential treatment center for Christian addicts and alcoholics? It's three states away, but I've heard good things. Apparently they approach recovery from a Christian position. Perhaps *they* offer what you are looking for. If you think Jon would consider going, I'd be happy to be a reference for him."

Picking up a yellow plastic chair I turned it upside down on the desk nearest the door. I struggled to keep a neutral expression. "No," I replied carefully, "I've never heard of it. Sounds pretty generic."

I would do anything to help Jon, but there is NO WAY we can pay for rehab in another state! And haven't we been through that already?

"The only reason I know about it is because a family member of Kyra's went there. They really helped her," he replied. "So, do you think Jon might be interested?"

"I don't know," I said continuing to turn over chairs and straighten crooked desks. "Another live-in program is out of the question. Last time we didn't have to pay because he was on my insurance plan, which will only pay for that kind of treatment once in a lifetime. If you mess up, there *are* no second chances. What you are offering is not an option. We don't have that kind of money, and with the way he's been blowing his paychecks lately, we barely cover our bills," came my frustrated response as I bent to pick up two broken crayons and a dirty tissue.

Pastor Josh turned toward the door, then paused saying, "Well, let's pray about it and see if he would at least consider it. In fact, let's pray right now."

"Good idea." I stopped being a whirlwind and bowed my head in the quiet classroom. After "amen," Pastor Josh handed me a Post-it note with The Rehab's phone number scrawled in blue ink.

"Thank you," I whispered, folding the note sticky-side-in and tucking it into my pocket as I turned back to the tasks at hand. In an elementary classroom there are many "tasks at hand." I did them all: sorting and filing papers, putting grades into the computer, checking student work, writing lesson plans, making photocopies. I would be the last person out of the building that night. Not wanting to go home to an empty house, I numbed my pain with work.

Days Later

"Jon the electric bill is overdue," I announced, lifting my bowl of oatmeal from the microwave. "If we don't pay it immediately, they will notify our landlords. Ooh! Hot!" As the bowl burned my hands, my voice got louder. "I really do NOT want Gary and Gloria to wonder what's going on over here. What are we going to do about it? Our checking and savings accounts are depleted. We dare not ask Bob and Aubrey for money since they *know* how much they are paying you each week!" I pulled a box of rice milk from the refrigerator. "What's your plan?"

Jon grabbed his favorite blue mug from the cupboard growling, "I don't have a plan. I have no idea what to do. All my good stuff's already been pawned. I can't get any more cash."

"How can two people . . ." I started the sentence, but he finished it.

". . . With good jobs not be able to pay their electric bill?" He mocked. "How about because one of them is a drug addict?" He raised his voice with those last words, angrily spooning sugar into his coffee.

"I'm not trying to fight with you, Jon," I pleaded around a blistering mouthful of oatmeal. "I just don't know what to do. Please think of a solution to this problem while you are at work today. We are out of time."

Jon carefully set his steaming coffee on the table and slid into the old school desk near the door to slip on his tennis shoes. Perpetually in a hurry, he rarely bothered to untie the laces when removing his shoes, so it took him only seconds to put them on again. He said nothing more. I swallowed my oatmeal in silence, flipping through our devotional book while secretly hoping he would stay long enough to at least hear one Bible verse from the top of a page. When I finally found the right date, Jon nabbed his coffee and opened the door.

"I'm gone!" He tossed the words over his shoulder, a bone to his wife; then added, "bye girls," to the dogs.

Jon only ate breakfast on special occasions. On normal evenings, he put his Folgers into the coffee filter before bed. In the morning, all he had to do was flip a switch. By the time his morning shower ran cold, my husband's liquid breakfast was ready. That coffee and a few cigarettes somehow fueled him until lunchtime. He never seemed short of energy.

I, on the other hand, am a breakfast girl. Without it, I am guaranteed a headache by afternoon. That morning, I couldn't enjoy my favorite meal. The pit of my stomach was as bitter as the dregs remaining in Jon's coffee pot.

"Good Morning again, God. Will You please solve this problem? Gloria and Gary have been generous landlords and neighbors. They see our comings and goings. They know we work. They know we only pay five hundred dollars a month to live here. If our electricity gets turned off, I will be mortified! Please intervene. Please!"

Darcy phoned me after school. "Wanna go walking?" Sometimes we met at the high school track to spend time walking and talking together. Two laps in, she realized something was wrong.

"What is it, friend?" She asked. "You're awfully quiet today."

"Do you really want to know?"

"Of course!" You can tell me anything. "Were the first graders givin' ya a hard time?" She fished.

I proceeded cautiously. "No. They were great. It's personal. I don't like to blab my business, but I'm not sure how to handle this situation."

"Well, shoot. I can't help ya if I don't know what's wrong," Darcy puffed. Poor thing, in my frustration I was walking the legs off of her!

Slowing down I said, "Here's the deal. Remember what happened after church last Sabbath? I'm discouraged things didn't turn out like we hoped. Instead of getting better, Jon is actually worse. He is using again this week. It's bad. He's blown all of our money, and our electric bill is overdue. I try to juggle everything, but I'm struggling to pay the bills by myself, especially when I have to keep bailing his tools out of pawnshops. I feel angry and embarrassed to share this with you. I am ready to explode!" I sped up again as we rounded the one mile marker.

Looking back, I can identify my codependent tendencies: control, taking responsibility for behaviors that were not mine, rescuing . . . Ouch! I should have given him an ultimatum, and followed through.

"Oh NO! I'm sorry! Although he seemed so normal the other day, we could sense something going on with him. I know this must be very stressful for you." Darcy responded with sincere surprise and concern. We walked and talked for another four laps before she glanced at her watch. "Ooh! I've got to go pick up Alan at the office. Thank you for walking with me, *and* for letting me in on your heavy secrets. Do you mind if I share with Alan? He may have some additional insights. He's a very wise man."

Even though nothing was technically different, I felt better on the drive home. The combination of exercise and honest communication worked wonders for my frame of mind. That changed when I noticed Jon's truck in our driveway.

Uh-oh. He's home early. I wonder what that means. I hope he's not still in a foul mood. I hope he's thought of some way to cough up a hundred and thirty two dollars by tomorrow.

When I walked into the house I heard him talking on the phone in the back bedroom.

"No, as far as I know we don't have any plans this evening. Yes, I remember how to get there in the dark . . . Okay . . . Thanks. I'll talk to Julie and let you know if anything changes. Otherwise we'll see you in about an hour . . . Okay. Bye."

I stuck my head in just as he hung up.

Boy, he sounds almost chipper. Wonder what plans he's making when we have no money.

"I'm home," I said coolly, bending to scratch the base of Snuffles' curly tail. "What's going on?" Jon, still wearing dirty work clothes, looked haggard as he leaned against the desk.

"Oh, that was Alan. He and Darcy want us to drive over there in a bit. Something about a proposal. Maybe he's got some A/C work for me to do. Are you up for it?" He asked.

Hmmmm. I wonder what Darcy is up to. I hope this goes well. Jon will be furious if he finds out I said something about our finances.

"Sure. Darcy and I just finished walking the track. I'm hungry, are you? Let's eat something first."

I can't recall what I fixed for supper, but I do remember driving to Dr. Alan and Darcy's home in my Cadillac. It was dark when we arrived. We parked on the grass instead of their driveway because my car leaked oil and we worried about staining the concrete.

Before Jon rang the doorbell, two miniature dogs, Pixie and Paintbrush spied our movement at the window and began barking furiously. Darcy warmly greeted us while she admonished Pixie to "Stop it!" and gave Paintbrush a firm bare-footed nudge.

"Come on in," she invited, scooping Pixie up and marching her toward the sofa. Dr. Alan, still in his stiffly starched work shirt, stood to give us each a hug. This wasn't our first visit to their home. We had shared several meals together. They *were* our friends, but we hadn't wanted to burden them with every skeleton in our closet, so there were things we'd never discussed openly. Jon's drug use was one of them.

By evening's end, they knew everything. How that happened could only have been Spirit-led. For the first time in a long time, I saw a spark of hope in Jon's eyes. He shared his problem and they still liked him. I think he expected rejection. Maybe that's why he hadn't opened up when they'd come over on Sabbath afternoon. Jon had the utmost respect for Dr. Alan. He felt unworthy to be his friend, but Alan had taken him under his wing ever since we arrived in town.

Dr. Alan listened intently as we explained our current dilemma. Then I told them about Pastor Josh's visit to the school and his suggestion of a second round of rehab. I felt safe mentioning rehab to Jon in that environment. He actually seemed open to the idea.

Dr. Alan encouraged Jon to consider his alternatives. The time he invested in Jon earned him the right to speak the truth in love. "At the rate you're going, brother, you could end up in a pine box. You are looking gaunt. If you've already had heat stroke once, you need to be very careful working in those attics and places where it gets to be over a hundred degrees. Summer is coming, and your body may not be able to withstand the pressure you are putting it through. These binges, where you don't eat or drink for days are dangerous, not to mention the toxic chemicals you are inhaling with crack cocaine. You need to stop before you die."

Jon listened without any sign of anger. I could tell by his fidgety fingers that he was jonesing for a cigarette, but he wasn't avoiding the conversation.

We prayed together before leaving. Just as we walked out the door Darcy handed me an envelope. "We want you to have this," she said. "It's not a loan. It's a gift. Pay your electric bill and hang on to the rest for emergencies."

"Thank you, Darcy," I whispered, hugging her tightly. "You are a true friend."

Jon hugged and thanked them both. The relief on his face was evident.

"Remember what I said," Dr. Alan reminded him as he closed the door. "Think about it."

Jon agreed to think about it. We opened the envelope in the car. They had given us five hundred dollars, in cash! Both of us wept.

"How can they be so generous?" Jon asked. "And they don't even want us to pay it back. Now *that's* Christianity."

We argued on the way home. Jon insisted on taking one hundred and forty dollars from the envelope to pay the electric bill. He said he would be passing "right by" the county electric co-op on the way to a job the next day. I was torn because I did not want him to have cash; especially that amount. There was no time to mail the payment. It had to be made the next day. The only answer was to have one of us take it. We argued about which one of us that would be. I was willing to take the day off in order to avoid giving him cash. Otherwise I'd be at work before the co-op opened and, because of staff meeting after school, I would not be able to make it before they closed.

He said, "That's ridiculous. Especially since I'm going past there anyway." Reluctantly I conceded, feeling like an idiot for doing so.

"*Thank You, heavenly Father,*" I prayed as I laid awake in bed that night, "*for proving Your promise that 'my God will supply every need . . .' [Philippians 4:19 ESV]. Thank You for these two gifts: the gift of Alan and Darcy's friendship and the gift of these funds. Please ensure they are used appropriately.*"

My prayers on the way to school the next morning felt like presumption.

"*God, am I nuts for praying Jon will make it to the co-op with that money when for months he hasn't been able to handle more than ten dollars at a time? Am I asking too much of You by handing him cash when he is so weak, and then calling upon You to give him the willpower to spend it in the right place?*"

All day I was restless with wondering.

In all there were three huge surprises that week. I listed them in my journal:

1. *God supplied our need, and more!*
2. *Jon paid the electric bill. I found out that evening when he came safely home.*
3. *He agreed to go to rehab if we could come up with the funds.*

Skeptically, I called The Rehab to speak with them about their program. It was expensive, but they claimed a high success rate among their graduates.

"Our next session begins two weeks from Monday," said the friendly voice on the phone. "Do you have a fax number where I can send the paperwork? We would need to approve your husband's application and receive payment prior to his arrival."

At the time, I felt as if everything fell into place for Jon to be able to get into that program. We spoke with Bob and Aubrey about the possibility of Jon missing a month's work. Bob was reluctant to relinquish his helper, but agreed it would be better for Jon to "get done with this mess" now rather than wait until warmer weather when the A/C repair calls became overwhelming.

For months, I was frustrated with Bob because he continued to pay Jon every Friday afternoon like clockwork, knowing Jon would go straight to the pawnshop to get his stuff out of hawk before someone else bought it and then directly to his dealer to spend every penny he had left. I cannot tell you how many times Jon pawned and repurchased his own expensive Swarovski binoculars, *and mine*, before I got smart and started keeping mine at school. I approached Bob, asking that he make Jon's check out to me so I could pay our bills, or at least give me part of the money, so it all wouldn't get blown.

Bob insisted, "A man's money is a man's money. If he works for it, it's his. No one can take that from him."

That was incredibly *frustrating* to me. I felt betrayed by them both.

Coming up with several thousand dollars for rehab was a huge hurdle. We had no free and clear assets, apart from Jon's truck. That poor truck was on its last leg after the way Jon abused it. He even beat the hood in with a sledgehammer in order to collect insurance money to smoke through his crack pipe. The truck certainly wasn't worth what a stay at The Rehab would cost, and I was still making monthly payments on my leaky Cadillac. The only asset I could think of was my teacher retirement fund. I accumulated enough there to cover the cost of the rehab, but would be charged a heavy penalty for dipping into it early.

I counseled with no one except Jon about robbing my retirement. He concurred with my plan. Tearfully I told him I was willing to access my retirement because, "I love you, Jon, and I really, really want you to be well. This rehab will be even better than the last one. These people are Christians. They will know what to do with the darkness inside you. You must promise me this, Jon," I said, searching his face, trying to make eye contact, "promise me you will let them help you. Promise me you will work the program. Promise to give it your all, Jon. Will you promise?"

"I'll give it what I've got," he conceded. That was the closest thing to a promise I could get, but I ran with it. Within days I cashed in my retirement account and mailed it to The Rehab. Jon's application was accepted, pending receipt of my payment.

Over the next few days, we had an ongoing argument about how he would get to The Rehab. I wanted to take him there and drop him off. There were two problems with that plan. The first being school was still in session, and I really could not afford to miss work. The second problem was Jon never wanted to feel "stranded" anywhere. He was like a donkey, refusing to budge. Jon always wanted a way of escape. He would not even consider allowing me or anyone else to take him to The Rehab and leave him without wheels.

I thought it imprudent to send him alone. I knew he would need money for gas, which was dangerous. I could not trust him with a credit card, either. He already ran the gas card up several hundred dollars before I froze the account. I don't know how he did that. Maybe he bought gas in exchange for crack. I'm not exactly sure the way the drug world works, but somehow he manipulated the system in order to get what he needed. With a regular credit card, he could purchase large items and pawn them, or return them to the stores for cash. Those were the days before most merchants wised up to scammers. Since The Rehab was so far away, I could not figure out how to get him there without giving him gas money for the trip, or running the risk of creating even more debt. We still shared joint bank and credit card accounts, but I controlled the finances apart from Jon's paychecks. I did not want to give him access to anything.

Listen, ladies especially. The Bible instructs us to seek godly counsel. Proverbs 15:22 (NKJV) says, "Without counsel, plans go awry, but in the multitude of counselors they are established." Hindsight reveals major flaws in the above plan. The main one being the only counsel I sought regarding liquidating my retirement account   was that of my drugged-out, demon-possessed husband. I was still trying to relate to him as a spouse who had my best interest in mind. I was still trying to respect him and the boundaries of our husband-and-wife relationship, but he violated those boundaries and left me in a vulnerable position, both financially and emotionally. I should have sought the wisdom of the people God placed in my life before making such a serious financial decision.

In the end, I loaned Jon my car for the trip. He took cash for food and gas and left early on a Sunday morning. He should have arrived at The Rehab by suppertime. I spoke to him a couple of times on his cell phone. By afternoon he was off the grid. Only much later did he tell me that while driving on an overpass in Nowheresville he glanced down on an inner-city neighborhood and the thought entered his mind, *go down there and buy drugs.*

"That was it," he confessed, "I took the next exit and found the nearest dealer."

He arrived at The Rehab by 10 p.m., "higher than a kite," as he explained it. "I faked it, though. Nobody knew why I was so late. They made me turn in my car keys. They wanted my phone too, but I told them I didn't have one. I wanted to keep it so I could talk to you sometimes."

That information came to me weeks later while he was explaining why he was kicked out. Yes, I said kicked out. Of rehab! After I cashed in my retirement fund to send him there! Livid would be an understatement for the emotion I experienced upon receiving that news. I think I was more upset about the betrayal of resources than I was about the betrayal of our marriage. I do not know the full details, but he alluded to the fact that he and a couple of other residents were asked to leave the program because they were caught with mixed company in a barn on The Rehab's property. Whatever happened there was the deal breaker with The Rehab's directors. Apparently, Jon was also written up for some other minor infractions. He said he was dismissed because he had too many strikes against him.

I called The Rehab to verify Jon's stories. They refused to speak with me because I was not their client. The friendly voice on the phone said, "I'm sorry. We will not be able to share any information with you regarding Mr. Miller. We understand he is your husband, but we are bound by confidentiality laws to protect Mr. Miller's privacy."

How can they refuse to speak to me now? They certainly didn't mind speaking to me when I was fronting the funds for this disaster! I'm his wife. I have a right to know what happened there . . . don't I?

My thirty-fifth birthday came and went while Jon was gone to rehab. I celebrated by buying myself a fabulous free-standing hammock with my birthday money. I knew it was an extravagant purchase, given our current financial situation. I justified the expense by avoiding the grocery store. My hammock had wooden bars that held the fabric wide, so two people, or one person and two small dogs, could comfortably lie there, staring at the stars for hours.

The night I learned Jon was asked to leave The Rehab I called the girls and fled to my hammock. We rocked there gently until the dogs fell asleep and the last tears seeped from the sides of my eyes down to the hammock's built-in pillow.

"God, are You there?" I whispered toward the Big Dipper. *"Didn't I tell You I don't know how much more I can take? I am so wounded by this. Even if he didn't do anything with another woman, just the fact he was out there when he knew it was against the rules shows a blatant disregard for the program . . . and for me. Why is he acting like a teenager? This was serious!"*

When I recovered from my initial shock, I asked Jon about the program. I wanted to know if there were any redeeming reasons for him to have gone there. "After all," I said sarcastically during another conversation, "you spent three weeks there. You must have learned *something.*" I know sarcasm is unloving. Unfortunately it is my sinful nature's default, and it comes out in moments of weakness. After that whole experience, I felt very, very weak.

Jon shared the story of how, as part of his therapy, he went into a room with some kind of a bat, whacking and breaking stuff while yelling and swearing at his invisible parents and anyone else he was angry with. I was not impressed.

"I thought this was a Christian institution. Is that how God calls Christians to resolve their anger issues? I don't think so!" I responded.

It took time to sift through Jon's stories for nuggets of truth. Finally, I pieced together a sketchy picture of what happened after he was ousted from The Rehab. To keep his dismissal a secret from me, he and another banished fellow decided to take a road trip until Jon's official release date. According to the story, Jon offered to take that guy home, only to discover his house burned down in his absence. They dug around in the ashes for the guy's safe and found it buried under the rubble. They survived on those funds until it was officially time for Jon to come home. That's the story to the best of my recollection. Whatever happened was inappropriate and sneaky. It was hard for me to find forgiveness for my husband. I was seething.

Guests

The dust had not yet settled from The Rehab incident when my six-month-pregnant sister came to visit. I desperately needed a distraction. Lucas was two and a half and absolutely adorable with his blonde curls and watermelon belly. Although baby Ariana wasn't due until August, Annie's belly was also quite ripe. Making that drive from Lexington was a sacrifice. I think Sis knew I needed her.

I made a cozy bed on the futon in our office for Lucas. My family of stuffed teddy bears huddled next to a stack of favorite picture books. Lucas, like me, was drawn to stories. He loved reading with his "Tia." Getting the house ready for company was a pleasant distraction from my inner anguish.

They arrived on a Friday. When Annie's blue Caravan pulled into our driveway, my excited squeal startled the dogs. They raced out the door in front of me, nearly getting squashed as Sis barreled into the yard. She barely came to a stop before I flung the minivan door almost off its hinges trying to get to Lucas. He had grown considerably since December. I released his seat belt and pulled him into a bear hug. "Lucas!" I shouted. "Look at you! You're a big boy now." Sister bolted for the bathroom after her long trip. "We only have one. You'll find it!" I shouted after her.

After we unloaded the van I gave them the grand tour of our home. Lucas discovered his bed immediately. "Read to me, Tia," he said, spying the books. "I will, Love. Tia will read lots and lots of books with you, but first, we are going to see Uncle Jon."

"Where is he?" Annie asked staring me square in the face and raising one questioning eyebrow.

"He's getting off of work early. He got paid today. I finally convinced Bob to put both our names on his checks, so we each have to sign in order for Jon to cash them. We're going to meet him at the bank first then we've got to go get a bunch of stuff out of the pawnshop in the city before it closes. Otherwise, it will be lost. I don't want to send him down there alone with the cash. It's five hundred dollars worth of stuff. If he goes into that city with five hundred dollars, we may never see him again," I replied.

"Right, so we get to spend even more time in the car today? Great!" Sis said unenthusiastically. "The only way we're going to get Lucas back in that car seat is to bribe him with ice cream."

"Lucas," I squatted down eye level with him and asked, "Wanna go get some ice cream with Mommy and Tia? If you do, I'll race you to the car." That's all it took. Soon we were all buckled in with Sis navigating us toward the local bank.

"I'm not comfortable with Lucas around you-know-who," Annie whispered, glancing into the rear view mirror to see if Lucas was listening. "After everything he's done lately, I'm nervous to be around him myself."

"I completely understand, but he'll be fine with Lucas," I assured her. "He's been acting fairly normal this week. He never does anything at the house, anyway. He always goes somewhere else, then comes dragging home when it wears off. Anyway, I can't imagine he'd try to pull any stunts while you guys are here. He's usually perfectly normal around other people. It's only when we're alone that he gets mean and weird."

Jon was waiting at the bank. I went inside with him and signed the check. He deposited it into our account, except for the five hundred dollars he needed for the pawnshop. "Hand me that money, please," I said, holding out the palm of my hand.

"You don't know where to go," he answered.

"I know, but you can tell me which pawnshop it is."

"But you don't know which stuff is mine," he retorted, still clutching the cash-filled envelope.

"You can go with me and tell me," I snapped. "Give me the money."

"You guys don't want to drive all the way into the city this evening. Not after Annie has already traveled for most of the day. Why don't you just let me go and get the stuff? I'll be home before dark."

"No way. I'm not letting you go down there alone. Now hand me the money before I make a scene in here," I retorted. "You did this to yourself. We could be doing a hundred other things with this money besides buying things we've already paid for. Now hand it over so we can get going. They are waiting in the car."

"I'll go ahead. You can follow me," he said, relinquishing the cash. "When we get there, you can give me the money and I will go in and get the stuff. I have to have my truck in order to haul it. Some of the tools are large. I'm not a child. You don't need to escort me into the pawnshop."

"We'll see," I said as I brushed past him. "Just don't drive too fast. We don't want to lose you."

Sis read my face as I got in. I tried to remain neutral but she knew me too well.

"Jesus, please don't let him ruin this visit. I hardly ever get to see my family. I don't want her to see me cry right now. Please just do some divine intervention so we can have a nice weekend together."

"Everything's fine," I smiled, turning to give Lucas a high five. "We're just going to follow him to the pawnshop. He's got some big stuff to get and he needs his truck to haul it. I'll go in and deal with the money part and then we can go get ice cream."

We drove thirty miles into the old downtown section of the city. No parking was available near the pawnshop. We circled around and around searching for a spot. Finally, Jon stopped near the side entrance and motioned for us to pull up behind him. I lowered the passenger window.

"You don't need to come inside with me," he said. "There's nowhere for her to park anyway. Just give me the money and I'll go in and take care of this. It will take a while to find everything and get it loaded. You girls just go on home and enjoy yourselves. I'll be there shortly. I promise."

I looked at Annie. She remained silent. "Fine," I relented. "I'm trusting you." I handed him the bank envelope with five hundred dollars in it.

"Bye, Lucas," he said, tapping the window and waving to his nephew with his left hand as he took the envelope with his right. "See you later, Annie." To me, he mouthed, "Thank you."

We silently watched Jon back his truck into a freshly vacated parking spot. As we drove away I told Annie, "I know he won't be coming home tonight. I'm tired of fighting it. We can just have a good time without him."

We did, for a while. We took Lucas to McDonalds and let him run around in the kiddie area. Then we went home to prepare supper. Even though we laughed and chatted together as always, there was an unspoken tension in the air as minutes turned into hours and still no Jon.

After supper, we went out back to swing in the hammock. Sis sat on the edge, gingerly rocking back and forth with both feet on the ground while Lucas and I were balanced in the center with the girls. Even our crazy cat, "Mama Kitty," came to hang out with us. Mama was a wildcat who sort of adopted us. She lived outdoors, but came around to eat and tease the dogs when they were outside. I was surprised to see her since she usually skulked about, trusting no one.

For those few moments, I felt content as I imagined what it would be like to have a happy family and swing together at twilight. As the darkness and mosquitoes came, we moved inside for bath and story time. My favorite part of the evening was lying on the futon with Lucas snuggled next to me as we read *Rooster's Off To See The World*, by Eric Carle, followed by a "Jesus story" from *The Children's Bible* and bedtime prayers. Those precious moments were irreplaceable. I refused to allow the silent drama to steal them from me.

Our family tradition is to celebrate the Sabbath hours by turning off the television and the distracting things of this world and focusing our attention on God and our relationship with Him and the people He has placed in our lives. Friday nights were generally quiet in our home, especially if Jon was binging. That particular Friday night was different because I had someone to talk to! Sis and I chatted and laughed and dreamed together about what Ariana would be like, who she would look like, and what kind of a big brother Lucas would be. She shared some of her pregnancy challenges then asked if I ever heard from Chloé.

"Did you only meet her once?" I questioned. "I can't remember."

"Yes. When Lucas was one and Chloé was two," she recalled.

"Well, now she is almost three and a half, eleven months older than Lucas. I can't believe that much time has passed. I still dream about what life would have been like if she was able to stay with me," I confessed. "I had a moment of nostalgia while reading *Rooster's Off To See The World* to Lucas. It was a book I read to Chloé over and over when she was a baby."

Hanging out with my sister did seem to make the time go by more quickly than if I were waiting alone for Jon. She kept asking me what time it was and wondering if he would ever show up. I tried calling, but his phone was off. This happened so many times in the past, I was numb to the strangeness of it all. Annie didn't like the thought of going to bed without knowing what happened to him.

"Welcome to my world," I said sadly. "But we can't stay up all night. We're going to church tomorrow. I want to show you off!"

Sometime in the wee hours, Jon came home. He showered before coming to bed, but he still reeked of the drug-life.

"Did you spend it all?" I asked as he crawled between our crisp yellow sheets.

"Yes. Every cent. I don't want to talk about it. I already feel like a failure." He rolled over, turning his back to me.

The next morning we all dressed for church. Even Jon. He looked bad. I could see Sis eyeing him as he poured his coffee. She didn't say a word. At church, Jon served as a deacon, taking up the offering and going through the motions of being friendly and interested in people. I was shocked! He even stayed for the fellowship lunch following the service. Afterward we all went home and crashed. Charades is an exhausting game, even for part-time players like my sister.

I cried when Annie left. The weekend was too short; too emotionally draining.

"Thanks for a nice time," she said dryly as she hugged me goodbye.

"Sure! Anytime," I answered. Then, "Sis, I'm really sorry it turned out like this. I know it was awkward for you. Please come and see me again sometime. You know I can't visit you. If I do, everything I own will end up in the pawnshop."

"You can do something about that, you know," she responded. "I love you."

"I know. I'll keep you posted. Goodbye." And then, "'Bye Lucas. Tia loves you."

Infuriated with Jon for ruining their visit, I long resented how he selfishly made the weekend all about him. It made no difference he had tried to redeem himself by playing with Lucas and giving him rides on the riding mower. I was ashamed by the pity in Annie's eyes as she witnessed my life. It was the only time my sister visited me in that home. I regret the drama that overshadowed her stay.

A Visit With Chloé

A few weeks later I drove to San Antonio for Jon's nephew, Robert's graduation from the Air Force Academy. Work wouldn't allow Jon to attend the ceremony, so I took the road trip without him. On the way, I got to see Chloé for the first time since our move. I knew it was a bad idea to leave Jon home alone because he would surely be drugging and pawning while I was gone. I didn't care. I needed to get away from the crazy.

It's not my problem, I told myself. *I need a life apart from trying to monitor Jon.*

That was something I was learning in the Celebrate Recovery meetings I sometimes still attended, even when Jon chose not to. I was increasingly aware he was not the only one in our family with a problem.

I surprised Carrie, Chloé's mom, with an impulsive phone call when I realized I'd be passing their home on my way to San Antonio. Although I did send cards and packages, it was rare for me to phone. Three years after losing her, my heart remained raw. I wanted to be a good god-mommy, but it hurt to have too much contact. Besides, I wanted Chloé, I still struggled to remember to call her Alexandra, to bond with her adoptive family more than with me.

"Of course you can come by! She will be glad to see you. *We* will be glad to see you! We've missed you," Carrie exclaimed when I shared my travel plans.

I planned for a quick visit, short and sweet, nothing too heavy. I thought I could handle it. Time heals all wounds. Isn't that what they say?

I was an emotional cyclone. The closer I drove to that town, the more I yearned to change my mind and keep on going. Too many memories lurked beyond the city limit sign. I didn't know if I could go back there and come out unscathed.

"God, help me please. Your Word says I can do all things through Christ who strengthens me. Can I do this?"

And then an answer came back strong and clear: *"You can do this, girl. You can get out of this car. Never mind the sweaty armpits or the weak knees. You can go in there and hold your head up and hold that little girl. I am with you."*

My heart pounded louder than I pounded on that door. I heard the sounds of children playing, and my friend, Carrie singing along with Kirk Franklin. She couldn't hear me. I knocked again, slightly harder. An "I've been here before" feeling greeted me when the door burst open and little ones gathered around my legs, searching my face with bright eyes. They were all taller than I remembered, but familiar. Carrie sat on the sofa next to a mountain of laundry. She got up to hug and kiss me on the cheek. I scanned the room for Chloé, I mean, Alexandra.

She stood apart from the group, eyeing me cautiously.

"She's super shy and kind of quiet with strangers," Carrie explained.

But I'm not a stranger. I'm her mama, my heart cried.

Years later, I wrote my baby an un-mailed letter as part of a grad-school assignment. I included a photograph of the two of us, taken the day of my visit. In the picture, we are standing on the front porch. I'm holding her on my hip with her long legs dangling. Her slender brown hand rests on my chest. We both smile for the camera.

6-14-08

Dear Chloé,

Yeah, Baby, that's you and me. You were three years old that summer. Bashful and "kinda quiet with strangers," your mother said. But somehow you sensed we weren't strangers, you and I. Something invisible drew our hearts gently toward one another. I knew you felt it too as you raised your eyes, though not your chin, to peek at me.

Slowly, as your mom chatted away, filling in the gaps since I'd seen you last, you made your way to me. Until at last you were enfolded in these arms where you fit just right.

Long ol' legs, girl! When you were three days old, I swore you'd be six feet tall. You come from tall roots, you see. Once I saw a photograph of your other mother—the one who birthed you. Lovely coppery skin, looong limbs and delicate features . . .

How can a child be so blessed as to have three mothers? You really are special, that's for sure.

I did long to take you home the day we took this photograph together. But as I took in your life, surrounded by playmates and your almost-twin brother, I knew you would be lonely in my world. I'm lonely in my world.

Of course I didn't know how things would turn out when I fell in love with you. I just wanted you for my own, and I poured myself into you for the first six months of your life.

You were everything to me. Each morning I awoke with a smile on my heart, unable to wait to just love on YOU! I drove to your mom's, only she wasn't fully your mom yet, to pick you up, and we'd spend the day together. I worked with you on responding and making eye contact. I read to you and sang to you and kissed you a million times. You had a few minor issues because of the substances your birth mother used while she was pregnant, but, Baby, you blossomed! I prayed every day God would heal your body and mind. And I believe He did!

I knew something special happened between us when you began to cry in the evenings, when, after your bath and jammies, I'd strap you into your car seat and take you 'home.' I'd try to talk to you and sing to you in the car, but you'd only cry louder as if to say, "But I just want to stay with you and sleep in my crib in your room tonight."

It broke my heart when you clung to my neck and I'd have to untangle you to give you back to your foster parents. I could not wait for the paperwork to be completed so you could be transferred to our home. It was six long months. I was ready to be your full-time mommy.

Someday, when you're older, I'll tell you the rest of the story. In the meantime, you need to know I loved you then, and I love you now. Not an ounce less, either. You are my baby.

Always will be.

My heart is yours,
Godmommy XO

Keying those last words into my laptop has sprung a well of emotion; tears I thought I could no longer cry, ending in dry wracking sobs. I'm grateful for solitude. No one should hear the anguish arising from the depths of these memories.

"God, heal my heartache. How can it be that she'll be thirteen in a few days?"

Perhaps these are the last of my Chloé tears. Now where was I? Oh, I remember . . .

Our visit ended too quickly, but I had a long drive ahead. After a final round of hugs and kisses, I was alone in my car, bawling my head off. That was the last time I saw Chloé in person.

An Intervention

It was mid-July when I returned from that trip, aware the summer's events marked a mental turning point. I decided not to continue crouching behind the wall of, "everything's just perfect" when things became sketchy with Jon. I was beginning to realize how much I needed spiritual allies in my day-to-day life.

Aubrey became just such an ally. She could see things were going downhill fast in our marriage. One afternoon she invited me to come over and do some gardening with her. We only lived three miles apart, but I'd kept her from getting too close to my pain. As we gathered huge lopsided tomatoes and prickly baby cucumbers, we discussed my life with Jon.

"I realize things have not been easy on the home front lately," she stated, tossing an oversized zucchini into the woods.

"It's been horrible. He lies all the time," I responded. "Ever since he came back from that rehab, it's like he has no conscience."

Aubrey and I chatted for a long time as we worked together. Every year she and Bob planted a huge garden. I learned much about growing and preserving things from her. That particular day, our conversation was about preserving my marriage. She and I both agreed the devil was out to destroy it and something drastic needed to be done.

Before sunset, we had a wheelbarrow full of fresh vegetables and a plan that just might work. All we had to do was convince Bob and Jon. We decided we'd each prayerfully convince our own husbands. Both of us felt Aubrey's task was the easiest.

"Listen to me." I sat down on the edge of the sofa next to Jon's feet, as he stretched out after work with one hand on the TV remote and the other mindlessly scratching the rolls on Snuffles' neck as she lay on the floor next him.

"What?" His eyes never left the news.

"I need to talk with you about something important."

My chest pounded as I silently prayed, *"Holy Spirit, please get through the walls he's built. Soften his hardened heart. Give him a desire to be free again."*

"I'm listening." Still no eye contact. The only movement was Whipper's tongue as she licked the back of Jon's hand as it gently rested on Snuffle's back. Snuffs was falling asleep, as indicated by the slow unfurling of her normally coiled tail. Were it not for the palpable tension between the humans, the familiar scene could have almost been a Norman Rockwell painting.

"Thank you. Please just hear me all the way out, okay? I want to ask you something." I lifted his feet onto my lap and scooted back into the sofa's comfy cushions. I guess he realized I wasn't going anywhere so his thumb found the mute button, silencing the background noise. Now my own heartbeat and Whipper's incessant licking were the only sounds I heard.

"Stop it, Whipper!" I barked. "Go lay down!"

Instantly three pairs of eyes fixed on me and immediately I was sorry. "Go lay down," Jon repeated softly, pointing in the direction of her doggie bed. Our eyes met. Mine teared up.

Shoot. So much for calm and neutral. Let me try this again.

"Okay." I knew I needed to speak while I had his undivided attention. "What I want to say is, do you *want* help?"

"You know the answer to that," he snapped. "Nothing works. I'm tired."

"But what if there was something that worked and we just haven't tried it yet?" I questioned.

"Like what?" He threw up his hands. "I've tried everything."

"What about prayer?" I almost whispered.

"Prayer?" He half rose from the sofa as he said it. "We pray every day. I ask God all the time to help me. He doesn't. I'm about done with prayer." Jon's face flushed red.

"I'm talking about a different kind of prayer. I'm talking about deliverance prayer."

Oh boy, here I go.

"Bob and Aubrey have some friends who pray for people who have with opened doorways for the devil to work in their lives through occult involvement or other strongholds, like addiction. Aubrey told me God has worked through them to deliver lots of people from the bondage of drugs, alcohol . . . whatever. She said she'd give us their number if we were interested. I know about this kind of prayer and I think it's worth a shot. Would you be willing to try it?"

Jon said nothing for about a minute. Then he simply stated, "I'll think about it," as he picked up the remote and filled the room with CNN.

The Next Morning

"So, that's what happened," I said to Aubrey the next morning as we stood on her wraparound porch comparing notes.

"Well, at least he didn't say no," she reassured me. "And if he does decide to go, Bob promised to give him the time off from work. We both feel this is a good idea. Some folks have the gift of intercessory prayer. If anyone does, it's the Stewarts. They genuinely care about the salvation of others. They also believe in the power of God to deliver people from bondage today, just as in Bible times. We still fight the same devil, you know."

Boy, did I know! Whenever Jon disappeared on a binge and reappeared sometime in the early morning hours, I could always sense the darkness entering our home. If I tried to engage him in prayer or read anything from the Bible to him, he became severely agitated, wanting nothing to do with it. Even his countenance changed. His facial features became harsh and his warm blue eyes, dark and hard. Between working in the heat, the crack cocaine, and his regular cigarettes and caffeine, Jon's blood wasn't flowing very well. His face was often red, but with this new relapse after The Rehab, his skin had taken on an almost purplish hue. This was more than a physical health problem. It was a spiritual health problem.

Sometimes Jon would attempt to break out of the darkness by attending church, praying, or listening to Christian music. Whenever his addictions came calling, it seemed he gave in more and more easily and it would take longer for him to return to "normal." Sometimes he'd stay in an evil funk for days after a binge, refusing to participate in any of our usual spiritual routines like prayers before mealtimes or bed. I'd never seen him in such dark spirits. I'd never seen such dark spirits in him.

During one of those malevolent spells I called my mom who now lived in Arkansas. I explained the spiritual battle raging in our home. We began praying together on the phone, and I shared with her what Aubrey mentioned about taking Jon to her friends for deliverance prayer ministry. Mom and Mr. P thought that might be a good idea and offered to go with us if Jon agreed.

When Jon disappeared for several hours one evening after work, I swallowed my supper with the overwhelming feeling he wasn't coming home that night. Something needed to change, quickly. School was starting in a few weeks. I was desperate not to begin another year with my husband making choices that affected my ability to function in the workplace. Working with young children became increasingly difficult as my home life drained my emotional and physical reserves. I slept restlessly until he returned, just before dawn.

The next morning I stood at our bedside with a glass of black liquid in my hand and a plan of action on my lips. "Wake up Jon," I said. "And sit up because you need to drink all of this."

The P's were already on standby, waiting for a phone call from me. I alerted them to what happened and asked them to pray as I again approached Jon about getting help. Jon opened his eyes and slowly sat up. He looked terrible: gaunt, gray and defeated.

"Drink," I offered again. "It will soak up any of the poisons that haven't yet been absorbed into your body."

I didn't really know how quickly crack cocaine absorbed into a person's body, but I knew activated charcoal would absorb any leftover toxins. Charcoal was in Mom's bag of tricks for as long as I could remember. As children, Sis and I hated it because it left our teeth black and our throats feeling chalky. But it sure relieved a stomachache! I prayed Jon would just drink it down and not fight it. It couldn't be any worse than some of the other stuff he took into his body.

Reaching for the glass, he asked, "What *is* it?"

"Charcoal and water. It will cure what ails ya," I tried to smile. "You definitely need cured."

He swallowed it in one shot, quickly lying back down as he handed me the glass, gray with charcoal residue.

"God, help me to say this well."

"Jon," I pleaded, setting the glass down next to the Bible on his nightstand. "You are killing yourself."

Oh boy, that didn't come out right.

"God, Help me, please."

I perched on the edge of the bed. Jon's eyes were closed again; the turned-down corners of his mouth sooty black. He looked so bad I visualized him lying in a coffin. I knew that was where he was headed without intervention.

"Will you please go to Illinois with me?"

"For what?" He mumbled.

"For prayer. For deliverance. For help. For whatever we can get Bob and Aubrey's friends to do for you before you kill yourself. Don't you want help? I can feel the battle. I can feel the pure devil when you are around."

So much for treading softly. But he's not leaving the conversation, so that's a good sign.

"This is worse than it was before we moved here. You look terrible. You are being destroyed and you don't even want to pray anymore!" Now my throat was constricting and I could feel the hot tears coming. "Please Jon," I pleaded. "Come with me to Illinois. The Stewarts will only be there for a few days before they head further north. This is the closest their ministry comes to us. I know it's a long way, but I'm willing to do anything. Aren't you?"

"What about work?" He questioned, eyes still shutting me out.

"I've already spoken with Aubrey. She says it's okay with Bob if you take a few days off. Aubrey says the Stewarts have a lot of experience praying for people with addictions and God uses their ministry to set people free. Isn't it worth a try? If nothing else, it will get you out of here for a few days. Mom and Mr. P are willing to go with us as prayer support. We can even visit Annie and Eddie on the way. Let's just have a little getaway. Please, Jon. Please?" I pressed for a commitment.

"Okay. Okay. Why not?" He conceded.

"Thank You, Lord! Thank You."

I jumped up and ran to call the P's. That's how the four of us ended up going on a twelve hour road trip through the plains and into the cornfields, in hope of finding freedom for Jon and relief from the oppression that seemed deathly close.

At first, Jon was surprisingly chipper about the trip. Once the decision was made and the plans came together, he seemed fine. We'd pick up and drop off the P's at Annie and Eddie's, so we could visit on both legs of our journey. Although we'd seen Sis in June, I hoped to make better memories this time.

I looked forward to spending more time with Lucas. I craved the opportunity to relax and enjoy my family for once, and hoped Jon wouldn't sabotage that.

I think he really did try to act normal when we stopped at Annie and Eddie's. He liked his brother-in-law and wanted to connect with him, but Jon's inappropriate remarks to Eddie's sister at Christmastime strained their relationship. Like many other Christians, Eddie was also skeptical about "deliverance." Although he knew why we were going to Illinois, he never brought it up. Jon also remained silent on the subject as we all laughed and talked together over dinner at Eddie's favorite Mexican restaurant.

Annie, always one to capture and scrapbook the memories, snapped some pictures on her new Coolpix camera. Jon embraced me and smiled, but when I later inspected the photo, I observed no joy in his gesture or expression. Jon's features formed the shape of a smile, but his eyes held only darkness. His skin was that strange purplish color and his countenance heavy. It appeared darkness took him over from the inside. I had not noticed how wretched he looked. Isn't it strange how we can become so acclimated to someone we stop *seeing* them? Or could it be that what we see hurts so much, we turn a blind eye to reality? I guess sometimes we don't perceive the darkness until the light is turned on. That is what the trip to Illinois did for us—it turned on the floodlights.

Our first day's drive was fairly uneventful. But that second night, when we stopped to rest at a roadside motel, Jon noticed the people in the room across from ours were trafficking drugs. His mood darkened as he struggled between outrage against what was going on, and the temptation to participate. We ended up changing rooms.

The next day there was a gloomy heaviness over Jon that worsened with each passing hour and mile. When we stopped for lunch, he went off alone to smoke a cigarette. His face was dark, scary even. Mom and I eyed him as we smeared hummus on rice cakes.

"I think he's having an internal battle," she said. "We need to pray."

Ten minutes later, Jon decided to join us again. We breathed relief when he jerked open the Cadillac door and got in.

"*Skirmish won. Thank You, Jesus.*"

We finally arrived at the modest cornfield church where the Stewarts would present their weekend seminar, all four of us exhausted by the unseen battle.

William Stewart met us at the car with a warm smile and a firm handshake. "Come on in," he invited. "Meet my wife, Barbara."

"I need a minute," Jon stalled, as the P's and I stretched and moved toward the tiny church. The church was an island in a sea of deep green cornstalks. I prayed that what was about to happen in there would be the lifeboat we needed in order to keep us afloat.

"*Oh, God,*" I silently pleaded, "*this has surely been a battle, but I believe You will prevail. We are here. Thank You. Please give Jon courage to get out of the car.*"

It was a relief to meet William and Barbara and to mentally pass Jon over to their care. I know that probably sounds strange, but I sometimes felt I was carrying him. I'd learned about codependency in the Celebrate Recovery meetings we attended and I realized those feelings were a red flag for me, but I didn't have enough tools in my tool belt yet to know how to support my husband without enabling him and disabling myself. I was mentally drained, and so were the P's. We needed backup.

William Stewart was a kind and calm man. He gently but firmly explained to Jon that no matter how much any of the rest of us desired his healing and deliverance, Jon's will was his own and only he could surrender it to The Almighty.

"Do you want to give up fighting and surrender every aspect of your life to Him?" He asked after Jon finally joined us in the church foyer.

"Yes. I do. I want to be done with this once and for all," came the reply.

"Good. Then let's pray together and ask the Holy Spirit to reveal to you every doorway you've opened in your life for the enemy to work. We will give God some time to work with your thoughts as you prepare to close those doors. After we pray this afternoon, I'm going to give you an index card. On that card, you can write down any relationship, habit, addiction, thought pattern, anything the Lord shows you has been an invitation for the devil to have the freedom to control your life. Plan to spend some time alone with God this evening and in the morning. He will make these things clear to you.

"If you have formed unholy sexual ties with anyone, just jot down the name of the person, or your age at the time of the incident, but don't dwell or strain to recall specific events. The point is not to focus on the sin, but to be aware of doorways. Sexual encounters or activities outside of marriage are always open doors. Tomorrow morning, we'll all come together for a time of prayer. In the meantime, Barbara and I will be fasting and praying for your deliverance."

It wasn't long before we were praying. Right there on the floor of the church hallway, the six of us knelt together. We each came humbly before God, asking Him to reveal any unconfessed sins so we could repent and receive His promised pardon. I knew I harbored pockets of anger and resentment toward Jon. Praying for release from the bondage of unforgiveness, I asked God's forgiveness so He would hear my prayers for my husband (John 9:31).

Mom was also bitter because of what Jon had put me, and our family through. She too, chose the path of forgiveness so that nothing could hinder the Holy Spirit's work among us. Psalm 66:18 (NIV) clearly states that unconfessed or "cherished" sin adversely affects God's hearing. No matter how much I justified my bitterness, it was wrong. I loved Jon enough to release it in hope of his healing. God immediately uprooted the ugly feelings as I confessed them!

After prayer, Jon went for a long walk by himself. The rest of us talked together about the power of God to set captives free. Barbara and William shared several incredible stories from their many years of working in the ministry of healing and deliverance. Their faith was inspiring. My hope soared high as we drove back to our motel that evening. I believed our mighty God would come through for us.

Jon remained quiet, even after we were alone. He appeared contemplative, thoughtful. We did not talk as we undressed for bed, but I noticed his index card, covered in blue ink, lying on the nightstand as he clicked off the lamp.

"Jon?" I whispered in the dark as I reached for his hand under the covers.

"Yeah?" came his soft response.

"Are you nervous?"

"Not really. I think I'm ready," he answered. "Are you nervous?"

"No. I felt the Holy Spirit's peace when we were all praying together tonight. I don't think there's any reason to be afraid. Goodnight."

Letting go of my hand, he rolled onto his side, his whispered 'goodnight' barely audible over the air conditioner's hum. "Night," I said again.

For most of an hour, I stayed awake, alone with my thoughts. Despite all of the lies and crazy behavior, I did love my husband. I just wanted him to be able to love me back. I yearned for him to be able to look beyond himself and to see me. Our relationship felt unbalanced. I was tired of being on the "good girl" pedestal where he so often placed me. I wanted to come down from the pedestal, and I longed for him to come up from the pit.

My final prayer that night went something like this:

"God, it often feels like Jon and I are 'unequally yoked.' But I know I'm not so great. I have recurring sin in my life. You are working it out of me. Jon's addictions always seem like they make him the worse sinner. He acts like he's so bad and I'm so good. You know that's not true. It's only because of Jesus that any of us has a fighting chance. Please help us both to find and maintain freedom in our lives. Please grow us both closer to You and closer to each other. Please set him free from these dark spirits. Keep me free from spirits of anger, bitterness and unforgiveness. Show me what doors I have opened to the enemy. I don't want Jon to be the only one who goes home free tomorrow. In Jesus' name, Amen."

Deliverance

Before we arrived at church in the morning, all four of us were convicted of our own sinfulness and anxious for the time of prayer. We each requested William put anointing oil, a symbol of God's Spirit, on our foreheads as we asked God to cleanse us of any and everything ungodly we ever opened ourselves up to. The P's had their own time of prayer with Barbara and William. Then Jon and I had our turn.

I'd become embarrassingly aware of some doorways in my own life where evil had entered. The Holy Spirit revealed to me I still felt guilty for how things ended with Bird Man, that I still blamed and resented Jon because we lost the opportunity to be Chloé's parents, and that I was protecting myself from further hurt by not allowing myself to love anyone unreservedly the way I loved that baby girl. I built walls around my heart, and that is not how God wanted me to live. I confessed my hardheartedness as sin and invited God's Spirit to fill me and give me a soft, loving, forgiving heart. I renounced guilt and false-guilt. I renounced an unloving, bitter spirit. I renounced and rebuked an unforgiving spirit. I experienced a warm peace as William and Barbara anointed and prayed over me, rebuking the spirits I named and any others that might be lurking in my life. Barbara specifically prayed for me to be able to have my own child, to love and nurture. I remember the tiniest spark of hope igniting in that walled off, I-long-to-be-a-mother section of my soul. Hope, it's one of those precious things that kept me alive on the inside.

I'm not sure what kept Jon's inside alive, because the things he chose to share from his index card revealed he had been semi-dead to abundant life for a long, long time. Barbara took a few notes as he poured out his soul. The anguish in his eyes hurt me as he expressed deep shame and regret for having wounded me in the crossfire between his addictions and his desire to be a "good Christian husband." He spoke of the open doors of rejection and feelings of worthlessness from childhood that led to other, more blatant strongholds, as he'd learned to use people and substances in order to numb pain and find a place of belonging. According to Jon, the enemy was present and vying for him from his earliest memories. The drug use was a symptom of something much deeper.

As William described it, Satan preys on the wounded. Evil spirits will attach to our wounds and create secondary issues that often mask the real ones. He said it is never God's plan for His children to be in bondage to the enemy. "God cannot force His will upon anyone. A person has to desire to be free. The Holy Spirit will give *even the desire* for freedom to a person who truly wants it. Then they must ask God to heal or deliver them." He said the next step is surrendering to the process of deliverance and healing, always believing by faith in the power and the name of Jesus, we are set free. It made sense to me.

William gave an example of a person whose will was so bound they didn't even *want* to ask for help. Like the man Jesus met in Mark Chapter 5, all they could do was fall on their knees.

"The good news is, even when our desire to be healed is broken, God will still honor the heart's cry of, '*Lord make me willing to be made willing*,'" he continued. "Sometimes, a person becomes like a puppet to the enemy, unable to even make the simplest decisions for themselves. That is when their very desires are in bondage. Certain substances and addictions, like cocaine or pornography, can eventually destroy a person's capacity to use their frontal lobe, where good reasoning and decision-making take place. Without intervention, Satan will wreak havoc on such a person's life. The power of the prayers of others can make a significant difference in that person's situation." Then, in a serious tone, he asked, "Jon, do you want to be free from the bondage of addiction, shame, abandonment, rejection, fear, and anger?"

"Yes, I do. I really do. I'm so tired of carrying all of this baggage around," came Jon's quick reply.

"Good! Then let's get started." William invited us to kneel around Jon, placing our hands on his bowed head and shoulders. I could feel his tension taut beneath my fingertips. Jon prayed first. Tears oozed from his closed eyes as he renounced and confessed sin after ugly sin to God, verbally closing every door he'd opened to the enemy. Step by step and word by word, Jon took back the ground he'd given to the dark side over the course of his lifetime. He asked God to wash each of those confessions with the shed blood of Jesus Christ.

William anointed Jon's head with oil as he prayed a cleansing prayer. He took authority over those spirits and strongholds, binding and rebuking them in the name of Jesus and commanding them to leave Jon's life and not to come back. Then he asked if Jon, Barbara, or I sensed anything else that needed to be addressed. Barbara mentioned a couple of items. William asked Jon if he agreed that those were areas where the enemy was working in his life, and he said, "Yes." So,

William asked Jon to renounce those as well and then he commanded any spirits that may have entered Jon's life through those doorways, to "GO! In the name of Jesus Christ of Nazareth."

During that time, I kept my eyes closed, but I could sense the battle. With each rebuke, I felt tension release under my fingers as Jon's rigid body relaxed. The oppression lifted and peace filled the room as God rescued my husband from bondage. William and Barbara must have sensed it as well because they both began thanking and praising God for His goodness and His deliverance. William then invited the Holy Spirit to come and fill the empty spaces and to bring the fruit of the Spirit into Jon's life. He especially asked God to give Jon self-control, and patience to wait upon the Lord to finish the good work He had begun in Jon's life. By the time we reached "amen," Jon was a new creation. He felt it, and we saw it. Gone was the strange, purplish skin tone. Gone were the sad, hollow eyes and the dark, heavy spirit. Jon's face was literally transformed.

After our prayer session, William offered to take a picture of us to remember the day by. He said, "It's good to document and remember the joy we experience when Jesus sets us free." That moment is branded on my brain. We used an Illinois cornfield as our backdrop. I was wearing new khaki capris and a silk polka-dot top. This time, when Jon put his arm around me, he drew me close with uncharacteristic enthusiasm. Both of us smiled for the camera as William counted, "One, two, three" and snapped two identical photos.

Over lunch at one of Illinois' not-so-great Mexican restaurants, Barbara and William spoke of maintenance. They shared experiences of people delivered from the enemy's bondage who maintained their freedom through a deep personal connection with Jesus. They said that spending time alone with God each day in Bible study, prayer and reflection was a crucial part of staying free. Barbara told us evil spirits constantly look for an opportunity to re-infest a place that has been "swept clean" and left empty. She stressed the importance of daily inviting the Holy Spirit to fill us, so there is no room for any other spirit in our lives. Both William and Barbara humbly reminded us that the deliverance we witnessed and experienced had nothing to do with them and everything to do with the power and authority of Jesus Christ.

They joked with us saying, "You really didn't need to drive all the way to Illinois to give God the authority in your life. The name of Jesus works in Texas too, and the Mexican food is definitely better there!" They encouraged us to put on the armor of God every day and to stand against the enemy's attacks by singing, praying and using praise as a weapon against discouragement and temptation.

As we finished the last few tortilla chips in our basket, William turned toward Jon and mentioned the percentage of people who relapse back into drug use is very high. He said when individuals experience freedom from spiritual bondage they must be diligent about maintenance, because to re-open doors once closed to the enemy can invite a host of problems that make one's life worse than it ever was before.

"Satan does not play fair, but he does play for keeps," he said. "So be aware of your weaknesses and never be afraid to ask for help. We can get into trouble when we try to do things on our own. If you feel the enemy closing in, call for back up."

"I will," Jon said seriously. "I don't want to ever feel like that again. Especially now that I know how it feels to be free. Thank you. Thank God!"

The atmosphere in our car on the drive back to Eddie and Annie's was definitely lighter. We sang along with our favorite Selah CD and joked with the P's about what happens when four people eat bad Mexican food and then go on a road trip together. Seeing Jon laugh with his eyes, and not just his mouth made the whole trip worth it for me. We praised God for His mercy and His deliverance. As we arrived back at my sister's house, my own heart felt light, as if I left my burdens back in the cornfields too.

A week after returning home I finally had the prints from that trip. I laid Annie's Mexican restaurant photo and one of William's snapshots side by side on our kitchen table. There was no mistaking the transformation in Jon's countenance and appearance. In the day between our dinner with Annie and Eddie and the time we posed for William, the Lord performed a miracle in Jon's life. I had pictures to prove it.

Chapter 11

The Last State of That Man

*"Then he goes and takes with him seven other spirits
more wicked than himself,
and they enter and dwell there;
and the last state of that man is worse than the first."*
Luke 11:26 NKJV

2005–2006

School years mark time for me. I love the fresh start: new notebooks, clean chalkboards, yellow roses on my desk for the first day of school. These things earmarked most Augusts since our marriage. August 2005 was not unique. Like clockwork, I ordered my materials, arranged my classroom, organized bookshelves, and wrote lesson plans. An exciting change was our district's transition from old-fashioned chalkboards to magnetic white-boards. Awesome! No more chalk prints on the back of my skirt. No more fine white dust on my computer keys. No more clapping erasers after school. I could now write the date in a different bold color every day of the week! My teacher-heart thrilled at the sight of that perfectly white "clean slate" that brightened our classroom each morning, inviting me to fill it with beautiful things.

Jon's clean slate lasted only briefly after our return from Illinois. By September, not only had he fallen off the proverbial wagon, it had run him over. The Bible's warning about unclean spirits returning is no joke. I was an unwilling eyewitness to that scenario.

Jesus said, "When an unclean spirit goes out of a man, he goes through dry places, seeking rest; and finding none, he says, 'I will return to my house from which I came.' And when he comes, he finds it swept and put in order. Then he goes and takes with him seven other spirits more wicked than himself, and they enter and dwell there; and the last state of that man is worse than the first" (Luke 11:24-26 NKJV).

In my Bible, the section just before that Scripture is titled, "A House Divided Cannot Stand." I tell you, those evil spirits divided *our* household. It was unable to withstand the onslaught.

I had no doubt Jon came home from Illinois a free man. His eyes were clear and bright. His countenance was peaceful. He was loving toward his wife. His heart was right with God. Jon's "house" was swept and put in order. The problem came when it *remained* empty.

It's like when we go to the gas pump to fuel our vehicles. If our car takes gasoline, and we put in diesel, that is similar to what we do to ourselves when we open up doors to the devil. We were never created to be the habitation for demons. Our hearts were created to be a home for the supreme gasoline—God's Spirit. 1 Corinthians 6:19-20 (NKJV) makes that very clear: "Or do you not know that your body is the temple of the Holy Spirit who is in you, whom you have from God, and you are not your own? For you were bought at a price; therefore glorify God in your body and in your spirit, which are God's."

Following such a deep cleansing, Jon needed to be filled with the Holy Spirit and to keep being filled. Going back to the gasoline analogy, if I put diesel in my gas tank, I have to completely flush the system before I dare try to run my vehicle. But that's not the end of it. Although my tank is cleansed and empty, I still cannot go anywhere. It is only when my car is full of supreme gasoline that I can move forward with my life. As life takes its toll, my gas gets used up. I must keep going back to the filling station for more.

Jon was aware of this principle. He read his Bible. He knew in theory what he chose not to put into practice. I'm not here to vilify him. Every Christian I know, including myself, is a leaky vessel. We *all* must daily choose Jesus. We get caught up in life and fail to connect to The Vine on occasion. Sometimes we go through the motions of abiding even though we aren't experiencing the emotion of abiding.

It's like a marriage. There are moments of intense, deep euphoria and there are deserts couples move through by faith, trusting they will come again to an oasis. I cannot begin tell you how I utterly longed for that oasis. How I ached for Jon to be victorious. How I prayed for him to allow Jesus to be Lord of his life. I knew if he connected to Christ and stayed filled with the Holy Spirit, he would make it.

After our Illinois experience, I begged Jon to keep all of the enemy's access points closed and sealed with the blood of Jesus. I watched him with eagle eyes to make sure he didn't fall back into a hole. Although I invited him to pray and worship with me, he insisted on going it alone. Isolation is the first step toward the dark side. We need each other. When a Christian husband and a Christian wife cannot consistently pray intimately together in their own home, that's a red flag.

The second red flag I noticed was when Jon began to avoid kissing me, a sure sign he was smoking again. When one of God's children is delivered from bondage, the enemy will seek to reclaim that which he lost. When we are set free, as new babes in our faith, we must again learn how to walk. Ephesians 5:8 (NKJV) spells it out like this: "For you were once darkness, but now you are light in the Lord. Walk as children of light." Verse 11 warns us to "have no fellowship with the unfruitful works of darkness . . . "

I think it was "fellowship" with cigarettes that re-opened Jon for inhabitation. There was a stronghold there that needed to stay broken. Those cigarettes were his lifelong comforter, but Jesus already promised to send him another Comforter. When we replace God's Spirit with an idol or a false god, we are walking on dangerous ground. My husband came to a crossroad in his life. He could no longer ride the fence or dabble back and forth with the things that wanted to destroy him. Once he opened that Marlboro door, the rest of his vices returned with a vengeance.

Jon relapsed so violently, he scared everyone, even himself. Bob released John from work; he was fast becoming a liability in the A/C business. We decided Jon should go away for a while, since between the devil and his drug dealer he was like a puppet on a string. Just before school started, Jon left for Arkansas to stay with my grandpa and work for Mom's brother, building a garage apartment.

It was during that quiet reprieve Ariana was born. Petite and perfect, she resembled her Nana, which is what the kids call our mother. I raced to Kentucky to fight for my turn to hold her.

Unfortunately, the drug drama did not stop just because a new baby arrived in our family. While Mom and I were in Kentucky, Mr. P called from Arkansas with disturbing news. My husband had already dredged up a crack dealer and worried Grandpa's new wife by going out after work one evening and never returning.

Jon somehow broke his crack pipe that night, deeply slicing into the meaty part of his palm. He didn't want to go to the hospital for fear of being arrested, and he didn't want to go back to Grandpa's house either.

He was scared, high, and badly bleeding from the wound. Because Mr. P was a nurse for decades, Jon decided to make the hour and a half drive to the Arkansas boondocks where the P's now lived, in hope of getting some professional wound care without involving the police. That was a real risk given the amount of blood Mr. P said he lost. Jon arrived on the mountain so late, the only creatures still awake were the ones who never sleep at night. Mr. P wasn't one of them.

Now you have to understand how frightening this scene was to a man who had previously only lived in European apartments in cities like London and Lugano. My mother, wanting to be a hands-on Nana, had dragged him to America after he retired from the nursing profession. Not only did she move him to America, she moved him to Arkansas—backwoods Arkansas! Their only neighbors were foxes, bears and panthers, unless you counted the people who wore camouflage and stocked ammo against the government.

So, imagine it's the middle of the night and you are alone in a cabin in the boondocks. It's exactly one mile from your mailbox to your front door on a dirt road that is only accessible with four-wheel drive, and a truck comes roaring up into your yard. You, unlike everyone else in the county, don't have a shotgun. All you have is a Swiss walking stick with a cowbell on it and a telephone. What would *you* do?

Jon was fortunate Mr. P didn't own a gun; he might have gotten a fright of his own. Once they both figured out they knew each other, the adrenaline rush significantly slowed. Mr. P took Jon inside to examine his cut. After he cleaned and bandaged the wound, he prayed over Jon's hand.

Let me tell you something about Mr. P. Some might say he has the gift of healing. I say he has the gift of faith, because he believes in *God's* power to heal. He takes Scripture literally when it says to lay hands on the sick and they shall recover (Mark 16:18 KJV). Because my mother's husband takes that whole passage in Mark 16, which gives "The Great Commission" to all Christians, very seriously, he has many stories of how God has worked through his prayers to bring healing to individuals.

Mr. P's faith has rubbed off on our family. Each of us has at least one tale of praying for a healing and witnessing no less than a miracle. None of us can explain why healing takes place sometimes and not others, but we continue to believe God calls us to do the works Jesus did while on earth. Healing is one.

After what happened when Mr. P prayed that night, Jon had no choice but to believe in the power of God to heal. He shared the story with me later. "I was completely fine the next day!" He incredulously exclaimed. "We went to bed right after he prayed. The next morning, I had no pain at all. I got up and got ready for work. By 10 a.m. I was wielding a hammer on your uncle's house."

Jon was always amazed that God would choose to heal him, a rebellious, addicted son. Yet, isn't that what Jesus did? Didn't he go around healing and forgiving the "lowest of the low," as Jon sometimes called himself? Aren't we called to be just like Jesus?

Sadly, Jon continued to use. Throughout that fall and into the winter, drug-related drama shrouded our lives. His behavior in Arkansas saddened and embarrassed me. Most of the money he was supposed to send home was spent on crack.

I spent the weeks Jon was away working on a scrapbook for him. This "Lifebook" was to be a surprise Christmas gift, an eleventh hour effort to show him how much I truly cared for him. I used some precious childhood photos Jon's sister Mona gave me to portray the positive, happy things in his life. I also included cards and letters, travel mementos and everything good from our courtship and marriage. It turned out to be a remarkable project. I was so proud of Jon's book I almost didn't wait until Christmas to present him with it.

In September, my other grandpa, a cherished man in my life died suddenly. Grandpa Kaiser loved me. I ached to attend his funeral. I wrote a tribute to be read at the service, but it wasn't the same as being there. I remember feeling angry with Jon because we had no money for my plane ticket. Grandpa's death was a great loss. I resented not being able to properly grieve.

November brought a chance to catch a free ride to Colorado with Jon's twin brother, Roman. Not wanting to pass up an opportunity to spend Thanksgiving with my Nannie, I took it. She lived with her son, my dad, his wife Janet, and their kiddos near Colorado Springs. I had not seen any of them in way too long.

My father and I struggle to be close, not because either of us want it that way, just because that's the way it is. Divorce disrupts relationships. Sometimes they never fully recover; even when people want them to, circumstances get in the way.

When Janet married my dad, I prayed for their family to stay intact, and it has. They've raised three extraordinary young people, whom I've loved from afar. We all had a memorable time together that Thanksgiving, even though my Nannie selfishly hogged me! I spent hours in her basement apartment, reveling in her wicked sense of humor; Nannie loved to tell tales on people in the family.

Between the scuttlebutt sessions, Dad and I managed to devour a whole pecan pie. Afterward we moaned about our misery and disparagingly laughed until our sides hurt. Between bites, he asked about Jon. I revealed nothing about Jon's drug use. I regret that now. Back then I just didn't know how to say it.

By Christmastime Mr. Ebenezer Scrooge had nothin' on me. I had the money so tightly clamped down Jon could barely rub two pennies together. I was learning new skills, like how to have my own checking account without John, and how to squirrel away dollars so I would not miss any more funerals.

We drove to Arkansas for Christmas, not to the boondocks though. The P's moved to the suburbs. I remember carefully packing Jon's Lifebook in a box and sneaking it into the trunk of my car among our other luggage. Even though he was negligent of, and absent from our marriage, I still hoped my gift would spark something inside him that might catch fire and warm our home again with love.

I wish I could say drugs didn't ruin Christmas, but they did. Not all of it, but most of it. These days the family jokingly refers to that year as, "The Wooden Spoon Christmas." Eddie especially likes to laugh and tease about it. When things are too strange to wrap your brain around, sometimes all you can do is laugh.

It all started like this: Jon worked with Bob up until the day we left. Yes, Bob took him back after he returned from helping my uncle. After Jon signed his holiday paycheck, I added my signature and deposited it into the bank. Then we loaded the car, whistled for the girls, and off we went to Arkansas.

"Lord God, thank You for allowing us to get away from here without Jon having an opportunity to buy drugs or do anything crazy. I've done my best to prevent him from getting his hands on any money or anything to pawn. You know how I've looked forward to this family time. Please protect us as we drive. Please let us have a nice vacation. I know You don't control people, but You can control circumstances."

The trip itself was uneventful. We arrived a day before Annie and Eddie. Jon insisted on going into town because he hadn't yet purchased a gift for me. I did not want him to go alone. He resented that. I stood my ground, finally convincing him to take Mr. P along.

I handed Jon fifty dollars. "You better get me something good. And bring me the receipt," I said jokingly, but not joking. Not wanting to risk any more shenanigans, I wanted him to account for every cent. Yes, I was controlling. That's what codependent people do when their world spins out of control. They find some dinky shred of something over which they can be a dictator. My shred was money. I became the Money Nazi. I asked Jesus to be in control, but I was trying to help Him.

Mr. P later told my mother Jon dropped him at Barnes and Noble, saying, "I'll be back in an hour or so." Mr. P likes bookstores. He'll grab a stack of European travel magazines and take a mental vacation. He can sit there for hours. And that's just what he did. He sat there . . . for hours. Jon disappeared. When he finally resurfaced with some lame excuse about how he drove all over the city searching for the perfect gift, suppertime was long gone.

On Christmas morning I unwrapped a feather pillow and about twenty different kinds of wooden spoons. I think Jon's reasoning was if each one were individually wrapped, it would appear as if he were inordinately generous. Granted, some of them were very nice. In fact, I still use the one with the extra long handle when I make large batches of pasta sauce for potluck. Sometimes I pray for Jon while I stir, wondering if he is able to pray for himself. I still remember Eddie's grin as he said, "Oh, and it's . . . another wooden spoooon!" or "Surprise! Another wooden spoon!" Over and over as I unwrapped each one. Embarrassment tinted my cheeks scarlet.

When I presented him with his Lifebook, Jon's reaction was similar to his response when I had handed him the truck keys the day he got out of Blue Sky Rehab. He crumpled, like a stringed puppet whose puppeteer walked away from the stage. Tears welled in his eyes, spilling over as he carefully turned each page. He paused for a long while on the page with the photograph of him smiling in his suit on ordination day.

Lucas and Ariana kept the energy high in the P's small home while Mom and I prepared the holiday dinner. Lucas played with Nana's tiny train set, or raced through the kitchen squealing with delight as Uncle Jon chased and tickled him. The baby smiled and cooed on the floor in the living room next to Annie. Sis was not well. I think the stress of having an addict in the family was getting to her. She and Eddie were no longer comfortable around Jon.

Christmas Eve brought more hoopla. Annie and Eddie drove to Wal-Mart for some last minute stocking stuffers. Jon went with them. He disappeared for a long time then, too. When they returned, Jon had such energy he greeted my mother by lifting her up and squeezing so hard he literally cracked her ribs. After that holiday, excruciating pain kept her laid up in bed for the rest of the winter. Jon always swore he wasn't high when he did that. Either way, Mom took years to forgive. She has still not forgotten.

I kept eyeing him, wondering where he was getting all that energy. Usually when we came away from home for any length of time, he got "the flu." At least that's what he told everyone by way of explanation for his sudden flu-like symptoms and loss of energy and appetite. For years, I believed him.

Paris 1999

I remember the first time he had "the flu." It was December 1999, the winter before Blue Sky Rehab. I had no clue Jon was snorting cocaine. I just thought he had chronic sniffles. All three of us, Jon, Annie and myself, worked around the clock for a year and a half trying to get Buona Notte Café off the ground. We badly needed a break.

The nomadic P's still lived in Europe at that time. How could we resist their invitation to spend a few days in Paris before heading to their cottage in Torquay, England for Christmas? When they even offered the money for employee vacation pay, we closed the café for two weeks and went!

"Thank You for this trip, God." I prayed as our plane lifted. *"We need this! Jon and I are growing apart. Hopefully we can reconnect on this vacation. Paris at Christmastime! How romantic! I'm happy Mr. P booked us our own hotel room!"*

Sometimes foreign situations and tight budgets dictate less-than-romantically-conducive sleeping arrangements, but this time was a score.

"And God, please give my sister rest while she's away from the café. She has been slaving too hard lately. She seems so stressed. Even though Eddie, that nice Army guy, brought her roses today, she's still in a bad mood. I don't understand."

What I did not know at the time was that our employees warned Sis that Jon was up to no good. They witnessed him sneaking money from the till and hanging out with questionable characters. She was suspicious, but had not yet figured out how to talk to me about it because I lived in a place she called "Oblivion."

Perhaps it was oblivion that made me thrilled to be going on a European vacation, thrilled Jon and I would have some special time together. I remember secretly hoping we might conceive a baby in Paris. During the flight, while everyone watched movies or slept, I dreamed up French sounding names for little girls. Chloé was my favorite. I held the name in my heart long before I held Chloé in my arms.

We met the P's in London and braved the Channel Tunnel together. Before our feet hit France, Jon had the full-blown "flu." He lasted surprisingly well through the long flight. Hindsight reminds me why. Jon disappeared just prior to check-in in Texas. I bet he snorted the last of his lines before boarding.

Paris was drizzly and gray. Unaware that Parisians don only black in winter, I wore a full-length white wool coat. I was the only bright spot in the frozen city as the five of us dragged our suitcases through the backstreets toward our hotel.

Mr. P inadvertently booked a declining ancient brothel. While the web site *had* mentioned a view of the Notre Dame, it failed to say that was the hotel's most redeeming quality. We wound around staircases and through narrow hallways up, up and up to the top floor.

"Will we ever get to our destination? I have never seen so many tiny doorways in my life!" I puffed.

Upon reaching our rooms, everyone was out of breath. Jon was out of patience. His nose had starting pouring at the airport in London. By Paris, he had the chills. He was shaky, grumpy and just plain miserable. The freezing, rainy walk from the subway to our hotel did nothing to enhance his mood.

So much for my idea of a romantic evening in Paris. Let me just leave him alone while I go visit Sis.

Her room had seven beds! We got the giggles as we bounced from bed to bed, joking about being booked in at a Parisian parlor house. Our laughter echoed down the passageway, inviting the P's to burst in and beckon us to *their* bedchamber. It was decorated in typical Victorian style with velvet-striped wallpaper, toile cushions with golden tassels and lush throw rugs. Nothing matched in their musty boudoir. "Oooh P's! Have fun in *here* tonight!" Annie taunted in a singsong voice, waving her hand elegantly over their lavish bed.

No fun was had in *our* room that night, or any other night on that vacation. Abstinence became our norm in the months and years that followed. I was clueless as to why Jon seemed so angry and aloof. "Lighten up, Jon. We're in Paris!" I'd begged.

Cluelessness doesn't prevent heartache. In fact, it exacerbates heartache. There is a strange comfort in knowing truth. It's in the *not* knowing, where one's soul is tormented.

Does he still love me? Am I not attractive to him? Has he lost his drive? Is there someone else?

Wondering can drive a woman mad. When she discovers the name of the other lover, at least she has a place to hurl her anger. It would be many more months before I knew her name was Cocaine.

From that vacation forward, our family subconsciously came to expect that whenever we visited, Jon would have the "flu." Everyone learned to carry on with normal plans, leaving him to his misery. If we tried to engage him too closely or invite him to be prayed over, he recoiled.

Jon was never openly hostile toward my family, but we all knew when to leave him alone. They were used to his need for excessive amounts of alone time, taking long walks with his binoculars or lingering outside with the dogs. Between his not-so-secret smoking habit, and the drug use, we all developed patterns of behavior that accommodated his addictions and prevented embarrassing confrontations. If anyone innocently asked, "Where's Jon?" One raised eyebrow brought an immediate, "Oh! Never mind."

Sometimes I lied, "covering" for him when he was supposed to be on the path of righteousness, but had lost his way. Sometimes I didn't realize I was lying when I tried to convince someone he "really had quit this time." I often believed the lies myself. I don't know if he ever quit anything, or if he just got better at hiding it. Codependent denial kept me too afraid to ask. Not much had changed in six years. Denial was still my default.

Springtime

The mystery of how Jon funded his drug use during The Wooden Spoon Christmas was solved in the spring of 2006 with Mr. P's discovery of a pillaged Swiss toolbox in his garden shed. *Someone* pawned his tools for a couple of highs. He was heartbroken about the ones inherited from his father.

I was heartbroken when my Nannie died on Mother's Day.

"*God, this hurts! Thank You that I got to spend Thanksgiving with her. I'm not about to miss her funeral!*"

Nannie came from Hot Springs, Arkansas, so my dad took her back there. Dad's extended family met there for the service.

Jon and I held hands on the front row. People I never met stood up to share their memories of my Nannie. I found it noteworthy that as a young girl in California, she pointed to a handsome sailor in uniform and whispered to her girlfriend, "See that dapper sailor over there? I'm going to marry him some day." She did, and she bore him a daughter and three sons, one of whom is my father.

That tidbit caught my attention because my other Grandma, Odessa, had also pointed and predicted. Only she, as she told it, was staring out the second story window of a girls' dormitory when she saw my handsome seventeen-year-old grandpa come walking across the campus. "I'm gonna marry that boy one day," she prophesied to her roommate. Their union lasted fifty-six years.

For me to learn that both of my strong-willed, independent-spirited grandmothers chose their husbands in such similar manners carried a strong warning. Neither marriage was a match made in Heaven. Both women lived out their marriages in volatile households.

"Oh God, wouldn't it have been better for them to have submitted to Your leading when it came to choosing a husband? Shouldn't they have waited on You rather than snagging the nearest eye candy they could get their hands on? I wonder how my life would have been different had both my parents not come from alcoholic or abusive homes? Has the apple not fallen far from that tree in my own life? Have I foolishly done what my grandmothers did by choosing a husband for myself when I was still too young and too wounded to make a wise decision? Will I continue to suffer, as they did, under the heavy hand of abuse and addiction? Why, oh why, did I jump from Bird Man's frying pan into Jon's fire?"

We ended that day in the cemetery, taking family pictures near Nannie's headstone. No one was ready to say goodbye. Not to her. Not to each other.

I was desperate for Jon to comfort me, as I imagined other husbands comforted grieving wives. He remained emotionally distant, choosing instead to party that night with my cousin's husband, who suffered similar addictions, and coming to bed long after I slept.

Isn't it interesting, I'd mused, as I curled around my pillow, *how people with common denominators manage to sniff each other out, even at funerals? I wonder if the common denominators are common demons?*

Speaking of evil spirits, I believe they were still hell bent on destroying our marriage. They used Jon to do it. But first, we had another small season of spiritual growth. God used it to prepare me for what was to come.

Dr. Alan and Darcy invited us to participate in a weekly Bible study on the book of Hebrews. There I began a journal called "Thoughts on Grace," where I recorded my gleanings from God's Word. Freshly conscious of the fact that my spouse was unable to meet my heart's desires, I carefully penned Psalm 37:4 (NIV), "Delight yourself in the Lord and *He* will give you the desires of your heart," on the inside flap.

My first Grace journal entry is a definition of "works." As in "faith and works." During our discussion on how, why and when to "do good works," Dr. Alan said, "Before we can do good works, we first need to know what good works are." Here's his definition. "When we are walking in the Spirit, good works occur when we sacrifice ourselves so others can have the blessing of Heaven."

I wondered about that. *Okay, but where is the line between sacrificing ourselves and enabling others? I really need help understanding the difference. I suppose that's where the walking in the Spirit part comes in. Maybe that's where I need to focus.*

With each passing addiction cycle I became increasingly aware of my need to stay in my cocoon with Jesus. Thanks to Gary Chapman's book, *The Five Love Languages*, I was aware my "love tank" was operating on a deficit. The emptier my love tank, the more vulnerable I felt. I knew I needed spiritual fortification. I knew it was only in walking in the Spirit I could stay sane through the "crazy" that had become my life.

I learned to begin each day with a Scripture-packed prayer I discovered in the back of a book called *Waking the Dead* by John Eldredge. Those forty-four Scriptures fortified my life. When I prayed them before my morning oatmeal, I felt prepared to face my reality. God's Word, prayed faithfully during that season of life, embedded itself in my mind. I continue to call out those verses in times of need.

In our Hebrews study, I found a new favorite verse. It says, Jesus is the "Captain of my Salvation" (Hebrews 2:10 NKJV). I loved that analogy. My ship needed a good Captain because I was feeling very tossed about by the stormy seas of life with a chemically dependent person. I was starting to figure out my husband was incapable of loving me and was actually abusing me. Although he never laid an angry hand on me, his negligence to touch me in appropriate, fulfilling ways was part of my abuse.

That realization brought me face to face with the spirit of rejection. When I felt rejected, I acted out of character: screaming, throwing dishes, and breaking glass. In the aftermath, the enemy guilted and shamed me into questioning *my* standing with God. I fought those lies with the Sword of the Spirit, finding comfort in my new favorite verse, which reinforced my spiritual position in Christ, the Captain of my Salvation—I *was* saved! Yes, I was broken, hurting, and acting out in my pain. But, my Captain rescued me.

Another Dr. Alan quote that ended up in my Grace journal says, "We are to live a life that vindicates the character of God."

If God's character is love, I reasoned, *then my life must vindicate love. Dear Jesus, how do I live a life that vindicates love to the universe, with a spouse who is incapable of loving?*

The answer comes a few pages later in my journal. *Mary was a worshiper—drinking in the words of Christ.* And then my simple written prayer. *Lord, let me be a worshiper. Make me thirsty for Your words.*

What God revealed through that journaling process was that by true worship, and the experience of a deep prayer life, He would guide my ship safely through the storm. Unlike Jesus, who rested in a storm-tossed boat while his friends panicked, I was not resting through my storm. I was restless. Restless.

As we studied Hebrews, I formed some new thoughts about rest. In my journal I wrote:
There are three steps of faith, which lead to obedience:
  1. Knowing
  2. Believing
  3. Surrendering
We can enter into rest when we surrender.

Jon's twin who happened to be visiting us the evening of that particular study, piped up. "Obedience because you 'have to' is not obedience. It's slavery." *Profound!* We were speaking of being obedient to God, which he was resistant to at the time. I wondered whether Roman had considered the fact that God never forces obedience. He *always* gives his children a choice.

Being obedient to the calls of addiction, on the other hand, *is* slavery because once his or her body, mind, and spirit are in the enemy's clutches—the addict virtually loses the power to choose. As the Holy Spirit's voice is drowned by addiction, it is practically impossible for the person's will to find the power to choose anything other than the drug of choice. Then all hell breaks loose in their lives. I would witness that firsthand in a matter of months.

Chapter 12

A Way of Escape

"And my God shall supply all your need
according to His riches in glory by Christ Jesus."
Philippians 4:19 NKJV

Fall 2006—Spring 2007

We again went to Arkansas for Christmas. Only this time it was to Roman and Kymberly's place. Jon's brother and sister-in-law were a twosome for years before Jon and I became a "we." They definitely survived their own struggles. Roman dealt with his lifetime disappointments in more legal, but no less destructive ways than Jon, yet he and Kym navigated life *together*. Kym encouraged Jon and me to do the same. She and Roman were well aware of Jon's addictive cycles. I suspect they both knew of them long before I did.

Roman and Kym are dog people. Breeders of Siberian Huskies, they always had several pups in various stages of growth, as well as the family Chihuahuas and other strays they took in from time to time. Our girls always enjoyed visits to homes where they had four-legged friends and kids to cuddle!

Although Cookie, Kym's teenage daughter, lived her life behind a closed bedroom door, Snuffles managed to sneak in and romp around on her unmade bed. Cookie's bed was so low Snuff's could jump up there all by her fat little self. Big eyes sparkling, curly tail wagging, she'd crouch with her bottom in the air, then race 'round and 'round in circles until she created a comfy spot to rest. Reggie, their middle schooler, preferred pets to people, so the girls were also welcomed into his bed each night. They were in their element! I was not.

As much as I had grown to love Kym and Roman, I felt like a fifth wheel when we were together. As the only nonsmoker, I struggled to breathe in their home. Although Jon didn't smoke indoors with them, he would have if I weren't around. He and Roman ducked outside a lot, even with winter temperatures in the teens. I felt like they were trying to get away from me.

Maybe I had grown insecure because of Jon's neglect. Maybe it was just my imagination magnifying the idea they kept secrets between the three of them. Whatever it was, my spirit did not rest well when we were there. No matter how I tried to fit in, I didn't. I felt uncomfortable. I couldn't quite pinpoint the uneasy awkwardness between Jon and me that Christmas.

I'm positive Roman knew things about Jon I could never know. Twins have impenetrable bonds. When either one of them would go off the proverbial deep end, then come up for air, his twin's number was the first one speed-dialed. I remember Roman's visit to our home the previous fall. Between his smoke breaks, he and I talked about Jon's drug use as I made a whole pan of chicken curry from scratch. We were waiting for Jon to come home from work. "Why do you think he's doing this?" I bravely initiated the conversation while taking my kitchen scissors to white globs of fat on the dead chicken's breast.

"I don't know, but I hope he quits before it gets the best of him," he responded, balancing his coffee in one hand as he leaned against our table.

"Just when I think he's done for good and I begin trusting him again, there he goes." I rinsed the chicken under cold water and continued scissoring the meat into strips. Making Jon's favorite chicken curry was truly an act of love because, as a lifelong vegetarian, I have never been able to touch raw meat without feeling queasy. Despite my qualmishness I plowed through the process of handling those slimy pink breasts, sighing relief when they were finally steaming in my stainless steel cooking pot.

Whew, the most disgusting part is done! The rest will be easy. I wonder what Roman is really thinking. He always seems guarded with me. I have a hunch he will protect Jon no matter what, even if it ends up hurting him. I wish we could work together somehow.

"Why do I usually end up feeling like the family bad guy? Jesus, where is Jon? He should have called by now to let me know he's on his way. Please don't let this day end badly. How much more can I take?"

"I kind of expected to hear from him by now." Roman glanced at his phone then gingerly folded himself into a wooden kitchen chair. Jon's fraternal twin is tall with a shock of brown waves and "Marlboro Man" features. Chronic back pain prevented him from being comfortable anywhere except his own La-Z-Boy chair at home. The four-hour drive from Arkansas to Texas set his herniated discs on fire.

Empathetically I suggested, "Why don't you wait in the living room? Our sofa is much more agreeable than those chairs. I'm sure he'll be here soon." Biting my lip, I whisked a whole bottle of Madras hot curry powder into my lemony mayonnaise mixture with a tad more zeal than usual. My heart was starting to do that rapid beating thing that eventually led to a tightened esophagus and the inability to speak without the fear of my words sounding strangled.

"Nawww. I think I'll go sit in the truck for a while," Roman declined then disappeared for forty-five minutes. I finished layering steamed chicken and broccoli into my spicy sauce. While the curry baked, I panicked.

"WHY, God?" I pleaded from the bedroom where I had gone to try and call Jon for the umpteenth time. *"WHY? WHY? WHY? This is so bad. Why would he disappear when his brother is here to visit? He's never pulled a stunt like this before! What should I do? Help me, Jesus. I don't know what to do."* I continued to pace and panic until the smell of that bubbling curry had even my vegetarian taste buds begging for a bite.

"Roman?" I hollered into the dark from the kitchen-to-carport door. "Dinner's ready. Wanna come eat?" Robert Plant immediately stopped singing about good and bad times from the other side of the carport wall. A few seconds later, Roman appeared in the kitchen.

"How often does the little turd do this?" he muttered, emptying the coffee pot into his mug. I stalled my answer, inhaling the pungent aroma as he scooped fresh Folgers into the filter.

"God, I wish I were a coffee drinker. How comforting that little drug would be for someone about to spend an agonizing night waiting for a loved one to come home. Help me to find my comfort only in You."

"More and more lately, it seems. Not just on weekends anymore. I never know when he's not going to come home. Looks like tonight may be one of those nights," I responded. "Do you want some curry?"

"No thanks. Smells good though. I think I'm going to cruise around and see if I can find him. I noticed the same vehicle slowly passing the house a couple of times while I was sitting in the truck. I'm thinking maybe it's him trying to get the courage to come in here, even though he knows I'm going to kick his butt."

That was a *long* night. Roman never did find him, but eventually Jon came skulking home. By that time, I was ticked. My flesh overthrew the Spirit in me and I threw a tantrum that kept Roman hiding in his truck for the length of an entire Zeppelin album. I screamed. I threw dishes. I cried. I screeched. I broke things. It was ugly. Embarrassing. I was too upset to care. My head was on fire! My tongue threw daggers. Like a dam whose network of cracks finally gives in to the pressure of a raging river, I broke. When I was finished, Jon stepped outside to grab the broom and dustpan from our laundry room in the carport and calmly began sweeping up broken glass in the kitchen. He did not utter a word.

That was the last time Roman ever visited us in our home. I can't blame him for that. Subsequent get-togethers were also awkward, at least for me. Everyone else seemed strangely fine.

In January, I began attending a Beth Moore Bible study at the local Baptist church. One of my good teacher friends, Shirley led the study based on Beth's book *When Godly People Do Ungodly Things*. Between that study and Dr. Neil Nedley's *Depression Recovery Program*, held at our own church, God provided me with several tools invaluable in keeping me sane and functioning through the next few weeks, as life as I had known it completely vaporized.

One of the greatest tools I gleaned from Beth Moore's study was a breakdown of 1 Thessalonians 5:16-25. I wrote it on a set of index cards and kept them on a metal ring along with other meaningful Scriptures I collected from my personal time with God. God spoke to me—encouraged and directed me through those verses. On page 104 in her book, Beth calls this powerful passage in Thessalonians, "A Concise Profile of a Seduce-Proofed Christian." I adapted and wrote the list on my index cards.

A Seduce-Proofed Woman:
- *Is happy in her faith.*
- *Abstains from evil.*
- *Is unceasing in prayer.*
- *Is thankful and gives thanks.*
- *Doesn't quench the Spirit.*

- *Does not despise instruction, exhortation, or warning.*
- *Tests and proves all things until she recognizes what is good.*
- *Allows God Himself to sanctify her through and through.*
- *Keeps her whole spirit, soul, and body blameless.*
- *Knows the One who called her is faithful to fulfill His call in her life.*
- *Knows she needs prayer.*

Those words became my mantra as I prayed daily prayers like this one.

"God, I am Yours. No matter what happens, I am Yours. I choose to thank You, even though I do not understand my situation. I choose to live by faith, and by Your grace, to abstain from evil. I will listen to the godly counsel You provide and will test all things before making rash decisions. I give You permission to sanctify me through and through. By Your provision and Spirit in me, I will live a blameless life. You are faithful. You are calling me and You will do these things in my heart as I submit to You. I know I am in deep need of prayer and I will not refuse Your constant invitation to meet with You in prayer, nor will I refuse others when they wish to pray over me."

Although I knew I hadn't been feeling quite right, I did not acknowledge the signs of depression in my mirror until Dr. Nedley's materials revealed them. Participants were to answer the question, "Have you experienced any of the following symptoms for two weeks or longer?" from a list under the heading, "How Can I Know It's Depression?"

- Deep sadness or emptiness
- Agitation or restlessness
- Sleep Disturbances
- Weight or appetite changes
- Feelings of worthlessness
- Fatigue
- Markedly diminished interest or pleasure in all or nearly all activities
- Diminished ability to think or reason
- Lack of concentration
- Decrease in your ability to make sound judgment

As I filled in the workbook at church that winter evening, I could not help but recognize myself as I checked box after box. After checking every single box, I knew something was wrong, had *been* wrong. Nedley's seminar helped me realize I never dealt with all the losses I experienced, I only buried them with busyness.

My grief from losing Chloé compounded with Jon's return to drugs. He was unable to comfort or grieve alongside me. My sense of isolation was a loss in itself. I hurt myself by not properly mourning Chloé, and by downplaying losing her to most people who knew me. I felt no one could understand why it was such a big deal to lose a baby that was never even mine. I don't think I fully understood how profound a loss that was.

Add to that the cycle of someone else's addiction, which caused me to give up my job, home, and proximity to close friends. Pile on the hopelessness threatening to overwhelm me after the devil appeared to have won Jon's soul back, and his last attempt at rehab left me broke and heartbroken. You may agree it is truly a wonder and a testament to the grace of God that I functioned in life as well as I did.

As a Christian who has always had a sense of responsibility for caring for my body, I was doing a lot of things "right" according to Dr. Nedley. Maybe that's why I did not fall completely into depression's dark, dark hole. During his seminar, he asked us to keep "Healthy Lifestyle Scorecards," which helped us monitor our exercise, sleep, breathing, negative speech, daily intake of water and sunlight, spiritual activities, and, interestingly enough, classical music enjoyment. Through following his program, I began to focus more on caring for myself rather than becoming consumed by rescuing Jon from *himself.*

By all outward appearances, Jon took care of himself pretty well. That new year he treated himself to a Flame Red 2006 Ram 1500 extended cab with the Hemi engine. "Because," as he said weeping tears of joy, "I've never had anything brand new like this." He didn't put me on any of the paperwork, although *my* car, which I had paid in full, had *his* name on the title. That purchase was one of those things he did on his own. "Buy now; tell the wife later." The payments were high, but it sure was a pretty truck.

I was happy for him to again have something nice to drive. His green truck took too much abuse; the last time being when he ripped off the driver's side mirror by driving too close to oncoming traffic while high one night. He said he never stopped. "Just kept on going. I'm thankful I didn't kill anyone."

Sometime in January, the P's returned from visiting family in England. A couple of weeks later they came to visit us, excitedly bearing gifts and stories from their travels. After they went to bed, I remember Jon angrily tossing a gorgeous Italian silk tie onto his dresser mumbling, "They always bring us the same stuff. Can't it ever be anything good?" Which I interpreted as, *"Why don't they give me something I can pawn so I can buy some more drugs?"* That's what he did with all the "good" gifts he received from people who cared about him. Jon's mindset was: "If it can't be pawned, it's of no value to me."

He did not hide his habits very well during their visit. In times past, he tried to be cordial, at least pretending things were fine. This time, he acted as if he did not give a hoot. "Jon," I warned him one morning, "Mom can see how you are treating me. Can you at least *act* like you care? I can see it's hurting her." Most mothers are sensitive to how their sons-in-law treat their daughters. Mine is particularly keen because she is a survivor of marital dysfunction. She does not want that for her "girls."

It was no use. Not only did Jon reveal his lack of love for me, he committed our family's unpardonable sin and had words with my mother! It happened on a Friday morning just before Jon left for work. I left some of my special Scriptures on the kitchen table, hoping Jon might read them. Mom attended the Beth Moore study with me that week and wrote a Scripture card of her own. She began to say something about the power of speaking God's Word over our lives as she pushed it toward Jon. He immediately pushed it back declaring, "No! It won't do any good."

Sometimes my mother says things in a joking manner when she is not joking. That's what happened next. Mom walked past Jon's hunched shoulders on her way to the sink and, placing her hands on each of his arms, she gave him a little squeeze, saying with a smile through clenched teeth, "Son-in-law, I could just beeeeat you!" That's all it took. Jon was instantly angered and defensive.

"What for?" He growled, "I haven't done anything." Rule number one: never growl at your mother-in-law.

Mother brought out all ammo, blaming Jon for everything from Ursli being stolen, to me having to drive an oil-leaky old Caddy while my husband zipped around in a brand new red truck, spending money like it was Monopoly paper. Jon denied knowing anything about why Ursli disappeared, claiming the puppet was simply part of the loot the robbers took.

Mom said, "I don't know what you're talking about, but that's just weird. What would robbers want with Ursli, or her baby book?" Mom almost shrieked the last question. Jon, never one for direct confrontation, quickly left for work and didn't come home until almost 4 a.m. The P's and I suffered an anxious night.

Mom recalls I got up when Jon came home. "You cooked scrambled eggs and toast and took it on a tray to him in the bedroom," she recently reminded me.

I'd forgotten. But I do remember feeling sorry for him when he came home hauntingly gaunt after binges like that. Never a big guy anyway, for years Jon wore Levis with 28x30 tattooed on the tag. More than a decade of marriage passed before he graduated to a 29-inch waist. After binging on crack for days without eating or drinking, he'd come home looking like one of those emaciated male *Yves Saint Laurent* models. I couldn't stand it. The first thing I wanted to do was poke some food into him.

When we were kids, that's what Annie and I did with fragile, fallen-from-their-nest birds. We force-fed those ugly, half-feathered creatures. We'd soak bread in milk until it was almost mush and force it down their scrawny naked throats. With me, it was instinct.

If it looks half-dead and half-starved, feed it, even if you don't feel like it, because you know you won't be able to sleep one wink knowing it is lost and miserable and may not last until morning.

Well, Jon lasted, but the P's didn't. By Tuesday morning they were on their way back home to Arkansas to prepare for their next adventure, a mission trip to southern Italy. Unbeknownst to them, that awkward weekend would be their final goodbye to Jon. "I guess I sent him over the edge," Mom said as we discussed the incident over the phone. "Maybe I shouldn't have said anything." Then, "Nawww. If it wasn't that, it was going to be some other excuse to destroy himself."

Why would anyone choose to destroy themselves with drugs? I mused after we hung up. *Most material things can be replaced, but what about their life? What about the relationships they destroy? What about all the holidays and gatherings and memories that just get put into permanently sealed mental vaults because no one wants to recall the pain?*

Whole families suffer heartache and loss as a result of one person's poor choices. That is why it is imperative God does our choosing for us when we decide to mate for life. That pivotal decision affects us, and our loved ones, potentially for generations. I hadn't thought about that when I married Jon. I wish I had.

February 2007

One Wednesday evening in February I went to church. Pastor Josh innocently asked if Jon and I would be interested in opening our home for a weekly prayer group. Less-than-hopeful, I promised to ask Jon about it. I did ask. He didn't commit.

"My spirit tells me it's a bad idea anyway," I prayed. *"How can we invite people over when Jon may never even show up? People really do not understand what my life is like, Lord. They think it's normal and that we can make plans. We can't. I never know anymore, what to expect."*

Just after the holidays, Bob accelerated his retirement plan. I wondered if that was partially to avoid the pressure of having an excellent employee who blew all his money on drugs. I was certain my quiet pressure for Bob to withhold some of Jon's check so I could at least pay our bills hadn't helped the situation. Sometimes Bob dropped by the house and pressed cash into my palm. It was above and beyond Jon's earnings—a band-aid for our gaping financial wounds.

After Bob's retirement Jon tried working for the husband of another church member. He lost that job after a few weeks because he couldn't consistently show up for work. When using crosses the line from "recreational" or "functional" drug abuse to the point of encroaching on a man's ability to hold down a job, the ultimate red flag begins to wave. Unfortunately, Jon was too far gone to heed the warning. He tried a different job. This time with Bob's brother Daniel, a very patient heating and air-conditioning expert who saw promotion potential in Jon. Initially Daniel even considered bringing Jon into his company as a partner. Jon was an incredibly hard and fast worker, especially when high on crack.

On February 8, a Thursday, I recorded in my journal: *Jon refused to pray with me. He went to the city. 'The city'* being synonymous with 'finding his dealer.'

I called Daniel, begging him not to pay Jon tomorrow because of his mental state, I wrote. Jon's behavior led me to believe he was on a mission to kill himself with drugs. I was afraid for him to have another week's pay to smoke through his crack pipe.

After realizing he wasn't coming home that night, I wrote Jon a note before I went to bed. It simply said, "I told Daniel what you are doing."

He arrived home around 4 a.m., furiously responding to my note, saying I "invaded his one safe haven" (work).

What about my safe haven? Must my own workplace be the only place where I feel safe from the insanity I live with?

We slept for a couple of hours. When the alarm buzzed, we got up and went through our "normal" morning routine.

My journal for that day says: *He prayed with me in the morning, and seemed happy and nice. After I left for work, Jon took my checkbook and wrote a check for $400 to 'cash' and went to the city.*

I arose early Sabbath morning and blearily got ready for church. Another sleepless night, but I needed to escape the house.

"Oh God," I moaned as I showered, "*I don't know how much longer I can do this. I have waited all night for that phone call—the one that means he is either dead or jailed. The silence is killing me! Where IS he? Please impress him to call me so I know he's alive. Please show me what to do. I'm exhausted with the dread.*"

Jon arrived home just before 8 a.m. He crawled into bed, sleeping all day and night, without drinking or eating. The next day, which was Sunday, he got up and moved to the living room to watch TV. The air in our home was thick. Even the girls were listless with the weight of it. In the afternoon I finally approached him pleading, "Can we talk?"

"I'm finished!" He responded with the most piercing monologue of our marriage. "I'm out. I don't want to be a Christian. I don't want to be your husband. I just want to live my own life and be myself and not have to pretend anymore. I'm a fake. Always have been. I used to do cocaine in Costa Rica. I used to party with my friends before we were married. The first time was NOT when my mother died. I've NEVER quit smoking. I'm tired of living a lie. If that's what keeps me out of Heaven, so be it. I am moving out."

That night we slept in separate beds.

My journal entry for the following day made me chuckle just now as I read it: *I had a migraine and missed the depression seminar.*

Poor girl! She couldn't attend her depression seminar because her reality was so depressing the iron claws of migraine had her head and neck in a vice grip that made her physically nauseous.

The entry continues: *I wept and cried, and cried and wept. I sat on Jon's lap, weeping for what was lost.*

That last sentence surprises me. I remember asking him to hold me, but it still surprises me. Why do we go for comfort to the thing that is destroying us? In my case it was a person, for others it is another addiction. We seek solace in the arms of the enemy and allow him to pat our backs while he rips our hearts out of our chests. Who can explain that oxymoron to someone whose every nerve ending is raw with unfulfilled expectations? We just need something to numb the pain a little—something to calm our nerves and soothe our souls until we are exhausted with the weeping. Perhaps then we can continue to function.

Knowing I needed help I made an emergency appointment with our new marriage counselor, Dr. Wayne Fox. I had already seen him several times. Leon felt too far away and I was desperately isolated in my disintegrating marriage.

At my insistence, sometimes Jon went with me, grumbling we were wasting money that could be used for something "necessary." I liked Dr. Fox. He wasn't Leon; he never hugged us or prayed with us. He did, however, offer good solid counsel about how to cope with addiction in the family. We needed an intervention.

My emergency counseling session brought little hope, but God had a plan in place. My journal says: *I told Jon he needed to move out. I felt okay saying that.*

"*God, I cannot continue to live like this! How can I teach little kids when I've had no sleep and am constantly worried something terrible is going to happen? I feel like I am cracking up. Please get me out of this. I don't know what to do.*"

I didn't see him again for ten days. In those ten days miracles happened. I could feel the Lord's hand all over my life. My journal documents the events.

Wednesday, February 14: I went to the Beth Moore Bible study. Opened up a little about my problems at home—about my husband acting like a teenager. I also shared at school there were problems in my marriage.

Why do we wait until the marriage is lifeless before letting folks know we are struggling? Wouldn't it be wise to have support all along the way? I suppose it was pride and fear that kept my veneer in place at previous Bible studies and teacher planning meetings. These women had become more than just colleagues to me over the five years we worked together. Why couldn't I trust them with my pain?

Once I revealed the truth about my crumbling home life our weekly public school planning sessions became mini prayer meetings. Those precious first grade teachers, sitting in tiny chairs around a kidney-shaped table took my hands and prayed over me with as much fervor as if I had been sitting with the twelve apostles. Those prayers sustained me week by week as the school year played out. It was a huge relief to realize I no longer had to hide my pain in the workplace. Removing that mask allowed me to breathe easier. It also created a team of allies who covered for me when I was having a particularly difficult day. There would be plenty of those before all was said and done.

I arrived home after dark, exhausted from corralling the kids at our annual Valentine's Day party and being vulnerable at Bible study.

"Hey girls! I'm sorry I'm late. I bet you are hungry!" I greeted the dogs as Mama Kitty came bounding to the door, in search of something. "Awww, Mama, are you tired of chasing field mice? Do you want some real food?" She let me scratch her ears before I went inside to drop my Valentine's Day loot onto the table. Grabbing some cat food from the pantry, I shook a little pile onto the carport floor beside the back door. "Where's your dad?" I asked the girls as we entered the empty kitchen. I poured two equal amounts of Kibbles 'n Bits from a plastic container onto the linoleum. Snuffles, as usual scarfed hers down without chewing and honed in on Whipper's pile, hoping for a stray Kibble. Whipper was picky. She meticulously separated her food, eating the softer Bits first, followed by the larger, harder pieces. If Snuffs crept too close, Whipper growled a warning. She never snapped, but Snuffles got the hint.

I'd left the door open. Mama peeked in at the dogs, her black-tipped tail twitching cautiously. When Snuffles got a little too close to a Kibble that wasn't hers, Whipper's snarl sent Mama Kitty fleeing into the night. We never knew where she went at nighttime, but I kept a cat bed on top of our deep freeze in the carport in case she ever wanted to domesticate. Mama had a mind of her own. We could not coerce her into being part of our family. She did what she wanted. She wanted to be loved, but not too much, held sometimes, but not too tightly, and fed only when the mice and birds became scarce.

Jon is a lot like that feral cat, I thought, rifling through the candy on my table. *I've spent years trying to tame him, but he always resorts to his own wild ways. He'll only come home when he wants to.* Bypassing the chalky conversation candy hearts and waxy Dollar Store chocolates, I dug up a couple of Reese's Peanut Butter Cups wrapped in red foil from the bottom of a goodie bag from one of my students. *Jackpot!*

I surveyed our quiet house while carefully peeling the pleated wrapper from the chocolate. In my heart I knew there would be no roses or romantic dinner that night, just me and the girls and a bag of random candy from which I had already robbed the good stuff.

"It's going to be another long night, Lord—one more sad memory to add to my bouquet. Please help me to get through this. My heart hurts. I just want to be loved."

Later I discovered Jon spent four hundred dollars on himself that night while I sat home alone with my bag of cheap chocolates. After a few hours, I couldn't stick around to see whether or not he came home. I was afraid and sick to my stomach. It wasn't from the Valentine candy. My journal says I spent the evening praying and organizing personal stuff. About 9:30 p.m., I called Darcy, asking if I could come over. "Bring your overnight bag," she insisted. I did.

Darcy's guest bedroom was light and airy with a white feather comforter on a firm double mattress. I remember sinking into that bed feeling safe and cared-for. She even left warm fresh muffins and juice on the nightstand. Love was in those muffins; I could taste it. And love was in that home; I inhaled it. For the first time in months I not only slept, I rested.

When I checked on the girls the next day, I could tell Jon had been home briefly, but had packed nothing. I scanned the bathroom. His toothbrush was still there. I went to work early and said to my next-door teacher friend, Donna, "I didn't sleep at home last night."

Donna, tall, thin and worldly-wise told me to get my paperwork in order. "You need to cover your butt. Get your ducks in a row. Don't leave anything lying around that you don't want him to have access to." She had always been blunt, but I liked her. Donna had some hardcore life experience under her belt. I listened.

That evening I drove home and packed a file box with important papers. The house was silent except for eight restless claws on the hardwood as the girls paced from room to room, sensing something was different. A simple phone call revealed the reason for Jon's absence. Daniel paid him a day early. He cashed that twelve hundred dollars and never even bothered to come home after work, just rushed straight for the city.

My mind raced as I packed a few personal things and placed the important papers in the trunk of my car.

"Lord God, I'm not sure what to do. I know Dr. Alan and Darcy said their home is my home and invited me to stay in their guest room for as long as I need to, but I don't know if I should go back there

tonight. It's not fair that I must be the one leaving my home, when he is the one who wants to leave our life together. I hated couch-surfing when he did this after we lost Chloé. I still hate it! It's just not fair."

The girls' restless pacing stopped as I began to wail. Immediately two tenderhearted dogs vied for space on my lap as I crumpled to the floor and bawled.

By 10 p.m. I could no longer handle the familiar feelings of dread and fear. I prayed, read my favorite Scriptures and rebuked the devil over and over. I was too tired to sleep and too lonely and apprehensive to stay awake. Even pulling the girls into bed with me didn't help. Finally I kicked them out and packed my school clothes for the next day—Friday. That meant jeans and an orange golf shirt with the school logo. Easy. I kissed the girls saying, "I'll be back in the morning." Then I left a Dr. Dobson-inspired, tough-love, note for Jon stating, "If you are not packed by tomorrow evening, I will do your packing for you," and drove eleven miles through dark windy roads to my friends' feather comforter.

I slept so well I woke up late and didn't have time to run home to let the girls out or feed them before school. All day I wondered whether or not Jon had come home. Whenever I dialed his number, voicemail picked up, which was "normal" for binge-mode. I became almost calloused by the familiarity of the cycle.

A recurring thought flashed through my brain as I gave my students their weekly spelling test, graded math assessments and made copies for the following week's lessons. *Rent a storage unit.* I repeatedly felt that impression. Finally, I searched the Internet for a storage unit while the kids happily buzzed in their learning centers. I found one on the outskirts of town. Jotting down the number on a sticky note, I stuck it to the outside of my purse. After good-bye hugs and bus duty, I ran to the office and called the number. "Yes, we have units for rent. What size do you need?" I had no idea. "Will you want a climate-controlled space?"

"What's the difference in price?" I asked. Adding that information to my sticky note, I thanked the lady and hung up. I decided to get the smallest, cheapest space, with climate-control. It was all I could afford.

Upon inspection, I realized I needed to go with the next size up. It would be impossible for my stuff to fit into that teensy cubicle. I *had* to get the larger unit, but that meant no climate-control. Although it hurt to shell out eighty-seven dollars for an empty metal space, I could not ignore the Voice in my head. During my prayer on the way to work that morning, I asked God to lead me step by step. I promised to listen and obey. I felt like this was the first step.

Later That Evening

Dog mess greeted me as I opened the door. The girls were frantic. Neither of them had pooped in the house since they were pups. Reassuring them it was okay and I still loved them, I sent them outside and inspected each room. No sign of Jon. I was irate. Not only had the poor dogs relieved themselves throughout the house, they were ravenous!

I found out from Aubrey Jon called in "sick" for work that day. I didn't tell her I had not slept at home for the past two nights. My journal says: *I packed Jon's personal things and some clothes and put them outside in the carport in boxes. I went to Alan and Darcy's and took more paperwork with me.*

I really thought Jon might die this time. I loathed leaving the dogs confused and alone, but I could not stay there waiting for the death call. Afraid to leave them outside all night for fear of them becoming Kibbles 'n Bits for coyotes, I locked them in the house again. Whipper's ears went back and Snuffle's tail drooped as I commanded, "Stay. Be good girls. I'll be back in the morning," before closing the door behind me.

Church was a blur. I could not concentrate. Jon still had not been home, and I hadn't heard a word from him. The dogs were noticeably upset by the change in routine when I went to put them out that morning. They weren't used to being alone in the house all night. I don't know if they pooped because they were upset, or if they just couldn't wait until I came to check on them. That afternoon I made the decision to take them to Jon's sister Mona's for a few days until I could figure out what to do.

"Until Jon is out of the house, I don't feel safe staying here. He's been going through a lot of money lately. I don't know how much more his body can take. After what he said to me on Sunday, I realize I mean nothing to him. There's no telling what he will do. He doesn't seem to have any remorse," I explained to Mona through the phone as I packed the girls' food, toys and bedding into my Cadillac.

They raced excitedly from the car to the house, and back again. Whipper leapt into the passenger seat settling herself in their bed. She was not about to be left behind. "It's not good for them to be left home alone, but I can't have them with me at my friends' house. They already have two dogs in the house and no fenced-in yard. I don't know what else to do right now. All I know is I have such an uneasy feeling in my gut I know I cannot stay here. What if he's not alone, or is still high when he comes back? He will be angry I put his stuff outside the house in boxes. I'm nervous. I do not want a confrontation."

Thankfully, Mona understood and convinced her husband Sergio that they should dog-sit for an indefinite period of time, even though their tiny house was already brimming with pets and people.

My journal says: *Jon's sister Laurel met with us at Mona's. We all cried and prayed together.* Jon's family, sensing my panic, invited me to stay the night. Their love was a solace. After my transparent explanation of current events, his sisters supported my decision to separate myself from him. They loved their brother, but feared what he was doing to himself, and to me. Jon's disappearance worried his family. Death lurked in the corners of our minds.

Late that night I emailed Jon's parents in Costa Rica. We had never been close. Some unnamed thing built a wall between us. I was hurt they had not reached out to me over the years, when they must have known how I had suffered because of their son's addictions. I wrote to them anyway, wanting them to know our marriage was failing and Jon was spiraling wildly downward. I felt like Jon's declaration that he no longer wanted me as his wife allowed me to transfer the responsibility of their son back to them. I figured they needed to know he was up for grabs if they wanted to try to rescue him. I was pretty much done with that.

Before I left Mona's on Sunday, Laurel and her husband Doug came over again to discuss Jon's situation with all of us. Doug, a former police officer, had much ugly insight into Jon's drug-binge lifestyle. He shared some things that left me in shock. He warned me against sleeping with Jon again, stating he was undoubtedly involved with people who would do anything for crack, and that Jon had become one of those people. He agreed I probably was not safe in my home, especially if Jon owed money to anyone.

"God, is this my life? I feel like I am watching a bad movie. I don't want to hear this. I don't want to feel this. I do not want to even know or think about this."

I took comfort in the loving support of Jon's sisters and their husbands. They expressed real sorrow regarding Jon's poor choices and how he affected everyone in the family. Leaving my girls resulted in both regret and relief. I knew it was better for them to stay with Mona and Sergio until things settled down, but I despised leaving them behind as I hugged everyone goodbye and returned to what was left of home.

There was a message from Jon waiting on the answering machine. It simply said, "I'll be home tomorrow." He left the message on Saturday night at 7. "Tomorrow" meant today. I spent the afternoon at home numbly sorting papers and files and organizing things that I may need to take with me when I left. I felt calm, but there was a heaviness in my spirit as I half-expected to hear his truck in the driveway at any moment.

"Lord God, I can feel You guiding me. Thank You. I can also sense a dense cloud of something I cannot name. Please give me clarity. Help me know what to do. I feel angry that I am doing all the work . . . even leaving my home, and Jon is off having fun—not caring about anything but himself. It's not right. I didn't ask for any of this."

Only later did the realization strike me that the hell I thought *I* lived was a cakewalk compared to the hell of being addicted to crack cocaine. Years afterward, I gleaned truth nuggets from the lips of other addicts. Jon wasn't having fun. Jon was flirting with death, battling demons I have *never* had to face. He turned his back on God and reaped the consequences of a series of painful choices—choices that crippled his will and taunted him with hopelessness. I could not see that at the time. Even if I could have, I wonder what difference that knowledge would have made in the events that happened next.

About 5 p.m. Jon called, crying. "I'm in trouble. I owe someone a hundred dollars," he spoke forcefully . . . fearfully. "Another guy and I got some drugs and cut them up. We were going to resell them for a profit and pay back the hundred dollars we borrowed. The other guy took off. I'm being held for the money. Can you help me? Please."

My mind raced. *Liar.*

"God, he's lying, right?"

"Let me talk to the person who's holding you," I replied. "Why don't you call the police? Call your brother. Don't call me."

159

"I knew I couldn't count on you to help me," he retorted. The phone went dead.

Immediately I called Roman and recounted the interaction. Roman phoned Jon and was convinced he was not lying. "I'd help him, but I don't have a hundred dollars," Roman stated matter-of-factly.

My emotions hit the panic button. Grabbing everything of value to me from the house, I began shoving stuff into my car. We didn't have much left as far as items drug dealers could pay themselves back with by pawning, but I wasn't taking any risks with *my* belongings. Frantically I moved from room to room, snatching up things I cared about and praying to avoid any confrontations.

"Father, I'm scared. And torn. I don't know whether I should help him or not. I don't want Jon to be killed for a hundred bucks! Even though I need that money to keep this boat afloat, I don't want to be responsible for his death."

Can you see the sick codependent thinking going on in my head as I responded to Jon's manipulation? All of a sudden it's *my* fault his life might be in jeopardy.

My faulty codependent mindset led me to decide to withdraw one hundred dollars from the ATM in town. I called Jon on the way to the bank. No answer.

"Oh, God! They've done something bad to him. Now I'm really scared."

"I can't help you, Jon, unless I know what to do," I pleaded to his voicemail.

A few moments later my cell phone rang. "Send the money from Wal-Mart to Wal-Mart. I'll let you know which one I'll be at," he instructed. After withdrawing five crisp twenty-dollar bills from the ATM, I drove to Wal-Mart. The parking lot was nearly vacant. My insides and outsides trembled with fear.

What should I do? This just seems so crazy. I think I should call the police. Yes, that's what I'll do.

Our sheriff's office asked how long he'd been away from home. "The only thing you can do at this time, Ma'am," the female dispatcher drawled, "is file a missing person report. Unless we can catch him in a crime, we cannot treat him as a criminal. Do you want to file a missing person report?"

"Yes. I also want to give you his license plate number in case you want to catch him with drugs in his car, or pull him over for driving while high."

Realizing Wal-Mart was going to charge a transfer fee, I went back to the ATM and withdrew another twenty. For over an hour I waited in my car with no word from Jon. Horrible thoughts paraded through my brain.

Maybe he's been hurt or killed. It's my fault because I didn't help him soon enough. I'm going to attend his funeral and know I could have done something different and possibly prevented his death. Why did I delay? I wasn't trying to be mean. I just didn't want him to be lying to me again, or using me.

I decided to go to my school and prepare substitute lesson plans for Monday and Tuesday in case I had to plan a funeral. Annie called me on my way to the school. "I can't talk to you right now. Can I call you later?" I asked.

"What's going on Sister?" Her antennae were up.

"I've just got to stay off the phone right now. I'll call you back later."

Jon's call came in just after I arrived at school. "The dealer wants to talk to you," he said. The man came onto the phone yelling and swearing.

"I have this man's keys. I need my @!*!#?! money so I can pay my man. I'm tired of this $@!*! He's been running me around and wasting my @!*!#?! time."

My heart pounded. "I can help you."

"Help me?! I don't need no @!*#ing help. This man needs the help." Jon came back on the line, explaining how to wire the funds from our Wal-Mart to the Wal-Mart on Highway 84. His voice sounded nervous and hurried. I could hear the dealer ranting in the background.

"Okay. Call me as soon as you get out of there so I know you are safe." Heart leaping with fear, I drove again to Wal-Mart and completed the paperwork to transfer the money. On my way back to school Jon called again, asking for the confirmation number so he could retrieve the funds. "I've misplaced it somehow," I explained after several minutes of frantically digging through my purse. "Just show them your driver's license. And call me please, as SOON as you are away from there. I need to know you are okay." He promised to call.

I returned to my dark, abandoned school. Not even the die-hards were there on a Sunday night. For the next two hours I planned lessons and tidied my classroom, not knowing what else to do with myself while waiting to hear from my husband.

By 9 p.m. I called the sheriff's office again. Explaining the whole story, I asked if an officer could meet me at our house because I was fearful since I had not heard from Jon. I wanted to go back home to see if he was there, but I did not want to go alone in case someone wanting payment was lurking there. They agreed to send an officer who was already on duty out near our place. Turning toward home, I phoned Dr. Alan and Darcy. No answer. I left a trembling message, "I think something terrible has happened to Jon. Please pray. I am going home to see if he's been there yet. A police officer is meeting me."

The thirteen mile-drive felt like forever. My mind imagined all kinds of horrors. When I arrived, the house was dark with no sign of Jon, or anyone else. The sheriff's office had some incident and could spare no one to meet me or help me. They took my number and said they'd call me back. They never did.

I phoned Roman. He had not heard from Jon again. "I'll call you if I hear anything," he promised. I did not go inside the house. Everything felt dark and strange. Fear began to engulf me. I could not get away fast enough. Looping around the driveway, I fled toward the comfort and normalcy of Darcy's house.

She met me at the door with concern. Annie contacted Mom and they both called Darcy to say they were worried about me because of the way I'd responded to Annie's earlier phone call. I'd forgotten to call her back. Dr. Alan and Darcy drove out to the house and then to the school looking for me. We somehow missed one another. They arrived home just before I got there. We were all upset, but I was distraught.

Once my family knew I was okay, I tearfully poured out the whole story to my worried friends. Alan did not believe Jon's tale at all. He said, "I don't want you to feel bad, but I think you have been taken for a fool." I could tell he was angry, not with me—with Jon. "He has preyed upon your love for him, and your trust."

I had a hard time wrapping my brain around that. *"Father, would he really do such a thing to me? Scare me, manipulate me, and run me through the wringer for a hundred-dollar high? I cannot believe that. He must have some decency left. Surely he would not stoop so low as to intentionally hurt me like this. Would he?"*

Around 10:30 p.m., while we were still talking, I heard from Roman. Jon just text-messaged him saying he was ten minutes away from home. Relief flooded over me as fresh tears pooled in my eyes. I went to bed thanking God for sparing Jon's life and for bringing him home. I still could not fathom the thought it could all have been a hoax.

I awoke at 5 a.m. with a distinct impression in my mind. *You must move out of the house today.* I began to pray, preparing myself for whatever the day held.

"Okay, God. I will be obedient to You. I can easily miss work since I've already planned for a substitute, but how can I move out by myself? It would be an impossible task! Please guide my every step. What should I do first?"

What happened between 7 a.m. and 7 p.m. was nothing less than miraculous. God's hand orchestrated so many details, I have goose bumps remembering them all. He was phenomenal! God wanted me out of that house immediately. Nothing was going to stop Him. Afterward, I wrote about it.

I had no idea the ways the Lord would work to have my entire household packed and moved by the end of the day. He saw what Jon did to me last night. His deceit was the catalyst that moved the hand of God.

After God and I talked, I called my principal, "Dr. V" to arrange for a substitute. Then I began unloading my car. Darcy came outside asking, "What are you doing? Do Alan and I need to help?"

"I have to move out today. Can you come over to my house at noon and bring a load of clothes back here for me?"

"Of course. Do you need any packing supplies or boxes? I can pick some up," she offered as she loaded her arms with odds and ends from my back seat and headed toward the pool house, where we had agreed to pile my personal belongings until I figured out what to do next.

I felt impressed to go out to my house first. I could see Jon had slept in the guest bed and left in a hurry. He unpacked some of his toiletries from the boxes I'd placed on the carport. As my eyes skimmed the household furnishings, I realized I needed Jon's truck in order to do what needed to be done that day.

I called Daniel, Jon's boss. "Some terrible things happened last night," I announced. "I have to move out of the house today. How late will you guys be working?"

"We should be out on jobs until about 5 p.m." he answered hesitantly.

"I'm coming to get his truck while he is out in the service van. I know where he parks. I'll leave him my car. Please do not say anything to Jon, but I need you to call me before he leaves your last job so I can be gone from the house and avoid a confrontation with him."

"Okay. I'll let you know." I could sense Daniel's reticence to be placed in the center of a domestic issue involving one of his employees. The woman-on-a-mission determination in my voice caused him to work with me anyway.

"Lord, You've got to be in this, because here I go to pick up Jon's truck and I don't even have a key! I'm trusting in You."

The next directive came clearly into my mind. *Call Donna at school.* I obeyed.

"Donna, I'm moving out today," I explained.

"I wondered about that when I saw you got a sub. Good. Call my husband, Ben. He's not working, and he has a truck and a trailer. Never mind. I'll call Ben and explain the situation. I'll have him call you back. Good for you, girl!" Donna cheered.

"Wow, Lord. Thanks for the man with a truck and trailer. That's awesome!" Within minutes, Ben called and said he'd pick up some boxes on his way to my house.

I reached out to Scott, our head elder, asking if he or his wife, Cheryl were free to help me move that day. I had been keeping them abreast of Jon's downward spiral so they could pray for him. Scott took a special interest in Jon and I knew he felt helpless about what was happening. "We're on our way!" was his immediate response.

Then came the strong urge to call Jon's sister, Mona. When I told her I needed to move out of the house that day she offered her son, Wesley, as a resource saying, "He was moving some of his stuff out of storage yesterday and hasn't turned in his U-Haul yet. He may be able to come and help. It will only take him an hour to get there."

"You are working so quickly, God, to pull a team together. You are magnificent!"

Arriving at Jon's workplace, I discovered his not-so-shiny-anymore red truck with the windows down and the keys in the ignition! Keys to our church were also on his ring.

I need to give these back to Pastor Josh. With everything Jon is doing right now, it's probably not a good idea for him to have keys to the church anymore. I wish he would just resign from being a deacon.

Sifting through the mess in his console, I unearthed a stack of pawn tickets for his binoculars and all the other tools he had pawned. I also discovered, and grabbed, two credit card statements, snuck from our files at home, and our 2006 income tax papers, still un-mailed. I left my Cadillac unlocked and took his truck.

It reeked. No wonder the windows were left down! I felt uncomfortable sitting behind that wheel, wondering where the truck had been and who had ridden in there.

"Heavenly Father, cleanse this vehicle of anything that is not of You. I bring the cross of the true Lord Jesus between me, and anything in here. I commit this vehicle to You and ask for Your protection as I drive it. I rebuke in Jesus' name any foul spirits that may have attached themselves to this truck or anything in here as it participated in illegal and ungodly activities. Thank You, Jesus for the power in Your name and the power in Your blood." Immediately I felt at peace.

As my heart rate slowed, the cell phone rang. It was Laurel. "Hi! Mona told me you were moving today. I have the day off and will come with Wesley so we can help you." Right after that Mona called offering to leave work early so she could help too.

"God, You are serious. Laurel rarely has a day off! The fact that Jon's own family is willing to help shows how much You are behind this. Thank You for providing seven helpers, two trailers and a U-Haul by 8:30 in the morning! You are truly God! You are giving me courage to go ahead with this hard, hard thing. I love You."

I stopped at the Brookshire's grocery store to ask for boxes. "How many do you want?" an aproned teen asked. "We haven't started breaking them down yet."

"All of them," I said. He loaded the back of the truck with every uncrushed box on the premises.

On my way back to the house I called Aubrey. She and Bob were still in Oklahoma visiting grandchildren. I filled her in on the events of the past week and asked if she would be willing to care for my plants if I brought them to her home. "Oh, Julie. Of course! I'm so sorry to hear this. What will you do?"

"Well, I need to finish this school year. That gives me three months to figure it out. Dr. Alan and Darcy have offered to let me stay in their pool house. It has a kitchenette and bathroom. I like that it's not attached to their home and I will be able to come and go without feeling like I'm bothering anyone," I explained. "I don't know what else to do. God has made it extremely clear I need to move out today. I know Jon will be angry when he comes home. I'm afraid of that. He has not been himself lately. Please pray today, that we can get everything packed and put in storage before he finishes work."

My next phone call was to our neighbor, Gloria. She and her family were incredibly gracious for the almost five years we'd rented from them. Certain Gloria noticed our erratic comings and goings, I knew I needed to reveal the embarrassing truth. It had to be done, especially if I was asking to be removed from the rental agreement. Shame and anger nearly strangled me as I apologetically explained the situation. Once more, I felt forced into a position of accounting for Jon's poor choices.

Ben and his trailer were waiting when I arrived. We prepared the larger pieces of furniture for transport. Cheryl and Scott showed up a few minutes later. Cheryl went to work quietly, steadily, carefully bubble-wrapping and packing my treasured possessions into boxes. Scott and Ben worked together loading the big stuff. I fluttered from room to room—giving instructions, answering questions.

Soon Darcy arrived, mountains of packing material hiding her contagious smile. She volunteered to wrap my paintings and special items, like Grandma 'Dessa's milk glass collection, and put them in her SUV so they would not end up in the storage unit. "You can keep these things in the pool house with you. We've already set up a bed for you there. Alan says you are welcome to stay for as long as you need to, in peace and solitude." Tears sprang to my eyes as her words massaged my knotted heart.

Mona, Laurel and Wesley showed up without the girls. I secretly hoped they would bring them. I missed my babies. Handing Jon's sisters two boxes, I asked them to pack things that were specifically his or that would have been special to him, if he was in his right mind. "Will you please keep Jon's bird books, his Life Book and his personal pictures at your house?" I asked Mona. "Just in case he dies. Or in case he gets well and begins to care again."

I wanted nothing expressly belonging to Jon put into my storage unit. On the other hand, I didn't trust he would care for anything I left behind in the house. The way his truck looked, I knew Jon was in no mindset to care for anything, not even himself.

I made the first trip to the storage unit, riding with Wesley in the U-Haul. Ben and Scott followed with the other trailer. "Wesley, thank you for coming today," I spoke to the young man in the driver's seat. "I know this is awkward for you—helping dismantle your uncle's home without him being present."

"It's okay, Aunt Julie. I'm happy to help. I know what drugs can do to a person. You are only doing what is best right now. I understand that." He spoke softly, without his usual smile.

All day, everyone worked together steadily, like bees or ants, each taking a job and doing it well. Disassembling a household in a matter of hours requires the perfect mix of personalities and resources. God brought that mix together under my roof that morning. I was so emotional I really was no help at all. At one point someone showed up with pizza. While they all ate, I disappeared into the bathroom for a weep. My phone rang as I perched on the edge of the tub with my head in my hands.

"Leon!"

"How did he know to call me today? Just now as I find a quiet moment to cry out to You, God? I haven't spoken to him in weeks!"

"You are doing the best thing for Jon and for yourself," Leon reassured me after I poured out my story. "Even God Himself says, 'Enough!' at times. You have given Jon ample opportunities through the years to choose a different life. He has chosen the life he wants, leaving you completely out of it. I'm sorry you are hurting, but God will provide for you. He already has. Let me pray with you so you can go back out there and finish the work before you today."

In my journal I later wrote: *Those words of affirmation and encouragement were exactly what I needed at that moment. God is so good!*

I drove Jon's loaded truck on another trip to the storage unit that afternoon. Mom called from Italy just as I arrived. "Mother," I said calmly, "You will hardly believe the blessings. The weather is perfect. God provided every detail I needed to be able to move today, including a storage unit. When I awoke this morning, I could not have imagined what God would do in a few short hours. I am totally at peace because of the ways He has orchestrated everything." Mom regretted she was so far away and unable to help, but my story of God's presence on moving day soothed her mama-fears.

After we unloaded at the storage unit, I cleaned out Jon's truck, discarding cigarette cartons, chewing tobacco, bits of copper scrubbies, broken glass and loads of trash. Wesley explained that some of the "trash" was drug paraphernalia. "Copper scouring pads are used as filters in makeshift crack pipes," he said.

"Oh. Ohhhh! *That's* why I'm always finding Chore Boy boxes around. I thought it was something they used in the heating and air conditioning business. Now I get it." A-ha moments like that brought both the understanding and mortification that came with realizing how incredibly naive I was.

I decided to hide both the truck and myself at Ben and Donna's for a few days. Jon would probably suspect I'd go to Darcy's. I didn't want to subject her or Alan to anything ugly. If I stayed somewhere else, they could honestly say they didn't know where I was if he came looking for his wife or his vehicle.

I wasn't planning to keep Jon's truck. I just wanted to double check with the dealership to assure my name was not on any of the paperwork before I returned it. I had a hunch Jon quit making payments. I did not want his irresponsibility to haunt me.

Texas is a community property state. That means creditors of one spouse can go after joint assets no matter whose name is on a title. I needed to hold onto that "asset" until I could get some legal counsel. If Jon overdosed or refused to pay his debt, I could become liable for a high payment on a truck I did not want.

Jon's family agreed with my decision, but, concerned for my safety, they advised me not to drive the truck. Ben took it directly to his garage.

By early afternoon, the ladies nearly had everything packed and labeled. Darcy and Laurel took a load to the pool house. Donna arrived from school around 3:30. By then Mona and Wesley had made several trips to Aubrey's, carrying plants in the U-Haul. "How in the world did you get so many house plants?" Mona asked as she wrestled a cathedral cactus with arms as long as her own.

"When my Grandma 'Dessa passed away, I inherited her plants. They make me feel like I still have a part of her with me. Succulents were her specialty."

"Obviously," chuckled Wesley, pointing to his cactus-scarred arms. "This will be our third trip!"

Within 45 minutes, Donna quietly packed the rest of the kitchen. I asked her to leave the coffee pot and Jon's mug. My eclectic kitchen contained mostly gleanings from foreign travels, or inherited treasures from my grandmothers. One set of flatware was a gift from my mother, the other I purchased with funds I received after my first article was published in the *Bird Watcher's Digest*. I wasn't about to leave either set behind. I regretted leaving stark cupboards though, so Darcy and I made a plan to purchase an inexpensive set of dishes for Jon.

"Pay attention to the time," Donna piped. "We need to be out of here in a jiffy." I raced through the house. Every room was virtually empty. Our bedroom was bare except for a few of Jon's clothes in the closet. Our dressers, handmade by my great-grandfather, were tucked safely in storage next to Nannie's antique mirrored dressing table. Our bed . . .well, I didn't want him to ever sleep on it again. Not alone, when he displaced his wife, and definitely not with someone else! *I cannot imagine that happening. Surely not that! Not in our home . . .*

I'd left the guest bed, the white sofa and chair in our living room, and the behemoth wooden desk in our office. Other than that, the place was stripped. The television stayed, but somehow the DVR and TV remote was packed into an unidentified box. Jon would be furious about that.

At 5 p.m. I called Daniel to see where they were on their last service call. "We're done and back," he announced. "Jon flipped out as soon as he spotted the Cadillac in his truck's parking spot. He's on his way home." My heart flopped around in my chest a few times as I shouted, "Clear out everyone! He's coming! We have fifteen minutes, maybe less."

In a flash, the final boxes were taped, the trash hauled out, and the last items placed on Ben's trailer. He'd been running around with a canvas bag, trying to catch Mama Kitty. I didn't want to leave her. Although she would never admit to it, she depended on us. When Ben and Donna offered to keep her, I'd said, "You can have her if you can catch her!"

Within five minutes everyone hugged me and cleared out. No one wanted Jon to know they participated in the move, especially his family.

"Where's the cat?" I hollered from the porch as Ben drove slowly away from the house.

"It's in the bag!" He answered. "Don't let it out." The three of us cracked up laughing as Donna handed me a writhing, yeowling canvas bag. I placed Mama in Donna's car and went back for one last sweep of the house.

Colorful vintage Pyrex mixing bowls nested in a corner of the kitchen among a mess of dried flower petals. Grabbing up my Nannie's bowls, I collapsed on the linoleum and started to wail. *My sweet little, homey hoooome. Destroyed and empty! That's how my life feeeeels. Just destroyed. And emptyyyyyyyyyy!*

"There's not time for wailin' now girl. We gotta go," Donna burst into the kitchen and pushed pause on my pity party. "We do not want to come face to face with the devil tonight. Come on." She pulled me up and flipped off the lights. I collapsed into her car, balancing the bagged cat and the Pyrex on my lap as she zipped around the driveway and onto the road, traveling the opposite direction from which Jon would come. Glancing back, I noticed the house looked abandoned. Even our bird feeder was gone. God worked a twelve-hour miracle. Jon would be downright shocked.

Donna and I stopped by the storage unit to drop off a few things. Scott and Cheryl were still there, unloading the last boxes from their trailer. The unit was packed from floor to ceiling, with barely a square inch to spare. Exhaustion etched Cheryl's face as she explained where they'd stacked important items. Scott hardly spoke as they climbed into their truck. I know they were disheartened by the realization that the "sweet young couple" they worshiped with nearly every Sabbath for four years was splitting up. They often ate and fellowshipped in our home. It was a challenging day for them. Scott was Jon's friend. I'm sure his heart was heavy as he helped pare down Jon's dwelling to the barest minimum.

I was exhausted as well. My emotions had run the gamut throughout the day. After we let Mama Kitty out of the bag and introduced her to Donna's other cats. I was ready to crash. There was not a word from Jon. That was okay by me. I was too zonked to care.

What I *did* care about was being within God's will. Of all the times in my marriage when I'd thought of abandoning ship, something held me aboard. Today was different. Every single thing that happened screamed, "Bail!" I knew my marriage was dead. God released me from my vows. I slept without a twinge of guilt. My Father in Heaven freed me. He knew when to say, "Enough!"

The following day was Tuesday, February 20, 2007. I took the day off so I could find a divorce attorney. Donna dropped me off at Darcy's house on her way to school that morning. We decided to leave Jon's truck in hiding. Donna's counsel was to make getting a decent attorney my first priority. So, Darcy and I researched local attorneys and decided upon one who came highly recommended from a client of Dr. Alan's.

John T. Rube, Attorney at Law, happened to have an opening for an afternoon consultation that day. Darcy took me to lunch and then to his office. Thanks to Donna's shrewd advice, I had my paperwork in order. "We can extricate you from any debts your husband has incurred without your consent. We'll also make sure you get a new last name and a legal divorce. Our fee for this service is twelve hundred fifty dollars," he said smiling. "I am confident you will come out of this financially unscathed. That's what we do here. We'll just need you to get him to sign the paperwork."

"That's a lot of money I don't have right now," I sighed. "But if you can rescue me from the debt of everything he's been doing lately, I will find a way to come up with your fee. I want a guarantee I will not be held responsible for what he has done. Every day he blows hundreds of dollars. The credit cards are maxed out. His truck payment is in arrears. He is stealing and pawning. I don't know what he's going to do next. I'm having a hard time keeping up the minimum payments on all of the cards so my credit is not ruined. I don't want to feel responsible for his debt any more. I need to separate myself from him as quickly as possible before people start calling me for money."

Darcy waited in the car while I met with Mr. Rube. She read my face when I told her his fee. "We can help you, if you need help with this," she offered. "It's important for you to do it right away. We can work something out."

Well, I get paid again in a few days and I won't have to pay rent for March. I could put that money toward the attorney bill. It's not fair that Jon's the one who wants a divorce, but he'll never pay one penny toward it. I always have to do everything. I'll be thankful when this is over."

That evening Dr. Alan and Darcy sat me down in their living room and made me cry. "We want to help you get on your financial feet again," Dr. Alan began. It's going to take time. Do you have anything in savings?"

"No. I don't have any cash. I've just been trying to juggle the rent and utilities and pay the minimum balance on the credit cards. That barely leaves me enough to buy gas and food," I admitted.

"Okay. Here's what we are proposing. Listen carefully," he said seriously. We're offering you our pool house. You and your dogs can stay there for as long as you like. You do not need to pay us any rent or utilities. We want you to pay off all of your debts and begin saving as much as possible. Only spend money when you absolutely have to."

"But . . . " I started to interrupt. He stopped me.

"You need to begin thinking about buying your own home. We'd love to see you save enough money for a down payment while you live here. You should never be put in a position like this again. You are a professional. You earn a decent salary as a teacher. You will live in your own home again. For right now, save, save, save! That's all I've got to say. You ladies can work the rest out." Dr. Alan stood up and walked down the hall toward their bedroom.

"Thank you," I called after him. "I could never repay you for your kindness. Never."

"You don't repay friends for their kindness," Darcy said as she hugged me. "That's what friends are for."

"You mean I can bring the girls to the pool house?" I asked.

"Of course! They're your babies, aren't they? I know you miss them," she gently responded.

I wept tears of relief. I *had* missed the girls; and I was so thankful for the financial advice and the generous offer I didn't know what else to do but cry.

"Let's have some chocolate cake," Darcy suggested. "This is a time to celebrate. I'm going to have my dear friend living right here in my backyard! Isn't that wonderful?" She chirped. "Come! I made homemade frosting."

Sitting on a bar stool in Darcy's English country kitchen, I enjoyed a piece of homemade chocolate cake with thick, creamy frosting and thanked my Jesus for His abundant blessings.

"Whatever happens tomorrow, Lord, I know You are going to provide for me. Thank You for the people You have placed in my life to support me. Thank You for Alan and Darcy. Please bless them because of their kindness toward me. I can see light, rather than dollar signs, at the end of this dark financial tunnel. I praise You! I praise You!"

The next day was Wednesday. Time to go back to my students. Dr. Alan loaned me his farm truck so I could keep Jon's truck hidden while awaiting instructions from the attorney. I feared his reaction if he spied it in Darcy's driveway or the school parking lot. I showed Vanessa, the school's secretary, a photograph of Jon and warned her to call the police if he came looking for me.

Late that afternoon, I drove to John Rube's office to sign a pile of paperwork and to pay him the twelve hundred dollars. Afterward I called Jon as I sat outside the Baptist church waiting for the Beth Moore Bible study to begin. I wanted to talk with him about the divorce papers.

"I want my DVR and my TV remote back," he demanded. "And my !@#!*!$ truck."

Ignoring those demands. I informed him I had been to see an attorney and some paperwork was being drawn up. I honestly had no idea where the remotes were. Jon proceeded to inform me that all of the stress he put me through on Sunday night was just a trick he and a friend devised to get another hundred dollars for drugs. "No one was holding me *hostage*," he spat. "Did you seriously *believe* that?"

"Yes. I did," I almost whispered. "I had no idea you were capable of doing something like this. You have devastated me. I didn't even believe the people I trust when they suggested you were lying. I could not imagine you would be so cruel . . . to me." Now my voice was cracking as the tears began to flow. "How could you prey on my compassion like that? How *could* you?"

I hung up the phone and bawled for an hour, just sitting there in Dr. Alan's truck in front of the church as the women in my Bible study group came and went. They just watched a DVD, *When Godly People Do Ungodly Things*. I experienced it first hand as I sat there in the parking lot imagining all kinds of wicked things I could do to pay Jon back for his meanness.

The deepest of wounds can easily fill with anger and revenge if left to fester and boil. I needed the cleansing balm of forgiveness to bring healing to my soul. I could not wrap my brain around Jon's cruelty. It would take days for me to process what happened and to accept that he manipulated my emotions and masterminded such a mean trick. It would take even longer for me to choose forgiveness over revenge. I felt broken as I pulled into Darcy's driveway. I wanted to see neither her nor Dr. Alan. I was too ashamed to admit they were right about Jon. Too ashamed to know he would treat me that way.

On Thursday, I stopped by our local post office to check for mail. The previous week, I opened up a post office box, transferring all mail from our rural route. My attorney said I must obtain the most recent copies of all credit card and bank statements. Jon intercepted the mail for weeks, hiding things he didn't want me to see. I hoped to find something helpful in my new P.O. Box.

As Jon's addiction escalated over the past few weeks, I found my naturally-reserved self revealing details of my life I normally would never have mentioned to strangers. That happened in our tiny post office the week before I moved out. I casually knew the head postal worker, Shauna, because her son was in first grade at our school. When applying for my own P.O. Box, I'd leaned over the counter and blurted, "My husband is on drugs and is hijacking our mail."

Shauna's eyes immediately filled with empathy. "I've been there," she said softly. "I understand." Todd, another postal clerk happened to overhear our conversation. They looked at one another knowingly. From that moment, I had allies in the post office. With them on my side, Jon would have no more secrets when it came to the mail.

Shauna called me at school the following day. "Right after you walked out yesterday, your husband phoned, demanding to know where his mail was. We assured him we had no idea."

Later when I went to check the mail, Shauna appeared beside me as I turned the key in my box, and whispered, "Your husband came in today and opened his own P.O. Box I made sure it was far away from yours. He was angry, insisting that he *must* have some mail here somewhere. I told him, 'The family mail takes precedence.'" She smiled as she said that. Then, "He looked at me with those blue eyes shooting daggers. Girl, I got a peek at what you are dealing with. It ain't cute."

"Thank You, Father, for providing that information. Thank You, for looking out for me. I know You see me and You are working all things together for my good, as Your Word says. I'm so grateful. So relieved I'm not doing this by myself."

After school, Darcy and I drove out to the house together. I knew Jon was working out of town that day, so there was no risk of running into him. We took the microwave back, since the pool house already had one. I also returned a feather duvet and some bedding to the guest room. A twinge of guilt pierced my tender heart that I left him without even a pillow.

Walking into the house was surreal. It felt completely different. Not like home at all. Jon cleaned up the mess on the kitchen floor and neatly organized his few belongings, meticulously arranging every book, mug and saucer, as if making order out of life's chaos. I felt sorry for him as I inspected his barren home. *I wonder if he feels sorry for himself, or if he's just happy to have me gone? I wonder if he will continue to rent here, or if they will ask him to leave. I wonder . . .*

"Come on. Let's go to Wal-Mart and buy a few things for the kitchen." Darcy's words interrupted my musing. "I know you didn't want to leave your copper-bottomed pots, but he needs *something* to cook with!"

"I know. I feel bad. But almost everything I own has sentimental value. I'd rather just buy him some cheap stuff than bring anything back."

We purchased a set of dishes, a couple of pots and pans and some utensils, leaving them at the house with a note.

Dear Jon,

I am so wounded by what you did to me that I don't know if I will ever get over it. You were never a cruel person. I cannot fathom how you could treat me like that. How could you lie and scare me on purpose for a few dollars? I am going to see Dr. Fox for counseling tomorrow at 5:30 so I can try to get past this. I'm inviting you to please meet me there. I think we need to talk about what happened, in a safe environment. I am afraid of you, but I need you to hear me. If you have even a shred of caring toward me, will you please, please come so I can have some closure? I am stuck in a very painful place. Please.

Sincerely,
Juliet

The next day was Friday. When I stopped by the post office after school, Shauna motioned for me to step into the back room. She handed me a bundle of Jon's mail saying, "I have not turned in his paperwork yet. As long as his paperwork has not been processed, you can still get all of his mail."

"Thank you, Shauna. You are an angel," I said sifting through the envelopes. Sure enough, there was a credit card statement! It was addressed only to Jon, but Mr. Rube, my attorney, would be thrilled to have *that* information. He needed it to help guarantee no one could ever knock on my door looking for that money!

"Honey," she drawled, grabbing my arm, "we can bind stuff up back in here."

When I got into my car, God and I shared a laugh together. Perhaps no one else would have understood the meaning of her words, but I got it.

"Yes, Lord. You can surely bind stuff up! You can bind up mail and demons, too. Thank You for protecting me from a confrontation with Jon in the post office. Please impress him to come to counseling tonight."

Jon beat me to Dr. Fox's office. He looked appalling. I sat as far from him as the space would allow. "Tell Dr. Fox what happened," I said, looking him in the eyes.

Jon explained how he and his buddy ran out of drug money and devised a plan to scare me into sending them some cash. He recounted the whole story from his perspective—how they had laughed after his friend jingled Jon's keys into the phone and cursed at me when I told him I could help him. They mocked my gullibility and the fear in my voice. They congratulated each other and celebrated when a hundred dollars arrived at the Highway 84 Wal-Mart. Jon purposely avoided calling me back to let me know he was okay.

Hearing him say the words, hearing the heartless thought process behind that series of events literally broke my spirit. I know what they are talking about when people say, "That was the straw that broke the camel's back." Something within me snapped that night. If there was any spider-web-thread of a bond between us, as husband and wife, even as friends, it was severed with Jon's face-to-face admission of what he had done to me.

In my mind, I always separated myself from the things Jon did. I justified the callous side-effects of his drug abuse. Before, it had always been Jon hurting himself and me getting caught in the crossfire. This was different. This was Jon hurting Juliet. On purpose. I took it straight to my soul. Poor Dr. Fox. I'm quite certain he never heard howling and wailing like what next came out of me in his neat, quiet office. Yes, he had a box of tissues on the table beside the sofa, but I'm sure they were meant for more than one client. I plowed through them ruthlessly as every tear I had never cried came forth in a hideous torrent.

Jon just sat there for a frozen moment. Then he apologized.

Afterward, Dr. Fox looked at him and said, "You are in full relapse mode. You are a danger to yourself and others."

He then turned to me and said, "Run like hell."

"I am running," I replied. "I've already been to see an attorney. There is no saving this marriage."

During the conversation that followed, Jon said some very harsh things like, "I don't want a kid. I don't even want to have sex. I just want to have a beer and a smoke and watch whatever I want. I don't want to feel pressured to be Mr. Christian. I am not and *cannot* be the man you want and need for me to be."

Dr. Fox proceeded to conduct a closure ceremony to commemorate our marriage's almost thirteen-year union. He had us tell one another what we had appreciated about each other through the years. Then he asked us to state our regrets and our wishes for the future. Jon's wish was that I not abandon his family. I cannot recall mine.

Forgiveness is the sharpest tool for cutting soul ties with someone from our past. It is bitterness that binds. Why have I so often seen it the other way around? My thoughts clarified as the round wall clock counted down our last hour of couple's therapy. I heard the second hand ticking like a time bomb. Side by side, we sat on the same gray sofa where week after week Dr. Fox witnessed the unraveling of our marriage. The dim lamp on the side table could not dispel the dark cloud hanging over us as we solemnly shared the memories and regrets of twelve married years. My mouth was dry and my eyes moist as I recounted a few of my favorite times with Jon and expressed my choice to forgive him for searing my heart with betrayal. As we hugged goodbye, I breathed in his familiar scent, a concoction of Acqua di Gio, sweat, and Marlboros. I released him. He released me. I was free.

Part Three

Chapter 13

On My Own

*"Trust in the Lord with all your heart
and lean not on your own understanding;
in all your ways submit to him,
and he will make your paths straight.
Do not be wise in your own eyes;
fear the Lord and shun evil."*
Proverbs 3:5-7 NIV

May–July 2007

I celebrated my release from the bondage of expectations for my marriage by attending a Selah concert. In January, when I purchased two tickets with some of my Christmas money, God already knew how much I needed a night of worship to soothe my soul after my emotionally exhausting move-out week.

As we left Dr. Fox's office, I reminded Jon of the concert that night. "I still have your ticket. Do you want it?" I asked.

"No thanks. You go ahead and enjoy your concert," he said as he struggled to unlock the driver's door of my Cadillac with the spare key I'd given him. "Why didn't you leave me the clicker so I don't have to do it this way?" He grumbled. "In fact, why don't you bring me my truck back? Where *is* my !@#!*!$ truck?"

"I'll get it to you once I get a few things sorted out," I answered calmly. "I'm not driving it either."

Jon's anger still blazed because Dr. Fox kindly told him in parting, "Call me anytime, when you are ready to get clean. Even if you have no money."

"I'll never end up on the street," Jon retorted. "You can bet on that."

Immediately Proverbs 16:18 (NKJV) popped into my mind. "Pride goes before destruction, and a haughty spirit before a fall."

Oh, Jon. I'm not looking forward to knowing where you wind up if you do not alter your course. "Dear God, please save him from himself."

Selah lifted my spirits. As I closed my eyes and sang with lifted hands, "*Be still my soul, the Lord is on thy side; Bear patiently the cross of grief or pain; Leave to thy God to order and provide; In every change He faithful will remain . . .*" Peace flooded over me, settled me. The spirit of forgiveness, which I extended to Jon began to take root. Tears of relief and regret flowed as I released him to God.

Suddenly, I found myself wrapped in the motherly arms of a stranger. "I can see you are hurting as you worship," she said. "May I hold you?" Certain she was an angel, I sobbed into her shoulder long before I looked into her face. As it turned out, she was simply a humble, loving member of the body of Christ who understood what the Apostle Paul meant when he said, "if one member suffers, all suffer together" (1 Corinthians 12:26 ESV). I never saw the woman before that moment, nor have I seen her since, but I will not soon forget her loving compassionate spirit.

Wherever you are, sweet stranger, thank you for being the arms of Jesus to me.

On Sabbath, after church, I drove to Mona's to pick up the girls. Our niece, Vicki, and nephew, Marco, met me at the door. Whipper dove through their legs, ecstatically leaping so high, she almost reached my chin with her tongue!

"Awww! Whipper kisses! Whipper kisses!" I tried to hold her, but she wriggled so much I could not contain her. Snuffles circled 'round and 'round as she did donuts on the living room carpet while I scratched the base of her tail and shrank from Whipper's merciless tongue. "Oh, girls! Your mama's missed you soooo much!"

Turning to Sergio and Mona I said, "Thank you! I know it's probably been a pain, but I sure appreciate it. I'm settled in the pool house now and I think they'll be okay there. My only concern is there is no fence, which means they'll have to stay indoors most of the time. They're not used to that."

Mona shrugged. "We're happy to help. The kids enjoyed having the girls around. Why don't you stay the night?" She invited. "Vicki and Marco would enjoy spending some time with you."

Our niece and nephew were afraid of losing me if their Uncle Jon and I divorced. I wanted to assure them of my love. They were the ones who ended up intuitively reassuring *me*.

"No matter what happens," Vicki promised, flinging suntanned arms around my neck, "you'll always be our Aunt Julie. Always!" Her sweet words soothed my fears. Since the day she'd held the train of my wedding dress, we'd held special places in one another's hearts. I did not want circumstances to change that.

Although I released Jon to God, I still kept loose tabs on him through the accounts of others. It wasn't control. It was concern. I longed to know he was still alive and functioning in a semi-normal way.

I learned from Darcy that Jon called Dr. Alan on Sunday night to apologize for his behavior. Dr. Alan spoke with Elder Scott and learned Jon had invited Scott to come over on Wednesday. I took those as positive signs since Jon was reaching out to men he had trusted in the past.

On the other hand, Mona shared that Jon called her on Monday, begging for gas money after spending the weekend doing drugs in the city. She and Sergio met him at our favorite Mexican restaurant to fill his tummy and his gas tank.

"He looked bad," Mona said. "I've never seen him so thin."

Wednesday, when Scott dropped by to visit, Jon ranted about his missing DVR and television remote. He was also steamed I *still* hadn't returned his truck and his rusty riding mower disappeared. I never told him I gave it away in a flurry of excitement on moving day. Scott reassured him he would speak to me about those things and offered to pray with him.

After church, Scott encouraged me to try to find the DVR and remote in my storage unit. "That's impossible!" I exclaimed. "You know how full that space is. I have no idea who packed those items or which box they are in. They could be anywhere. Jon may have to replace them. Please tell him I didn't do it on purpose."

Although I hadn't purposefully vanished his treasured electronics, *something* inside made me secretly happy he was so upset about it. I had to take that something to God.

"Father, please forgive me for feeling like that. In the precious name of Jesus, I bind and rebuke the spirit of revenge from my life. I break any agreements I have made with the enemy when I think things like, 'He deserves to suffer a little after what he's done to me.' I know, God, that those thoughts are not from You."

On March 3, I wrote in my journal: *God has given me peace. I feel like I am resting under His feathers. I have no idea what Jon did this weekend, but I wish he experienced the joy and rest of the Sabbath as I have. There's something healing about spending quiet time with the Lord.*

That peace and quiet prepared my heart for the ultimate betrayal. I thought I experienced every ounce of pain my husband could offer me. What happened next trumped every card he previously dealt.

Mr. Rube called me in for a consultation prior to completing the divorce papers.

"You do not need to worry about the truck anymore. Since your name is not on the paperwork, and you filed for a legal separation prior to the third skipped payment, you will not be held liable for any portion of the balance; however, I would suggest holding on to it until we can get Jon's signature on these documents. As far as the rest of the debt, anything incurred on credit cards solely in Jon's name, you will not be responsible for. The joint account is the one my people are still working on. The sooner we get the divorce papers signed by both parties and filed, the sooner we can clear your name from any portion you did not incur. Your student loan is still yours. Everything else should be cleared."

"Thank you," I said. "I will try to get these signed and returned to you within a few days. Sometimes Jon is difficult to pin down. I'll do my best."

I did not desire any more face-to-face meetings with Jon, so I planned to drop off the paperwork at the house while he was at work. I still had a key. Besides, I'd left my favorite sparkly flip-flops in the laundry room. I wanted them.

Late afternoon sun filtered through my favorite oak's branches as I pulled into the driveway. I missed that tree. A twinge of sadness sprang up within as I walked toward the carport. It was littered with unfamiliar boxes and two tattered, mismatched lawn chairs were set up under the windows where my plants had been.

That's strange. I wonder where he got those? Our lawn chairs are yellow.

Dismissing that thought, I began searching for my forgotten flip-flops. What I discovered hanging in the laundry room were several pairs of panties. They were not mine.

"What in the world?" I said out loud. Then, "Oh, God. Oh, no. Not this! Not in my house!"

Maybe they are his sister's. Maybe Mona and Sergio came to visit. Or maybe Jon has started wearing women's underwear. Nawww, I can't imagine that happening. Surely he wouldn't be with another woman . . . Would he?

"*Ohhhh, Jesus! How could he? We're not even divorced yet!*"

My stomach queezed as my heart pounded so loudly in my ears I couldn't even hear the terrible thoughts I was thinking. Knowing Jon would be home shortly, I should have bolted to Dr. Alan's truck and disappeared. The 'woman scorned' within me needed to see the truth—all of it. So I unlocked the kitchen door with my key and flipped on the light. Nothing much changed since Darcy and I dropped off the dishes. I looked in the fridge. Pepperoni pizza and sliced bologna. A carton of milk. One beer and a Starbucks coffee drink. No vegetables.

Turning from the fridge, I spied my flip-flops. One of their turquoise sparkles caught the kitchen light, beckoning me into the guest bedroom through a narrow doorway next to the pantry. Without a thought, my hand found the switch and flooded the room with light. *My* favorite blue and turquoise sparkly flip-flops sat side by side neatly facing *their* rumpled bed. I say *their* bed because it was obvious more than one person slept there. Unfamiliar lotions and potions stood on the makeshift nightstand. His and her articles of clothing were strewn about. I felt like one of the three bears discovering evidence of Goldilocks's presence as I wondered who had been sleeping in *my* bed. Or, rather, my not-quite-ex-husband's bed.

Leaving my flip-flops and the divorce papers behind, I fled toward the refuge of the pool house as fast as I dared drive my friends' farm truck on winding back roads at twilight. My emotions were street fighting. One moment, Anger seemed to have the upper hand. Then, Despair came in with an undercut and sent me wailing. Betrayal and Abandonment snuck up from behind, threatening to suffocate the life right out of me.

"*Oh, my Jesus, how could he bring her into my house? I know I'm not there anymore, but that's his fault. He's the one who should have moved out. He's the one who wanted the divorce. He doesn't really belong there. She surely doesn't belong there. Who is she? Is it just one she, or a series of she's? Why would he so blatantly disrespect me? How dare she wear my shoes and hang her skanky panties above my washing machine! How will You ever help me to forgive this? What did I ever do to deserve this?*"

Before reaching my teeny twin bed in the pool house, I was heaving dry tears. The girls knew the drill. Sometimes I think they *hoped* I would be upset just so they could jump into the bed with me. There was barely room for *me* in that bed, let alone a fat pug and a wriggling Boston terrier. They didn't last long. I quickly threw them out as I fitfully wrestled my emotions.

Hours later my heavenly Father, and my poor dogs, had heard every cry of my heart. He reassured me of His love and protection as the Holy Spirit reminded me how long it was since Jon and I had been intimate. Although it stung when Jon verbalized he wasn't interested in sex, the pain of the contrary evidence he and Goldilocks left behind was comparable to an attack by a hive full of hornets. My only relief was the hope that marital celibacy rescued me from any potential sexual diseases. That's the one thought I took comfort in as I finally fell into a restless sleep just before my alarm woke me for school.

That morning I inspected myself in the mirror. Apart from the dark circles under my swollen, red-rimmed eyes and my super thick glasses, I thought I didn't look *so* unattractive.

I wonder why he really didn't want to sleep with me. I wonder what she looks like? Why was I so repulsive to him? What would cause him to choose her over me?

Sad, self-deprecating thoughts plagued my mind as I dressed for the day. I felt worse about myself than I had in a long time. It was bad enough to have lived with the fact my husband "didn't want to have sex." Those two additional words, "with me," from yesterday's revelation, added to the sentence and gave an extra twist to the dagger in my heart.

Dealing with eighteen first graders takes energy. I had none. For weeks, my students suffered the consequences of having an emotionally drained teacher. I would forget to check their folders for parental communication, misplace their homework, or make-do with skimpy lesson plans. Sometimes I snapped at them for misbehaving. Sorry I had so little to give, I tried to make it up by bringing them treats from the Dollar Store, or allowing extra playtime. Fortunately I had taught for so many years I could almost run my classroom on autopilot. The day following my discovery that someone else was wearing my flip-flops and sleeping with my husband in our home was an autopilot day. I was completely numb.

"Mrs. Miller, you have a phone call in the office." Dr. V's voice came loud over the intercom a few days later, interrupting the silence of my planning period. It was Jon. He signed the divorce papers.

"I'll meet you at the McDonald's on Main Street this afternoon," I said, not wanting him to come to the school, yet not wanting to be alone with him anywhere.

"McDonald's is a safe, neutral place, right, Lord? I'm not sure I trust myself to refrain from attacking him if we are alone. I am so angry! I'd just as soon slap his face as see it! Please help me to get through this."

I ordered an ice cream cone and sat down in a booth. I felt his presence before I saw him. He slid into the seat across from me, tossing the manila envelope containing our divorce papers my direction. "Here," he said. "I've signed everything. I'm not happy that I don't have a stinkin' thing to show for twelve years of marriage. You took it all."

"There was nothing to take," I spat defensively. "You pawned all the good stuff. Everything I took belonged to me, not to you. *And* you are making me pay for this divorce. I didn't ask for that."

This wasn't the conversation I planned to have with him. Just as our voices began to escalate, we felt a hand on each of our shoulders. Dr. Alan's brother, a man we casually knew, stood at the end of our table. He stared at us before stating, "A cord with three strands is never broken. If you allow God to be the third cord in your marriage, it will be strong."

"It's too late," Jon said. "It's just too late." He stood up and walked out, leaving the envelope on the table.

Walking Away

Early Friday morning, March 23, 2007, Jon called the school again. That was the only way he knew to reach me since I forbade anyone to share my new cell number with him.

"I want my truck back. Today!" He demanded. "I gave you the papers. You have everything else. Give me my truck!"

"Okay," I consented.

I'd been driving it for a few days. What a gas hog! I was ready to have my Caddy back. Besides, my attorney gave me the all clear. There was no reason for me to continue holding Jon's truck hostage.

"Daniel and I are working in the new subdivision behind our . . . I mean *my* house today. I will leave the Cadillac in the driveway at home. Drop off my truck and pick up your car. There's nothing else to say." He hung up.

It sounded like a good plan. I needed to stop at Aubrey's to check on my plants anyway. I missed Aubrey. Our relationship was strained since Jon and I separated. She and Bob were friends with both of us. It was hard for them when we began pulling from opposite sides of our emotional tug-of-war. Jon fed them lies. I felt betrayed when they bailed him out and helped him, even though they knew he continued to use drugs.

"How can I be upset with them, Lord? They are just doing what I did for so long, enabling and rescuing . . . prolonging the agony of addiction. I understand. It just smarts to see Jon's family and friends stepping in to save him now, when it felt as if I was carrying that load all by myself for years!"

"Where's my Cadillac?" I said quietly to myself as I turned into our familiar driveway. "He said it would be here. What should I do, Lord? I don't want to go to where he is working. I don't want to see him. How will I get my car? Should I wait? Should I leave?" I prayed aloud.

Spying my deep freeze on the carport, I remembered the fresh blueberries Aubrey and I picked together last season. There were still several bags in that freezer. *I know Jon's not ever going to use those. I may as well take them and eat them on my cereal. It's almost blueberry season again. How quickly this year has gone.*

"What the @!!*" I heard him swear just as I realized he was slumped in one of those lawn chairs under the carport windows. I froze three feet away from him on my way to the blueberries.

"What are you doing?"

"I'm getting high, what the *!@* do you think I'm doing? Where's Nemo? Where's Beth?" Jon appeared startled and confused.

"Who's Beth?" I asked, glancing around nervously.

Suddenly, Jon realized who I was and jumped up, yelling, "I want my @!*#ing truck." As he sprang toward me I spun around and ran to the truck, locking the doors behind me. I laid some rubber on what was left of the crumbling asphalt in our driveway as I headed for the road. Pulling over at the entrance to the new subdivision, I phoned him. He ranted and swore and threatened to call the police if I didn't return his truck immediately.

"Where's my car?" I countered.

"I got some cash for it by letting the bank have the title. You forgot about *that* little piece of paperwork, didn't you?"

Oh, Lord, did he sell my car? I thought frantically as he continued stabbing me with words.

"Beth is driving it. Getting it detailed for me. She can go anywhere she wants. I don't care what she does in your car or when she's coming back." Then he persisted like a spoiled child, "I want my truck. I want my truck! I want my truck!" Deepening the verbal puncture wounds, he continued. "You are no longer my wife. I'm not living for anyone except myself now, and the ONLY thing I care about is my TRUCK!"

At that moment, emotional adrenaline took over. Without stopping to think or pray, I made a 180 and flew back to the house. Jon's red truck screamed into the driveway, my foot heavy on the gas. He stood in front of the carport with a cigarette in one hand and his phone in the other.

Run him straight over! came the thought from hell. Instead, I slammed the brake, ripped the gears into park and jumped out, leaving the door open and the engine running.

My legs started walking toward the road as my eyes burned with the tears I did not want to cry.

"Julie, don't do this." His voice came from behind me. Too close. I didn't turn around. Just waved my hand twice, like I was shooing away a hound, and kept walking toward the road. Jon climbed into his truck and rolled down the windows hollering, "Who's coming to get you?" as he caught up to me on the county road. I kept walking. Didn't even look at him.

"God, I do not want to talk to him. Do not want to cry. Just need to get away. Help me to get away from him. He's scaring me. Help me, please!"

Jon drove past me and pealed into the subdivision entrance. He got out of the vehicle repeating, "Who is coming to get you? Julie, get in the truck. Julie! Julie! Just get in the truck!"

He called my name over and over in a mean, yet pleading way. I went to the other side of the road and kept walking. Jon jumped back into the driver's seat and pulled up beside me. "Who did you call to come and get you?" He demanded.

"NO ONE! I'm too embarrassed and ashamed for ANYONE to know you are treating me like a DOG. Worse than a dog! You HAVE the most important thing in the world to you now, so LEAVE ME ALONE!" I screamed without stopping or looking at his face.

"Get into this truck. NOW!" he commanded. Then, using a different tone, he said, "Here come Daniel and Glen. They must be finished with the job."

I kept walking. Jon pulled over to the side of the road as one white service van drove slowly past and turned onto Highway 39.

Fine. Just let me walk.

It was Daniel. I knew Jon would be embarrassed by this scenario. I did not care.

As he watched from his truck, the second service van pulled alongside me. It was Glen, Jon's other workmate. I only met him once.

"Get in. I'll give you a ride. Where are you going?"

I crawled in and started bawling even before the door closed. Poor Glen. I unabashedly wailed and sobbed and wailed some more. It was ugly. I wiped my nose on my arm and attempted to choke back the sobs when his phone rang.

"Yes. I've got her . . . Okay . . . Okay. Bye." He flipped his phone closed and turned to me. "That was Daniel. He saw you walking and wanted to make sure I picked you up. Now, where are you going?"

"I . . . don't . . . knooooooow where I'm going," I wailed.

"I'll take you in to town," he said.

"That's okaaaay. I'm not sure where to go. I don't want anybody to see me. I'm too sad. I'm too devastated that he would be so mean to meeeeeeee. I've never done anything bad to him. How could he do this to meeeeee?"

I proceeded to pour out my deepest hurts to Glen-the-air-conditioning-man as he slowly drove the thirteen miles into town. Before we reached the city limits sign, Glen said kindly, "I believe you are a Christian woman. You don't need to live like this."

He went on to share his own story of suffering when his young first wife decided she wanted to go clubbing and partying after she gave birth to their baby. He said, "I just couldn't do it. I was a deacon in the church and a new dad. We ended up divorced. I went the devil's way for a couple of years, but then I got right again."

"Thank you for sharing. And thank you for picking me up. Thirteen miles is a long way to walk," I said, raising my forehead from his dashboard.

"Well, by the way you were going, you might have made it. I don't think I've ever seen anyone walk so fast in my life," he chuckled. "Daniel and I just finished the job in the subdivision. It took us longer than expected because Jon cut out on us after lunch. He can no longer function very well on the job, especially doing attic work. He's worked about twenty hours this week, but he was worth maybe half that. Those drugs are really taking a toll on him."

That was the first time I heard anyone say Jon was not worth his salt at work. Despite all of the drugs he'd done through the years, he somehow managed to be an asset on the job. I felt an additional sadness in my spirit to hear those words from Glen.

"I could definitely tell his brain was fried when I saw him today," I said. "I mean, he gave my car to his girlfriend! Who, in their right mind, would do *that* to their wife? I paid for that car! What am I gonna do noooow?" Fresh tears flowed until Glen dropped me off at the front door of Dr. Alan's office.

"Thank you," I whispered, closing the van door. God sent that man to me at the precise moment I needed a way of escape. I never saw him again.

"Thank You, Lord God, for hearing my cry and for rescuing me."

As I closed my swollen, puffy eyes that night—March 23, 2007—I had no way of knowing how my Savior would redeem me from all I thought was lost that day.

Now, exactly seven years later, I have goose bumps as I realize how He has taken the 23rd, the date I literally walked away from Jon, and vindicated it! I've only just unearthed, in the writing of this chapter, the realization of how God lovingly and perpetually redeems that awful date in my life. I am moved to tears by His thoughtfulness. He is truly the "Lover of My Soul!" I want so badly to get ahead of myself and give you a sneak peek into the future, but I will save it for the final chapter.

Now where were we? Oh, yes . . .

I was technically homeless and car-less and virtually penniless, with a wounded ego and a broken heart. And I was about to get snared in a trap I didn't see coming. Hold on for the ride. It's a bumpy, bittersweet one. You'll want to rescue me from myself because you've either been there yourself, or you've loved someone who has. Unfortunately, many of us must learn lessons on boundaries the hard way, through the experience of digging our own post-holes and setting our own fences. That, my friends, is terribly hard work.

Boundaries

I read Cloud and Townsend's books on boundaries. In fact, I had so many boundaries in place even my boundaries had boundaries. Still, not long after the day I walked away from Jon, I noticed someone in my small town world noticing me. How that soft-spoken Harley-rider leaped my fences and got through my barbed wire is still a mystery.

If I could avoid telling you *anything* about what happened next, I would do just that. I don't *want* to tell you. But I'm ignoring shame's hot breath on my neck, choosing instead to include this part of my story in hope of perhaps helping some dear reader to sidestep a similar pitfall.

Let me begin by saying this, I don't care how wonderful he is, if you put all your broken pieces in one man's basket you leave yourself open for heartache—unless that man is Jesus. This man was surely not Jesus, but he did try to be my savior.

After walking through years of marriage as an invisible woman, it took only one yellow Post-it note from a man I highly respected, but hardly knew, to let me know I was no longer invisible. One Post-it note, written in neat, black Uniball, read, "An observation. You are a beautiful woman." I was smitten.

Every repressed girlish emotion I had was unleashed upon that unsuspecting man. How could he have fathomed my heart's hunger for attention and affirmation? Of course, *he* had no way of knowing, but my enemy knew. The enemy, whose very existence revolves around destroying God's sons and daughters was fully aware of every level of my vulnerability after the death of my marriage. He wasted no time before moving in for the kill. A lion never waits for the wounded to recover before attacking.

I'll call him Chris. Chris Roberts. He was our well-loved assistant principal, the only male on a primary school campus of twenty-five females, including custodial and cafeteria staff. The shift in dynamics between us was so subtle no outsider could have noticed. At times even I wasn't sure if something was different. Our exchanges began innocently enough. An extra second or two of direct eye contact, a brush of arms when passing, increasing reasons to hold a brief conversation.

When Mr. Roberts was in a room, I suddenly felt alive. Like a dormant flowering tree whose winter was finally over, something deep within my being began to awaken.

My sister was the first to notice. Annie could hear the difference in my voice over the phone. "How come you sound so happy?" She asked one afternoon in April.

"I don't know. I'm just ready for something new."

"Hmmmm." She remained silent for a moment.

"I think someone likes me," I finally admitted. "I'm not certain, but I think so.

"Who is it?"

"Oh, just someone. His name is Chris." Saying his first name felt strange. Then I added, "He rides a Harley."

"Oh, a Harley, huh? Sounds like danger to me."

"It's just nice to be noticed. I've been invisible for far too long."

"Well, be careful. I don't want you hurt again."

"I'm not doing anything."

Silence . . .

"Seriously, Sis. I'm innocent."

"I can tell you are smiling."

"I'm just counting the days until the divorce is final. That's all."

"How many days?"

"Thirty-seven."

"Are you for real? You have literally counted the days?" She asked incredulously.

"Yes. I can hardly wait for that day. Can't wait to get my maiden name back. Can't wait to be cut loose from Jon. I. Can. Not. Wait."

During the waiting, the Lord used another man, a kind Christian gentleman, to show me how a woman should be treated. His name was Tom. Tom was born on March 20, 1927. For his whole long life he loved the same precious wife, until she left him a widower not long before we met.

When he noticed Jon no longer attended church with me, Tom asked a few pointed questions. Observing my heartache, he wanted to do something to help. "Would you mind," he inquired, "if, in light of your husband's neglect, I respectfully showed you how a man should treat a woman on special occasions? I still miss my wife so much. I long to do special things for someone on birthdays and holidays." I told him I didn't mind at all.

So, what did Tom do? Over the next three years, for my birthday and special occasions, he faithfully delivered roses and fancy gold boxes brimming with Godiva chocolates. Occasionally he took me out to dinner. God used an unlikely World War Two veteran to lavish me in a way I would never be able to accept as unadulterated from anyone else. On those dinner dates, Tom instructed, "You should *expect* to be treated like a queen. Never settle for less. You deserve the best." He never expected anything in return. I wish I paid closer attention to Tom's wise, gentle words.

Those thirty-seven days to divorce seemed to fly. Several things happened with Jon that drove me to my prayer journal. On April 21, I wrote: *"Lord, why do I feel so angry that Bob and Aubrey paid for five nights in a motel for Jon after he lost our rental house? Why am I angry Roman sent him eighty dollars to get his stuff out of another motel room after he didn't pay the bill? Why do I even care Jon used that money for drugs rather than to salvage his belongings?"*

I feel betrayed knowing Bob and Aubrey met Beth when they took Jon out to eat at Olive Garden. Why would they even tell me that? Don't they know how I'm struggling to forgive Jon for moving her into the house and giving her my car? Rumor has it that broad has already been in prison for being one of the highest-ranking drug dealers in this area. Why Jon wants to be with her, I don't know!

Maybe it's because she knows how to earn money. Bob says they are renting out my Cadillac to a dealer for fifty dollars a day, so she must know how to earn a buck when necessary. Here I am bumming a ride with a teacher friend every morning because I can't afford to buy another vehicle, and they are earning cash by pimping my car! It's all so crazy foreign to me. I can't bear to know about it.

Yes, I am saddened by the report that Jon has boils all over his body and can hardly walk, but boils are a direct result of his choices. A body can only take so much. I do hope he goes to the emergency room as Bob suggested. I don't want to go to his funeral. Please help me to forgive. I'm just not feeling it.

For a long while, I wrestled to fully release Jon. I would release him then take him back into my heart's tender places. I struggled to forgive him after those last two or three harsh blows. I didn't forgive Beth for a long time. I loathed her. Sometimes I would think I had forgiven, and then a surge of emotions would cause me to second-guess myself.

Forgiveness is both a choice and a process. I learned more about myself and that process, through subsequent counseling sessions, recovery groups and Bible study. I longed to cut the soul-ties I still had with Jon, but at times unforgiveness was the knot that held us together. I remember making a conscious choice to actively pursue my own freedom and the lifestyle of forgiveness. I believe that is why I am who I am today. By God's grace, I am free from any bondage to Jon, Beth and anyone else who has hurt me. Unforgiveness keeps us bound to the past. Forgiveness sets us free.

Just three days later I journaled again: *"Jesus, I'd ask You to take Jon into Your hands, but I know he is already there. So, I guess what I'm really asking is for You to take him out of my hands . . . out of my heart."*

Jon phoned me at school that afternoon. "I'm calling to say good-bye," he ranted. "I don't give a !*!@ about anything anymore. I want my life back. I am going to run into a semi." His contradictory tirade continued. "I have boils all over my body. All of my clothes are dirty. I'm supposed to be helping Beth get out of the drug life and into college . . . "

"DON'T talk to me about her!" I interjected.

"She thinks I still have a job. What am I supposed to do with that?" Jon moaned. "I'm never going back to our house. Never." Then he hung up.

I didn't know what to say. The words "I am going to run into a semi" resounded in my brain. I remember rocking back and forth on the floor in Mr. Roberts' office, where I'd taken Jon's call, the phone cradled in my hands.

"God, is he threatening suicide? Is that what this is about? What am I supposed to do with that? How should I respond? Why would he call me at work to blurt all of this to me?"

I made an emergency appointment to see Dr. Fox. Counseling with him had proven immensely helpful as I navigated the emotional turbulence that came toward the end of our marriage. Even if I had to borrow a car to get there, it was worth it!

On my way home afterward, Annie called. I told her about Jon's upsetting phone call. "What did Dr. Fox say?" She asked.

"He said it's common for addicts to use threats of suicide as manipulation. We talked about releasing any sense of false guilt I might have and letting go of feelings of shame related to Jon's choices. I cannot be Jon's savior. He already has a Savior. Somehow he has forgotten that. I wonder if he is truly reaching out, or just trying to manipulate me. I really don't want him to contact me anymore."

Apart from speaking with Dr. Fox and Annie, I also talked to Mr. Roberts about Jon's phone call. He had noticed I was visibly shaken by Jon's suicidal monologue. I accepted his offer of a sympathetic ear and a warm hug.

Confiding in him crossed one of my invisible boundaries: "Persons who are in the process of separation or divorce shall not pour out their hearts to someone of the opposite sex who has flirted openly with them and who is also in the process of separation or divorce."

In my journal that night, I scribbled: *Chris Roberts does something for my soul, my heart, my very being; something that I cannot explain. He has such a steady, calm spirit. I'm drawn to him. "Is this okay with You, God? I'm begging You—make him go away if it's not. I don't want to end up wounding him, or he me. I am a basket case right now."*

I was a *very* wounded girl. Hurt people hurt other people. I recognized I had the potential to harm Chris, and I wanted to avoid that. When I mentioned him to Dr. Alan and Darcy, they'd immediately repeated the same things Annie had said.

"Be careful. We don't want to see you get hurt. Wait."

Unfortunately, infatuation deafens a person to godly counsel. When emotions rule, we cannot hear the warnings of the people who know and love us best. The Lord graciously removed me from temptation with a mission trip to Italy. Before I escaped, though, I had to get divorced.

Lessons and Regrets

The divorce was final on May 16, 2007. I processed my thoughts in my journal: *Today is one of those milestone days in my life. Usually, I would guess that divorce day is not a happy day, but I was pleasantly surprised at the feelings I experienced—definitely not the doom and gloom I would have expected upon finding myself in Divorce Court.*

I felt an overwhelming sense of relief and freedom as I walked down those courthouse steps this afternoon. I praised God for bringing me to this place in my life. He's used these years to teach me some difficult lessons; lessons I may have never learned otherwise. So I thank Him and praise Him for the experience. More than that, I praise Him for setting me free from the bondage I've been under. What relief! I want to remember the lessons I have learned. I don't want to repeat the mistakes of the past.

Here are the lessons:

1. Bitterness and unforgiveness cause depression, which leads to my own addictions and allows Satan to have strongholds in my life. God has taught me the importance of forgiving over and over again. He has allowed me to experience a tiny taste of what He goes through with us.

2. Unconditional love is a choice, not a feeling. Sometimes when I chose to love, I did not have the feelings to accompany my decision. Sometimes God did allow me to feel, but I had to make the choice first.

3. I learned how to have a life of my own within the dysfunction of my marriage. I learned how to find joy and fulfillment elsewhere—from my family, my church, and my workplace, and especially my alone time with God.

4. I learned how to get up and get dressed and do my job well, regardless of the havoc of my personal life.

5. I've learned how to walk with God, independent of anyone else's input or opinion.

6. I learned how to pray God's Word and expect answers to His promises. I learned to trust Him. Am still learning this one . . .

7. I've learned how to put on the Ephesians 6 Armor each morning and not be afraid to use it when under attack during the day.

8. I've learned how to pray from the heart because I want to, not just because it's the right thing to do.

9. I learned how powerful the name of Jesus is and that I am covered by His blood. I can come against evil spirits in His name and they have to leave. What a truly amazing and untapped resource . . . The name of Jesus! I never want to use His name "in vain" again.

10. I learned to show restraint when extremely angry. God is still working with me on this, but I have had lots of practice!

11. I learned how to talk with other people about how I really feel. This has been a slow and difficult process. I'm getting better. I trust a handful of people with my "authentic self" these days.

12. I am still learning to "speak the truth in love." I have had plenty of experience with that. It is getting easier.

13. I learned I can live without sex.

14. I learned God is able to give me self-control in areas where I have cultivated or have hereditary weaknesses. I just need to call upon Him in the moment. Or better yet, prior to the moment!

15. I learned Jesus cares immensely for me as an individual. He has shown me His tender love and mercy throughout these lonely years.

I am thankful I have learned, and continue to learn these valuable lessons. I pray my character is a bit closer to that of Christ's. It has been a painfully tedious process, with many failures, but I praise Him that He never gave up on me. Others have shared that they have actually seen Christ in my life. It's a miracle.

Although I've grown through these years of being married to Jon, I still have my regrets:

1. I regret I allowed him to get away with so much lying from the very beginning, and I didn't confront him with it.
2. I regret I am 37 and haven't been a mother.
3. I regret I didn't finish my master's degree because of Jon's drug use.
4. I regret I didn't keep a tighter rein on him when we had the café.
5. I regret my family has been wounded by this whole process.
6. I regret the wasted years of my life . . . especially all the sex I've missed.
7. I regret letting Jon talk me into being deceitful on the paperwork when we wanted to adopt Chloé.
8. I regret having to let Chloé go because of his drug problem.
9. I regret hurting Chloé.
10. I regret cashing in my retirement plan to pay for his second stint in rehab.
11. I regret being silent when he hurt my feelings or ignored me.
12. I regret losing all of the assets we worked so hard to gain.
13. I regret not listening to Leon four years ago when he told me to, "Get out!" But I know God has His own timing.
14. I regret being naive when Jon flirted with other women over the years. I feel stupid and embarrassed for defending him.
15. I regret all of the times I didn't go to visit friends or family because I had to stay home and baby-sit Jon.

Having said all of that, this is my prayer tonight, along with a list of what I'm thankful for:

"My dear Lord Jesus, You have been such a faithful Friend to me. I cannot imagine having to go through these experiences without You.

- *Thank You for the hard times.*
- *Thank You for teaching me to trust You.*
- *Thank You for helping me to grow, rather than become bitter and self-destructive.*
- *I praise You for making Your presence known to me in real ways.*
- *Thank You for the people You have put into my life who have shown Christ to me.*
- *Thank You for the provision of a home through Alan and Darcy, and a borrowed truck.*
- *Thank You for all of the people who have prayed for me, called, or sent cards of encouragement on just the right days. I know You orchestrated everything.*

- *Thank You for my family's love and support of my decision to divorce Jon and move on with my life.*
- *Thank You for everything You have done for me today.*
- *Thank You for releasing me from my marriage without any hint of guilt.*

I love You for that! Amen.

After I removed my wedding band, my hand felt as bare as my soul. Almost immediately I noticed men responded to me differently than when I wore that tiny diamond. Being targeted as "single" made me feel like prey. I promptly went to the Christian bookstore and purchased a simple pewter ring with the inscription, "I am my Beloved's and He is mine." Placing it on my ring finger, I vowed to God I would accept His promise to be my Beloved Husband in the absence of an earthly husband. I also sincerely promised to remain sexually pure, and faithful to Him.

Three weeks later, I was on my way to Illinois in a rented red Mustang to drop the girls at Annie and Eddie's for the summer. Sandwiched between May and August were seven wonderful weeks in Italy!

The foundation for that trip may be best explained by sharing parts of a letter I sent to everyone I knew.

April 30, 2007

Dear Family and Friends,

Many of you are familiar with the recent events of my personal life. If you are not, I can only describe the past few months as devastating on many levels. However, the Lord has promised in Hebrews 13:5, "Never will I leave you; nor forsake you" (NKJV). He has made His presence known in my life in many comforting ways and I've been able to say with confidence, "The Lord is my helper; I will not fear. What can man do to me?" (Verse 6) I know that my material loss and heartache is temporary. Through Jesus, I have hope in a brighter tomorrow.

That brings me to the purpose of this letter. Incredibly, as I've walked through these recent months, the Holy Spirit has laid upon my heart a burden for a group of people from Northeast Africa who have suffered even more loss than I ever could imagine. These suffering souls have less than nothing when it comes to material possessions, family, friends, or even documentation that they exist on this planet.

I became familiar with this group's story back in the fall when my mother, who was doing volunteer literature evangelism in Italy, discovered them in Bari Park. Mom began sharing their plight with me via phone calls and emails. Before many days passed, her husband, Mr. P literally gave the shoes off his feet to a young man. Mom spent their grocery money to buy personal products and medicine for some of the young women.

As their stories were unfolded to me, in the midst of the unraveling of my marriage, I learned that many are educated, Christian young people who chose to escape their homes rather than be compelled to kill their "brothers." They were forced to leave universities where they studied medicine, commerce or information technology because all eligible fighters were drafted to war. They could not go home and they did not want to fight, so they escaped.

Conditions were so terrible many died in the fleeing. Of the ones who actually made it to Italy, some had lost their paperwork and some their integrity. The Italian government was unwilling, or unable to help after their initial stay in the refugee camp. In fact, they were left to live as homeless street people. Some found their way to Bari Park, which they quickly renamed "Parko Inferno," which translates as "Hell Park."

Mom and Mr. P felt an urge to do something for these suffering people. Most Italians were wary of assisting refugees and refused to become involved. Through prayer and determination, Mom has obtained some help from church friends in Switzerland and Italy.

They've received an invitation to plant a church in the Southern Italian city of Lecce. Their plan is to include Christian refugees as initial members of the congregation, with the goal of nurturing their faith as well helping them become established in their new country.

I want to assist in this project. I plan to fly to Italy as soon as school is out and spend the summer there. I will do what I can to serve these suffering souls and to help restore some dignity to their existence. Currently, I am working with Mom to network some resources so that we can meet their most pressing needs.

Our goals are:

- *Show Christ to the refugees in practical ways*
- *Provide loving Christian fellowship including Bible study and prayer*
- *Obtain food daily*
- *Find permanent housing*
- *Provide them with proper clothing*
- *Teach them Italian*
- *Refine their English skills*
- *Assist in getting their legal documents in order*
- *Help them find work*
- *Help them contact their family members*
- *Provide assistance in school enrollment to continue their higher education*

Yes, humanly this is overwhelming, but "With God, all things are possible" (Matthew 19:26 NIV). We will move forward in faith and watch the Lord move these mountains. The best part is that we can all be tools that God uses to do His work. That's why I'm officially inviting you to participate in this project by supporting it financially . . . I am excited about the challenge and encouraged by the support we've already received. I solicit your prayers beginning today. Please pray that we might show the love of God to these people.

Thank you and may God bless your life as you consider blessing others.

With love,

Juliet

That letter generated a flood of empathetic cards, letters and phone calls, and enough cash to bless the refugees in some beautiful, practical ways. In addition, my friends Ryan and Meredith convinced *their* friends on the board of the Live It Foundation, a nonprofit organization, to support our ministry by collecting tax-deductible funds and donating items for me to take to Italy.

Their son, Riley, a web designer and graphic arts student set me up with a blog called "Julie In Italy" and created a T-shirt that said, "Ciao! Jesus loves me too!," for us to distribute to the refugees as a way of stating we all are equal in the eyes of God.

Before I left, the Live It Foundation presented me with a new Nikon D40, so I could digitally document my journey on my blog as a way of inspiring financial and prayer support. I was elated! God was opening doors that would take me out of my place of hurt and set me on a path of healing. My journal records the state of my heart as I began my journey. Here are some snippets of my talks with God:

- *You are the God who sees me . . . I have now seen the One who sees me (Genesis 16:13 NIV).*
- *I surrender . . . I abide . . . I seek You . . . and I trust You. Thank You, Lord. It all begins with surrender.*
- *Idols are those things that come before You in my life. I cease to occupy the throne of my life. I choose to let You, God, occupy that throne.*
- *Make me a living sacrifice, holy and acceptable to You (Romans 12:1 NKJV).*

I was completely in love with my God after everything He had so boldly done to declare His love and watch-care over me. I wanted to do nothing to displease Him. However, simultaneous to the above journal entries, are other entries, which expose my vulnerability and some of the tactical moves of the enemy as he set me up for a fall. Here's a sample of *those* entries:

- *The blessing and wonder of this day was that Mr. Roberts told me he was falling in love with me. He demonstrates wonderful restraint when it comes to me and I'm blessed to have him in my life right now.*
- *Keep your servant also from willful sins; may they not rule over me. Then will I be blameless, innocent of great transgression (Psalm 19:13-14 NIV).*

And a piece of a poem:

- *You left me at the table, a thousand things unsaid. Things I'm not ready to hear. So I reflected on the things I read . . . in the lines around your mouth and beside your eyes.*

Then some notes from a sermon I drove two hours to hear, as God sought to rein me in:

- *Everything has its effect. Our own mistakes are the first source of wisdom.*

- *"Failure is failure only if we fail to learn," John Maxwell.*
- *Learn from the mistakes (life experiences) of others. Who are the 'wise' people in your life? Listen to them.*
- *Are you ready to humble your heart enough to trust God?*

I honestly thought I *was* humble and ready to trust God. Early in life, though, I had developed a dangerous pattern of going from relationship to relationship without any space between. My marriage was simply part of that pattern. Now that it was ended, I defaulted to my faulty wiring, which was a result of deep insecurity and childhood wounding. I was desperately in need of time and space to heal. Italy would provide that, but before I could get away, the enemy wove a spider's web with my name on it. It awaited my return.

Italia

Italy was an adventure. Between ministry opportunities, I savored the local food and culture. The P's made mission work interesting. They would often strike up a conversation with a person who seemed lonely or unconnected. Once they handed ten Euros to a young man, who shouted, "Woohoo!" and ran to call his mother in Africa. His joy infected all of us. Experiences like that taught me a beautiful way to live—always looking for someone to bless, always sowing seeds for God's kingdom.

After spending several weeks listening to heart-wrenching stories from refugees, my own story started to seem less painful. The hours I spent in Internet cafés, telling their tales on my blog brought the realization that everyone has a story. I began to see how every story is important to God. The miracles, small and great, woven throughout each person's life are the hooks upon which we hang our faith. When we share those miracles, faith increases. I believe that is why we overcome the enemy by the blood of the lamb and the word of our testimony as Revelation 12:11 says.

Testimony is powerful. My faith in God's tender love for us as individuals increased tenfold that summer as I learned of the ways He sustained those brave and brokenhearted young men and women some people referred to as "refugees." Hearing their testimonies brought the certainty He would sustain me too.

In quiet moments between the flutter of activity, I thought about my "real" life—the one I'd have to return to once summer was over. One July afternoon, Mom and I snuck away for some "girl time." Over gnocchi and pesto, I decided to tell her about Mr. Roberts. He and I had been emailing back and forth every few days, since my arrival in Italy.

My heart quickened at the sight of his name in my inbox. He wanted me to come home. He'd texted once, asking for prayer for a family crisis. I responded by calling him from a pay phone with my credit card. He sounded so familiarly Texan, but so far-removed from my life with the refugees and the P's. It was two different worlds.

Soon I would be back in his world and Italy would be an ocean away. As the summer wound down, I knew I needed to let Mom in on the secret of Mr. Roberts. She doesn't like surprises.

"So, he's your boss?" Mom chose her words carefully as we sat side by side in front of our favorite gelateria, licking cioccolato fondente from homemade cones.

"Well, yes. I guess he is, in a way. He supervises our instruction and deals with disciplinary issues and anything else we need help with. He's exceptional at his job. I tell you what, the little boys' restroom has stopped reeking since we've had a man on campus telling them how things should be done in there!" I joked.

"I wondered how you could be so lighthearted this summer after what you've gone through. One wouldn't know your heart was ever broken. I thought it was because it was wrapped in angel wings. Maybe those were Harley wings instead," Mom quipped. "I'd like to talk with him."

Mother was wary of my news about the appearance of a man in my life so suddenly after Jon and I divorced. "I've been there," she warned. "You know what Mamaw said about the frying pan and the fire. I understand your need to be loved after the way you've been treated, but you and this man have some major differences when it comes to religious beliefs. Will he understand the way we keep the Sabbath? Or will ball games and television fill the day God set aside for worship? These are things you need to find out now, because they can become huge issues later, no matter how nice he is."

When I emailed him about my conversation with Mom, Mr. Roberts responded, "I want to speak with her, too. We need to get to know one another's families. In fact, I'd like to come to Illinois and pick you up when you get back to your sister's. What do you think about that?"

"Wow, Lord! He must really care about me if he's willing to drive from Texas to Illinois to get me. Mom seemed calm as she explained her reservations over lunch. I understand completely. What is Your will concerning this, God?"

My journal reflects my internal roller coaster as I chronicled life that summer. In one entry, I was writing passionately about the plight of the refugees, begging God to make a way to relieve their suffering. A page or two later, I'd scribble bits of Mr. Roberts-inspired poetry, raw slivers of emotion with lines like: *Insecurities laid bare, starvation of my soul sticking out like bones . . .* and *The only pain is the distance between us, my sorrow from being apart.* On the following page, at a prayer's end a desperate, *"Lord! Save Jon's soul!"*

Speaking of Jon, on July 8, 2007, Annie emailed with a link to his mug shot and a police report revealing his recent arrest for drug trafficking. Bond was posted at fifty thousand dollars. A wave of relief washed over me. I believed the only way Jon's life could be spared would be for him to go to jail or court-mandated rehab.

"Praise God!" Mom shouted when she heard the news. Then she shook her finger at Jon's memory and said, "You sit in there you little man, until Jesus rattles your cell doors!"

I don't know why, but we both got the giggles after that. Mr. P couldn't understand why we were laughing after receiving such awful information. I guess it was just a way for us to process the shock and relief that he was safely behind bars. Just as love takes time to grow, it takes time to die. Despite everything, part of me genuinely wanted Jon to be okay.

I did not laugh, however, the day I learned he received a twelve-year prison sentence for his crimes. I was shocked! Wondering how much my ignorance and enabling had prolonged his consequences, I prayed: "*God, what would have happened in Jon's life if I had not continually rescued and bailed him out? Did I just extend everyone's agony? Would he have gotten to this place years ago if he'd been unable to come home to a warm bed and a loving wife who paid the bills? Please help him to get clean and stay that way. Please heal his brain so that he can think normally. Please help him to make it, God. You love us all just the same. There's no difference. We're all Your children, Jon, me, the refugees, all of us.*"

On a sticky note in my Bible, I keep this quote from Francis Frangipane, "The singular objective of our faith is Christ-likeness." Loving people is the most Christ-like thing we, as Christians, can do. If nothing else, my 2007 summer in Italy taught me to love complete strangers and to have compassion for people whose stories I do not yet know. I learned to live outside of myself, and my own pain, looking instead for ways to bless others and to sow seeds for God's kingdom. As one beloved refugee said, "Speaking words is not important. Loving is something. Knowing is something."

In subsequent years, Italy has been inundated with refugees to the point where the tiny country has had to get help from the United Nations to handle the influx of asylum seekers landing on it's shores. Many of the individuals we ministered to that summer have since fled to other countries. The P's and I hear most of them, by God's grace and provision, are making decent lives for themselves. Some still consider us "family" and remain in contact to this day.

If Victor Hugo was correct in saying "to love another person is to see the face of God," then I believe Italy taught my broken heart to see God more clearly.

Chapter 14

Full Circle

"So, if you think you are standing firm,
be careful that you don't fall!"
1 Corinthians 10:12 NIV

July 2007—May 2008

Illinois in July is nothing but cornfields. I remembered that from Jon's and my desperate 2005 trip with the P's—acres and acres of Crayola crayon green on both sides of the road for countless miles. As the summer breeze caught the corn's broad leaves, they seemed to wave good-bye to the girls and me as we headed back to Texas in Mr. Roberts' heavy diesel pickup truck. Reaching for my hand and smiling through his goatee, he said, "It's gonna be a loooong day, but I'm thankful I can bring you on home."

For most of twelve hours, with Snuffles and Whipper happily snoring on my lap and Little Big Town harmonizing in the speakers, we talked of his life, my life, and the possibility of making a life together. I was excited about meeting his six-year-old daughter, Penelope.

She caught her dad reading my blog one day and had asked about me. "Who is she, Dad? She's hot. You should marry her. Can I write to her?" My first email from adorable pig-tailed Penelope was as straightforward as a kindergartener could be. She wrote, "Dear Juliet, Do you love my dad? Do you like me?"

We arrived at Mr. Roberts' house late in the evening. "Why don't you stay? You can drive my truck to your pool house in the morning. Keep it for as long as you need to. I've got the Harley," he offered. I slept in Penelope's pink twin bed that night. She was still at her mama's. I wanted to meet her when she came home, so I accepted his invitation.

Although no hanky-panky took place, I knew spending the night did not follow the Biblical principle of abstaining from the appearance of evil. I did it anyway. I felt safe with him.

A poem I'd penned from Italy expressed my thoughts this way: *It's your insight and integrity, so much more than flesh and bone. In your character and strength is where my heart has found its home.* After eight weeks away, I was still smitten.

To me, Mr. Roberts represented everything Jon turned out not to be: respectable, professional, law-abiding, God-fearing and really into me. On the way to Olive Garden one evening, I discovered he was also a pretty good kisser. How could a girl *not* be smitten? I say "girl" because that's exactly how I felt after my divorce. Somehow my emotions reverted back to those almost-teenage highs and lows and I became all googly-eyed and butterfly-tummied whenever he was near.

Penelope adored me, and I her. "I love you, Ms. Juliet," she said one Sunday afternoon, as we lay shoulder-to-shoulder on the carpet coloring pictures in her Strawberry Shortcake coloring book. From the sofa, Mr. Roberts took turns watching us and watching the Texas Rangers thrash Kansas City.

It's a bittersweet memory. Children cannot understand the adult world of romance and relationships. They only know one day you're there asking for the yellow crayon so you can finish Lemon Meringue's hair, and the next day you have vanished from their life. No amount of explaining can make it feel okay. Even when they fiercely rip all the pages *you* colored from their coloring book, there are still shreds stuck in the binding. We leave a shred of ourselves in the binding of each life we touch.

Two weeks after school started, Mr. Roberts invited me to go to DQ with him late on a Thursday. His invitation stunned me because he'd insisted our relationship be clandestine in order to protect our jobs. District policy frowned upon administrators becoming romantically involved with teachers under their supervision. Both of us loved our work and neither wanted to be "reassigned," so I agreed to keep things "hush-hush" until we figured out the most appropriate way to break the news to everyone.

I was bursting to tell my first-grade-teacher friends, especially Shirley, who was my wheels to school for several days after I'd returned Mr. Roberts' truck. Always interested in all the details of my life, Shirley had a way of making me want to tell her everything. It was tough to hold my tongue about Mr. Roberts. I felt almost guilty for saying nothing, but I didn't want to get him in trouble. I knew if I leaked, the word would spread like wildfire! Small towns are like that.

It was difficult pretending I didn't have affection for him as I went through the normal routines of my school day. I found multiple reasons to pause at Mr. Roberts' office door on the way to and from the teacher workroom. He never failed to put a smile on my face. It's a wonder intuitive Shirley never suspected a thing! That's why I was surprised by his risky suggestion of going to Dairy Queen, a place continually crawling with students and parents from our district. I went because I'd missed him since school started.

Besides that, since my favorite treat—the world's darkest chocolate gelato—was far away in Italy, I suppose the small-Texas-town alternative would be visiting the local Dairy Queen. It didn't happen often, because I knew the hazardous effects of those concoctions on my thighs, but mmmmmm, a Blizzard sure made a hot Texas afternoon almost bearable. I waffled between choosing their Peanut Buster Parfait or the Reese's Peanut Butter Cup Blizzard.

"I'll have a small Reese's Blizzard, please," I told the happy high-schooler behind the counter.

"Let's go out to the nature preserve," Mr. Roberts suggested after receiving his own candy-filled Blizzard, served upside-down, in true DQ tradition. "I want to spend some time with you." I nodded as I grabbed a handful of extra napkins and headed for the door. "You'd better meet me out there, since we probably shouldn't be seen getting into the same vehicle," he'd whispered into my hair as I brushed passed him.

Dr. Alan loaned me his farm truck until I could save enough for a down payment on my own vehicle. I cranked down the windows and followed Mr. Roberts' familiar taillights out to the local nature preserve where ours were the only two vehicles in the parking lot.

"*Oh Father,*" I prayed aloud between licks as my fast-melting ice cream dripped onto my hand, "*I'm looking forward to having wheels of my own again. Thank You for the kindness of those who have helped me get by until I could save enough money for a down payment on something decent. Thank You this school year is beginning much better than last year ended! Thank You that Mr. Roberts wants to spend time with me. I love this man . . . honestly and hopefully. Please help me to be wise.*"

We both still had some Blizzard left in our cups as we made our way toward the picnic pavilion near the river bottom wetlands. Mr. Roberts knew the peaceful preserve was one of my favorite hangouts. I loved spending Sabbath afternoons there with my binoculars, spying on Indigo and Painted Buntings. Our long-handled red spoons made similar scraping sounds as we sat on a splintery picnic bench, finishing our ice cream. The silence between us was not uncomfortable.

"Guess what?" I asked. Without waiting for a response, I went on to update him on the latest news from Italy. "Mom says Nadeem is going to school and Aazim has a job! Isn't that wonderful?"

"Yes. It is. What about the others?" He responded, kissing my sticky fingertips.

"Well, Teddy has moved out of that rundown building and is in a safer place. The P's are trying to help him get some paperwork done so he can become legal. They have a few loose ends to tie up before they come home in September. With the donation money we raised, they purchased Bibles, a washing machine, a computer, vitamins, phone cards and clothing. My mother would literally give the shirt off her back to help someone in need. I swear she is Mother Teresa's twin!" I answered passionately.

"Her daughter isn't so unlike her. I haven't met your mother yet, but I believe her daughter is the kindest person I have ever known." Mr. Roberts eased off the picnic bench and onto one knee. Before I could say banana pudding, he pulled out a square-cut diamond ring the size of Texas. "Will you be my wife?" He asked, looking up into my face with soft, serious eyes.

That was August 30, 2007.

On September 28, I snuck into Mr. Roberts' office and left a manila envelope on his tidy desk. It contained the barely-worn engagement ring and a good-bye note. The month in-between those dates was an emotional whirlwind. Since I ripped chunks out of my journal from that time frame, I can only rely on snippets that did not get cropped, and what's left in the margins of my memory to tell the tale of one more heartache.

After I said, "Yes!" We perched atop the picnic table like two lovebirds, holding hands and making plans until a ranger stopped to inform us the preserve gates would close at dusk. As the horizon swallowed a bright orange sun, the golden rays made my new diamond sparkle proudly on my hand as I turned the steering wheel of Dr. Alan's truck toward home.

Within days, Mr. Roberts and I were house hunting. My journal says: *We looked for houses together before Parent Night. He told me he cherished me today. I loved that. Love him.*

On the twelfth of September, we went to see the gifted songwriter, Mark Schultz, in concert. I wore navy pants, a white blouse, and my diamond. It had lain on my nightstand most days since I'd said, "Yes." We weren't officially announcing our engagement yet, so I was careful to only wear my new ring among strangers. The only people I shared my happy news with were Darcy, Alan and my sister. As I recall, none of them had much to say. I do remember Darcy asking, "Are you ever going to call him by his first name?"

"Probably not," I answered, laughing. "It's such a habit to call him Mr. Roberts. Chris just does not easily roll off my tongue."

A few days after the concert, Mr. Roberts invited me to come over and hang out with him and Penelope after I finished with church. Although he visited my church once, and I'd accompanied him to his sister's church a couple of times, worshiping together was not something we established as routine. I prayed about that as I drove the fifty miles from my place to his.

"Lord, I know ideally You want families to worship together in spirit and in truth. I've spent too many Sabbaths lately sitting alone in a pew. Is this the way my life with Mr. Roberts will be? I don't know if I like that much. Switching worship days doesn't seem to be something either of us is willing to compromise on. Why does everything seem to be so perfect, except for this? When will I be able to tell people about our engagement? I want to stop hiding the best thing that's happened in my life for a long time. I want to shout about it! Please, God. I just want to start living out loud again."

My shiny-silver 2005 Toyota Rav4 hummed down the highway as I prayed. I couldn't wait to show off my new Rav to Mr. Roberts. I *knew* the car was a gift from the Lord. I returned from Italy with the notion that a Rav4 was just the vehicle for me. It was sporty, but not a gas hog, had room in the back for a packrat teacher to haul her stuff around, and was easily capable of keeping me on the road for at least 300,000 miles, with very little maintenance.

Purchasing a new one was not in my budget, but I found a dealership in a nearby city that had two used Ravs within my price range. Dr. Alan and Darcy went with me to test drive and advise. I immediately fell in love with the more expensive silver one. The salesman wasn't budging on the price. I knew it was going to be a stretch to make the payment every month and stay within the budget Dr. Alan helped me set up. When I briefly left the negotiation room for the restroom, God must have moved in, because when I returned, Mr. Car Salesman reduced the price of *my* Rav4 to match the other one. Darcy and Alan sat there silently beaming. I have a hunch they had something do to with the radical reduction!

"Lord, I love those two people. I love You, too. Thank You for Your provision."

Trouble

"I have a new puppy!" She exclaimed. "Come out back!" Penelope led me by the hand to the sliding glass door. Because her daddy wasn't overjoyed with the pup's chewing habits, we spent most of the afternoon outside with the little girl and her needle-toothed pet. I tossed a rubber ball again and again, mindlessly listening to Penelope's happy chatter.

Mr. Roberts seemed strangely quiet. I didn't know if it was because of the dog, me, or what, but he definitely wasn't himself. When I left for home, he barely gave me a peck good-bye. I knew that was a bad sign, but the more I hinted the more silent he became.

"We'll talk later," he said closing my car door. Then, looking closely at my Rav, "I like your new wheels."

"I like you," I replied, clicking my seatbelt. "But today, you don't seem like you."

That was the beginning of trouble. The next time I saw him, he was speaking about leaving education to become a preacher, like his father. Then, within a matter of minutes, he was going to quit being a principal and become a flight instructor.

"I'm just not sure what the future holds," he said ominously. I could not put my finger on it, but something was definitely different. I began to panic on the inside.

Within days, we broke up. I had to beg for a good-bye meeting with Penelope. He finally conceded. We met at a park, taking some bread to feed the ducks.

"Your dad and I are not going to be seeing each other anymore, so I think this might be the last time I see you," I said, squatting down to look her in the eye. "You are a precious little girl and your daddy loves you very much. He wants just the right step-mommy for you and I may not be the best choice, okay? I still care for you and am so happy we got to spend some time together. I'm sorry today is a good-bye day." Writing this paragraph resurrects the warmth of Penelope's chubby hand in mine. My heart holds her for a moment as I try to imagine her now as a teenager.

Eight months later, Mr. Roberts wrote me a note.

One particular paragraph said, *"I thought I was all cried out, but I sat on the side of my bed the other night and just wept and wept. Not for me, or for us, but for Penelope. She loved you, and more importantly, felt YOUR love for her. I have tried my best to explain to her why you and I cannot be married and I think she understands, as well as a seven-year-old can, but she still asked me the other day, just out of the blue, 'Will I ever see Juliet again?' It was difficult for me to answer over the lump in my throat. Thank you for loving her so genuinely. I'm not sure I am better off experiencing that. I didn't know it was possible for someone to love my child as their own, and now that I've seen it, I doubt that I will ever find it again."*

It's difficult to find words to describe the next few months as I tried to make sense of what happened. Hindsight gives me great peace because temporary conflict pales in the light of what could have been another 'till death do us part' fiasco. If I boiled it all down to two words, they would be these: religious differences. History tells us many wars are fought and lives lost over those two words. Our casualty wasn't the first, but it didn't lessen its impact.

Mr. Roberts maintained he loved me. He just could not marry me, nor would he speak to me or acknowledge my existence. It was as if overnight I once more become an invisible woman. No one else knew I was invisible because no one else had seen how *visible* I was in his life those few short weeks. Sometimes I wondered if I imagined it. The silence drove me insane. Literally. I do not know how else to explain what I did to get his attention.

On a page from October, my journal says: *I want to be understood. I feel terribly misunderstood. This is the first time I have been made to feel as if I'm not good enough for someone. How can he just cut me off? Even God says, "Come, let us reason together."* The Scriptures I wrote revealed my agony. Next to Psalm 116:11, which says, *"And in my dismay I said, all men are liars (NIV),"* I scrawled in red ink, *Yeah, they abandon me. I let them hurt me and I still love them. I believe what they say when they use words like, "forever" and "I promise."*

On subsequent pages, I continued, writing Hebrews 13:6 (NKJV), *". . . The Lord is my helper, I will not fear. What can man do to me?"* and Psalm 119:28 (NIV), *"My soul is weary with sorrow; strengthen me according to Your word."*

Those were some long days at school and even longer nights in the pool house as I slowly processed my latest of heartbreaks. Since my workplace and my students had always been my refuge, I was at a loss for emotionally safe places to go. I could only go home. I couldn't break down at school or in front of my friends because nobody knew Mr. Roberts had hurt my heart. I didn't want them to know. I didn't want anyone to see him through the wrong-colored glasses, especially in his place of work. I respected him.

Unfortunately, respect did not long remain intact. In losing respect for Mr. Roberts I lost respect for myself. You see, the sick mixture of pride and insecurity festering within caused me to loathe being ignored. I began to hate it. That mixture was sin. It was dangerous, and should have been dealt with immediately. At some point I wrote in the margin of my journal: *Unless we are surrendered daily to God, sin will cause us to do reckless and foolish things.* My hurt hardened into anger and some of that anger spit in God's face. I began to spend less time in His Word and more time trying to figure out how to get Mr. Roberts' attention. It was a costly mistake.

I stopped avoiding Mr. Roberts and calculated ways to make our paths cross on campus. I spent more time in the mirror before leaving for school. I started eating lunch in the lunchroom rather than alone in my classroom with a stack of ungraded papers. One Friday in October I sent him a text message inviting him to dinner. By Monday he still had not responded.

I guess that's a no. What part of no am I not understanding? "God...help me."

On Wednesday, I received a texted reply. It said, "I miss my *wife*. I have been in anguish for weeks."

Those eleven words opened wide a doorway, which led to consensual sin. He called me his wife even though I wasn't. We did what husbands and wives do, even though we weren't married. I was like a starved trophy bass in an overstocked fishing pond. When the bait appeared, I took it - hook, line and sex-with-a-man-who-was-not-my-husband. Haven't I mentioned that wounded people find ways to wound each other? That intimate act hurt us more than any words we had exchanged. We also wounded our relationship with our heavenly Father by engaging in *one* of His sacred acts without the protective covenant of the other. Marriage and sex were never created to stand alone. I had experienced the hollowness of each, without its counterpart.

The grief, guilt and shame I was left alone with afterward were devastating. Hindsight reveals neither of us allowed the proverbial time that heals all wounds to bring us to a place of readiness prior to engaging one another in our whirlwind romance. The emotional high of being newly released from a difficult marriage, combined with the adoration of a man I respected and admired resulted in some hasty decision-making. A rushed engagement ultimately led to second-guessing and a breakup that reopened my barely scabbed-over wounds, still reeking with the infection of rejection.

Our ultimate adversary knows just how to set us up for each fall by preying on hereditary and cultivated tendencies. Obviously the enemy studied my weaknesses well, for he won a huge victory by assaulting my integrity, a victory he did not allow me to easily forget. Even now, I cringe to write these paragraphs. There is redemption in the sharing if only *one* reader will allow my experience to make them pause at the threshold of sexual temptation and ask God's Spirit to reveal the way of escape Heaven has promised to every child of God.

After pouring out my heart to Jesus in the emotional aftermath, I picked up Beth Moore's book, *Praying God's Word* from my nightstand and flipped to the "Overcoming Sexual Strongholds" chapter. There I found these words, "Since the Spirit of Christ now dwells in the temple of believers' bodies, getting a Christian engaged in sexual sin is the closest Satan can come to personally assaulting Christ." She continues by saying, "Sins against the body also have a way of sticking to us and making us feel like we *are* that sin rather than the fact that we've committed that sin." I knew exactly what she was talking about. I felt filthy. So, why did I do it again and again?

What I know for certain is, once those doorways are opened, they are tough to close. Once compromise creeps in, it becomes easier to justify the once unthinkable. A popular Casting Crowns song, *Slow Fade,* perfectly describes sin's slippery slope. I had the CD, but I missed the message.

My first step into seduction's quicksand began with one thought that escaped being brought into captivity, which led to another . . . then another. Those thoughts created a boldness to act in out-of-character ways.

And then there's the whole "soul tie" business. Beth speaks of it in that same chapter, saying, "A soul tie to *anyone* besides our spouse is outside the will of God and becomes an open target for the continuing, destroying schemes of the devil." Mr. Roberts and I had several strands of emotional and physical soul ties entangle us during our intensely brief romance. Although I had handed back his engagement ring, I hadn't broken the tie. I still clung to hope. We now had a *sexual* soul tie that opened all kinds of avenues for the enemy to work in my life, because I had become "one flesh" with someone who was not my spouse, regardless of what his text message said.

Immediately, I began to suffer spiritually. An ungodly guilt plagued my prayer life. My church life was cloaked in shame. Fear-of-being-found-out walked the halls with me at school. I did not feel like myself. For weeks I spent my non-working hours locked in the pool house with the girls. They took advantage of my dark mood and cadged their way into my tiny bed, sensing I had no energy to resist their bug-eyed begging. From that place of quiet solitude, I let the Lord break my heart.

Up to this point, all of my life I allowed boys and men to break my heart, leaving pieces of myself behind in the binding of each of their souls. That breaking only resulted in tearing me down. There was never any of the restoration that comes from being broken by the One who formed my heart in the first place. I was surely broken in the past, but this God-experience brought a new kind of brokenness, a brokenness that eventually resulted in complete and utter surrender. With that surrender, came the full ugly realization of just how far I strayed from the blood-stained pathway of purity that begins at the foot of the cross.

I needed to find my way back to the place of humble repentance, deep confession and complete forgiveness the cross of Christ represents. From there, I would once again be able to live the life of integrity Jesus calls His followers to live. I knew the way back to freedom, joy and peace. I don't know why I dragged my feet to find it, but I suspect pride had something to do with it. Why are we so full of ourselves that we often live our lives begging to be noticed, but ignoring the One who savors every detail and loves us beyond all measure, no holds barred? Perhaps it's because we become so caught up noticing the "specks" in the eyes of other people that we miss the "logs" in our own eyes (Matthew 7:3 NKJV).

I focused on Jon's poor choices the entire time I participated in that Bible study entitled, *When Godly People Do Ungodly Things*. While I was busy trying to figure out why *he* did what *he* did, my soul's greatest enemy was plotting how to get *me* into a different kind of sinking ship. God used that Bible study to give me an opportunity to prepare myself for what was ahead, but I missed the boat. I also ignored the other warning signals He blasted my way. It's easy to go deaf and dumb when we are tossed about on a sea of emotion. That's why it's important to openly seek and heed godly counsel.

Although my feelings for Mr. Roberts were real, our common ground wasn't enough to do life well together. We hadn't given ourselves enough time to figure that out before our hearts became entangled. We only exacerbated the pain of reality by crossing the physical boundaries God has so wisely commanded humanity to reserve for the sanctity of marriage. The aftermath was messy. Thankfully, God understands messy. He's been cleaning up sin's messes for thousands of years.

Unable to play charades with God any longer, I stayed home from church one gray Sabbath and literally wept on my face before my Father. He gently reminded me of King David's Psalm 51 prayer of repentance. I made it my own, adding several other Scripture references (2 Corinthians 5:17, Ephesians 2:6-9, Ephesians 6:10-18, Colossians 3:9-10, Romans 6:13, and Romans 12:1-2) as well as insight from my studies. It was a long prayer, but when I emerged, I was a brand new creation.

"Have mercy upon me, God. Wipe away my sins. Cleanse me completely from every stain my selfishness has left on my heart. I know what I have done is wrong. I renounce every impure thought and action regarding Mr. Roberts. I renounce the pride, fear, doubt and unbelief that caused me to entertain those thoughts in the first place. I choose to trust You with my future."

At this point, I had to stand up off the floor because Whipper wouldn't leave me alone. She kept pawing past my hair to lick the tears from my face. Snuffles jumped on my back and settled down as if I were a rug. "Go lie down," I said, rocking to one side and sending Snuffs for a tumble. They headed for their own bed. Crawling back into mine, I continued my prayer.

"*I acknowledge my sinful choices. I think about them continually. I know it's not only Mr. Roberts and myself I have hurt. I know I have sinned against Youuuuu. After all Youuuuu have done for meeeee.*" I sobbed those last words into my pillow.

"*When I was younger, I sinfully sought the attention of guys. I let them kiss and touch me, unaware my behavior was the result of deep woundedness. I thought being married for all those years would cure that. But, now I can see I am still a broken person. Heal me, dear God. Make me whole.*

"*You have shown me who I really am without You. I am a foolish girl. But You want me to be wise. You accept nothing less than my complete honesty with You. Cleanse me with the blood of Jesus and I will believe that it is done. I am tired of this heaviness in my spirit. Please 'Create in me a clean heart, O God; and renew a right spirit within me' (Psalm 51:10).*

"*I never want to be without You. I cannot stand the feeling of knowing my own willful sin separated me from You. It wasn't worth it. Please do not take Your Holy Spirit from me. Instead, fill me that I may have the fruit of the Spirit in my life. Restore Your joy to me. Help me to learn from this experience, all my experiences, so I can help others to avoid the pitfalls that have shaped my life.*"

Mid-prayer I felt four round brown eyes peering at me from the edge of the bed. The girls were standing on their hind legs begging my attention. They knew the wailing usually meant the rules were bendable and they could wheedle their way under my covers. Determined not to be distracted from my prayer, I clapped my hands and commanded, "Go lie down!" The eyes disappeared.

"*I choose to praise You, even though I don't know where my life is going. You are righteous. I put on Your righteousness because I do not have one shred of my own. I certainly see that now. I will faithfully put on Your armor every day before I leave my home. I know that I have no chance of standing firm without it.*

"*My heart is broken, Lord, for what I have done to You. My spirit is broken, Lord, with the realization of what I am capable of. I never want this to happen again. So now, in the name of Jesus Christ, I break any soul ties or sinful bonds I have with Mr. Roberts, with Jon, or with anyone with whom I have used my body or mind as an instrument of unrighteousness. I want to be fully cleansed, and only bonded to You.*

"*I bring the victory represented by the cross of Jesus Christ between them and me. Thank You, Jesus! I choose to forgive them for their part in this mess. I choose to release them from any holds I have on them because of words, vows or promises I have spoken or written. I choose to be released from anything they have spoken, written or done that would bind me to them in ungodly ways.*

"*I plead the precious blood of Jesus over my life. I accept Your forgiveness. I believe I am redeemed and restored. I choose to present my body as a living sacrifice. I put off my old self and my old ways, accepting Your promise that I am a new creation in Christ Jesus. I can come boldly to Your throne of grace. I am seated with Christ in heavenly places.*"

I sat crisscross on the bed and spoke in a voice that caused the girls to perk up and take notice, although they did not budge from their spot.

"In the holy name of Jesus Christ of Nazareth, I command every spirit of fear, doubt, unbelief, pride, and lustful thoughts and actions to get out of my life. You have no place here. You have to go."

Raising my hands toward Heaven, I turned my face upward as the blanket of sin and shame lifted off of me and I was delivered from the oppression I had been under.

"Thank You, heavenly Father, for redeeming me. Thank You for giving me another chance, for not leaving me in the pit. Praise Your holy name! Praise You for Your power. Praise You for Your mercy, Your tenderness, and Your grace. I feel Your love for me. I feel it. I believe it. Please help me to live it. For Your glory, and according to Your will, I pray. Amen."

That afternoon, I took the girls for a long walk. They, happy to get outside, didn't mind the gray day. Neither did I, because the cloud I had been living under was gone. I could breathe again. Somehow I knew I was going to be okay. I had a deep peace that carried me through the next few months. Even though I still had tears to cry, I was committed to trust God with my future and not try to manipulate it in any way.

When we got home, we discovered a dozen deep-red roses beside the pool house door. Tom, my dear veteran friend, had been there. His gift reminded me of the One who loved me most extravagantly. How could I not trust Him? Tom's roses were a physical reminder that God heard the cry of my heart that morning.

My journal collected my thoughts afterward: *Regardless of the depth of our loss and our sorrow, those who walk by faith choose to give thanks in everything. Strength comes from rejoicing. I will give thanks. I will trust Him. I will have the joy of the Lord. That will be my strength.*

Wanting to remember the ways God was speaking to me through His Word, I dug up my 3x5 Scripture cards and began to copy even more verses, adding them to my ring. Those Scriptures became my lifeline to joy, courage and strength as I navigated my way through life for the first time as an unattached woman. Since I consistently overlapped one romantic relationship with another, that kind of aloneness was something I had not experienced since middle school. With every bond to my past broken, I was finally in a place where God could fully heal me and redeem my life.

During my morning quiet time a few days later, I discovered a powerful verse to add to my index card ring. It was a promise that carried me through the next two years, found in Ezekiel 36:36 (NIV). "Then the nations around you that remain will know that I the LORD have rebuilt what was destroyed and have replanted what was desolate. I the LORD have spoken, and I will do it." That promise reminded me I did not need to strive—God would do it! Applying His promises was burden relieving during the following months as I watched Him open doors to life transforming opportunities.

Before the holidays came again, I knew I must leave my school, and very likely, my town if I was serious about moving forward. There were reminders everywhere of my life as Jon's wife, or as Mr. Roberts' secret love interest. Even though I appreciated my precious friends and my tiny church family, I had the ominous feeling I could easily wake up ten years later in the exact same place, doing the same things. That thought depressed me.

On January 1, 2008, my journal entry says: *I long to begin and end this year with my heart connected to God's heart.*

"*Lord, I commit my life to Your keeping and Your timing. Help me to be patient.*"

I continued praying similar prayers as God began to move me in a new direction. I remembered the master's degree I abandoned when Jon's drug use escalated, just before he went to Blue Sky.

"*Lord, do You think any of those credits would transfer if I am accepted into another program? Is my work lost? What about the Graduate Record Exam? I remember how difficult it was for me and how much I studied to prepare for it. I'm not sure I could pass that test again if those scores are expired. I am mentally drained after all of the drama. My concentration for critical and mathematical thinking is almost nil. What would You have me to do?*"

By February, I researched several graduate programs and made a delightful discovery. Every program I looked at required me to re-take the GRE. The only exception was my alma mater, a small Christian university near the Tennessee/Georgia border. The administration agreed to use my outdated scores if I could procure original test results and begin my summer classes on campus in June. Grateful, for once for my packrat bloodline, I unearthed the genuine document in its original envelope from the depths of my beat-up metal filing cabinet. Finding that piece of paper was a gift from Heaven. It represented confirmation I should go back to school and established which university I should attend. Rather than a campus I was completely unfamiliar with it would be a place that felt like home.

Once God starts opening doors, watch out, He swings them wide! The first weekend in March I flew to North Georgia to interview for a teaching position at a private Christian school. "We encourage all our teachers to obtain master's degrees," stated the superintendent. "In fact, if you sign a two-year contract, we will pay for you to get yours."

"Show me the dotted line," I responded when the school board offered me a first grade position. As I drove to my hotel afterward, the calm presence of God's Spirit washed over me. Even though I was in a strange city, I was not alone.

Over the next three months, my heavenly Father spoon-fed me from His banquet table. Sermons, Scriptures, songs, everything I heard seemed custom made for me. My journals are filled with verses and teachings, which sustained me through my life-altering transition time.

When the enemy brought thoughts of shame or condemnation I refocused my eyes upon Jesus. I stuck a Post-it on my bathroom mirror, declaring, "God is the 'Lifter of my head' (Psalm 3:3, ESV), I do not need to be insecure or ashamed." One journal entry proclaimed: *The Power that works in me is Jesus! That's how I overcome. If I'm not plugged in to Jesus Christ, I have no power (Ephesians 3:20 NIV). I am His workmanship (Ephesians 2:10 KJV) and He's not done with me yet. For it is God who works in me to will and to act in order to fulfill His good purpose (Philippians 2:13 NIV).*

My reflective writing from that time frame reveals the Holy Spirit's work to restore and grow me spiritually and emotionally. I was learning to get everything I needed from God, realizing it was only from that place of fullness that could I give to others. I no longer wanted to feel needy or to be motivated by what I could *get* from another person. I longed for God to heal me completely and was willing to do whatever it took.

My prayer journal toward the end of March reflects my heart: *I want Your presence all over my life. Nothing I hang on to will be bigger than what I stand to lose. I give You permission to pull out every rebellious root in me. No person can be as real to me as You, God. I will be faithful wherever You place me. Please prepare me for my future.*

Part of my preparation prayer was answered when I accepted an invitation to attend a Captivating Women's Conference in Colorado just before I moved away from Texas. I asked God to meet me there. Over the course of three days, He filled my exhausted love tank as I invited Him into every hurting broken place.

I came away from that experience with a renewed sense of my individual worth in the eyes of my heavenly Father. From my firm renewed stance as The King's beloved daughter, I decided I would never again accept scraps from the enemy's table. *Rather than taking matters into my own hands, I will wait for my Father's very best gifts,* I'd journaled as my airplane flew home from Denver to Dallas.

May I share a few morsels from that weekend with you?

Let's start with a prayer from my journal, written April 4, 2008: *I need to find the healing You have for me here. Open the eyes of my heart. Give me ears to hear You, eyes to see You, and the voice to praise You—even though I am broken. I am not abandoned, alone, unloved, betrayed or at the mercy of the world, because You promise, in John 14:18 (NKJV), that You will not leave me as an orphan, but that You will come to me.*

"Sin is adultery of the heart. It's what we give our hearts away to instead of Him." The first speaker's words stung like lemon juice in a paper cut. I knew what she was talking about. I'd been giving my heart away for my whole life. During the outdoor reflection time following that session, I propped myself against the base of an evergreen and penned this prayer in my journal: *"Father, give me the courage to hang on until You rescue me fully. I do not have to pretend to be strong. I need only to depend upon Your strength. Help me to trust Your heart, but not my own. Help me to follow Your desires for my life, not mine. Help me not to settle for less than the best You have in mind for me."*

On an afternoon hike, I captured a Mountain Bluebird in my binoculars. His rich cerulean feathers sparkled as he posed on a fencepost between swoops to snatch insects mid-flight. I relished discovering the chunky Red Crossbills with their crisscross beaks, and tried to identify a female hawk in flight. God's presence surrounded me in the grandeur of the snowcapped Colorado springtime with its azure sky and crisp air. This beauty was different from the familiar Texas fields of April bluebonnets and Indian paintbrushes. This was wild and vast, raw and majestic, like the heart of God. I wanted to know it . . . wanted to know Him.

Some of the questions I felt God asking me stemmed from a talk by a speaker named Sue. "What kind of woman do you want to be?" Sue asked. "Do you want immediate gratification, or true restoration? If you really want more, choose more. It will require more of you, but it will be worth it. Rise up and walk out of the darkness. Our fallen-ness is not the deepest thing about us. We do not need to hide there. We don't need to believe the lies."

In my journal I asked: *"God, what am I hiding? What is the lie I'm believing about the story of my life?"*

The answer came instantly in the form of one loud thought. *"Abandonment."*

It was true. I *believed* men would leave me, reject me, lie to me.

Early in life I made some dangerous internal vows to protect myself. Everything I experienced with Jon and Mr. Roberts reinforced the abandonment lie. I was tempted to renew those vows and construct an impenetrable shell around my tender parts.

I'll never place myself in that position again. I won't depend on anyone. I won't need anyone. I can never trust a man.

Those were vows of death, best friends to bitterness, resentment, anger and unforgiveness. I broke them in prayer and then re-made them many times over the years. The Holy Spirit was prompting me to renounce those lies yet again.

"God, lead me through this valley without bitterness," I wrote. Knowing I must *say* the lies were untrue before they began to *feel* untrue, I continued.

"I'm inviting You to come in and to let me know You as the Father and the Husband I long for. I break the agreements I have made with the enemy . . . the ones that say I will always be abandoned and I am not worthy of keeping. I renounce those lies, in the name of Jesus Christ. You will never leave me, nor forsake me. You did not spare Your own Son, but gave Him up for me. I am that worthy" (Hebrews 13:5, Romans 8:32 NKJV).

As the weekend unfolded, I could feel *myself* unfurling as my Savior gently spoke healing into those fetal-positioned places inside, where my soul curled around itself in protection from the pain that nearly crushed me.

As my heartache flowed onto the feet of Jesus, He neither cringed nor pulled away. He stayed close, grieving my losses with me. When I tearfully wrote: *My husband spent twelve years trying to get away from me. I want someone who wants to be with me,* my Savior spoke to me through Isaiah 63:9 (NLT). I personalized it to say: *In all Juliet's suffering, I also suffered, and I personally rescued her. In My love and mercy I redeemed her. I lifted her up and carried her through all the years.*

I begged Him to give me beauty for ashes and to redeem the dreams I thought were lost. At that time, I had no way of knowing how perfectly He would answer my plea; all I knew was I wanted to go home and live life differently than I ever had before.

The final thrust of the weekend was a class that could have been called "How To Be A Godly Wife 101." Although I was no longer a wife, the wisdom and experiences shared proved crucial to my future. I embraced the concept that whether I am married or not, Christ is to be the first and foremost Love in my life. My validation does not come from man, but from Him. I also took to heart the fact that I cannot be the validation of a man's soul. He too must find his worth in God.

"Father," I prayed from the depths of my sleeping bag the night before I headed home, *"if I ever love a man again, I realize I must enter his life with an open hand and heart, not descend upon him from a grabbing, controlling, needy place. Please don't let me be afraid to trust. I want to be vulnerable in the right way. Please make my heart soft, but help me to guard it, not just throw it out there for anyone. I want total healing in my life so I can love more extravagantly. Help me to remember I am worth fighting for, and to never recklessly give myself away. Let me live what I have learned."*

I returned to Texas with that prayer on my lips. It carried me through the transition of leaving all that was familiar and moving into a university community as a single, divorced woman. By the time Mom and I packed up my classroom and shoved everything that wouldn't fit in my Rav4 into my storage unit, I felt ready to go.

April and May were tough. Even though I knew it was time, saying good-bye was difficult. I was leaving my entire support system: my therapist, my job, my friends and my church family.

Over those last few weeks I tried to connect with everyone dear to my heart. Janet, my precious friend from church made it easier by planning a fabulous Mexican-themed going away party for me. She invited everyone she could think of, including some of my students. They lavished me with songs, gifts, cards, and even gas money for my long drive to Tennessee!

I came away feeling truly loved by my church. Even though they had not always understood what I was going through as I suffered the consequences of an addiction that wasn't mine, they *did* love me. Love, as the Bible says, covers over a multitude of sins (1 Peter 4:8 NIV).

If I had it to do over, I would have been more open with my church from the beginning. Perhaps we could have worked together to support Jon without supporting his habit. Perhaps they would have ministered to us differently had they known about the addiction. I know some folks, especially the young people, were hurt by the discovery of Jon's "secret," and our subsequent divorce. Maybe transparency all along would have been better than a bad surprise. It's hard to say. What I *do* know is healing takes place in community, not in isolation. We need one another. We cannot go it alone. God designed us to walk with Him and with others.

I will not easily forget the feelings of isolation, loneliness, and fear of exposure that marked each time Jon relapsed and I went to church without him. I remember the sting of the stigma that came with divorce. It wasn't spoken. Maybe it was even imagined. Overnight I went from being part of a couple to being single. Things changed. Loyalties divided. Invitations decreased.

Never wanting anyone else to feel that way, I committed myself to creating my own personal culture of vulnerability and acceptance of people who experience real struggles in their lives. I decided when I became involved in another church I would initiate opportunities for people to be authentic about what was happening in their lives. I would choose to be part of ministries God could use to bring healing. Those decisions were deliberate. I didn't know how they would eventually play out, but I knew I wanted to make a difference within the body of Christ. I knew it had to begin with me.

"No longer," I vowed, *"will I hide behind the pillars of pride and fear."* I wanted to be willing to live transparently in my new community. Only God could help an introvert like me to break down my self-imposed barriers in order to reach out to others who might be hurting. It wasn't long before He provided my first opportunity to do just that, but first I had to get out of Texas.

Mom and I hugged and kissed and waved our way out of town with a loaded down Rav and two restless dogs. We happily chatted all the way to Arkansas. Seven hours and three potty stops later, we were finally parked in Mom's driveway.

"Thanks P's," I said, inching out of their carport the following morning. "I really appreciate you taking care of my girls. What else could I have done with them? Extra food is in the shed. Please don't feed them anything but Iams brand, and *nothing* from the table. It will make them sick."

"Okay. The dogs will be fine. We'll take good care of them. Promise! Love you. Jesus be with you. Safe travels." Mom held a copper watering can in one hand while flapping the other up and down in her familiar wave. I could tell she wanted to cry. So did I.

I hated leaving the girls. The P's aren't dog people. It was a sacrifice for them to keep the girls for the summer while I attended grad school in another state. I knew being away from me would be hard on Snuffles and Whipper, but the dorm where I'd be staying had a NO PETS policy. My options were limited. I trusted they'd all survive for eight weeks. Hopefully, by then I'd have a home again.

Mom's tearful good-bye triggered buried memories of a much younger me heading off to university for the first time. I was eighteen and carefree, excited to embark on a new adventure.

"Oh God, where has twenty years gone? Here I go again, in a car loaded down with clothing and a heart loaded with regrets."

My tears came as I turned onto the winding two-lane road that led toward Tennessee and I could no longer see Mom's pale hand fluttering in my rear view mirror.

"Father, forgive me for remembering the regrets. Let me view them as milestones. Please protect the P's. Protect my girls. Protect me on this new adventure. I'm definitely older—please help me to be wiser than when I first arrived on campus."

Two Days Later

The dorm room door's familiar click messed with my mind. Déjà vu . . . again. It's interesting how a single sound can trigger a flood of memories. Since I'd returned to my alma mater, many experiences had an eerily familiar tone. Sixteen years had passed since commencement weekend, when I'd happily marched the very same halls in a black cap and gown. I felt like everything, and nothing, had changed.

Kicking off my sparkly sandals, I surveyed the ten by fifteen foot space that was my new home. *Is this what my life is reduced to; a few square feet of rented room, a laptop, and enough clothing to overflow two dormitory closets?* Memories of my former life leapt from behind the safety of busyness, pouncing on my unsuspecting soul. Rather than flinging them back, I allowed them to draw me to my Texas home where I mentally wandered through a life no longer mine.

Memory persisted in placing Jon's haunting mug shot from last June before my mind's eye. Although I viewed it only once, I will neither forget the hollowness of his face, nor the steel coldness of his once-lively and loving eyes.

"He's still there, isn't he, Lord? After all I've done this year, it's hard to imagine he's still sitting in that cell. Please visit him there. Show him Your love now that his mind is substance-free. Heal him, God."

"That's what drugs do to a person." I thought about how many times well-meaning observers repeated the phrase in search of something to say that would alleviate the ache of knowing what happened to Jon.

What drugs do to a person, I wanted to shout, *is cause far more damage than that person may ever acknowledge. No addicted person lives a life solely unto themselves. The residual effects of chemical dependency run through the veins of anyone who dares to love them. I KNOW what drugs do to a person!*

Finding myself enclosed by four bare walls, sharing a bathroom with a stranger, and staring at the underside of a bunk bed, I wondered if Jon was even cognizant of the fact that his choices had placed me in a cell-block too. *Do you have any idea what you've done?* My mind screamed the question multiple times since the disintegration of our marriage. It was difficult for me to accept that another thing certain drugs "do" is continue to anesthetize the user to the pain they have caused long after the user is removed from the drugs or the drugs from the user. Sometimes the drug of denial numbs for a lifetime and prevents a person from making amends.

As my dorm room door clicked closed, I remembered the thousands of times I'd heard its familiar sound as an undergrad student on that very campus, and of how many nights I'd flopped onto my narrow dormitory bed, with its plastic-covered mattress crunching through the sheets, begging God to bless whatever relationship I was in. I'd prayed for many things back then, but mostly for a good husband and a home of my own.

Thirty-eight is not much different than eighteen, I thought, scanning my surroundings. *I am right back where I began, with the very same heart dreams I had twenty years ago. I have come full circle.*

Chapter 15

Beauty for Ashes

"To console those who mourn in Zion,
To give them beauty for ashes,
The oil of joy for mourning,
The garment of praise for the spirit of heaviness;
That they may be called trees of righteousness,
The planting of the Lord, that He may be glorified."
Isaiah 61:3 (NKJV)

June—July 2008

"Are you a teacher?" I innocently asked a petite platinum blonde as we stood awaiting our student ID snapshots.

"Noooo," she responded slowly, eyeing me all the way up and then back down to my platform wedge sandals. "My husband flew the coop and my nest is empty, so I came back to school."

Smiling, I stepped closer.

"This is my chance to try on transparency for the first time in my new surroundings. I'm ready, Lord. I'm real."

Feeling awkwardly Amazon-womanish, at five foot nine and high heels, I bent toward the petite lady's sparkly headband and almost whispered, "Mine did, too. I know exactly what you mean."

That brief, honest exchange was the beginning of a precious friendship between Nancy and me. She, like Meredith, Aubrey and Darcy, would become a season-pass holder to all God was redeeming in my life. For me, one of the worst things about starting over is finding new face-to-face friends. It's hard to strike that just-right balance of trust, transparency and spirituality, let alone discover someone with enough silliness to prevent me from taking myself too seriously. Nancy turned out to be all of those things, with a Latina verve that could dazzle the Pope. Her God-story, as I soon learned, is a book of its own. I was grateful to have discovered a kindred spirit so soon after arriving on campus.

"You promised to give me the desires of my heart." I wrote to God on the June 5, 2008. He gently reminded me the second part of his promise in Psalm 37:4 (NKJV) begins with the phrase, "Delight yourself also in the Lord . . ."

"I am delighting in You, God. I heard You when You said I needed to seek You first and then everything else will be added to me (Matthew 6:33 NKJV). I keep hearing You every time I come across one of those "seek Me" verses You keep giving to me. I promise. I won't allow anything to separate us. I will "Seek the LORD while He may be found, call upon Him while He is near" (Isaiah 55:6 NKJV).

My desire to please God outweighed anything else that summer had to offer. He and I continued our conversation about my heart's desires three days later. Beneath a Maya Angelou quote in my journal, which says, "A woman's heart should be so hidden in God that a man has to seek Him just to find her," I wrote this simple prayer: *"Lord, hide my heart in You. Don't let me wear it on my sleeve."*

I was beginning to get used to having God as my only lover. I could certainly trust Him to handle my heart with more care than anyone else ever had. Speaking of caring for my heart, remember that verse Isaiah 65:24 (NIV), where God says, "Before they call I will answer; while they are still speaking I will hear?" That's exactly what happened next as God answered one of my deepest, most private prayers. Like me, if you've ever experienced abuse from someone who was abusing drugs or alcohol you may have wondered if they *intended* to treat you badly.

Perhaps they didn't really mean it. Or perhaps they don't even remember what they did. We try to ease our pain by pretending they're too inebriated to know what they're doing. *It doesn't seem so bad if they don't know they're doing it,* right? I'd done that, innumerable times, with Jon's neglect. I'd even done it with Mr. Roberts' shunning. As my perpetual emotional dust storm settled into stillness at the beginning of that life-transforming summer, I began to realize I longed for at least an acknowledgment from Jon.

"Father," I prayed one evening as my Asics ate up another quarter-mile of track. *"I know we cannot expect other people to apologize to us. You know I've forgiven Jon and released him from the bondage of my expectations. Sometimes I just wonder if he remembers anything, anything at all about our life together. Anything about how he hurt me."*

I continued my one-sided conversation as I left the track and headed for a set of steep concrete steps leading to the university promenade. I loved finishing my workouts with several runs up and down those steps. My body, as well as my mind became more fit every day as I burned off the side effects of years of emotional-eating.

You know about emotional eating, right? That what-can-I-do-to-make-myself-feel-better stress-snacking that happens when we choose to numb our empty souls with empty calories? I hate admitting those donuts I'd sworn to consume every time Jon smoked a cigarette turned out to be more than just idle threats after all. It may not have always been Krispy Kreme that calmed *my* nerves through the years, but it was usually something on the sweet side, consumed in secret and remembered with shame when my body didn't know what to do with the extra calories and stored them in places my bathroom mirror ruthlessly revealed.

"I'm truly sorry about that, Lord. And not just because of the physical consequences. But because I chose to have other gods before You."

My prayer swung like a pendulum between asking for some shred of admission from Jon, proving he realized how much he hijacked my dreams and hurt my soul, and repenting of all the times I'd turned to food instead of turning to Jesus. When I finished running those steps, I was physically and mentally "tuckered out." That was the seventh of June.

Almost two weeks later, I received a letter from Jon in jail. It was postmarked June 3, 2008, four days before I called upon God to jog Jon's memory so I could experience full closure. Isn't our Father incredibly gracious? I realize the rarity of the gifts of remembrance, reconciliation and closure. I've participated in several 12 Step groups where members mourn the fact they've never received any such grace from those who wounded them. I don't know why I became one of redemption's recipients, but I do know the weight that came off my soul with every sentence in Jon's eight-page handwritten letter. Glimpsing my name on that envelope in Jon's familiar all-caps printing triggered a vivid memory of the last time I'd seen him in person.

Flashback

I was summoned from staff meeting by the school secretary to answer a pleading phone call that included trembling phrases like, "I'm hungry" and "I need you to help me." Initially thinking it was a parent, I'd answered the phone in my confident teacher voice. When I heard Jon's near-tearful requests, my professional façade crumbled into panic.

"Where are you?" I asked. No one had heard from him for weeks.

"I'm in the city. I've been living on the streets. Ran out of money a while back. Made some enemies and can't seem to get back on my feet. Nobody wants to help me. I'm so hungry."

I mentally prayed, *"Should I go, Lord? Is it safe to meet with him? Will he hurt me?"*

I heard nothing from Jon since we'd said our good-byes in Dr. Fox's office. I'd only learned through the family grapevine that he hit everyone up for cash until his phone calls were no longer welcome. According to Mona, he was living a rough lifestyle and could not be trusted. Of course, *I* knew that better than anyone. I went to meet him anyway.

Entering a filthy Main Street Mexican restaurant 40 minutes later, my eyes adjusted to the dim lighting, but not to the marked change in the face, demeanor and countenance of the man I'd married barefoot on the beach thirteen years before. A red tropical-style shirt with martini glasses and Spanish olives scattered over it in a busy, gaudy pattern swallowed his thin frame. He slumped alone at a table for four. As our eyes met, he motioned toward a debit card on the edge of the table, muttering, "There's no account to go with that card."

"Then why is it out here?" Our conversation began with his explanation of the debit card's presence. The card was a hollow promise of payment so the waitress would get the chips and salsa started for the "hungry, homeless addict," as Jon referred to himself.

When the chip basket came, I reached for his corpse of a hand in an automatic gesture that brought tears to two pairs of eyes. Holding hands in prayer before a meal was something we'd done countless times at home and in restaurants over the years. Rather than recoil from the pain of connecting on that level, Jon let me pray.

He ordered the enchilada dinner and ravenously devoured three or four bites before pushing the plate away. It was unusual for him not to clean his plate, but everything about him that day was a paradox. While I finished my chile rellenos, Jon, a normally quiet person, talked incessantly. He bragged about being a "man of my word" on the streets and told of "important people" he'd rubbed shoulders with, as if I *cared* that he met the "kingpin" of the North Texas drug trade.

Jon was not at all the Jon I'd known. From the strange jeans—I'd never seen him in anything but Levi 501's—to the loud shirt and even louder talk, *he* was a stranger. I felt like I was on a bad blind date and just wanted to escape as fast as I could.

After I paid the bill, Jon asked if I could please take him somewhere. "Where?" I cautiously inquired.

"Well, I don't really have anywhere to go. And my sisters won't even talk to me, after all I've done to help *them*. Do you think you could take me to Bob and Aubrey's? I bet he's got some work I can do."

"I don't know. You can use my phone to call and ask." Handing him my phone, I silently prayed for wisdom as we stepped outside into the sunshine. Part of me wanted to run, part of me hated to leave him in his emaciated state. I didn't know what to do, but I'm the kind of person who gets out of my car to move a snapping turtle off the highway so it won't get squashed. I felt like Jon was a snapper with a semi headed straight for him. I couldn't just walk away.

When Bob said, "Come on." I again defaulted to rescue mode. *Jon needs help. Don't Christians always say, "Yes"?* Sometimes enabling is all we know. It would be years before I understood the roots of my own inability to say, "No." Hindsight tells me I only prolonged Jon's ability to abuse himself and others by continually providing a way of escape from the messes he created. My final encounter with him was no different.

An Apology

After all that happened between us, seeing Jon's handwriting on the envelope released an uncontainable flood of memories and emotions. Although I was reticent to open it, I couldn't resist. Perhaps I can best share the gist of Jon's letter by sharing my response.

June 19, 2008

Dear Jon,

Today I received the three weeks worth of mail our Post Office finally decided to forward. I stood in line at the university deli with this giant armload of mail, ordered a couscous salad and some roasted-red-pepper-and-tomato bisque, then sat down to eat my lunch and sift through the pile before class. Of course, my whole day came to a halt when I saw the envelope from you. I never expected to hear from you again. I wondered what angry, hurtful things you had to say this time about the superfluous things of life.

Although you caught me off guard, I was pleasantly surprised with the way you began your letter . . . with memories, pleasant ones, ones only you and I know about. I nearly choked on my couscous and bisque as I ate up every word you wrote. As painful as memory lane is, you were the witness to my life for nearly 13 years. That's a lot of history. You mentioned things I was sure you had forgotten and things I HAD forgotten—like that we both loved the same wedding dress from those enormous, expensive bridal books. That dress still haunts me because I cannot seem to garage sale it or give it away, and here it hangs, in this dormitory closet, in the same pink bag it traveled to Costa Rica in the very first time.

I really don't know what to say. I'm scanning your letter now. It's nighttime and I've gone over and over it in my mind. I know I cannot sleep until I respond and lick the envelope, and there is just a lot of pain on these pages.

Yes, I remember the beautiful letter you wrote to Chloé while you were at The Rehab. And I do recall telling you I wished you would write me a letter like that. I just wanted to know you thought and cared deeply for me like you did her. I didn't understand why you couldn't say something meaningful to me after a decade of marriage, but you could pour your heart out in apology to her after only loving her for 8 months. You said, "I knew if I ever wrote you a letter like that, it would be to say good-bye." Why did "I'm sorry" have to mean "good-bye?"

Thank you for your long list of "I'm sorrys." I forgave you as the list happened. I couldn't bear to hold it all against you. I never expected you to be "my perfect husband." I just wanted you to love me, to want to be with me, to enjoy me as your wife. It felt like you spent our marriage trying to get away from me. I never truly understood that, but it was the most pervasive feeling of our life together. That hurt more than any one act—just the general impression that somehow I was unloved by the one who promised he loved me with words, but whose actions continually denied it. It really affected the way I viewed myself as a woman. I felt unattractive and unlovely, undesirable, and I struggled with self-esteem because of the continual rejection. I loved you and I just wanted you to love me back.

Of course, the assaults against yourself, me, and our marriage and life together became so great that I had to begin shutting my heart down in order to survive it all. That one scary, manipulative phone call you begged my forgiveness for was the final straw for me. From that point forward, I just started cauterizing all the wounds and begging God to set me free from the pain. I couldn't do anything else. I'm sure you can understand that. But thank you for acknowledging you would take it back if you could. I'm glad you regret making the call. It really, really hurt to be used like that.

Enclosed is a copy of my journal from the day our divorce was final. You can pretty much see by that time, God was already starting the healing process with me. I'm still in that process because I too, have memories to deal with and regrets to overcome as I face turning 39 without realizing many of the dreams I had for my life

From your words, I gather that you and God are doing similar things. If all this is what it takes to refine us and fit us for a life of total dependence on God, then Eternity will be worth it. Maybe this is the way it had to be. Maybe we weren't supposed to live comfortable, normal lives because we'd have forgotten Him. This process has forced us to cling to Him because we have nothing and no one else. Maybe that's where we need to be. It's my only source of comfort.

I pray for you whenever the Holy Spirit brings you to mind, which is pretty much daily. I know this has been a difficult, lonely year for you. I've never wished you harm and hate that you've suffered in so many ways.

. . . Jon, I wish you only peace. Accept my complete forgiveness just as I offer it, no strings attached. You are a child of God. You are precious to Him, and you are precious to me. I'm glad you remember some of the good times and the happy things of our life together. I will try to do the same. May God bless you as you pick up the pieces, and I hope it will be a little easier knowing that I accept and appreciate the extreme effort it took for you to write what you wrote to me. I am thankful for this opportunity for us to make a drug-free closure.

Love and prayer,
Juliet

Sealing that letter to Jon sealed my freedom from the chains of our shared past. His prayerful, purposeful attempt to make emotional amends completely released me from any binding threads of uncertainty regarding his memory. When I dropped it in the mailbox on my way to class the next morning, an invisible barbell lifted from my shoulders. I felt so light I skipped up three sets of stairs to the Ed/Psych building without stopping to catch my breath.

Perhaps my new workout routine is paying off! Or perhaps my heart is just so free nothing can slow me down.

"Thank You, Lord God! You saw my deep need for healing in those dark, secret places and You answered even before I asked. You've got my back, Lord . . . You've got my heart. I love You."

Wanting God to make me wiser than I had ever been, I sought His counsel for everything, including house hunting. In-between studying for *Action Research* and *The Art of Teaching Writing*, I'd managed to locate a realtor who, on the cusp of the 2008 real estate crisis, became an advocate for a first-time home buyer like me. Vivian was as southern belle as her name, but she meant business. When I shared my "dream list" with her, she scanned it and said, "There aren't many Cape Cods around here, darlin', but we'll see what we can do."

While I was still living in the pool house, I'd drawn up another list. This time it was a list of things I wanted in a home. Dr. Alan and Darcy, believing God cares even for details like dormers and porches, kept a copy on their refrigerator door. They joined me in praying over it for months, while encouraging me to save every spare penny toward a down payment. We prayed with faith, believing that far more than a garden tub and a cook-friendly kitchen, I needed a place where I would feel safe as a single woman living alone. A place that *felt* homey. A place to heal.

By the twentieth of June, Vivian scored. I made an offer on a four bedroom, three bath Cape Cod style home with a rocking chair front porch that would have made Scarlett O'Hara smile. It was way too much house for me, but the price and location were irresistible. I loved the neighborhood with its half-acre lots and older residents with their flowering trees and well-kept lawns. I loved the privacy of a cul-de-sac.

In duplicate emails to Aubrey and Darcy I wrote, *I made an offer today. Someone else made one this morning and I made one this afternoon. Vivian is sending them together to the bank which owns the home because it's a foreclosure. It is a lot of house for $132, 900, but it needs carpet and paint. If they accept my offer, I'll have it inspected next week and we'll go from there. Please pray.*

To God I said, "*Father, I love this place. Yes, it needs a lot of work. But I'm not afraid of work. It feels like home. Please, please, please . . . I mean, if it is Your will and within Your plan for my life, make a way for me to be able to purchase this house. Amen.*" Then I waited.

Just as my first summer session closed, I got a contract on the house. We were set to close on July 21, 2008. Because the lender initially frowned upon the fact I had not paid rent for almost two years, I wrote an honest email to the loan officer, explaining I'd lived with friends since my husband bailed on our marriage. I described Dr. Alan and Darcy's generosity, "which included not charging me rent," and my savings plan, "which enabled me to accumulate a sizable down payment on a teacher's salary."

The bank called me in for a face-to-face meeting, requesting a printed, notarized copy of the emailed letter. "*God, this is humiliating,*" I prayed while nervously crossing and uncrossing my legs as I sat across from a no-nonsense woman in her freezing-cold, glass-fronted office. "*Please vindicate me from the consequences of Jon's choices.*"

"I must admit this is the first time a potential buyer has been so forthright about their circumstances. But all of your paperwork is in order, your earnest money is good, and your teaching contract guarantees a salary which will enable you to make the payments on this property," she said after several excruciating minutes of flipping through my file and crunching the numbers with flying fingers. "Let me gather a couple of signatures and I'll be right back." She left the office on a high-heeled mission while I continued my prayer.

"Okay," she startled me with the suddenness of her reappearance, "If you would just sign here . . . and here, you can be on your way. Thank you for the opportunity to let us help you begin your new life in a new home." For the first time, she looked me in the eye and smiled as I pushed the paperwork back to her. We stood to shake hands across the desk. The atmosphere in that office had definitely shifted from subzero to almost tropical.

"*Praise You, Father! You do melt even the skeptical hearts of bankers!*" Ninety miles evaporated under my Rav4 as I flew back to campus on the wings of hope.

Our heavenly Father's willingness to honor my dream-list for a home revealed His tenderness toward the dreams of my heart. Ever since I'd been a gangly girl playing *Little House on the Prairie* in a Texas cow pasture with Annie and the neighbor kids, I'd dreamt of living in a home with a massive front porch and enough space to invite all my loved ones for sleepovers. When I called Darcy to announce God's answer to our prayers, I exclaimed, "If He can see my heart about that, I'd better get busy making my list for a godly husband!"

I wasn't joking. Being single was something I neither enjoyed nor envisioned myself doing forever. My "Godly Husband" list began filling pages in my journal. But it morphed into something more, because as I searched the Bible looking for references about husbands, the Holy Spirit revealed even more Scriptures about wives. So I divided my journal pages in half and wrote, *"A Godly Wife,"* on one side and *"A Godly Husband"* on the other. Then I made a bulleted list with Bible references for each side. The whole project took several days of my morning time with God.

Out of that initiative came the realization that if He were to one day grant my request for a husband who remotely reflected my wish list, I probably needed to allow Him to refine me into the kind of wife I'd discovered in Proverbs, First Peter, and Ephesians.

"Lord, I want to have the beauty of a gentle, quiet spirit," I prayed, *"Please help me to cease striving. Mold me into a woman who is ready for the kind of man who puts You first. Make me more like You and less like the wife I've been in the past. Grant me the patience to wait for the man on this list, and the courage not to compromise in the meantime."*

With that prayer, I held up my journal to God. Here's what He saw:

A Godly Wife

Proverbs 31

- *Is a crown to her husband*
- *Is rare*
- *Will do her husband good and not evil all the days of her life*
- *Works willingly*
- *Brings food from afar*
- *Gets up early and takes care of her family*
- *Has a business mind*
- *Makes wise transactions*
- *Is strong*
- *Invests in quality*
- *Works into the night*
- *Helps people in need*
- *Cares for her appearance*
- *Has strength and dignity*
- *Speaks with wisdom and kindness*
- *Is not idle or lazy*
- *Is praised by her husband and blessed by her children*
- *Fears the Lord*

1 Corinthians 7:3, 11 and 35
- *Fulfills "benevolence" (sex)*
- *Doesn't depart from her husband*
- *Cares for how she may please her husband*

Ephesians 5:23 and 33
- *Submits to her husband*
- *Respects her husband*

1 Peter 3:1-2, 4
- *Wins her husband by submissive (not dominating) behavior*
- *Has the beauty of a gentle, quiet spirit*

Titus 2:4
- *Listens to the counsel of older women on how to love a husband*
- *Self-controlled*
- *Pure*
- *Busy at home*
- *Kind*
- *Submissive*

A Godly Husband

Proverbs 12:4, 31:10-11, 23
- *Is proud of a virtuous wife*
- *Trusts his wife in his heart*
- *Is respected*

Genesis 26:8, 24: 67, 25:21
- *"Caresses" his wife—even when they are old*
- *Finds comfort in loving and making love to his wife*
- *Prays for his wife*

Titus 2:6
- *Is considerate of his wife*
- *Treats her with respect*
- *Is self-controlled*

Proverbs 31:23, 28, 31
- *Is a leader*

- *Praises his wife and notices what she does*
- *Talks about her in an honorable way with friends and peers*
- *Praises his wife with words of affirmation*

Matthew 1:19
- *Does not shame or humiliate his wife in public*

1 Corinthians 7:3, 36
- *Fulfills "benevolence" (sex)*
- *Doesn't take a hundred years to decide whether or not he wants to marry her*

Ephesians 5:28-29, 31
- *Loves his wife as himself*
- *Nourishes and cherishes her*
- *Doesn't allow his relationship with his parents to interfere with his marriage*

"And God," I continued confidently, *"if You could please give me a husband who has a heart for ministry and helping others, I know we could really make a difference for Your kingdom. I don't want a man who is only interested in spending his weekends watching sports and entertaining himself. I want someone who really cares about the suffering in this world, someone who will work with me to help alleviate it."*

In addition to all of that, I also slipped in a request for a couple of minor details in the "externals" department. Hey, it never hurts to ask, right? The Lord didn't create our sense of sight for nothing. He knows what pleases the senses He gave us.

A few days later Vivian called to say the bank accepted my offer on the house and had moved the closing date up by two weeks.

"Woohoo God! Praise You for Your hand in this! Forgive me for doubting. I know that according to Psalms 91:9 (KJV), You are my habitation. If You are my home, I never need to feel homeless. I also know I shall weep when Vivian hands me the keys to my new house on Cooper's Cove. It feels like forever since I've had my very own space."

Statistics

Although I anxiously anticipated my closing date, I'd have to tread through four weeks of statistics before I moved in. Statistics gave me grief. I still recall the nail-biting anguish of taking a graduate level stats course after thirteen years of teaching first grade math. I felt like I had flown to a foreign country where everyone spoke a language I'd never heard, yet expected me to respond fluently. Talk about culture shock! I was more lost than Gilligan ever thought about being. Thankfully, my professor, Dr. Kevin Green, was a patient man. My Savior also provided a tutor named Tizzana. Without her, I may not have survived the shipwreck that was EDUC 566, also known as *Statistics*.

Everything hinged on that particular class. In my graduate program, if I got a grade lower than a B, I would technically not pass. If I "failed," I would not have enough credits to renew my private-school teaching certification, which I needed in order to reach the pay scale that would allow me to purchase my home. All of the financial information in my contract was based on the salary I would receive if I passed every class and renewed my professional certification.

To add additional pressure, EDUC 566 was an "intensive," which meant it met from 1 to 5:15 p.m. each day. Dr. Green explained the material we would cover every single DAY would be what is normally covered in a WEEK during a regular semester course! I was terrified.

My experience may resonate with those of you who are not "math people." Here's how I shared it with my friends via email when I sent out an SOS for prayer:

On Tuesday I cried during Statistics class. The volume of information and the rate it was being introduced overwhelmed me. Afterward, I told Dr. Green he may as well be speaking Chinese.

I had absolutely no clue what he was talking about. I asked if I should withdraw. After explaining the grade is based on four components, each worth 25%, Dr. Green recommended I try to stick it out through the first week and see how the test goes.

I'm torn. I've never made a failing grade, and I do not want to make history now. As you know, I tend to be stubborn. I don't "throw in the towel" without a good fight. The problem is . . . I'm worn out. I don't know if I can do this. I feel like my only choices are to fail or give up and drop out.

I begged my mother to specifically pray for God to place someone in my life who could help me through that class. The following day I met Tizzana, a high school math teacher who was also taking EDUC 566 for certification renewal. Observing my stress, that angel-girl invited me to her apartment after class to help me with homework.

In order to save cash, I was living on peanut butter and bread. Tizzana not only spent four hours tutoring me, she also cooked steamed asparagus and mashed potatoes and gravy, serving my plate as I sat at her table working problem after problem. Her kindness was a direct answer to Mrs. P's plea.

"Thank You, Lord, for Tizzana," I prayed after a tutoring session. "*I asked for someone to walk me through this without being condescending. Forgive me for not believing such a person existed. I prayed, but lacked the faith. Yet You still came through!*"

My *Art of Teaching and Writing* course turned out to be even more satisfying than Tizzana's mashed potatoes. It was there I met Joelle Callahan. God would use her to forever alter the course of my life.

Joelle was brilliant. Her comments in class and the way she carried herself set her apart. She was young, blonde, and zippy, headed for a Ph.D. She wasn't someone I'd naturally hang out with. Especially when I was feeling dumb and outdated, thanks to my Statistics class. But God had special plans for our friendship. Joelle was more down-to-earth and deeply spiritual than I initially guessed. She was a pastor's daughter, which proved to be an interesting tidbit she used as a conversation opener one day after class.

"Hey, I'm not really one to do this kind of thing, but . . . " As soon as the professor assigned our collaborative project, Joelle had marched directly across the room, stopped at my table, and bent close to my ear. I thought she was going to ask for my notes or something, but she finished her sentence with, ". . . are you seeing anyone? As in a guy? As in dating?" Without stopping for a reply, she continued, "You see, I know someone in the ministry with my father in Florida, and I think you two would really hit it off."

"Uhhhh. No. I'm not seeing anyone. I'm just not interested right now. I've recently come out of some rough stuff and I'm trying to give myself time to recover."

"I understand completely. I don't want to pressure you, but the Holy Spirit has impressed me strongly about this ever since you shared your poem. I think you two might be kindred spirits. Would you at least be willing to give me your phone number to share with him?"

I'd written a poem for class, about Christ's ministry to Mary Magdalene. Several people, including Joelle, asked for a copy afterwards. I called it "Sermon in the Sand." Unbeknownst to them, the poem was really about me. How gracious of our God, to take my simple words and use them to impress a pastor's daughter, who saw my heart and wanted to connect it with another similar heart.

"Thank you for your interest, but I'm not comfortable with passing my phone number to a stranger." I was flattered, but resistant.

"I'm scared, Lord. And I don't know Joelle well enough to completely trust her judgment. Florida is a long way from here. I don't have time to fiddle with trying to get to know someone far away."

"Okay. Well, please let me know if you change your mind." Joelle stood up and gathered her things. We walked out of class together, chatting mundanely, thinking deeply. Joelle's deep thoughts persisted until she acted upon them a second time.

Two days later, she again approached me, this time with her laptop open to a church web page. "I know you said you weren't interested," she began, "but I just wanted to show you his picture. He's really handsome and he has a great South African accent, in addition to being passionate about God, of course."

I couldn't help but look. He *was* appealing to the eyes, but I had learned that eye-candy can cause cavities of the soul.

"Isn't he good-looking?" Joelle prompted.

Several females had now gathered around the screen.

"I'd sit in his pew in a heartbeat, Honey," Caroline said with her Tennessee accent.

"You'd have to ask me twice what the sermon was about, though," another chimed in. "I think you should take Joelle up on her offer."

"I'm sorry," Joelle apologized for causing a commotion. "I just wanted you to see him for yourself. I recently went on a mission trip to Mexico. He was in our group. I got to know him a little and he seems like a wonderful guy. He's never been married."

"He *is* cute," I conceded, "and I'm sure he's very nice. I'm just not sure I'm up for this right now."

"How about if I just give him your email address?" She pressed. That way there's no obligation to actually speak with him." Joelle should have been a salesperson.

"Okay, okay. You can give him my email."

The ladies cheered. Joelle danced a victory jig.

On Saturday night at 8:14 p.m., his name showed up in my inbox. André Van Heerden. *Hmmm.* Apparently Joelle had been using her gifts of persuasion on him as well. I immediately Googled him.

Oh, here he is . . . Pastor of the Lime Grove Christian Church in Smalltown, Florida.

"Lord, please don't let me get tangled up in anything that is not of You. You know I can't handle any more drama in my life. Statistics class is enough for right now."

Following my prayer, I opened the email and read these words:

Hello Juliet,

My name is André and I'm writing to you after Joelle mentioned she met you and suggested we become friends. I'm sure you also prefer to consider only a friendship, with nothing more right now, asking God to impress us both if there is to be anything more in the future.

Great start. I guess Joelle warned him of my skittishness. I don't have any agendas, but hey . . . Sounds like he's just as nervous as me. Good.

His email continued:

I am very excited and very passionate about preaching, one-on-one nurturing, and about creating a website for people who are facing divorce, the loss of a loved one, past abuse, addictions, financial problems, depression, etc. There isn't much help available within churches in general for people facing personal and private issues and pain. If you want to check it out, the web address is www.relevantlifesolutions.org.

"Wow! Okay, Joelle. I see where you are coming from. He's speaking my language right here." I spoke aloud to my laptop. "How many times, God, have I desired in the past for a pastor to seek to understand and have compassion for people who suffer these things? How interesting these issues are this man's passions."

I also connect well with children and enjoy the way they appreciate silliness and respond when we are real and open with them.

To prove that point, he attached an image of himself surrounded by happy school kids. Everyone made silly faces for the camera. The next paragraph made me choke a little, because, seriously, who mentions the words "life partner" in an introductory email?

I would enjoy building a friendship on a spiritual foundation where we can encourage each other in our walk with God. I'm sending you some pictures that best depict my personality. Please be assured I am praying for God to make it very clear to me regarding a life partner, and that there will be absolutely no pressure from my side for anything more than just friendship.

André
P.S. My parents live in Chattanooga and I might be there this week.

I scrutinized the pictures he attached, especially the one of him on his bicycle. I tried *not* to like anything too much. The following afternoon, I responded. But only after forwarding André's email to Annie and Eddie and receiving Eddie's no-nonsense green light to proceed with caution.

"Go ahead and have a conversation. He doesn't sound like a pervert or anything," Eddie said.

Part of my email to Sis said, "*Please, just read and delete. If I ever do date this man, I don't think he should know I sent him through the weasel-screening process first.*"

I simply did not trust my own judgment. I was taking God's Word practically when He says there is safety in a multitude of counselors (Proverbs 11:14 NKJV). That's why I also forwarded his email to Dr. Alan and Darcy, and to my father.

Dad's response was typically concise.

Okay, so he's handsome, muscular, runs, bikes, swims, believes in God and loves kids. Big Whoop! Love you, Dad.

Thanks, Dad. I figured you wouldn't be impressed. That's what happens to parents, whose child's heart has become a casualty of someone else's addiction. They trust no one. I didn't hold my father's indifference against him. I was simply trying to include him in the conversation.

Darcy's reaction was by far the best:

Juliet,

Do I love this? Of course I love this!!! This guy is smokin' HOT! HOT! HOT! You better save some of that house-fixin' up money for a plane ticket to paradise! Good grief, girl, when God gives you a reward for being patient, He gives you the WHOLE ENCHILADA! I've been wondering if you've met anyone . . . So, as your nosy friend, I want to know:

- *How old is he?*
- *Why isn't he already snatched?*
- *Have you talked to him on the phone?*
- *And what's his deal about "FRIENDSHIP?"*

You tell him your friend from Texas said that his little biography and those pecs, oops . . . pics, and the Lord Himself impressed her enough for everyone. So no dilly-dallying around! Time's a wastin'. The "future" is NOW!
(Hey, don't actually tell him all that. He may never want to meet us!)

You sure he's for real? If God isn't involved, André is too good to be real. But I'm sure God is, so maybe this is finally the one out there for YOU! God is probably grinnin' and sayin' 'See, I told you I still have some good ones out there. You should listen to your friend Darcy more!'

Of course, you DO deserve the best. HE would be the lucky one. I know God has been looking out for you. Like Abraham, you stepped out in faith, moved everything to where God said to go, and took on a whole new life. Whatever happens, God will bless you with happiness.

Alan and I and so many people who love you are praying for you. I have had no doubt of God's plans for your life since that morning He woke you and told you to take action and pack up your house. You are so precious to Him. He has proven Himself over and over as you have trusted Him. He will not stop now!

Keep me updated.

Love you lots,
Darcy

I texted my reply. No time for long emails when I had a Statistics test to study for.

You made me laugh out loud. I don't know the answers to your questions. Haven't talked with him on the phone. Taking it easy. Will keep you posted. Love You. Thanks for prayers.

I did send an email to André, though. Texting felt too personal.

Hi André,

I've had to smile at Joelle's persistence. She was quite apologetic for her forthrightness when she chased me into the hallway last Thursday with her laptop open to your church website. I see she followed through on your end as well! Since she doesn't really know me, I find it brave of you to make contact.

I checked out your website. I know from personal experience how few resources are available within the context of our church for people who are dealing with some of those issues. I'll be interested to see how that resource is developed and used.

Walking with God is something I'm learning to do in new ways. I'm asking Him to give me ears to hear Him lately . . . pausing more to listen, trying to monologue less. Have you read John Eldredge's book, "Walking With God?" I've gleaned some things from it I'm trying to put into practice. If you have any experience in "listening" to God, I'm interested in someone from my generation's perspective, if you truly want to begin a dialogue.

Thank you for sharing your photos. I was trying to think of pictures that depict my personality. The ones on my blog from last summer's trip to Italy give a fairly accurate image of who I am. If you can wade through tons of writing, there are some pics of me dispersed throughout. It was quite an experience. Here's the link: www.ciaodirect.blogspot.com.

Juliet

A few hours later, his response came back:

Hello Juliet,

Well, I must say I am impressed with your blog. I really regret not having documented the mission trips I did to Peru in '06 and '07, and the ones I went on to Ukraine in '07 and Mexico in '08. What a great idea.

Yes, I have been very conscious of listening to God's voice. As a matter of fact, I was just listening to a sermon I did on the first Sabbath of the new year about that very thing. Elijah wanted to hear from God after his great victory on Mt. Carmel. There was an earthquake, a tornado, and a raging fire. But God never spoke through any of those dramatic events. He spoke by means of His still, small voice.

I have not read Eldredge's book, Walking With God, but I have read Wild at Heart and Waking the Dead. I find that getting up early in the mornings and spending time alone with God, studying His Word, meditating and praying is when I can get the closest to where I can hear Him. I find that any other time there is too much noise and distraction that muffles God's voice. When I spend that time with God, first thing in the day, it's as if the connection between us remains close for the rest of the day. When I don't, there is a lot of static.

It is also my deep desire to hear God's voice. It is truly the ultimate gift any human can receive. People on this planet strive for so many things that seem to be so important, not realizing that hearing God's voice would mean having all the resources contained within the mind of an all-wise, ever-present, all-powerful God right at their disposal. Unbelievable!

Right now I have come through a season of deep, earnest, committed petitioning before God. I want to hear His voice in very specific areas of my life. In the broad parameters of my life I have heard clearly from Him, but there are a few areas where I need clarity.

I am so excited to see that you love traveling and serving on mission trips. I absolutely love doing that! Please tell me more about what you see yourself doing in the future in this regard. Thanks for the email, and thanks for sharing your thoughts with me.
Seems like you enjoy writing?

André

I was hooked. I responded immediately.

André,

Glad you enjoyed the blog. It was a ministry project to encourage people at home to pray and to continue their support. Encouragingly, when I returned from Italy I went to the post office and one of the workers said, "Hello Juliet. Welcome home. I've been keeping up with you on your blog."

Someone in my church had put it in the local newspaper and it was widely read in the area. I think it had a positive impact on my local community because I was invited to share my story with different audiences. It also served as an icebreaker for several of my students and their parents at the beginning of last school year. Those who were Christians expressed thanks that I would be their child's teacher, based on what they had read on my blog.

As I sat in those Internet cafés in Italy, I had no idea how many people would be impacted by my stories. I feel blessed to have had the opportunity to be used by God in that small way.

Thank you for sharing your sermon points with me. I'd be interested in hearing the whole thing. Do you have a way to share?
Please forgive my brevity. There are other things to say, but I must log off and finish my Statistics homework. Taking five graduate level courses in eight weeks is not a very good idea, I've discovered. The next three weeks may finish me off!

Would love to chat more about your take on Eldredge's work, mission trips, your obvious passion for God and seeking His ear. Maybe in a future conversation . . .

Juliet
P.S. Yes. I must admit to being a closet writer. It's my best form of communication, I think.

I enjoyed the back-and-forth we were having. Email communication gives a person time to think and respond. I wasn't ready for phone calls yet, too much pressure. It wasn't long before André suggested a bridge between the two. Texting. He offered the bait in his next email. I took it.

Hello Juliet,

Phew . . . uuuh . . . I had no idea that you guys were busy with Masters programs! Thanks for responding. Please, please don't feel like you have to respond soon, or even write more than a line or two. If you send me your cell number, we can text back and forth . . . and finally, when you are at peace and have a bit of time . . . we can talk. My cell number is at the bottom of this page. Text me and I'll be able to text you back with some words of encouragement during your hectic days . . .

At the bottom of that email André included a poem he'd written six months before, along with the question, "Do you write poetry, too? I haven't metered out the rhythm of this one yet, but it seems to flow okay."

"Seriously, Lord. This man writes poetry? In addition to caring for hurting people and spending his own daily quiet time with You? And he's read two of the books that have recently impacted me spiritually? I'm intrigued, and I haven't even met him yet. Please protect my heart. This just seems too good to be true."

His poem was called "Three Strands." I liked it. In my emailed response to its author I used words like, "powerful," and "insightful." The last two stanzas went something like this:

> *Internet websites, an introduction or blind date,*
> *Everyone is trying to meet their perfect mate.*
> *Possibilities are endless, yet few find what's right.*
> *Couples meet and part. They know not their plight.*
> *Divorce, separation, loneliness and pain.*
> *Are relationships under some curse that won't wane?*
>
> *The answer is yes, when the strands are just two.*
> *Where is that third strand, seen by only a few?*
> *The third strand was woven into the first romantic pair,*
> *When God created them so perfect and fair.*
> *He Himself was the third strand. They were the two.*
> *His love would bind them forever and be their strong glue.*
> *When He opened their eyes to see beyond human love,*
> *They learned to practice it like God from above.*
> *A cord of three strands can't be broken or torn apart.*
> *And that's the secret to ultimate-love in your heart.*

I could sense both trepidation and hope in André's lines. How well I knew what could happen in a relationship with only two strands in place. And, although he'd never been married, he probably understood it too.

"Perhaps that's why he so carefully pads his emails with "spiritual friendship." He's surely been burned a time or two himself. Don't let us hurt each other, Father. Please make us wise. It's so easy to get caught up in conversations like these and allow emotions to get out of hand when we really know nothing about a person except the pictures they paint, and send, of themselves. I'm too tired to paint a picture. All I can be right now is me. Take me or leave me."

I plowed into the next three weeks with all the gusto I could muster. It had been a long time since I'd been on the other side of the "teacher desk." Although I loved school, no matter which side of the desk I was on, I was feeling the burn as finals approached. I wasn't as young as I'd been the last time I'd pulled all-nighters before my exams.

The day before our Statistics final, I brought an industrial sized roll of toilet paper to class as a joke because of all the tears that had been shed there. Poor Dr. Green, I'm sure he wasn't used to working with such a group of crybaby elementary school teachers. Eyeing the paper roll, he turned his palms upward and shrugged, "Should I even ask?"

Tizzana invited me to come over so she could help me with the last homework assignment. Her clock said 9:15 p.m. by the time we finished. As I was leaving, she handed me a copy of a practice test she had created.

When am I going to have time to do this, Father? I still have a paper to write and a project to complete!

Overwhelmed, I finally flipped through that practice test around 11:00 p.m. My mushy brain held three weeks worth of statistical information, which had been crammed into the past three days of class. In fifteen hours, I'd be tested over all of it. That one test was worth a quarter of my entire grade. I was distraught.

My mood lifted when I discovered André's name in my inbox. His email was short, but encouraging:

> *I'm not going to put you under any pressure by sending many emails right now. I'll just pray quietly in the background, asking God to impart special measures of strength, wisdom and support to you at this time. May He give you a tangible rush of Divine Energy that will invigorate and revitalize you.*
>
> *May you be able to rest in the knowledge that God is working all things for your good and that you have absolutely nothing to fear, but failing to surrender to His offer to carry all your burdens. May His Word fortify your mind and fill your being with courage and hope. There is nothing too difficult for God to handle, nor any problem too big for Him to solve.*
>
> *I'll be praying He gives you great wisdom and unusual composure as you wrestle through issues on multiple fronts. I know He'll help you through your stats test and that He will continue carrying you in His powerful, unseen arms of grace.*

To have a handsome, single man encourage me and pray with me like that was both inspirational and dangerous. All I'd ever wanted from Jon was that he be present in my life. That he support me in the things I was going through. That he pray for me and with me about real issues. To have a virtual stranger reach out and empathize with my stress, and be willing to pray for and with me about it—well, let's just say that whether or not André meant to touch a chord within my heart, he did.

That's why it's dangerous for men and women who are not in a God-ordained romantic relationship with one another to pray intimately alone together. If either person has a void in their life, prayer breaks down barriers and creates bonds the enemy can use to cross boundaries that should remain intact.

"Father, I am committed to You and You only. I trust that this man is too. Please help me not to read anything into his words that is not there. Don't let me be so needy that I depend upon his or anyone else's prayers. Help me to trust You."

When I could no longer stay awake, I went to sleep with a prayer for God to wake me early so I could spend time with Him before my big day began. Usually, when I think "early," I'm thinking 5 or 6 a.m. Guess what time He woke me up that Thursday? 2:45 a.m.!

"No, God! Don't You know how tired I am? Let me sleep."

I rolled over on my crackly, skinny dorm room mattress. But then I remembered what André shared about how God's voice cuts through the "static" when we get up early to spend time with Him. In my case the static was Statistics. I needed Him to cut through *that* and make it clear to me. I got up.

God impressed me to get my Bible, my Statistics book, notes and practice test and go down the hall to the lounge area of the dorm. I spread everything out on the desk.

"Well, Lord? Now what?"

Isaiah 50:7. That's what He gave me. I wrote it on an index card. *For the Lord God will help me; therefore shall I not be confounded: therefore I have set my face like a flint, and I know that I shall not be ashamed* (KJV).

I read that verse several times.

"I understand what You are saying. You want me to try. You are promising to help me. I will not be confounded. I will set my stubborn, pit bull jaw like a rock, and I will NOT be ashamed of the results of this test because I TRUST YOU."

Tears run down my cheeks as I write this, for even six years later His presence through that experience is tangible. I could feel His Spirit right there with me. Can feel Him *now* as I recount His goodness.

"I Love You, God. Thank You for this memory of how You care for the details of our lives. Oh, how You love us!"

God and I sat there together for hours. He helped me work through Tizzana's practice test, finding the formulas from my homework and the textbook. I wrote them on a three by five inch card in teeny-tiny handwriting with a mechanical pencil. Dr. Green allowed us to bring one index card, with anything we chose to write on it, to the test. I worked on mine until it was time to get ready for class.

At André's suggestion, Joelle and I met before our first class for prayer. It was a good idea to tap into the power of intercessory prayer. Although Joelle had aced Statistics in a previous semester, she sympathized and lifted me up. I felt such peace afterward, certain God was with me no matter what.

In our 8:00 a.m. class everyone from Statistics was in a panic. Our second period teacher caught wind of our distress and brought us chocolate. She also dismissed us an hour early so we could all go to Tizzana's to cram for the exam.

Tizzana's apartment was wall-to-wall with desperate teachers. She flitted from person to person, answering questions, explaining, and providing background knowledge to help the problems stick. My brain was so full NOTHING new was going in. I sat on my new friend's floor staring at my index card, praying no tears would smear my teensy-weensy formulas.

By 1:00 p.m. we transitioned to the classroom where Dr. Green conducted an hour-long review session. I was so sleepy by then I nodded off. I awoke with a jerk, fearing I drooled on my card. I hadn't.

At 2:15 p.m. the test began. We had until 5 p.m. When I received my test, panic returned. The test was thick.

"Help me, Jesus."

At the top of the first page I wrote, *The Lord God will help me, therefore I shall not be confounded, I have set my face like flint and I will not be ashamed.*

Then I wrote my name, worth 3 whole points.

Taking that test was surreal. I had a mental picture of Peter, walking on the water toward Jesus. As long as I kept my eyes on Him, trusting His hand to guide me, I felt okay. If I mentally disconnected from Him, I felt as if I were drowning in a sea of numbers. Continual prayer moved me from one problem to the next as I searched my index card for a formula that looked like it might fit. I worked methodically, knowing I could not afford even one careless mistake. The presence of the Lord was powerful within me.

The speedy people soon finished and exited. The average students dwindled until a few tortoises remained. Finally, only Dr. Kevin Green and I remained. He finished grading our homework and sat behind his desk in front of the huge, deserted classroom, clicking his pen, click-click, click-click, while the second hand waltzed around the clock.

By 4:45 p.m. I had done every problem I could do with my purple, plastic Dollar Store calculator. Too late, I'd discovered everyone else had hundred-dollar machines with all kinds of fancy formula buttons. I couldn't afford one of those, so during the test, mine kept saying EEEEEEE for error because it couldn't handle what I was asking it to do. I approached Dr. Green's desk and showed him my paper. "My calculator won't allow me do these problems."

"May I see it?"

When I presented my calculator, his mouth quickly concealed a smile that his eyes could not hide. Nodding with understanding he said, "You can use mine," as he handed me his two-pound calculator. I walked slowly back to my seat.

"Oh, Lord God. This is so humiliating. I don't know what to do with this thing. Should I ask for help, or just fake it? I will not be confounded. I will set my face like flint . . ."

I u-turned and humbly approached Dr. Green again. "I'm sorry, but I don't know how to use this. He patiently showed me which buttons I would need to press in order to discover the calculator's different functions. I'm positive he wasn't breaking any rules. It was a mini-lesson called "How to Use a *Real* Calculator 101."

Returning to my seat, I completed the last few problems moments before the clock ticked 5 p.m. Between that industrial wall clock's ticking and Dr. Green's mindless click-clicking, it's a wonder I finished. But God and I had done it! At the bottom of the last page I wrote, *This is one of the most difficult things I've done in my life, and I've been through some tough stuff! Thanks for your patience. I really wanted to finish.*

As I stepped outside into the July heat, I realized how frigid that classroom had been. A warm wave of relief washed over me.

"No matter what my grade turns out to be, Lord, You were with me. You guided me. You woke me early to prepare me. I'm so thankful I tried. I did my best. I am not ashamed."

Although my archenemy most certainly tried to use the whole Statistics experience to make me feel stupid and crush my spirit, he was defeated. I walked away with stronger faith and firsthand knowledge of what it meant to depend upon God moment-by-moment. I learned He can give us victories in the wounded-brain places where years of emotional stress have done serious cognitive damage. I felt so loved as He took the time to be with me in that numerical valley. There have been few seasons when I've experienced His presence so strongly as I did during that Statistics final. Each time I hold a calculator, I remember His faithfulness.

On Friday I received a "test results" email from Dr. Green. I seriously had no idea what my grade might be. When I saw it, I melted onto my dingy dorm-room carpet and wept on my face before God. Then I called my friend Nancy to make a date to celebrate.

"Woohoo!" I shouted into the phone as I shared my good news with her. "I got an 87%! Can you believe it? Not just enough to get by, but *exceedingly abundantly above all that I asked or thought!* Just as Ephesians 3:20 says. Isn't God gracious? Hallelujah!"

Nancy and I "partied" that Friday night like godly girls who have been through hell—we went to church and raised our hands and voices in worship! After two hours of solid praise, we prayed quietly together in my car, thanking God for His goodness and mercy. Even though we were both broken by the unfaithfulness of our spouses, we had met the Faithful One. His love had carried us to higher ground. From that stance, we could see the promise of a future, and not only the pain of our pasts.

André phoned on a Tuesday to announce his soon arrival in town to "visit his parents." We'd been texting back and forth and had prayed together a few times on the phone. I was convinced his parents were a smokescreen and he really just wanted to visit *me*. Joelle jumped up and down when I told her we were finally meeting face-to-face.

I wrote in my journal the night before our introduction: *André called. We talked about his website, chatted a little, and prayed together. I strongly feel the Holy Spirit when he prays. I cannot wait to get to know him better. God, give me wisdom and discernment.*

In an email to Annie the following morning I wrote, *"He's coming to Chattanooga today. We'll get together sometime this weekend. Whatever happens, I think he'll be a great spiritual resource."*

I'd been encouraged by his response to my complaint of feeling overwhelmed: "It will be great to meet you," he'd texted, "and hang out when you have time available that, eh, won't detract from your studies. I'll arrive Wednesday evening and leave Monday morning. As we continue in prayer on each other's behalf, be assured God will continue unfolding His awesome plan as you sign for your home, complete your studies and take your new job."

We made a plan to meet in front of the dormitory after my last class on Thursday. Joelle would join us. She and Colin, André's longtime friend, would come with us to P.F. Chang's for dinner. A group date felt safer to both of us.

"Lord, I'm so nervous." I prayed as I gathered my armload of books and began walking from my Rav to the dorm, thinking I'd have time to change and primp before everyone arrived. *"Help me to be calm on the outside. I don't care if I am thirty-eight, I may as well be eighteen the way my heart is pounding and my pits are sweating. What's wrong with me? It's only a man . . ."*

When I rounded the corner from the parking lot to the sidewalk leading to the dorm's front doors, I saw two men in dark sunglasses standing under a tree.

Is that them? Which one is which? Oh, the one on the phone must be André. Yes. That's him. I recognize his face now.

"Help me, Jesus. He really is more handsome than I thought."

"Hello. You must be Juliet." Colin reached out his hand and shook mine firmly. We chatted a moment as André finished up his phone call.

"Hi. I'm André. Sorry about that, I was just finalizing some church business." We shook hands and tried not to stare at one another.

"I'll just run in and drop my books off before Joelle gets here," I suggested, searching for a momentary escape. "Do you guys want to wait in the lobby where it's cooler?"

"No thank you," they chorused in matching South African accents.

How quaint. How awkward. How can I keep my eyes from popping out of my head? How come I've forgotten how much I hate the whole dating scene?

"Oh, Lord, I think I'm going to throw up."

I smiled and nodded as they decided to wait outside for Joelle, who was "two minutes away." The sidewalk to the dorm's front doors seemed endless. I could feel eyes behind sunglasses following me all the way.

"You know, Lord, there's a reason I hid behind a long distance relationship when I came to this campus, years ago. I don't like dating. I don't like the uncomfortable awkwardness of getting to know a stranger and being grilled like a piece of zucchini, with too many questions about things I don't want to answer. At least we're not going out alone. Remind me again why I'm doing this?"

I checked my hair. Scrutinized myself in the mirror on the back of the bathroom door. Brown pants, colorful gypsy top. Tall shoes. Smile. *Okay, no one will notice my nervous perspiration in this blouse. Casual is a good choice. It's only P.F. Changs. I don't want to appear overly-anxious-to-impress.*

On the way to the restaurant, spontaneous laughter erupted several times between the four of us. My edginess disappeared by the time we were seated. André sat to my right, reading the menu over my shoulder. We ordered several items to share around the table. I chose the coconut curried vegetables with tofu and suggested the stir-fried spicy eggplant as an appetizer. Neither Joelle nor Colin liked the eggplant. André and I had no problem scraping the plate together.

"*Wow, Lord, this isn't as awkward as I anticipated. I'm actually enjoying myself!*"

Dusk settled over the campus when André's tan Honda Accord pulled up in front of the dorm.

"Who wants to take the leftovers?" He asked, pushing a brown bag toward me.

"I don't have any way to keep them. You go right ahead."

"No thank you," Joelle replied as he tried to hand her the offering. "I'm good. But, why don't you guys plan to come over to my place for supper tomorrow night. I usually have a few people over on Friday evenings." Then she looked at me. "Some of the teachers from class will be there. You are welcome to join us. That way you two can continue that religious conversation you started earlier." She smiled and winked.

"Sounds like a plan," I replied just a little too quickly.

"Thank you, Joelle. I can't be there because I'm going to meet my daughter and son-in-law tomorrow evening, but I'm sure André will be happy to take you up on it." Colin turned sideways in the passenger seat, smiling broadly at Joelle while giving André the elbow. A moment of awkward silence later, both gentlemen jumped out to open our doors for us. We'd decided beforehand it would be most comfortable to travel with the men in front and girls in the back.

We all shook hands again, repeating, "Thank You" and "Goodnight" over and over. André finally found his tongue and promised Joelle he'd be there for dinner.

Back in my dorm room, I couldn't concentrate on the final assignment I needed to complete. My brain was a ball of electricity. It had been much easier to keep that man at arm's length before the chemistry kicked in. Isn't it funny how you just click with some people? You don't even have to touch. You just *know*.

I sent an email the following afternoon to Scott, the elder from my church in Texas. He'd written to say he'd gotten an encouraging letter from Jon in prison and wondered if I'd be interested in the contents. Here is part of my reply:

I'm realizing more and more God WANTS all of His children in Heaven and He will do WHATEVER IT TAKES to bring us to surrender. He does not force, but allows our own choices to take us where they do. However, He's always right there for the asking. I'm thankful to see this evidence of a positive change taking place in Jon. It's what I prayed for over a decade. Thanks for sharing.

On another personal note, I've been introduced to a single pastor. We had dinner last night. I don't know what will become of it, but he's definitely someone I'm interested in getting to know. He has experienced the transforming power of God's love. It's obvious in his countenance. That, to me, is very attractive.

Friday evening at Joelle's passed too quickly. Although her apartment was full of people, André and I only had eyes for each other. When the group gathered for prayer at the end of the Bible study, he took my hand in the circle. I don't remember who was on my other side. I only know I kept my head bowed and my eyes open, staring at our two hands with their fingers laced together.

"He's holding my hand in an intimate way, Lord. This is not your typical churchy side-by-side-we-stand-in-a-circle-of-prayer way to hold hands. Is this what he does? Or am I special?"

I dared not crane forward to see how he was holding the hand on his other side, but I wanted to.

André and I made plans to meet for church the following morning. He knew several South Africans who attended the same church I'd been visiting all summer. They'd invited him to a picnic that afternoon. He suggested Joelle and I come too.

We met in the lobby and took an elevator to the second floor where the Bible study classes were held. Issey Miyake's men's and women's fragrances mingled to fill the small space within seconds after the doors closed. We compared notes and chuckled about choosing the same brand.

"I get headaches with most perfumes," I explained. "This is one I *can* wear. I love it! But I save it for Sabbaths because it's pricey. The men's version seems very nice as well. I'll let you know if I get a headache from being near you."

When the elevator opened, I spied Nancy across the hall, adorably dressed as usual. She turned from her conversation and did a double take.

"André?" She called his name as a question as she looked from him to me, and back again. "Juliet?" Nancy's short legs and tall heels quickly crossed the carpet to embrace first André, then me. Looking up at him, she inquired, "What are YOU doing here?" Then she looked from his face to mine and said, "Ohhhhh! Oh. Ohhhhh!"

We all laughed as she immediately put two and two together, making us a couple in her mind. André put his arm around her shoulders and said, "It's so good to see you, Nancy. Let's talk more after church." Then we ducked into one of the classes, already in session.

I enjoyed our study from Deuteronomy, taking notes in my journal as André sat smelling-so-good beside me. I felt God speaking to me through verse thirty-one of chapter one. *The Message* puts it like this: ". . . you saw what he did in the wilderness, how God, your God, carried you as a father carries his child, carried you the whole way until you arrived here."

"God, You have carried me like a father through my wilderness experience. Thank You for bringing me to a new place. Help me to depend upon You for every step forward."

My heart's desire was to please the Lord. I did not want to get caught up in the religion of performance, but I knew I wanted to make right decisions. Especially when it came to men. Something else I wrote in my journal that morning speaks to me now, as I face fear, pride and shame head-on with the writing of this memoir:

Perfection is not a performance. Perfection is perfect dependence. Am I trustworthy with His power? Not caring what others think? Being myself and allowing Him to fill me with Himself?

André confided later that he was "deeply attracted" to the way I listened so intently and took notes during class and church that day. He wasn't used to seeing someone so hungry and thirsty for God. I wasn't used to someone staring at me so unabashedly.

After church, I discovered Nancy's life puzzle had a small André piece in it. The last she'd seen him was at his pastoral ordination ceremony, where her husband had been an officiating minister. Much happened in both of their lives since then. On the wall of André's office hangs an ordination certificate that bears a signature with Nancy's last name, although she no longer bears the burden of being *that* minister's wife.

As Nancy began sharing the saga that split their marriage, André's eyes filled with tears that spilled over onto his angular cheekbones. "Oh, Nancy! I had no idea. I am so, so sorry."

She began sobbing as we both embraced her in an effort to comfort her deep sorrow at remembering the loss of her marriage and the "pastor's wife" life she had known for twenty-five years.

As we wept together in a tight circle, André began praying over Nancy. His words were God-given and Holy Spirit driven, right into her soul. She later confided that André's tears were "Jesus tears," poured out for all of her suffering.

"When he prayed and wept over me, I strongly felt God's presence. It was as if Jesus Himself was weeping and praying over me. I desperately needed that compassion from a man. A safe, godly man. I will never, ever forget those Jesus tears."

We invited Nancy to join us for lunch in the park. When we arrived, a festive picnic was spread over two tables. Joelle came. So did Colin, who also knew several of the other South Africans. Everyone chatted and ate and laughed together. Although I didn't know anyone well, I felt comfortable enough to hang out for a couple of hours.

Observing André interact with friends he'd known since his university days was enlightening. I could see he was well loved. For me, that was an important bit of information, because Jon had never formed healthy, long-lasting relationships growing up. He didn't have deep roots with godly friends. To me, that void is a red flag for brokenness. It was good to check that box off my invisible checklist. *Has solid, longstanding friendships. Check.*

Nancy and I excused ourselves from the picnic when things started to get quiet. We were both exhausted from being single. I needed a nap. The institution of marriage is a wonderful protection. A buffer. A haven. Facing the world without it always wore me out. After comparing notes with Nancy all summer, I'd come to realize I wasn't alone in feeling that way. By mid-afternoon we were each snoring in our own rooms, trying to recharge so we could join Joelle and the guys later for Thai food.

I have a photograph from our Thai date. Three smiling ladies sandwiched between two semi-serious South Africans. I look a little nervous. André is wearing black, his best color. The spiky crest in the front of his hair is perfectly gelled. He is tanned and Hugh Jackman handsome. But there's a dash of Mr. Bean lurking around his edges.

By evening's end everyone's stomach ached, not from the spicy green curry, but from André's Mr. Bean antics. It had been years since I'd doubled up with laughter. It felt strangely surreal to just let go and howl in a good way. I wish I could tell you what was so funny, but, as they say, "I guess you had to be there." I was sad to see the evening end.

André called me on Sunday morning. "How would you like to lose the group and go out again, just the two of us?"

"I'd like that. Very much."

"How about Carrabba's? What time do you think you might be finished with your studies?"

"Ooh! I love Carrabba's. I can be done by 6 p.m. Is that too late?"

"No. It's perfect. That gives me some time to spend with Mom and Dad today. I'll pick you up at 6 p.m."

"Okay God, this is it. An official first date. No buffer crowd. Obviously he wants to get to know me better. I cannot keep my eyes off of him. But it's his insides that truly matter to me. As long as his heart is hidden in You, I know I'll be okay. I will continue to find out, but it seems like he's the real deal. I hope so."

I could barely focus on finishing my final class project. *"What should I wear? Should I pull my hair up, or have it down around my face? What will I say if he asks me questions about my past or being divorced? Help me, Jesus."*

I yearned for the discomfort of all the "firsts" to disappear. I could count on my fingers every first date I'd suffered. For me, starting new relationships usually felt like trying to get a lawnmower going after it's been in the garage all winter. Someone keeps pulling the cord over and over trying to spark a topic that will fire up a conversation. I hated it. Fear always choked me on first dates.

Not so with André. Two hours at Carrabba's passed too quickly. He leaned forward in our dimly lit corner booth to catch every word I expressed. He offered pieces of himself and his story that softly paved the way for me to share part of mine. We happily dipped our bread in a shared plate of spicy olive oil and sopped up one another's histories. By the time the tiramisu arrived, my fears were allayed.

"So, do you mind telling me your age?" I felt I'd earned the right to ask the one question I was *dying* to know the answer to. After hours of observation and internal guessing, I couldn't be certain. His silence magnified the sound of my spoon scraping the last bit of swirled chocolate off our plate.

"I'm fifty."

"You're lying."

"No. I am a fifty-year-old bachelor who has had Jell-O for brains most of my life. God has taken a loooooong time to bring me to maturity. I'm still a work in progress."

Fifty!? He cannot be fifty. That's not even my generation. Not possible. Seriously? No way. How can he be so well-preserved? Fifty? That's only nine years younger than my mother. Ouch! That hurts my brain.

I may have missed part of André's monologue about being fifty because *my* brain immediately began a familiar childhood pastime. When I was a kid, I used to lie underneath my yellow and white tulip-covered comforter playing a game in my head that went something like this: *I'm ten, my sister is six. In four years, I'll be fourteen, and she'll be ten. When she's fourteen, I'll be ready to graduate from high school. And when she's eighteen, I'll be twenty-two.* I'd continue on until I reached about thirty. Then my mind would go blank, because I could not even begin to fathom what my life would be like at thirty. That was the age of my mother, whom I believed to be ancient.

That's what I did while André explained his "Jell-O." Before he finished, I had our kids graduating high school with their father in his seventies. It was almost a deal breaker. But not quite.

"*Wow, Lord! That was an answer I was not expecting. This is twice the gap between me and Bird Man. And I thought he was old. Never mind. It's not like I'm a teenager or anything. I just feel like one.*"

I rejoined our conversation with what I thought was an appropriate response. I think I embarrassed myself. Or him. He later confided that when I mentioned my mother's warning about older men, he'd taken it quite personally.

Thankfully, that little exchange didn't spoil our evening. In fact, it ended just the way I'd dreamed—with a long walk on the promenade. As a student who had hidden behind a curtain of long-distance relationships, I never had the opportunity to take advantage of the university's romantically inviting grounds. I always envied the couples strolling hand-in-hand along the winding walkway that stretched the length of our campus. A winsome desire of my heart had never been fulfilled, it was something small and secret, known only by my Savior.

"I'm not ready for the evening to end. Are you?" André asked as he carefully parallel parked his Accord directly opposite my dorm.

"Not really," I replied.

"*Oh, Lord, don't let him try to kiss me, or anything. I do not want to like any of this too much. Help me to keep good boundaries, even though I really cannot help but notice all the kissable things about him.*"

"Why don't we walk off some of those carbs we just ate? It will be a nice way to close our time together," he suggested, pointing toward a set of steps leading to the promenade.

"What's at the top of those stairs?"

"A really long walkway. They call it "The Promenade.""

"Perfect."

We exited the Honda and walked toward the steep steps I'd been running each evening. My heart pounded. Hard. As if I'd just completed my workout.

The night was perfect. Darkness cooled Tennessee's July heat and humidity down to something bearable. The moon was on the cusp of full. As André took my arm and looped it through his in a formal old-fashioned way, I felt a bit like Mary Poppins. Although we didn't break out in song together or anything, I nearly could have. His Dick Van Dyke good looks, captivating personality and deep love for Jesus were all sugar that delightfully sweetened the shock of his age.

My journal from that night says: "*Lord, hide my heart in You. I need wisdom and discernment because I definitely had a spiritual connection with this man. I cannot deny that. Thank You for the work You are doing in him. The zeal, the power, the energy . . . I'm attracted to all of it. Very intrigued.*"

André sent me a final text just as I crawled into bed. "Juliet, thanks for being willing to meet me and for hanging out tonight. You inspire me, you stretch my mind, and you encourage my quest for greater intimacy with God. I left wanting more. Good night."

Sermon in the Sand

Skin weathered brown
Bending down
Sun on the back
Of His neck.

Pointing out
Beyond shadow's doubt
Secret sin
In shifting sands.

Backs turn
Faces burn
Truth pierces
Blistered hearts.

Silencing her accusers
Hypocritical users
With insightful,
Truthful script.

Bleary eyes raise
Meeting gentle gaze
Forgiveness blows
Her sin away.

Sermon in the sand
By weathered brown hand
Speaking her soul
To freedom.

Chapter 16

Ghosts and Roses

"... We went through fire and water,
but you brought us to a place of abundance."
Psalm 66:12 (NIV)

July—October 2008

It was nearly move-in day! My plan was to drop a load of plants off on my new front porch as soon as I signed all the paperwork and had my house keys in hand.

Four years after my lips last-kissed Grandma 'Dessa good-bye, nostalgia moistened my eyes as I remembered her red-hair and her green thumb as several of her still-thriving houseplants accompanied me to my first ever house closing.

"I cannot wait, Lord! My cup feels full to overflowing. A home of my own! A safe haven. A place that I can dedicate to You and to helping others."

It was the day after my dreamy date with André; my head was full of questions and my heart was full of butterflies, their tiny flutters making my cheeks turn crimson if I took too much notice of them.

"I cannot stop thinking of him. Is that a good thing? Is it normal? Is it possible I am missing him after only four dates? I like him. I really do, even if he is twelve years older. I think I'm okay with that. Are You okay with that, God? I've never felt such peace in the presence of a man. It's only now, with him gone, that I'm all fluttery. When he was near, I felt safe, because his heart and my heart are both hidden in You. If we must go to You to find each other, then everything should be just fine, right?"

I chatted with the Lord as if He were belted into the passenger seat of my Rav4. He had become such a Friend; I couldn't imagine the drive without Him. I felt like I had been through the fire and water, but finally He was bringing me to a place of abundance (Psalm 66:12 NIV).

Those brass keys Vivian placed in my hand were symbolic of the doors God was opening to my future. I could barely swallow back tears as I thanked Him while carefully arranging Grandma 'Dessa's begonias on the wide white railings of my new front porch. My heart brimmed with gratitude as I hung the last of three new ferns on silver hooks. I surveyed the homey scene through my windshield while backing out of my driveway.

The next few days brought a Texas-sized whirlwind of activity as I wrapped up summer school and transitioned from dormitory living to moving into my very own needs-a-facelift-in-a-hurry home. There was much to do before Bob and Aubrey arrived with my belongings. Bob's generous offer went something like this: "I don't think a lady should have to drive a loaded U-Haul 700 miles alone. Why don't Aubrey and I work with our friends from church to unpack your storage unit and load the truck for you? I can drive the U-Haul, and she can follow in our Camry."

"Oh Bob! That would be wonderful. In the meantime, I can get some of the indoor painting done in preparation for your arrival. Thank you! What a blessing."

"We're glad to help. We're so happy for your fresh start. Just mail us the key to the storage unit and we'll take care of the rest."

God placed many helpers in my path to ease my transition to homeowner. Although my house was perfect in so many ways, it was abandoned for a year or more, and the previous owners left parts of it in shambles. Between my down payment and closing costs, I spent nearly every cent I'd obediently saved. My lender informed me I qualified for something called a "first time home buyer tax credit." Basically, that meant I got an interest-free loan from the U.S. government, which I could paid back over fifteen years. It sounded like a great plan. That would give me $7,500 to purchase carpet, paint, and appliances. I took it!

After several days and multiple trips to Lowe's and Home Depot, I ordered new carpet, a new washer and dryer, and a stainless steel refrigerator. I also purchased several gallons of paint in warm colors with names like "Vanilla Bean" and "Provence Crème." I could not wait to begin the painting my new kitchen "Lemon Chiffon."

I camped on the floor in my sleeping bag for a couple of nights before the U-Haul arrived. My body was too tired to care. Memories of my painter days returned as I popped open the first can and emptied it into a metal tray. Almost no tool makes me happier than a new Purdy paintbrush with angled bristles. I trimmed out my huge kitchen in no time, following myself with the roller, top to bottom, always leaving a wet line of paint as Mr. Lutz, my paint boss had taught me back in college.

In an email, André offered to come and help me. But I declined, not yet ready to have him scrutinized by any of my "peeps." Although he'd begun phoning me each evening so we could pray together, I wasn't sure quite where we stood. I felt nervous about exposing my crush to anyone, especially the close friends and family who would soon descend upon my home like a swarm of the busiest bees.

Just after Bob and Aubrey arrived with all of my earthly possessions, the P's showed up with two very fat, happy-to-see-me dogs, and a load of furniture. We decided they'd store their best belongings with me, so they could sell their place in Arkansas and use mine as home base when they returned to Italy in January for another round of mission work. My grandpa and his new wife Jean followed close behind with a truckload of tools and a wealth of remodeling knowledge.

It was our own *Extreme Home Makeover* episode. Bob power washed layers of Georgia mildew from the external siding, cleaned pine needles out of gutters, and re-vamped my air conditioning system. Grandpa re-set a leaky upstairs toilet and repaired multiple holes in the sheetrock of one of the bedrooms, where an obviously irate person kicked and punched through the walls in several places. Jean and the P's scrubbed down everything that could be scrubbed and began unpacking kitchen boxes while Aubrey and I finished the interior painting.

Before Bob and Aubrey were ready to return to Texas, my home was inspected from top to bottom and everything a husband would have done for me was done. Between everyone's expertise and elbow grease, they saved me thousands of dollars. My twenty-two-year-old home felt almost new.

We all held hands in my Provence Crème-colored living room, praying prayers of thanksgiving and dedication before saying good-bye. Grandpa and Jean would have a long drive back to Oklahoma. The P's had some pre-mission trip planning to do and a couple of grandkids to spend time with before they'd return to spend the holidays with me. I hugged and waved to each one from my fern-filled Southern front porch. My heart felt full, but my house felt empty, except for two overstuffed girls named Snuffles and Whipper.

"What in the world did your grandma feed you for the past two months?" I questioned Snuffs, lugging her onto my lap as I plunked into my Nannie's rope-bottomed rocking chair. Whipper tried to leap up, too, but fell backwards onto the porch. "Goodness! You two used to fit up here just fine. You are both going on a major diet. Effective immediately. Snuffles! You can hardly breathe for that collar of fat around your neck!"

I had fussed at Mom as soon as the dogs waddled up the walkway to our new home. Snuffles was so overweight I had to carry her down the stairs to go outside.

"Well, they *were* bad girls," Mom explained. "They discovered our compost heap and we didn't realize they were sneaking out there to scavenge until they had put on some pounds. We just thought they were exploring the woods when we let them outside."

Snuffs, always prone to chubbiness, already had one knee surgery in the past. Rather than forking over six hundred dollars for another blown-out knee, I lugged her down the stairs several times a day until we got a handle on her weight and she could do it by herself. I was worried about her, about both of them, really. They seemed older than I remembered, and more clingy—refusing to let me out of their sight.

I placed their bed next to mine in the tiniest upstairs bedroom, which I'd chosen for myself. It was furthest from the staircase and had a great walk-in closet in the hallway just outside the door. I loved the cozy tucked away feeling I had when I snuggled into my new queen-sized bed, a gift from Dr. Alan and Darcy, which basically filled the room. I was not planning to allow any beggar dogs into *this* bed. No way!

With everyone gone, and most of my boxes unpacked, I had a couple of days to catch up on correspondence and adjust to living alone before it was time to begin setting up my new classroom. When I emailed my elderly friend Tom to tell him about school and let him know of André, I had to chuckle at his encouraging response.

"I've been praying for over a year for you to find a single pastor, and will continue to do so without fail. Go for it, girl! Yes, your plate is full with what you have to do before school starts, but you're a capable teacher."

"God, please bless Tom. Thank You for praying friends. May his prayers be answered! According to Your will, of course."

André phoned each evening around 10 p.m. to catch up on the day's happenings and to pray with me. I planned my bedtime routine around that phone call, making sure both fat dogs had been outside and the house was secured before my phone rang. I felt safer knowing everything was finished and the last thing I'd do in my day was have prayer with André.

He also emailed, making me smile out loud with flowery compliments like this one, "You have been and are in my thoughts and prayers constantly. I do love your heart for Christ. And that wonderful heart bubbles over into your radiant smile, out of your sparkling eyes and emanates from your whole demeanor. The beauty from within beams to the exterior. So, from whichever way one looks, from the outside in, or from the inside out, it's beautiful."

Now who wouldn't go to sleep with a dreamy smile on her face after praying with a man who spoke like that? I cannot imagine any tenderhearted girl whose love language is "words of affirmation" not letting her heart get all twitter-pated when she reads and hears the very words she's spent a lifetime longing for. I was no different. Somehow my big new home didn't seem quite so hollow with André's words and prayers to keep me company.

After a few nights alone in my cherry-wood sleigh bed, I caved to Whipper's begging eyes and Snuffles' pleading tail and pulled both girls up by their armpits into my forbidden bed. They were ecstatic. Rapturous rooting and twirling eventually led to settled-snoring as they each found a perfect resting spot.

They're old. I reasoned with myself. *I don't know how much longer I'll have them. Eleven is ancient for a pug. I never noticed how gray the fur around Snuffles' face has become. Her muzzle hardly has any black left. And I'm worried about Whipper. Her seizures seem to be more frequent. What if something happens to her? What will it hurt if we cuddle together in bed? Who really cares?*

Since the divorce, I was learning to release myself from self-imposed rules and to enjoy life as it comes, rather than trying to control everything so much. I was learning my need to control and create façades of perfection were really smokescreens for mountains of shame. God was healing me. Setting me free from myself. He was releasing me from the bondage of shame and the unrealistic expectations I'd held over myself and others for most of my life. It was a liberating process. The dogs in my bed were just one of the fruits of God's labor in my life. Admitting to myself I craved their close company as much as they did mine was a big step, a healing step.

There I was one night, not long after moving in, that the girls and I had a colossal fright. I was in a deep, deep sleep. It was one of those wee-hour kinds of sleeps when you are literally "dead to the world." I'm normally a sound sleeper who doesn't remember dreams, but that night, I thought at first I *might* be dreaming when I heard heavy footsteps slowly ascending the stairs. The dogs beside me didn't stir. Then I heard the steps coming down the hallway toward my bedroom.

Do you know that feeling when you are coming out of hibernation and you aren't sure what's real and what's not; and that feeling of oppressive darkness that's more than the absence of light? Well, that's the feeling I had as I struggled to awaken. My experience suddenly became more than just a subconscious feeling when the extra pillow I kept between me and the headboard came down over my face with force, and I was being smothered right there in my own bed in my own little room in my lovely new home in Georgia.

Even in my suffocated state, Mom's lessons from childhood kicked in immediately. She always taught me the first response to danger and evil is to call upon the name of Jesus. In milliseconds I knew I was in the presence of both danger *and* evil. "In the name of Jesus, GET OUT OF MY HOUSE!" Although my shout was pillow-muffled, it managed to scare the girls nearly to death. Instantly, the pressure on my face ceased and I was able to inhale. Heart pounding, I jumped up and flipped on the light. No one was there. Together, Snuffles, Whipper and I inspected every cranny of the house. There were no visible signs anyone had been there. But someone *had* been there. And I wanted to know why!

"Jesus! Thank You for the power in Your name. Thank You for rescuing me from the darkness that tried to smother me. But I'm mad! Why would the enemy dare to come in here to haunt me when I belong to You and I have not opened any doorways to welcome anyone from his camp into this home? Please reveal what's going on so this creepiness does not happen again. I never want to feel afraid in my own home. I will not be afraid."

I claimed the "power, love, and sound mind" of 2 Timothy 1:7 (NKJV) as I rebuked the spirit of fear and once again lay down to sleep. Soon the girls and I were again snoring. In the morning, I went on a mission.

When I was being smothered in my bed, I am quite positive it was the work of an evil territorial spirit who was working with a spirit of fear for the purpose of trying to frighten me into leaving, or getting me to acknowledge the presence of darkness and do nothing about it, therefore inadvertently allowing it to continue to live there with me. We are never safe when we turn a blind eye to darkness. Unfortunately, ignorance doesn't protect us when the enemy is trying to move in.

In the Bible, we find references to evil angels who were long ago cast out of Heaven. Ever since then, they have been looking for other places to dwell. Some impersonate loved ones who have already died, some live inside of living people, and some live in places.

On an airplane recently, I picked up Inflight magazine from the back of the seat and flipped through it. Toward the back there were advertisements for "Haunted Bed & Breakfasts" in Europe. The reviews said guests could see, hear and experience the presence of the "ghosts" in various ways. *Ummmm, no thanks!*

You might just think it's a gimmick, but I'll tell you this—when the P's were looking to purchase a thatched-roof cottage in England some years ago, their realtor very seriously asked if they wanted one with a ghost or without. She offered to show them a home with a ghost who would turn down the beds each night. They firmly declined the offer. Mother did not want any "ghosts" in her house—friendly or otherwise!

I also didn't want a house with ghosts, so after my disturbing experience I did some research. From my new next-door neighbor, I found out the previous homeowners had gone through a messy divorce while living in my home with their two teenage sons. After the father left, the sons "lost their way" and apparently became involved in substance abuse and other unsavory activities because, according to the neighbor, the police had visited the property several times before they finally moved. That bit of information explained a few details I previously ignored.

When Grandpa was repairing the trashed upstairs bedroom, he noticed a tweaked trapdoor leading to the attic and mentioned someone had used the attic as a hangout. I hadn't paid close attention, nor had I gone up there to investigate the evidence. After Grandpa repaired the trapdoor and patched the walls, I re-painted the room and was using it as an office.

I assumed my home became mine when I signed all of the paperwork with the realtor. And it did, in the physical realm. But in the spiritual realm, my home still belonged to the spirits who had been invited there by its previous owners through whatever ungodly activities they engaged in on that property and in those rooms. I didn't need to worry though, because I knew that through Jesus, I had authority to drive out those spirits and reclaim my property for God and His purposes. I was just sorry I had not been more thorough early on.

After chatting with the neighbor, I searched my kitchen for a bottle of olive oil. Sitting down at the table, I asked forgiveness for my sins, claiming the cleansing blood of Jesus Christ over my life. Then I prayed over that oil, asking God to anoint it, sanctify it, and make it representative of The Holy Spirit's power and presence.

If you Google anointing oil, you can find several Biblical references for what I did and lots of oils you can purchase. Some of them are even from the Holy Land and significantly more expensive than others. I believe anointing oil is merely a symbol, and God will work with what we've got. What I had that day was a large measure of faith, and a small bottle of extra-virgin olive oil I purchased from my local Wal-Mart Supercenter.

I took my little bottle of oil and prayerfully anointed the door frame representing each room in my home. I said aloud, "As the legal owner of this property, I claim this territory for the Kingdom of God and no evil spirits are welcome here. In the Name of Jesus Christ of Nazareth, I command you all to go NOW! And do not return. I invite the Holy Spirit of God and the holy angels to come into this home. You are welcome here. Bring a sense of calm and peace and the very presence of God into my home. I dedicate this place to You, God. For ministry, or for whatever purposes You have for it. Please protect me. Protect my belongings, my vehicle, my finances, and everything on this property." Then I went outside and walked the perimeter of my property, rebuking, anointing and praying all the way around.

That's it. That's what I did. And do you know what? I never had any more creepy late night visitors after that, and I never felt afraid in my home again even though I spent many nights there all by my human self.

Keeping our homes spirit-free is fairly easy when we live alone and are committed to not bringing anything ungodly onto our property. It becomes more difficult when we share a space with other people who may not be quite so diligent. That's when one's home can become a battleground, as I experienced when I shared a life with Jon. I never again want to live with or be taken by surprise by that kind of darkness. Even now, I like to pray, rebuke, and anoint any unfamiliar place I sleep so I can avoid confrontations with "familiar spirits."

I was curious about André's home and his lifestyle. It's one thing to meet someone online or away from their own turf, but quite another to step into their home, read titles in their library, and see what "recently watched" Netflix are in their queue. Naiveté hadn't managed to convince me all pastors are saints. In fact, I'd been privy to some quite-the-contrary evidence in the past. As badly as I wanted to believe everything about this man was perfect, I knew that wasn't realistic. I just prayed his imperfections would be ones I could possibly live with and not ones that invited nighttime visitors from the dark side. That *would* be a deal breaker.

By August, I'd shared with André that many people drop the "t" from my name and simply call me Julie. He responded by saying, "Once we get to know each other a little better, I will probably have ten different names for you. I do like the elegance of 'Juliet.' It has a classic ring to it, but I'll probably lean toward Jules eventually."

He never did call me Jules, but through a progression of emails and phone calls I acquired a pile of nicknames, "Girl in Ten Million" became one of my favorites. I only called him André. Or Pastor. It would be a long time before "Honey" left my lips, even though I secretly thought him the sweetest man to ever walk the planet.

When my little Christian school was looking for a speaker for our September Week of Prayer, I suggested Pastor André. Before I knew it, they arranged for him to spend five days with us. I floated to cloud nine! He arrived on a Sunday night and took me out to dinner at Provino's, where the garlic rolls are so potent no one would dare consider a first kiss afterward.

André and I hated to see our evening to end, and mutually complained about Monday's daybreak start, which warranted an early "good-night" before he returned to his extended stay hotel room. He called for prayer just before I fell asleep.

André did a fabulous job with the students. Although I previously listened to several of his sermon CDs, watching him engage a live audience was enlightening. Pastor André was obviously serving God within his gifting. In my journal I penned: *"Lord, I love the way You used this man to speak with the kids. He poured himself out and they responded openly to the altar call. I'm so sad he had to leave early because of the storms."*

When you catch wind that a tropical storm, which might turn into a hurricane, is heading toward your home in Florida, and you are the kind of person who stores food, water, sandbags and a backup generator, you probably won't stay in Georgia to finish a Week of Prayer at a Christian School. Neither did André.

Just after Thursday morning's worship, he slipped into our classroom to say good-bye. My first graders crowded around as he gave them high fives and hugs. I busied them with an independent activity so André and I could have a quiet moment. I was disappointed he was leaving early. The tears that pooled in my eyes as his hands squeezed mine surprised both of us. I'd wanted to be more reserved, but the abrupt ending to a beautiful week sparked emotion that gave my heart away. That raw reaction frightened us both—just a little.

I journaled about it later as I embarrassedly wrote: *I think André feels the need to retract or rethink. Maybe I was too open about my feelings, too unguarded. I think I maybe scared him.*

"*Lord, help me to be balanced in my responses to him. Help me to be patient until You show him, beyond a shadow of a doubt that it is me You have brought into his life. I need for him to be completely confident of that.*

"*Until that time, Lord, make me be still, patient, and a source of encouragement and blessing to him, but never a source of stress, temptation, or a drain on his reserves. I know He is a man of God. I also know he's a man. Help me to honor him and respect him.*

"*I love that he calls me "Girl in Ten Million." I love that he cares for me and sees the details of how You, God, have provided so many blessings to me in my new little world—my home, job, people, church. He noticed how beautiful my life here is. Thank You. What is Your plan? Help me to trust You completely.*"

As I mentioned earlier, I'm not one who normally has visions or dreams. When I'd dated Bird Man, Jon, or even Mr. Roberts, there was never any handwriting on the wall telling me I was on the right, or wrong path. I just moved forward with what I felt, thought, or wanted. Yes, I prayed, but I wasn't particularly obedient or in tune with reality. I didn't listen to godly counsel. I'm not sure I even listened to God. This time, I wanted to be certain. I didn't want any second-guessing down the line after it was already too late to salvage the pieces of my fragile heart. I had been through quite enough. I wanted this to be perfect; however, it wasn't. In fact, it turned out to be a bit more complicated than I'd imagined it could be.

After my encounter with God in Colorado, I had a constant sense of His presence. I felt I was learning what it meant to walk in the Spirit. My summertime Statistics experience only solidified His voice in my very marrow. So, when God responded to my questions about André, His answer was undeniable. Beyond any shadow of a doubt, I knew He had spoken to me.

It happened as I stood at my bedroom window one evening, watching a White-breasted Nuthatch complete his final feeding frenzy of the day. Standing there, absently listening to the nuthatch's constant nasal yammer as he foraged for insects before bed, I had a distinct mental picture of André and I working together, side by side, for souls. I could almost hear Jesus say, "You will stand beside this man and support him in ministry until I come back." I got goose bumps as the hairs on my arms stood up. Then a warm peace washed over me. From that moment, I knew God was in control. I did not need to strive or fret. I would never have to resort to an ungodly female arsenal, with its traditional weapons of wheedle, cajole, and manipulate. I was not yet 100% sure if I could trust André, but I had complete confidence in my heavenly Father.

In September, André arranged a visit because he wanted to take me to Chattanooga to meet his parents and a sister who was visiting from California. He also helped me with a problem I'd been having with the girls. Learning a new curriculum and meeting the extra academic requirements for my new job kept me away from home for nine or ten hours a day. If I did any errands after school, it was sometimes longer. I didn't have a fence, so they were alone indoors for all that time.

When I lived in the pool house, Darcy usually let them out during the day. Before that, they'd always had a fenced-in yard, where they could freely roam until somebody came home from work.

Staying alone inside all day was new. They did not like it one bit, and were letting me know by tearing things up and pooping in weird places rather than the potty paper where they were supposed to go.

In frustration, I devised a plan and I asked André if he would go with me to Home Depot to choose materials for an outdoor doggie playpen. That's all I could afford, but I hoped it would help my situation. He kindly insisted on paying for my purchase and carefully helped me assemble the makeshift structure under some trees in the backyard. When I put the girls inside the pen they looked miserable. Whipper stood there with her ears flattened against her head and Snuffles' tail drooped pitifully. I wanted to try the playpen out briefly before I left them for a longer period of time, but they could sense I was in the house watching, so they barked their heads off until I rescued them. We ended up leaving them indoors while we went to Chattanooga for the evening. We were running late.

Just before we arrived at his parents' home, André stopped at the grocery store to grab two bunches of pink roses for his mother. "Oh! They're beautiful!," she exclaimed after he hugged her and handed her the blooms. "Just beautiful! Thank you. Thank you so, so much!" Her enthusiasm lit the room. When he introduced me, she again cried, "Oh! She's beautiful! Really, really a beautiful girl!" I shook her hands and smiled into her eyes. Her whole face smiled back.

His father entered the room with a shawl for his wife. "I'm sorry André, but we aren't able to visit for very long right now because Mom and I are on our way to a wedding," his father announced.

"Dad, I apologize. We were caught up in a project for Juliet's dogs, and we got away later than expected."

"It's no problem," his father answered. "I just wish we had more time to spend with you, but we mustn't be late to this thing." Then he turned toward me, "Juliet, I've heard good things about you, and I can see why André is so enamored. Please come again when we can get to know you better."

After they left, André explained his mother's declining memory while he arranged her roses in a cut glass vase. "She started forgetting things about three years ago. At first it was just small stuff that could happen to anyone, but then she stopped remembering how to get home if she drove somewhere in the car. And she couldn't recall how to do things she'd done a thousand times before. Eventually she quit going places alone, and has declined socially. Her physical health is great, but she's no longer able to carry on a conversation, or do many things for herself. Each time I see her it's more difficult. I hate it."

There was a sadness in his spirit as we drove to Carrabba's to meet his youngest sister, Leesa and her husband for an early dinner. Leesa and Anthony are a fun couple exactly my age. We laughed and talked about mutual acquaintances over Zucchini Fritte and Insalata Fiorucci. I loved the attractive vibe of their marriage—mutual admiration and a California cool I couldn't quite identify. By the end of the appetizers, Anthony and Leesa lifted André's mood. He let them know how much he missed them and how he despised the distance between California and Florida. We took a few snapshots together before saying good-bye.

Although I thought it significant that André wanted me to meet his family, throughout our brief visit I'd noticed a coolness in him. But it wasn't cool in a good way. It was cool in an aloof way. I wasn't sure what to do with it, so I did what I usually do with things like that, I wrote about it. My journal says: *He's a bit distant. We talked on the phone after our day together and I jotted down these words from our conversation. He said I was "attractive, alluring, and magnetic." If that's true, why do I feel like he's holding back and being reserved? More so even than our first weekend together.*

After he returned to Florida, André called me. I grabbed a yellow Post-it note and scribbled two sentences from our conversation. "I caught a window of a future that looks very attractive. I'm overwhelmed a bit." My journaled response was a question: *Why is he overwhelmed?*

The answer unraveled over the next two months. It was long and complex. I was thankful for the peace my "together till Jesus comes" vision afforded me as I treaded those waters. My first clue should have been a poem André shared early on. In an email, he'd written, "This is a poem I wrote about my life and the life of a good friend of mine and how God wove a beautiful, glistening Golden Thread amidst our sadness and sorrow, turning it all into peace and praise."

The rhyme explained how he lost his father in an accident at the age of four, and how he lost his mother to her job as a school principal as she struggled to support him and his baby sister after her husband's tragic death. It goes on to reveal how André cried desperately for God to fill the aching void left by his absent parents in childhood. One verse reads:

> *"I know the plans I have for you," I heard the Skilled Weaver say.*
> *"From when you are born, I work the Golden Threads every day.*
> *No matter the loss, the hurt, the disappointment or pain,*
> *I weave my Golden Thread in-between till all is new again.*
> *I send my Spirit to comfort, to strengthen when you cry,*
> *To make you more like Me, even when you cannot try."*

It was a touching piece, but I hadn't paid enough attention to the verses about his "good friend," who is mentioned in the last lines this way:

> *She cried desperately to God, needing her soul to be filled.*
> *Another Golden Thread was woven, by a Hand so skilled.*

How do we miss truth when it stands directly before our eyes? I should have raised a questioning eyebrow when he sent me a poem co-written by a female "friend" with a needy soul. Once oblivion's fog began to lift, I realized André's good friend might be a hindrance to our forward movement. I remained in the dark for several confusing weeks until the full reality was revealed.

In the meantime, he went on a mission trip to Guatemala and I had a drastic decision to make. My decision had nothing to do with André and everything to do with my girls.

Long, long days alone were taking a toll on them both. I tried leaving them outdoors in their little pen, but the neighbors complained because they barked incessantly. Regardless of whether I left them indoors or out, they acted angry with me when I came home, either nipping my hands or sulking in corners. I began to imagine awful scenes like discovering that one of Whipper's seizures had killed her, and she'd lain there all day while Snuffles freaked out until I came home. Guilt began to gnaw at me as I struggled to balance my work and graduate classes with caring for two beloved aging pets.

Late one afternoon, Jon's sister Mona called to check on me and to let me know she'd forever treasure me as her sister, regardless of anything that happened with Jon. She asked about my new life and then, "How are Snuffles and Whipper doing?"

"Not so great, to be honest. I'm worried about them. They aren't adjusting well to our lifestyle. I have to leave them alone too much, and they are making me pay," I confided. "I'm especially concerned about Whipper. Her seizures seem to be more frequent, and Snuffles is angry with me for being gone long hours. I really don't know what to do."

"Why don't you call Roman and Kymberly?" She suggested. "I bet they would be happy to take the girls for a while. Someone is always home at their place, so they would never be alone."

"Hmmm. Thanks for that suggestion, Mona. I think it would be incredibly hard for me to take Snuffles and Whipper there. I haven't seen them since Jon and I divorced. But, you're right, they are definitely dog lovers, and they would never let the girls lack for anything. I'll pray about it."

The whole time André was gone to Guatemala, I prayed about the situation concerning the girls. Between that, and his pre-trip aloofness, I was feeling down. I journaled my thoughts:

"God, my prayer is that You will show this man beyond a shadow of a doubt what Your will is concerning me. I have many questions concerning the future. Yet, I DO have peace. My life has been so unlike anything I dreamed for myself. I still have so many girlish dreams left in my head. So many desires in my heart continue to go unfulfilled. Many hopes lie dormant and I dare not even think about or dwell upon them, or the dam will break and I'll surely drown.

"To be loved completely and unconditionally, to be cared for, to be cherished and appreciated, to be tenderly looked at and touched . . . to plan, to hope, and dream together, to weep and grieve, and forgive, and grow together. To have a witness to my life—this is my heart's desire. When will I ever experience this oneness with a man? How long will I have to wait, oh Lord? Help me to be patient and to continue to grow into the woman You want me to be. I'm tired of being independent. I'm tired of being strong. I feel like leaning on someone."

A few days later, my spirit was still restless as I wrote, *"Please make Your will exceedingly clear. Help me to trust You and not to second guess You. Something is not right. I am hesitant to see André again without Your answer to him. I'm battling spirits of rejection and fear, and lies that tell me I'm not worthy. My shield of faith feels heavy. Please put Your hands over and under mine and help me lift and hold the faith shield when I am under attack."*

A week after returning from his mission trip, André boarded a plane to Portland, Oregon. He was going on a motorcycle road trip with a couple of buds from college in celebration of their 50th birthdays. We barely communicated before he left. He'd gotten sick in Central America, but I wasn't convinced that illness was what was keeping him quiet. I felt uneasy.

While he was out West, I made up my mind about the girls. In response to Mona's suggestion, I gave Roman and Kym a call. Immediately after I explained the situation, they offered to take Snuffles and Whipper. "We'll love them like our own babies. Don't you worry about it one bit. Older dogs need more TLC, and you aren't in a position to give them that right now. I know it feels like a hard decision, but you'd really be doing what is best for them," Kym reassured me.

With a heavy heart, I made arrangements to drive to Arkansas on my next long weekend. Seeing how stressed they'd become in just two months, and knowing I had two years of grad school ahead of me, I realized it was the best I could do for them under the circumstances. It just really hurt. I felt like a bad mama, but I didn't know what else to do.

André was still in Oregon when I told him. I was surprised when he offered to go with me, saying, "I don't want you to travel all that way alone. I'll make a way to go with you. You are special and deserve to be looked after."

Wow! Where did that come from? Is this an answer to my "I'm tired of being strong and independent" prayer?

Although it was tempting to bring him along, I declined André's offer. The main reason being I felt awkward about introducing him to Jon's family, and the secondary being I thought I would wail for most of the nine-hour drive home.

I did wail. It was an ugly, ugly cry, reminiscent of those following Chloé's disappearance from my life. Even though it was not directly Jon's fault that I released Snuffles and Whipper, I battled the temptation to blame him for my pain. And, just like with Chloé, I had no idea when I would ever see them again.

I wept until I had to pull over and vomit beside the Arkansas highway. Then I wept some more. The enemy messed with my mind and tempted me to numb my pain in myriad ways. I kept driving.

I'd decided to make the whole trip without stopping—all 18 hours—only pausing in the middle to drop off the girls. They'd immediately recognized Roman and Kym, and raced through the house looking for the kids. When I left, Snuffles was snuggled on Kym's lap as she sat in her La-Z-Boy. Whipper lay sprawled on the sofa next to my nephew, Reggie. I kissed them each goodbye. Nobody moved as I made my way to the door. That was my sign the girls would be happier right where they were, rather than forever waiting for me to come home from my crazy-busy new life. Still, I carried the weight of guilt, shame, and sorrow as I walked to my car. Hours later the heaviness had not lifted.

Then André called. "Why don't you just keep driving when you get to Georgia? Come down to the Sunshine State for the weekend. I'm concerned about you. I shouldn't have let you do this alone. You don't sound good."

He didn't have to ask me twice, but I needed to go home and get some sleep and some clothes first. Knowing I wasn't staying made entering my unoccupied house bearable. I immediately fell asleep and left for Florida in the morning. Six hours later, I stood at André's open front door. The sun shone from behind me onto his shiny tiled entryway. André greeted me in a black tank top, shorts, and bare feet.

Welcome to Florida. This should be interesting. Just guard your heart, girl. Guard your heart.

While I was busy guarding my heart, André was finalizing arrangements to guard our reputations. He'd organized for me to stay with some church members, Peter and Lynda, a young couple who immediately liked me and graciously opened their home for whenever I came into town. Abstaining from any appearance of evil (1 Thessalonians 5:22 KJV) was a priority for André. I respected him for that. He never wanted to give reason for tongues to wag when we visited one another. I agreed.

The weekend flew by too quickly. Before I knew it, I was driving home on memories of a St. Augustine sunset carriage ride, dinner on the patio of a quaint Italian restaurant, and some solid answers to my nagging questions; painfully solid answers that prompted me to leave André with some tough decisions to make.

Tremendous peace blanketed me as I headed north to Georgia. We'd experience a wonderful time together. I'd tasted his life as a pastor: the oatmeal-in-the-car-on-the-way-to-church routine as he rushed to preach at one small church, then another, the potluck, followed by an afternoon hospital visit, and then an evening program where he featured the Guatemala Mission Trip slideshow. I'd also glimpsed his heart, and his library. That's what gave me hope as I left him with an ultimatum.

Perhaps I should let André tell the truth in his own words, as he shared it with me. It went like this: "I need to speak with you about something. It's a long story, but I feel you deserve to know the whole thing. On December 23, 2006, I renewed a contract I'd made with God and broken. The contract said I would no longer search for someone to date or marry. I was giving up and trusting God to bring someone into my life in a miraculous way, without me looking.

"I spent years in the dating cycle, always making a terrible mess of things, never able to commit to one girl for the long haul. I was broken. Tired of breaking hearts. Tired of having mine ripped out of my chest. At one time I was talking to about twelve different women on Internet dating sites. It was insane. I knew something was wrong with me. I wasn't doing it on purpose, but time and again I'd reel a woman in until I knew she really cared for me. Then I got cold feet and dropped her like a hot potato. I could not commit.

"That's when I made a decision to stop looking and to get help. I saw a counselor over the course of about two years. She really helped me to understand my problem. It stemmed back to losing my father at the age of four, and grew from various other emotional wounding that occurred throughout my youth. Anyway, as you could see from my library, I've learned a lot about what I did not want to be like. And a lot about what I truly desired.

"So that brings me again to December 2006. On the twenty-third, I renewed my contract with God, believing that only through miraculous divine intervention would I ever engage in another relationship. I promised not to look anymore. I would wait until God brought someone to me.

"The next day, December 24, 2006, I received a phone call. It was from a man I'd met eight months prior, on a mission trip to South America. He approached me on that trip to ask if I'd be willing to meet his daughter. He thought we would be compatible. After I agreed to meet her, she refused the invitation. I let it drop. Now, here was her father, the day after I renewed my vow with the Lord, calling to say she had changed her mind and wanted to meet me after all and would I come to his home to celebrate the New Year?

"To cut a long story short, the Lord allowed that girl to spend the next 17 months doing to me what I'd spent a lifetime doing to others. It was painful. I would not call it a romantic relationship by any means, but I was thoroughly convinced God miraculously brought her into my life, so I was positive that she must be 'the one.' She didn't seem to think so. But I continued to pursue her. Every time I became frustrated and ready to give up, she'd offer me another little carrot of hope, and off I'd go again, trying to get her to love me.

"The last straw for me was her refusal to allow me to join her and a group of friends on a European trip last spring. That was it. I ended our friendship, for that's all it ever was, despite my best efforts to woo her into something more. She was still away on that trip when I angrily broke my contract with God . . . again, and went on another dating site. I contacted a pretty girl and sent her an email similar to the one I sent you the first time. Just after that was when Joelle called to tell me about you.

"I knew my going on the Internet again to look for someone was wrong, and not a sign from God. But having Joelle contact me out of the blue to tell me about a beautiful, godly woman in her class . . . now *that* was more like divine intervention. You know most of the rest of the story.

"But what you don't know is that Vacation Girl kept sending me post cards while she was away. Then she began texting me as soon as she arrived back in the States. I became confused again. After you and I met and had such an amazing connection, I wasn't sure what to do, because I believed from the beginning she was a direct answer to my prayer. I had not gone looking for her. She came to me.

"The other thing you don't know is my church collaborated with her medical team to go on the mission trip to Guatemala. It was planned long in advance, and I could not easily extricate myself from the trip. Part of me didn't want to. I wondered if I should give it one more chance to develop into something more than platonic friendship. I cannot understand why the Lord would have brought her into my life in such a bold way, just after I prayed for Him to do something like that.

"Anyway, I've never felt so insecure in my life as when I was with her. She never gave me anything solid to hold on to. I'm always left guessing. It's a terrible feeling.

"And then there's you. Whenever we're together we have a beautiful time. You are truly a Girl in Ten Million. I nearly swallowed my Adam's apple when you came floating up that walkway the first time I saw you! Our ministry together that weekend with Nancy was so incredible. I felt like

I got a true view of your compassionate heart. I love our prayer time. I get a surge of joy coming into me whenever I hear from you.

"I know I initially said I just wanted to be spiritual friends, but after just four months of knowing you, I already love you and sense we could share a future together. My only question is, 'What does God say?'

"The problem is, I do not have complete closure with Vacation Girl. It's that little hesitation I need peace about. I'm sure you have a little hesitation about me too. God will give us the peace we need. Can you please be patient with me until I hear very clearly from Him? My mind knows you are best for me. I just need confirmation in my spirit."

I had several aha moments as André poured out his story. I also had compassion for him, as I could see his struggle was real. He aspired to be obedient to the Lord and to follow through if the other woman was the one God sent him. Unfortunately for André's tender heart, he was coming to realize he cannot coerce love from another human being. Not even God can do that. As much as I longed to embrace him and comfort him in his very real distress, I chose to give him an ultimatum instead.

"André," I said, just before I pointed my Rav toward home. "I do not want to be your friend. I have plenty of great friends in my life. I honestly don't need any more. And my heart has been through too much to take another beating. I understand what you're going through, but I cannot be a part of it. I want what is best for you. And I must do what is best for me. What I believe is best for me right now is to go home and let you and God sort this out. I'm not going to enter an arena to vie for your affections."

Following that statement with "Thank you for a wonderful weekend," I backed out of his driveway. It was one of the most difficult decisions I'd ever made relationally, but I knew it was the right one. As much as I wanted to beg for his heart, I couldn't. I knew if God wanted me to have him, He would give him to me. I did not need to grovel.

I calmly processed the weekend's details on my way home. My little vision kept me steadily between the lines on the road ahead. I would do my studies and teach my students. I would pray without ceasing. I would wait upon the Lord to heal André's heart and prepare it for mine. I trusted my Savior.

When I arrived home on Sunday evening, I hunted my index card from Statistics and taped it to my bathroom mirror as a shield against the enemy's lies. "For the Lord God will help me; therefore shall I not be confounded: therefore I have set my face like a flint, and I know that I shall not be ashamed" (Isaiah 50:7 KJV).

Monday and Tuesday dragged. I kept a running monologue to Heaven as I sought to remain steady. It was hard to practice faith and surrender when I'd spent a lifetime trying to control people and situations. I knew this situation was beyond my control. All I could to was trust.

"Lord, I'm tired. It's hard to be put on hold when everything seems so right. Please do not let me be hurt again. I don't want to be a pawn in the game of love. Part of me wants to jump in with both feet. But I can't, because everything is not right. It's up to You, Lord. More than anything, I desire to do Your

will. Help me to just be still and wait on You. I feel Your impression to be quiet. It's hard. I miss him. But I will be obedient. I will wait."

When I arrived home from school after dark on Tuesday, I was greeted at my front door by eighteen perfect red roses and a note which said, "To the most beautiful angel in the world. My mind is made up. Please call me. All my love, André."

My knees buckled beneath me. Realizing I had been holding my emotional breath waiting for an answer, I exhaled. The relief was overwhelming. Sinking to the floor, I wept into my hands under the yellow porch light. It had been the longest three days of life.

Chapter 17

Same Dress, Different Day

"For the LORD delights in you . . .
and as the bridegroom rejoices over the bride,
so shall your God rejoice over you."
Isaiah 62:4-5 NKJV

November 2008–May 2010

"Too many cooks spoil the stew!" I hear Mamaw's voice in my head as I picture her gingerly backing out of her daughter's overpopulated Thanksgiving kitchen. In Odessa's kitchen, things went Odessa's way. There was no other way. Even if you were her mother!

I love Thanksgiving. When those familiar aromas mingle in my kitchen, it's like having each of my grandmothers in the same space at the same time. I always make Nannie's sweet potato crunch, Mamaw's creamy green bean casserole, Grandma 'Dessa's extra salty version of Waldorf salad, and Grandma Kaiser's bread dressing. When all those smells rub shoulders, I imagine my family's matriarchs measuring, sprinkling, chopping and stirring the pot together.

I'm smiling, remembering each of them and how they've contributed to the "me" I've turned out to be. Strong women. Tenacious. Resilient. Each had an invisible line you never wanted to cross. In modern psychological lingo, that line would be called a "boundary." I first heard the term years ago, in my 12 Step group.

Boundaries helped me navigate the end of my marriage to Jon, and to draw the line in the sand with André when he couldn't make up his mind. If I had not done so, it's possible I could still be one of those long-haired-Barbie dolls he'd juggled for a lifetime, being tossed and caught like a circus act.

As much as it hurts, tough love reaps some good results. Sometimes people need to be firmly helped off the fences they're used to riding. We must never be so wounded that we allow someone else's wounding to keep us stuck in a holding pattern. God has higher purposes for His children. We've got to break free from our codependent cycles and begin to have healthy boundaries. Otherwise we become somebody's victim.

Our heavenly Father calls and equips us to be victorious, never victims. My decision to drive away and disconnect communication from André until he decided I was worth pursuing was a personal victory for me. I'd always been a beggar-girl, willing to take whatever crumb of attention was tossed my way. Allowing him the freedom to make a pressure-free decision, and being okay with the outcome demonstrated a quantum faith leap. When my soul freely echoed Job 13:15 (KJV), "Though he slay me, yet will I trust in him," I knew I was cool with whatever happened.

"It's a good place to be, God. When Job got there, You redeemed the things he thought were lost. I want to live my life from that place. I want to trust You that much."

In the weeks after André sent the roses, he made peace with God regarding Vacation Girl. "Perhaps she was allowed into my life to reveal to me what I'd done to all the girls whose hearts I broke in the past. Those months of chasing her kept me from chasing anyone else and gave me a healthy dose of my own bitter medicine," he confided into the phone one November night as icy wind whipped through the branches outside my bedroom. "I'm actually thankful for the experience. Men and women can really hurt each other trying to 'just be friends.' Someone's going to get hurt, because somebody always wants more than friendship. I get that now. Let's not be friends, okay?"

"Okay," I laughed. "I'll do my best. Are you coming up for Thanksgiving? The P's will be here. You can stay with us and save your hotel bills. I have plenty of rooms."

After giving me the runaround for those confusing weeks, André made up for it with his wholehearted devotion. In one of his texts, right after the roses, he said, "It has been rough, but God has taught us a lot. You are remarkable. Your handling of this shows pieces of the puzzle I wouldn't have seen otherwise." A few days later, he continued, "Jeweliet, You are such a beautiful, special and precious woman of God. I know He will not disappoint us."

Once I was assured of his commitment to moving forward with me, I spoke my mind. Explaining I had enough rejection for a lifetime and wasn't about to play second fiddle to anyone, I exclaimed, "I'd rather be alone than to be a beggar for affection ever again!"

He got the message. Although it was a long time before he broke down and kissed me, André never kept me guessing about whether or not he wanted to. Given my recent history lesson with Mr. Roberts, I knew it best to keep all things physical on the back burner until everything else was on the fast track to the altar. *Besides, when you're dealing with a slippery fifty-year-old bachelor, there is no fast track to the altar.*

Just before Thanksgiving, André messaged, "I wish you knew what an impact you have had on my life. How much I respect and appreciate you. And how deeply I love you, even though it hasn't been that long since we met. My heart aches to be with you. I trust God's plan for both of us and I know He'll bring us together in His time."

"Now that's what I'm talking about! Woo hoo, God! Way to move Mt. Bachelor!"

In the meantime, the P's returned to Georgia, their Jeep loaded with treasures from travels abroad. "Goodness Mom, did you leave anything behind to stage your house with?" I asked as she dragged a ceramic Italian pedestal up the sidewalk. "Let me help you. At least I have space for all this stuff!"

Between their things and mine, four bedrooms filled up nicely. My home had a warm, cottagey feel. I loved it. I also loved that the P's were back, if only for a couple of months. I'd been lonely without my girls to keep me company, lonely and a little bit hungry. I grew tired of cooking for one.

Mom took care of that problem right away. "You are not going to just live on lentils with me in the house," she said, inspecting my scant cupboards and stark fridge. "Mr. P and I will go to Whole Foods tomorrow and fill this thing up!" They did. It was awesome to come home to yummy smells and tasty treats. My jeans grew tighter. I didn't mind one bit.

When André proposed splitting the Thanksgiving holiday between my home in Georgia and his sister's in Tennessee, Mom and I got busy in the kitchen. "Now listen," she stage whispered to Mr. P in a serious tone, "*my* mother always said, 'The way to a man's heart is through his gizzard.'" Facing her husband, she placed a hand on each of his shoulders, looked mischievously into his eyes and asked, "Do you know what a gizzard is, Mr. P?" She gave his shoulders a little squeeze and shake as she said his name. "Do you?"

Confusion danced across his face. Wink-winking my direction, Mrs. P continued, "You men are about to find out where your gizzards are. Just you wait until these pies come out of the oven. Then I'll ask you again."

My mother had a scheme. I went right along with it. Mr. P definitely reaped the culinary benefits of her plan, but we weren't cooking for him. André would arrive late Wednesday evening. Mrs. P's objective was to entice him with food. "We'll have the most tantalizing holiday aromas greet him at the door. He needs to feel so at home here that he never wants to leave," she said. "We will treat him like a prince! He will fall in love with my daughter, and he might even like his future mother-in-law!" With that, she kicked up one heel and waved her wooden spoon like a magic wand. Mr. P and I spewed laughter.

As André's headlights hit the driveway, I bolted for his car, still wearing my blue and yellow French apron. He hugged me. Twice! Warm light and Vivaldi spilled from the open front door as we ascended the steps together.

"What is this deliciousness I'm smelling?" He stopped, sniffing the air Mr. Bean style. Though the P's were sworn not to spy, I could hear them chortling from somewhere inside.

Suddenly they appeared at the door all smiles and Italian greetings, "Ciao! André! Welcome! It's wonderful to finally see you." After hugs and handshakes all around, just like that, he was in our lair.

Soon Mom and I were back at our pie-making posts. I could feel André's eyes on me as I flattened a dough ball with Mamaw's old wooden rolling pin. He didn't know my Martha Stewart side. My cheeks flushed. *Can he see through our ploy? I hope not. Why is he staring?*

At Mom's invitation, he taste-tested everything in sight. Then he peeked under tinfoil at delicacies we'd reserved for the holiday dinner. "Wow!" He exclaimed, lifting the cover on a tray of turnovers. "Wow! And wow again!" I'd never known him to be at a loss for words. He seemed to be stuck on "Wow!"

By the time we ate our way through the weekend, both men had happy gizzards. Mom's scheming, which she preferred to call "wooing," worked wonders on André. He later divulged this tidbit: "When I saw you and your mom cooking together in your aprons, I felt so happy and at home. I spied a mirage of a future I wanted to be real."

André ended up enamored with the P's, and his family fell in love with me. We divided our holiday between my place and his Tennessee sister and brother-in-law's bustling home, where four teenagers vied for their uncle's attention. Meeting the rest of André's family felt daunting.

Thanks to South African hospitality, daunting didn't last long. Marie and Abe were gracious hosts. I tasted the family's loving spirit the minute we arrived, when their only daughter, Elise, happily removed her leopard print slippers, offering them (still warm) to my freezing feet.

"Thank you, Elise. How thoughtful! My shoes are soaked."

"We don't want anyone around here to have cold feet," André's dad joked as he joined the conversation. Giving me a wink and a warm hug, he said, "It's nice to see you again. Please, call me Mervyn. Call my wife Trudi. There won't be any 'Mr.' and 'Mrs.' around here, okay?" He immediately introduced me to everyone else. I noticed André didn't look up from untying his soggy shoes until the conversation turned toward something safer than cold feet.

Thanksgiving's most poignant moment was when Trudi broke free from dementia's grasp long enough to share her heart with me. It was the only time she and I held a deep conversation.

"I am so thankful my son has found you. You are a lovely, lovely girl. God has answered my prayers. We want you to be our daughter," she confided quietly as we linked arms in the brisk after-dinner air. November's incessant drizzle momentarily ceased and we ladies went for a walk while the men tidied the kitchen. For me, that motherly moment of clarity confirmed my earlier vision. In my spirit I felt the Lord reassuring me. He had things under control.

Marie, holding her mother's other hand, agreed wholeheartedly. "I would love for you to be my sister. Our family has seen so many girlfriends come and go through the years we've become afraid to get attached. Next thing we know, they're gone and André has another. May I give you some counsel about my brother?"

"Of course."

"Don't chase him. He will run!" She and her mother both chuckled knowingly.

"I don't have time to chase him. He is too far away and I am too busy," I replied.

"Good. That's for the best. Just let him do all the work. In the meantime, we will pray."

"I will pray, too. Nobody wants to be hurt."

After we circled the neighborhood, Trudi slipped back into her own world, sweetly smiling and nodding, but rarely engaging.

"Father, thank You for the touching transparency of that conversation; may she still be with us when our wedding bells ring. Help me not to try to help that happen any sooner than it should.

"He's still smarting a little from being wrapped around Vacation Girl's finger. I know love is not a game, but please help me to play this well. I've always messed up before, trying to force things that shouldn't be forced. Now is the time to practice everything You've taught me. Let's win this man's heart. Forever."

Christmas 2008

"Did he kiss you yet?"

"Mr. P! Don't ask her that," my mother scolded. "It's none of our business."

They sat on the sofa, watching old English movies with a bucket of popcorn between them. Mom was taking a break from the kitchen as our last tray of ginger snaps puffed up in the oven. André, back in town for Christmas, went outside to unload his car.

"I don't kiss and tell. Besides, whose lips can stretch 400 miles? It's not like we've seen each other much since Thanksgiving or anything." Blushing like a teenager, I brushed passed the giggling P's, grabbing a handful of popcorn on my way out to help André with his bags.

A lot can happen in a month, even if it's *not* kissing. Our communication escalated from once-a-day prayer to a running dialogue via text, email, and phone. I continued listening to André's sermon CD's and falling in love with his brain. His transparency and passion for God were refreshingly authentic. Our prayer time was my absolute favorite time of day. I was jubilant about praying together in person for the next few days, as we spent the holiday together.

This time, Marie invited the P's to come with us to Tennessee. "Don't leave them home alone on Christmas Eve! We're all anxious to meet them," she urged. The P's didn't mind. They were as curious about the South Africans as André's family were about them.

We definitely got a taste of South African culture in a houseful of Afrikaners at Christmastime. The family's strong Dutch heritage showed up when Afrikaans words popped into the conversation and traditional foods landed on the table. When André's cousins, Vincent and Madelyn arrived with a huge tray of "koeksisters" (pronounced cook-sisters), everyone cheered! The syrup-soaked fried dough was a huge hit, especially with Mrs. P.

"These little twisted sisters are delicious!" She said, swiping "just one more" from the shrinking pile.

Mine isn't the only nostalgia-kissed kitchen during the holidays. Familiar recipes also awakened childhood memories in André's family. I sensed their homesickness for a time and space that no longer exists as they "Mmmmmmed" their way through homemade fruitcake and peppermint crisp tart made with South African style caramel.

"It's lekker!" His father exclaimed between bites. Lekker is Afrikaans for great or tasty.

As a Southern girl, I grew up with Eagle Brand sweetened condensed milk. Without exception it shows up at picnics and potlucks in everything from banana pudding and peanut butter fudge to homemade ice cream. We know about our Eagle Brand. But I can promise you this, what the South Africans do to sweetened condensed milk trumps every scrumptiously sinful thing my Southern grandmothers dreamed up. Who knew placing the cans in a water bath and baking them for hours transforms it into dulce de lecce?

Our evening ended, as all South African gatherings should, with rusks and rooibos tea. Contentedly dunking my crisp homemade rusk, think biscotti, into my steaming tea, I gazed at the faces surrounding me. Gentle, content faces spread with laughter. Loving eyes. Genuine smiles. A sense of peace entered my heart as I contemplated becoming part of such a family.

André caught my eye and moved toward me. Placing his arms around me from behind, he whispered, "Merry Christmas Precious Angel. I always wondered what it would be like to have an angel in my life. Now I know. Thank you for being here with us. I treasure every moment."

Surprises

Good-bye is hard. Especially after creating such cozy holiday memories. After André went home and the P's left for Italy, my house seemed strangely desolate. I missed André's laughter. I missed Mom's cooking. I still missed my girls.

I often cried for Snuffles and Whipper. Every time I called Kym to check on them, guilt gnawed my stomach into knots. "They are doing great here," she assured. "Don't worry. We received the food money you sent. Everything's good."

I had conflicting emotions when I'd hear they were "happy" and "great." I wanted them to be. I also wanted them to miss their mama, just a little. It was hard to let go. I'm thankful I released them because 2009 was brutal. Between André, work and grad school, I was hardly home. They would have suffered.

One afternoon during parent-teacher conference week, I got a text from André. "Don't make plans for tonight. I've bought supper that I want you to pick up at Carrabba's around 6:30, okay?" His thoughtfulness always touched me. I wasn't used to a man worrying about whether or not I got enough to eat or enough rest or exercise. As André and I grew closer, I felt nurtured in new ways.

"Carrabba's takeout? Awesome!" I responded. "Back-to-back conferences after a whole school day . . . exhausting. Last one finishes at 6:30. Thanks for thinking of me. XO."

I parked in a "takeout only" spot and waited. André called to say they were running a few minutes behind with my order and would bring it to the car when ready. Pressed with an assignment for my online class, I hijacked some Wi-Fi and opened my laptop.

A knock-knock-knock on my window startled me before I remembered I was waiting on a waiter. Gazing into the smiling face on the other side of the glass, I shouted, "André! What are *you* doing here? You nearly scared me to death!"

Opening the door, he kissed my cheek. "Surprise Sweetie Peeps! No one should work as hard as you're working and eat dinner alone. I've come to take you out. Sorry I'm late. Atlanta traffic is terrible this time of day." Within seconds, I was out of that car and in his arms!

"I still can't believe you drove six hours to have dinner with me." We lingered side-by-side in our booth for an hour after the entrées arrived. I knew I should be tired, but joy kept my eyes open.

"When you're young, you can do these things," André joked. "Besides, I wanted to see you before I leave for South Africa. A month is a long time to be away from my Sweetie-Little-Darling. I don't want you to forget about your Honey."

Forgetting him was impossible. Marie's advice was spot on! Her brother wouldn't let me forget him. He was doing all the chasing while I focused on my job and got A's in my classes. It was easy to respond and reciprocate to André's attention.

The only thing I couldn't do was think of anything to call him, besides "Honey." He had tons of nicknames for me. He even strung them together into a song he left on my phone. While he was out of the country, I'd play and replay it from my voicemail box, "Sweetie-Little-Darling, darling little Angel, angel little Honey, honey little Sugar, sugar little Precious, precious little Jewel . . ." Then he'd whistle at the end. Every time he sang it, I ended up grinning. I felt adored.

In April, I turned thirty-nine. Annie and the kids came to visit for my birthday. Too many months passed since Lucas and Ariana had seen their Tia. I yearned to be part of their lives. Lucas was already on the downhill side of Kindergarten, and had a gaping hole where his two front teeth should have been.

Seeing Lucas made me think of Chloé, even though she was a whole year older. *I wonder how many teeth she's lost?* Watching him chase his sister around my backyard, I imagined Chloé, a full head taller, with long brown legs, running and laughing alongside them.

"*When, God, will this ache ever end?*"

"Where do you want to go for your birthday dinner tomorrow?" Sis asked, jerking me from my musing, "Or do I already know?"

"Who has my favorite Fiorucci salad?"

"Carrabba's."

"You got it. Is there anything the kids will eat there?"

"You can never go wrong with a place that serves pizza."

"Great. Can you guys come by the school tomorrow so I can show you around before we go out? Carrabba's isn't far from there."

"Sure, Sister. We want to see everywhere you spend your time these days. I know Lucas will be curious about your classroom."

On my birthday, I wore a favorite orange top and a knee-length denim skirt to school. "Tia, you look pretty," Ariana said, hugging my legs when she saw me.

"Thank you! My students threw a surprise party for me today. Can you help carry my presents to the car?"

"Yes. What did you get?"

"I'll show you when we get home, okay? Right now, I want to load up and get out of here. I'm ready for some supper. I didn't take time to eat much today."

I wanted to get to the restaurant before the dinner crowd, but Sis kept stalling. Then she stepped out to take a phone call just before we ordered. I'd nearly devoured a whole bread loaf by the time dinner arrived.

"Who wants to pray?" I asked.

"You do," Lucas said, "It's *your* birthday, Tia."

"Okay. Let's bow our heads." I thanked God for my family and the food and prayed a blessing over each person at the table. When I said, "Amen" and opened my eyes, André was sitting next to me!

"Surprise!" Ariana shouted and clapped.

"Surprise, my Angel. I couldn't let you celebrate without me. Besides, I had to meet your sister." Then he turned and waved a Mr. Bean hello saying, "Hello everybody!," as his eyebrows did a dance for the kids. They giggled. I blushed.

"André, you've got to stop doing this to me. I don't like surprises you know."

"You better get used to surprises if you're going to be with me. I'm full of them, Sweetie-Little-Darling. Watch out. You never know what's going to happen!"

He was right. I didn't. His unpredictability kept me guessing. For a list-making planner, it threw me slightly off-kilter—in a good way. My controlling rigidity was a byproduct of a low self-esteem and an out-of-control marriage. God was working to build me up and lighten me up. André's carefree adventurous spirit helped speed up the process. In the months that followed, he surprised me with many generous random acts of kindness.

When he realized I was mowing my hilly half-acre with a push mower, he gifted me with a red riding lawnmower. When I needed my wisdom teeth extracted, he paid the part of the bill my insurance wouldn't cover. André discerned what needed to be done and took care of it. He took care of me. Although I tried not to depend upon his kindness, I appreciated the ways he relieved my burdens and spilled joy into my life.

Christmas 2009

By the time I was rolling dough for Thanksgiving pies again, our relationship stood solid on all levels. We had big holiday plans. We would spend Thanksgiving in Tennessee with his family, and Christmas in Europe with the P's. Ecstatic about returning to Italy, when Mom called to invite us, I happy-danced in my kitchen.

"*Great idea, Lord! I hope André goes along with this plan. There's no more romantic place on Earth!*"

"Of course I'm in! What kind of question is that? Who wouldn't want to spend Christmas in Italy? Tell me how to pack." It took only seconds to make up his mind. Within days, we had plane tickets, thanks to André's credit card.

Next to those plane tickets in my journal is a scrap of rhyme that asks: *Are you and I - ready to fly - hand in hand - through life's sky?* On the same page I wrote, *I'm ready to move forward with this man. Why do I love him so?*

Then there is an unfinished list. It has seven reasons:

1. *Proactive regarding personal growth and healing*
2. *Kindest person I know*
3. *Compassionate*
4. *Unselfish*
5. *Sensual*

6. *Deep Thinker*

7. *Spiritual*

Apparently André came across my list at some point, because there's a number 8, in his handwriting. It says, *Goofy.*

The P's met us in Rome with hugs, kisses, and stories galore. We caught up in a coffee bar while waiting for our train in Stazione Termini. We told them all about the blizzard that delayed our flight and they shared stories of working with earthquake victims in L'Aquila, where a deadly April earthquake claimed more than three hundred lives and left 40,000 homeless.

"We were among the first responders to feed the people from makeshift kitchens on site," Mr. P said. "It was incredible to work alongside volunteers from all religions and walks of life."

"After that ministry, we moved to Sperlonga. That's where we're going now," Mrs. P explained. "It's halfway between Rome and Naples, quaint and precious. You will love it there!"

André's eyes sparkled as Mr. P laid out the itinerary for our ten-day stay. When I heard the word "Assisi," I cheered with delight.

"Assisi! I love Assisi! It's my favorite place in Umbria."

Soon our train raced toward Sperlonga. We fought jet lag, trying to stay awake so our body-clocks would match Italy's time zone in the morning. By the time we transferred from our train to a bus, which left us just outside of town, we were fading. I remember blindly following the P's down dark narrow streets, dragging our suitcases behind us.

Morning light filtered through white lace curtains and crept across my face. I smiled before opening my eyes.

"I'm in Italy. It's Christmastime. My Honey is in the next room. What, Lord, could be a better way to start this day? Thank You for safe travels. Thank You for time to relax after a jam-packed semester. I needed this. Thank You that my life is in such a better place than last time I was here. You have brought me a long way. I'm so thankful to be in Your hands."

"Good morning, Angel Baby Doll!" André greeted me from his room across the hall when I opened my door. "How's the most beautiful girl in the world this morning?" Jokingly, I looked around quickly as if trying to see who else was there.

Obviously he hadn't looked very closely. I was still in sweats, with hair askew and coke-bottle glasses weighing down my face. There was only one bathroom. I claimed it. One downside of traveling with someone you're trying to woo is the fact they will probably behold you at your very worst. The good part is if they are only into superficial beauty, you might scare them off before it's too late.

I felt better once my contacts were in. "Good morning," I answered ten minutes later. "How's my favorite preacher?"

"Buongiorno!" bellowed Mrs. P from the kitchen. "Buongiorno ragazzi! Avete dormito bene?" We laughed at her attempt to sound like an Italian mama and followed our noses to the table, where fresh croissants were waiting. Mistaken in thinking I'd been up first, I realized Mr. P already went for a seaside prayer walk and raided the corner bakery on his way back home.

"It's hard to keep him indoors when we are in Italy," Mom said. "He's more at home here than anywhere. I can barely keep up with him!"

Neither could we. Mr. P kept us running nearly the whole vacation. It was marvelous! Our first day in Sperlonga, we donned sweaters and scarves before exploring our surroundings. Sunshine peeked through thin clouds as we overlooked the sparkling Tyrrhenian Sea from the top of the village.

We walked for hours, from one picturesque scene to the next, stopping to pose for the camera in front of antique doors and bougainvillea-covered walls. André's excitement was contagious as he tried out the language, "Ciao!" and the food, "Mmmmmm! Bellissimo!" He even tried to kiss me like an animated Italian when the P's weren't looking.

They disappeared after lunch, leaving us to get around on our own. My Italian was horrible, so we ended up laughing and gesturing more than speaking, but usually managing to get our point across. The townspeople were friendly and helpful, without making us feel like fools.

Since December is not prime tourist time, we had the place to ourselves. It was surreal. "Maybe we're on a film set!" I laughed as, holding hands, we made wishes at an ancient well in the villaggio's center.

My wish came true! Perhaps it was more prayer than wish. Here's how it happened, just like a movie. After dinner that evening, André suggested we go for a short walk on the seaside promenade, "Just to get a taste of the town at night."

"Take a brolly," Mr. P suggested, placing an oversized umbrella in André's hands. "It could mist a bit."

He was right. As we reached the promenade, a light rain began to fall, creating colorful halos around Christmas lights and street lamps. The nighttime view was enchanting as reflections danced across the water and Sperlonga's medieval fortress stood illuminated against a darkened sky. We walked arm-in-arm, the whipping wind threatening to pull a Mary-Poppins on our "brolly."

"I remember the first time we walked arm-in-arm on a promenade," I recalled.

"Yes. So do I. That was the night I first wanted to kiss you."

"But you didn't."

"I was nervous. We weren't ready for kissing."

"I know. I'm glad you thought about it though."

"I could kiss you now."

"You could."

"Or we could just walk up a little higher so we can take in more of the view."

We continued up the wide walkway toward the fortress. Arriving at a lookout point, we stopped.

"Let's pause here for a moment," he said. We stood side-by-side, gazing down at the sleepy village in silence.

My heart flip-flopped as André turned to face me. When I looked into his eyes, I knew.

This is the moment I've wished and waited and prayed for. He's really going to do it! "Hold me, Jesus. I think I might pass out." *Oh, yeah, I'm holding my breath. Breathe, girl. Breathe.*

"Thank you for experiencing such a beautiful place with me," he began. "How would you like to share many more incredible days like today? How would you like to always travel with me, minister at my side, share my joys and share my sorrows? How would you like to be my life partner?" A fraction of silence, then, " Juliet Louise, take off your left glove."

With trembling hands, I removed my glove.

"Can you hold the umbrella a moment, please?" I took the handle firmly in my right hand as André produced a white gold band from one of his pockets. Baguette diamonds caught the street-lamp's light, matching the sparkle in his eyes as he popped the one question he'd never asked anyone.

"Will you marry me?"

My "Yes!" echoed off the fortress walls, upsetting a couple of sleeping seagulls. André slipped that ring onto my finger and made up for the kiss he didn't give me on our first date. Then the wind suddenly whipped up, inside-outing our umbrella, so we hurried toward the cozy apartment to share our excitement with the P's.

"We knew it! We knew it!" They danced joyfully around and around their tiny kitchen. "Congratulations! Tomorrow we shall celebrate in Assisi!"

I slept very little that night, knowing the man in the next room was my fiancé.

"Father, You are gracious. You know how much Italy means to me. To have this be the place of our engagement is redemptive! I remember coming here a lifetime ago, head full of girlish plans to find the perfect fabric for an imperfect union. What I didn't realize is the fabric of a marriage is so much more than brushed silk or Italian lace. It is You who binds two souls together. Only You, who can take a pair of sinful, selfish human beings and weave something holy. You cover our shameful nakedness with Your white robe of righteousness. I know that now, Lord. Thank You for giving me a man who knows You too."

In the morning, we boarded a northbound train to Umbria. André and I sat next to each other, facing the P's. Our fingers laced and unlaced as we fiddled with the ring on my finger. "My Baby Angel is happy today," he proudly announced to no one in particular. I guess my grin gave me away.

"Well, why wouldn't she be? She's in Italy!" Mr. P responded.

"She's happy because her mother's prayers have been answered," Mom said. "Of course, we knew a year ago this would happen, didn't we Mr. P? We saw *all* the signs." She wagged her finger at André to punctuate her last three words. "Now when is the wedding?"

"It has to be a twenty-third. That is my special covenant day with God. I proposed to Juliet on the twenty-third because that's the date I promised the Lord I would trust Him to bring someone into my life in a miraculous way," André answered. "He honored that covenant, so I want to always remember His faithfulness on that date. That's why we'll not only celebrate our wedding anniversary on the twenty-third, but we'll also celebrate each month with a 'monthaversary' in remembrance of what God has done for us."

The Lord knew the twenty-third was also an important date for me. Remember that awful twenty-third of March, when I physically walked away from Jon after giving his truck back? Just look at how He redeemed it with a perpetual celebration of His grace in my life, on every twenty-third of the month.

Waving my diamonds Mrs. P's direction, I spoke.

"I love his idea. If we do it, he'll never forget our anniversary. The problem is, I only have a week between school getting out, and starting my last round of graduate classes in June. Unless we wait until the fall, the only twenty-third that works for me is May. That leaves us just five months to plan a wedding.

"André wants a real wedding, too. Bride. Groom. The whole nine yards. No cheap and easy Justice of the Peace stuff. That will be a lot to plan with short notice. I might need you P's to come home and help."

Little miss Type-A-list-maker was starting to manifest. My mental gears began spinning the moment André proposed. I even brought pen and paper on the train to jot down ideas.

"He deserves a real wedding, he's waited fifty-some years for this. We will help you pull it together. This is so exciting!" Mom clapped her hands and squealed, causing the gentleman across the aisle to glance up from his paper.

Something happened in Assisi that made *me* squeal. It was a thumbs-up from God, one of those gifts, so tangible and rare, I will never forget.

Our train halted just outside the medieval city walls. We entered Assisi on foot, again rolling our luggage down cobbled streets behind the speedy P's. André "oohed" and "aahed" at everything Italian along the way to our hotel. Gorgeous pastry-filled shop windows beckoned us to stop in for a treat. First, we needed to drop off our gear and get our bearings.

Mr. P was proud to have scored a great off-season discount on our hotel, which was built right into the thick city wall. "This is unbelievable!" André exclaimed, running his hand along ancient stones as we were shown to our rooms. Tiled hallways led us up a set of stairs and down a few doors to the room where I would stay. I grew weak-kneed with emotion to discover the number above my door was "twenty-three."

"Oh, André! Look!" I pointed, tears tightening my throat. "God is showing His approval. He's placed me in room twenty-three!" We paused before that wooden door, arms entwined, prayers of gratitude ascending to our Father, who reminded us of His presence in our every decision.

"*Lord,*" I prayed later, "*thank You for affirming our decision to be married on the twenty-third. Thank You for caring for the details that matter to us. This is confirmation that You see us. I feel loved! Amen.*"

Our engagement photos exude joy. Assisi's thirteenth century Basilica di San Francesco stood behind us as we laughed cheek-to-cheek, overlooking the Umbrian countryside. No staged, professional photo shoot could have captured the euphoria of those sacred days following our engagement. Mr. P's camera caught them all as we explored Assisi, Sperlonga, and Rome together.

"We better go home while we can still fit into our clothes," I joked as André and I spooned scalding cioccolata densa into our mouths for the umteenth time in ten days.

"I've never had anything so delicious!" André declared after sampling Italy's extra-thick version of hot chocolate. "These miniature cups hardly hold enough. I need more!" With Italian-style bravado, he'd exclaimed, "Deliciosa!" to the girl behind the counter as he ordered round two.

We left Italy with our heads full of wedding plans and our suitcases stuffed with packets of cioccolata densa. In following months, no matter how we tried to re-create those moments, it never tasted quite the same at home as when sipped from tiny mugs in foreign cafés.

"We shall return to Italy!" André vowed each time we reminisced about our engagement trip.

"Yes! We shall." I'd agree, toasting my fiancé with a souvenir Assisi mug.

Wedding Plans

The Tortoise and Hare of time raced one another as five months simultaneously dragged and flew. Swallowed by research for my semester-long literacy project, I prayed for longer nights to write, while wishing away the 144 days that kept me from my Honey.

True to their word, the P's came home to help with wedding details. From behind an armful of faux tulips Mr. P joked one afternoon, "As many times as I've been to Hobby Lobby to buy tulips, *I* should be the flower girl!"

In an effort to maximize my generous groom's dollars, since he offered to fund our wedding, I was planning a do-it-yourself event. Thankfully the "yourself" wasn't just me by myself; the Ps and other friends were a great help. As I tapped into the skills of my friends and loved ones, we devised an intimate church wedding on a pastor's budget.

"I want white horses and a carriage!" André exclaimed on our homebound plane ride, as we listed our wedding wishes. My inner Cinderella perked up. So did the ears of fellow passengers.

"That sounds fancy. I wonder where I can find glass slippers?" We chuckled together as he kissed my forehead. "Why do I love you so much, Sweetie Peeps?"

I savored glimpses of André's sentimental heart as we planned together. Our budget nixed the horse and carriage, but I was still a princess on our wedding day.

Royal preparations began in January, with a hunt for the perfect dress. I tried them all: puffy white clouds with armholes, slinky walk-like-a-geisha dresses created for mermaid bodies, itchy-bodiced gowns with plunging necklines. Nothing worked. By March, I was ready to give up. Feeling like Cinderella's stepsister after weeks of stuffing myself into dresses designed for someone else, I left a trail of tears from David's Bridal to my car.

Throwing up my hands to the Lord, I cried, *"I don't have time for this, God! I want to look on the outside the way André makes me feel on the inside—young and excited and beautiful. These dresses make me feel like Snow White's grandmother!"*

Resisting the temptation to seek comfort in *Häagen-Dazs*, I returned home. The Father spoke to my heart on the way.

"Yes, Lord, I know what's in that bag in my closet. You already know I've thought about peeking. But what if unzipping that bag unzips the past? Isn't it sacrilege to consider wearing my wedding dress twice? Yes, it's beautiful. Yes, it's 'me.' Yes . . . I will try it on when I get home."

From the recesses of my closet, heart thumping, I pulled out that same pink bag I hauled from house to house for sixteen years. Folding back the plastic, I scrutinized my dress. Not one spot or blemish marred its beauty. The lace felt true beneath my fingers, not stiff and scratchy like those other dresses.

I wonder if it still fits?

The mirror revealed truth. Although I couldn't zip myself, I was in. *"It's perfect,"* whispered my reflection. *"I love it!"*

The Princess Diana sleeves could disappear, but the rest was a dream. Kneeling beside my bed, enveloped in silk taffeta and Italian lace, I prayed.

"Thank You, Lord. This is the dress I've been looking for. And it's already mine."

Emotion erupted as I remembered purchasing that lace with my mother.

"It seems so long ago. I had high hopes at twenty-three, didn't I? Thinking I could make a marriage work. I'm facing forty, Lord. Yet I feel like a girl . . . a girl finally learning to trust her Father."

Peering again into the mirror I questioned, "Why does this dress make me giddy? How will I explain that to André?"

When anyone asked, "Do you have your dress yet?" Invariably, the inquiry followed, "Where did you get it?"

Embarrassed to admit I was revamping my original dress, I learned to avoid the second question by answering, "Still looking," to the first. I was looking; looking into the mirror each time the seamstress called me in for alterations.

Mrs. Cho worked diligently. She removed the puffy sleeves and fitted the bodice to my torso, modernizing the dress without compromising the design. She and Gold's Gym had become my new best friends. In order to get my forty-year-old body into sleeveless-wedding-dress shape, I began stopping on my way home from school each day for a quick workout, arms one day, legs the next.

"Ooh! You looking good!" Mrs. Cho exclaimed when I showed up for the final fitting. "I take dress in here. And here." She pinched the fabric at my waist and underneath my arms. "Come next week. You like it."

After Italy, André introduced me to weight training at his YMCA. Prior to that, I had never worked out in a gym. After all of my body trauma, I was just thankful to be running. Building muscle to increase metabolism never occurred to me. Within eight weeks after incorporating weights into my workouts, I noticed the difference. Next time André came to visit, so did he.

"Wow! Wow! And wow again!" He twirled me around, trying to whistle through a grin. I blushed.

"She's been running herself ragged!" Mom eavesdropped from the porch. "Take her out. Feed her. All she does is study and work, work, work!"

"Looks like she's been working out, too Mrs. P."

André could not keep his eyes in their sockets on our way dinner. "Why did I wait so long to ask you to be my wife?"

"I don't know, but you better watch the road," I replied, both pleased and uncomfortable with the extra attention.

"How are the wedding plans, My Angel? I'm afraid I haven't been much help."

"Everything is falling into place. Just keep sending money. That's the best help you can be. If every potential guest RSVP's, we'll be hosting a crowd."

Over dinner we finalized ceremony and clothing details. I feared André would ask too many questions about my dress. He didn't. Whew!

When shopping for his suit, I'd brought along a piece of lace, to make sure our colors blended. We bantered about whether he should wear a cream or white shirt with his coffee-colored Italian suit.

"I think your shirt should match my dress. My dress is not white."

"I look sickly in yellow. Surely white is the better choice."

"But my dress isn't yellow. It's cream. There's a difference."

He bought both shirts. I don't remember which one he wore on our wedding day. Perhaps we both had wardrobe secrets as we dressed for our vows.

Initially only Mom and Annie were in on my secret. They thought it unwise to advertise the dress's history. Already overwhelmed with year-end teaching responsibilities, graduate finals and wedding details, I agreed. Unsolicited opinions, especially negative ones, are potentially hazardous to bridal nerves.

I have always welcomed my friend Meredith's opinions, however. She's generally wise. She also has a nose for chocolate and secrets. If either is in proximity, she will know. Inviting her to be our wedding coordinator meant inviting her into the minutiae of the entire operation. As the twenty-third of May inched closer, we communicated almost daily, discussing countless details, from the guest book to the getaway car.

The only thing we didn't discuss was where I got my dress. Not wanting to lie, I awkwardly diverted those conversations. Meredith didn't push. She waited. Eventually I caved, sending her a tell-all email explaining my evasiveness.

I don't plan on advertising it, I wrote. *Of course I would NEVER tell André, but I can tell you. You can keep a secret and I don't care if you think I'm weird.*

Meredith's response surprised me.

Thanks for letting me in on the dress secret. I don't think it's completely weird. You always said you already had your dream wedding, just not your dream marriage. What better dress for an Italian-themed wedding than a personal keepsake made with fine

Italian lace? You are supposed to be making you and André happy, not everyone else. So it does not really matter what anyone else thinks. With that, I felt impressed to encourage you to consider telling André. That way you will have no worries—ever.

"Oh Lord. How can I tell him? This will be awkward. What if he doesn't understand? What if he gets upset? No, I'd rather carry the secret than risk hurting him."

Stubbornly, I chose not to heed my friend's advice. For weeks my emotions ranged from giddy to guilty when anyone mentioned the dress. Hindsight reveals a lack of trust in the heart of the man who would become my husband, and the heart of the God who was granting the desires of my heart. I should have told him. I should have trusted. Fear blocked my faith. I still had much to learn about love.

It's like that when a girl grows up without consistent fathering. She's rarely sure if the hearts behind the words of men are trustworthy. Trust is like a Greek phyllo dough pastry, its paper-thinness strengthened only by multiple layers, held together by authentic sweetness.

André definitely had the sweetness. He adored me. The layers of trust between us grew with every interaction. He deserved my honesty. Still, I held out, with no plan of how or when I would reveal to him the history of my dress.

Speaking of the dress, Mrs. Cho and I had a verbal skirmish when I went to pick it up.

"You try on," she said, whisking me into her dressing room.

"Okay, but I'm in a hurry today."

"We make sure everything okay."

I undressed and re-dressed as she helped me navigate the silk and lace. The long zipper stuck midway up my back.

"Suck in you air," she commanded.

"I am."

"Hold you arms up."

"Okay."

Zzzzziiiip. "We got it!" She cheered.

I. Could. Not. Breathe.

The mirror told me the bodice was too tight. I told Mrs. Cho what the mirror said.

"You no eat for three days. You fine."

"If I don't eat for three days, I will die," I retorted. "You have to loosen this. If I breathe or laugh or move, I'm going to bust a seam. Please."

"Okay. Okay," She consented. "You pick up next week."

"Thank you. I'm sorry. Thank you. I have to eat food. Every day."

She chuckled as she un-shrink-wrapped me. "Okay. Okay. For you, I will do again."

Almost There

All other plans were taking shape, thanks to my notebook filled with lists. "Guest lists, gift lists, food lists, countdown lists with day-by-day to-dos . . . I'm in list Heaven!" I laughed with Darcy on the phone as we finalized the flower order. "When will you be here?" Darcy, a former florist, was in charge of every blooming thing. Literally.

She and Meredith were flying into Atlanta a week early, to help pull it all together. Their husbands would follow later, in SUVs laden with eleventh hour items, including a huge metal trellis we "needed" for the reception hall. Ryan would be our videographer, and Dr. Alan would be a behind-the-scenes peacemaker when pre-wedding blood pressures escalated. God bless them both!

Last minute RSVP's arrived in the mail a few days before my girlfriends arrived on my doorstep. "Mom! You're not going to believe this." I shouted, sprinting from the mailbox. "Dr. V, my former principal is coming! I'm honored that she would make the effort."

"She always did like you. You have quite the guest list, don't you?"

Mom was watering plants on my porch. I sat down in the rocker beside the front door.

"Mother?"

"Yes."

"Are you going to be okay with everyone on the guest list? I know it's never easy, being in the same room with ex-spouses. I don't want to create stress for you. I just want everyone who worried about my life before to see how happy I am now. I want them all to taste and see what God has done for me."

"I will be fine with Mr. P here. Last time you married, I was alone. I didn't like that. The past is the past. We all have different lives now. I have forgiven and forgotten what needs to be forgiven and forgotten. We will be fine."

"Thank you for your help. I never could have done this much preparation without you. I'm going to miss you P's."

As our wedding date grew nearer, my enthusiasm showered André every time we spoke. "I can't wait for you to see the church and reception hall. It's all coming together! I'm so excited!"

"That's great, Babydoll. Tell me everything!"

So, I did. Well, almost everything, except for the teensy-weensy dress details.

Between André and me, our favorite idea was to include in our ceremony those friends who had spiritually mentored and inspired us. Rather than an awkward row of groomsmen and middle-aged bridesmaids in matching dresses, we chose to honor our special friends by seating them on the platform during the ceremony. We wanted them to encircle us during the prayer of blessing, laying hands on us, anointing us to be a godly couple who would inspire others, as they inspired us. We each chose twelve.

Wanting our close friends and families to get acquainted, we also planned a lakeside picnic for the day before our wedding. Blue skies greeted me through the bedroom window on the twenty-second of May, as I gathered my thoughts for the testimony I wanted to share. André suggested we each tell our story so loved ones could see our hearts and recognize God's hand in our lives. I'd agreed, although public speaking makes me nervous.

"I wrote mine out," I confided in his ear at the picnic.

"That's okay. You'll do fine. They aren't public. They are family."

"God, I want to do fine," I prayed as I deep-breathed my nerves away. "I love my people. I want them each to see how You have led in my life and I want them to love André, too. Please speak through us. Let our joy be a testimony of Your goodness."

As we stood up to speak, emotion overwhelmed me. Each familiar face was significant to our life stories. "These are our peeps," I whispered to my love.

André surveyed our parents, our siblings, and our longstanding friends as they happily chatted together. We already spent some time introducing our guests to one another, now we wanted to introduce them to the depths of our grateful hearts as we shared our stories.

André went first.

"Every relationship I pursued of my own volition failed . . . badly," he shared. "On December 23, 2005, I was staying with my parents in Hixon, Tennessee. Exhausted with being my own advisor, I laid on the floor in their guest bedroom and surrendered to God.

'God, it's over,' I said. 'I can't do this anymore. I'm going to stop pursuing. Fourteen failed relationships in six years! I'm done.'

"I made a covenant with Him that night.

'I will not pursue any more relationships. You will have to miraculously bring someone into my life if I am ever going to be married.'

"Ever since, on the twenty-third of each month, I celebrate with God. He often gives little nods of recognition in remembrance of our covenant. For example, there were exactly twenty-three tables available for our reception tomorrow."

André proceeded to preach a sermon to his captive audience, highlighting the importance of surrounding ourselves with godly advisors. He thanked the people whose counsel has impacted him, whose marriages have remained strong.

Then it was my turn to speak. I read my script, anchoring my thoughts in 2 Corinthians 2:15 (NIV): "For we are to God the pleasing aroma of Christ among those who are being saved and those who are perishing."

"You've been the aroma of Christ to me," I said, directing my words to the achingly familiar eyes that wept with me through the valley of Jon's addiction. "When we are single, God loans us husbands from the body of believers, to help us in areas where we would normally lean on a spouse. Several women here have generously shared theirs with me." I paused to gaze at Meredith, Aubrey and Darcy.

Then to each man in my tribe I said, "I'm humbly grateful for the men God used to help me get on my feet again. Thank you for being the 'aroma of Christ,' for showing me what Jesus smells like. And Tom, thank you for raising my floundering expectations with your unselfish gifts of flowers and candy after my divorce. You reminded me how it's supposed to be, without ever asking anything in return. André . . . you have some big shoes to fill."

Sunlight glistened in my father's tears as he reached to hug me afterward. "I'm angry with you," he blurted. "Why didn't you tell me you were living like that? I feel so stupid. I had no clue!"

Shocked by the intensity of his emotion, I searched for a response.

Although I loved my family, they were often the last to know of my suffering. Even now, with the writing of this book, I realize how much I hid. Why do we hide our deepest pain from those closest to us?

"Dad, I'm sorry. I was often in denial myself. Or I was hopeful things would change and I didn't want you to hate Jon if he got better. It's hard to know why. I just couldn't call you up and say, 'My life is out of control.' It was easier to say nothing; less humiliating to accept help from people who hadn't walked me down the aisle and witnessed the making of those vows I couldn't keep."

"Well, I'm glad I'm here to witness the vows that will take place tomorrow. André seems like a guy who's going to love, honor and cherish my daughter." He shot that last sentence André's direction. "That's what she deserves."

The Wedding

Excitement awoke me early for a quiet moment with God. Grabbing my journal, I curled up in bed and wrote: *May 23, 2010, "Thank You, Lord, that today I will marry, in front of everyone, the man of my dreams. My Love. My Heart. My Soul Mate. I praise You for who You are and for what You've done in my life . . ."*

My heart rejoiced, even as butterflies flitted through my insides in anticipation of the hours ahead. Over breakfast, I said to Nancy, "Can you believe, my friend, how gracious God has been? I do not deserve this! Yet, He has given me the desires of my heart. I believe He will do the same for you."

"He will, my sweet friend. In His time, He will. Right now I am celebrating with you. Now, how can we get you to the hairdresser's on time?"

"Right," I laughed, wiping mango from my chin. "That's why you're here, isn't it? To keep me focused, and moving. Thank you for staying here with me, even though everyone else was enjoying their hotel hot tubs last night."

"Of course! Somebody had to drive you to the salon this morning. A bride should always be chauffeured." Nancy held out her hand for my keys. She started hauling my bags to the car, while I slipped on some jeans and packed a snack for later.

We were only two minutes late.

Jennifer, my trusted personal stylist for the day, was waiting with hot curling irons and magic hands. We agreed on hair that was, in Jennifer's words, "sexy, classy, elegant and movable."

We had a few quiet moments of intense makeup application before the party burst through the door. First came Ryan, rolling video, followed by Ariana, who shyly crawled onto my lap with a crayon drawing of André and me standing outside "The Love Hotel."

"It's for you, Tia!"

I oohed and aahed, as my face flushed pink with the adult innuendos that accompanied Ariana's gift.

Then Eddie stuck his head in, "I'm heading to Starbucks, anybody need anything?"

Annie and Lucas found a corner and began rehearsing "Love Story," a modern-day Romeo and Juliet song the kids were performing at our reception.

Intent on making me gorgeous and getting me out the door on time, Jennifer ignored the hoopla and kept curling and spraying until my hair was perfection. Finally, she started on Ariana's, transforming her into a petite prima donna.

"Are you ready to be my flower girl?" I asked after several minutes. The five-year-old smiled at her own reflection, nodding as tight blonde ringlets bounced, "Yes."

"Time to go, folks!" Ryan announced soon after Eddie returned with a tray of steaming paper cups. "We've got a wedding to get to."

I glanced in the mirror and caught Annie's approving eye in the reflection.

"I'm overwhelmed! I feel like a kid. I feel like a princess. I'm gonna cry." Tears threatened to mess with my makeup as joy swelled my insides. "It's great to be forty and feeling like a teenager," I said as a final dot of lip-gloss was professionally applied. "I cannot wait for André to see me!"

My emotion went deeper than excitement over curls and the flawless finish Jennifer created with her cosmetic palette. Those were but tiny branches on a solid taproot of delight that anchored me to the heart of my heavenly Father. I was thrilled with the gifts He was giving me.

"God, I feel Your delight in me. Thank You for bringing me out of darkness. Thank You for each joy in today's journey toward the altar."

"We have a surprise for you, Tia!" Lucas grabbed my hand, pulling me out of my prayer and my chair.

"What is it sweet boy?" I smiled into enthusiastic seven-year-old eyes.

"We got you a limo," Eddie grinned, winking at Lucas.

"You what?" I stopped at the door, confused.

"Yeah, we ordered you a limo. The driver will take you to the church now, then chauffeur you and André to your hotel after the reception. We just couldn't let you two go off on your honeymoon in a Honda Accord. This is too big a deal for that!"

"Awesome! Thank you!" I hugged Annie and Eddie. "I've never ridden in a limo before! Who's going with me?"

"I am!" Ariana pulled me toward the parking lot where a white stretch limousine sprawled across five spaces. Lucas was already inside, his grin as wide as the chassis.

"Wow! This is crazy awesome!" I ducked through the door after Ariana. Annie and Nancy joined us. Ryan videoed as we giggled and romped inside the fancy car, then he followed us in my Rav and shot video out the window as we hogged the highway on our way to church.

"I'm reminded of Psalm 18:19," I said after our excitement settled. "It says, 'He brought me out into a spacious place; he rescued me because he delighted in me' (NIV). This new life is definitely a more spacious place than the soul-restricting circumstances I used to live under. I feel free. I feel loved. I feel joy!"

We spilled out of the limo just in time to duck into our dressing rooms before the early-birds arrived. One early bird, a man who fathered me from age seven to fourteen, received a tender hug. "Thank you for being here, "I beamed. "Your presence is significant."

Nancy took her post at the guest book. My two younger brothers stood guard at the sanctuary doors, while inside the church my soon-to-be nephews and niece rehearsed Pachelbel's "Canon in D" on stringed instruments.

André and I tapped into the talents of several young people who loved us enough to give of themselves to make our wedding day extraordinary. From the handsome doormen to the teenagers who volunteered to work our reception we were blessed with their youthful energy. Little Lucas even had the distinguished honor of escorting me down the aisle. He took the job seriously. "Tia, I would love to," was his exuberant response when I asked.

Meredith, my efficient wedding coordinator, poked her head into our bridal chamber as my photographer friend, Sarah, captured the chaos. "You have ten minutes ladies," she warned. Annie and Ariana were peeking through the blinds into the sanctuary, giving play-by-play coverage of arriving guests.

"Ooh! There's Grandpa and Jean. Who is that lady in the blue dress? She looks familiar . . . " Marci, my friend since fourth grade, had the back of my dress stretched taut while Darcy attacked it with a hand-held steamer.

Somehow, the not-so-tiny detail of steaming the bride's dress was overlooked. I'd been in a pretty panic since the moment I arrived to notice the creases. Mother was so busy reassuring me she forgot to take down the pin curls on the sides of her own hair. We only noticed when we studied the pictures together, weeks later.

My friends finally gave up with the steamer when we realized the humidity was wilting everyone's curls.

"Air! I need Air!" Annie fanned herself in the corner.

"You look beautiful Tia," Ariana's sweet voice soothed my inner wrinkles. She wrapped willowy arms around my waist, leaning her head into my hip. Sarah's Canon caught Ariana's wistful expression against a backdrop of lace. That image remains one of my favorites from the day.

"Thank you, my little princess. Are you ready to drop some petals on that carpet out there?" She nodded. I turned toward the mirror for a final inspection then spritzed my wrists with L'eau D'issey. I was ready.

Everyone else cleared the room when Eddie knock-knocked to exchange Lucas for Annie. The kids and I spied through the blinds as André seated first his mother, then mine.

"Thank You, God, for allowing André's mom to participate in this day. Seeing her bachelor son marry has been her lifetime dream. She appears so elegant on his arm."

Watching him walk the length of the aisle was sheer delight. He. Was. Gorgeous. My heart did that little skippy thing when he turned around and smiled at one of his friends.

"I'm crazy about him, Lord. I really am. Each time I see him it's like the first time!"

I chuckled at what happened next. Rather than the groom entering on his own, he walked the aisle surrounded, bodyguard style, by his posse, as if they were preventing an escape. His friend Colin later commented, "I wasn't letting him out of my sight. The only time I've seen him walk down an aisle is after preaching the sermon, and that's going the wrong way."

"Okay Ariana, you're next." Meredith waved the three of us into the foyer. I winked at my brothers at their posts then backed out of sight when they opened the doors for Ariana and her flower basket.

Lucas and I held hands, waiting for our cue. He was a tiny man in his dark suit and yellow tie. "Are you nervous?" I asked, kissing his forehead, then rubbing away the lip marks with my thumb.

"No, Tia. Are you?"

"Yes."

"Why?"

"I just feel nervous. But it's the good kind of nervous. Thank you for walking with me."

"You're welcome."

"Remember how we practiced? Not too fast. We want to make it take a long time to get to Uncle André."

"I remember."

The doors opened wide as the string quartet began Mendolsohn's "Wedding March." We paused for a moment as everyone stood and turned to stare. Some snapped iPhone photos. Lucas' palm was warm against mine. My eyes scanned familiar faces from a lifetime of friendships. *Oh! There's Dr. V. And my Aunt Candice. Oh! I see my friend Sandy!* I smiled. Not for the camera, but for the joy of knowing my loved ones were witnessing the happiest moments of my life.

Step. Step. Step. We marched toward giant pedestal urns cascading with white tulips and wisteria. *Darcy sure did a great job with those.*

Step. Step. My spiritual mentors smiled from their places. Dr. Alan, with his arm around Darcy. Bob and Aubrey. Tom. Eddie and Annie. Mr. P. Shirley, my Texas teaching-buddy. Sweet Nancy. Meredith. Scanning for Ryan, I found him behind a video camera. Marci, my grade school girlfriend.

"God, bless each of these praying people. Thank You for using them to counsel me through life's thick and thin."

Step. André's eyes, moist with joy, found mine. From that moment, I was captivated. Everything else faded as I focused on him. Trading Lucas' little-boy hand for André's arm, I stepped to the top of the platform and turned to face my bridegroom.

He smiled and winked at me, mouthing the word, "Beautiful" as Joelle's father, Pastor Callahan, welcomed our guests. *"Joelle was so right to insist on introducing us. I'm sorry she couldn't make it today. She would be pleased with the results of her obedience to Your Spirit."*

After prayer, we stood like statues while André's buddies, Steve and Randy, sang Dan Fogleberg's "Longer Than." Annie later joked, "That song described your ceremony. Longer than life!"

Neither of us noticed. Enveloped in our own little bubble, we floated through the ceremony and reception, our mutual adoration palpable. Pastor Callahan commented afterward he'd never seen a couple so in love on their wedding day.

"There is a great need for two people like you to share God's love with others," he explained before we took our vows. "By choosing to make 'The Prayer of St. Francis of Assisi' the theme of your marriage, you reveal what is in your hearts. How beautiful that God has inspired you to serve humanity rather than being served."

Behind me sat André's special people, those who had served *him* during difficult times. Every once in a while, he'd glance over my shoulder to share a smile with one of them. I'd take that opportunity to sneak a peek at *my* peeps. Having them all together in one spot was precious. Each time I looked, the emotion in their faces mirrored their hearts. They were thrilled for me. For what God had done in my life.

As we knelt together, those loved ones encircled us, laying praying hands on our heads and shoulders. Closing my eyes, I drank in the moment, allowing the reverence, the solidarity, the revelation of the healing power of community to soak into my spirit. I knew André and I were not alone. We had a combined force of godly, longstanding marriages to glean from as we began our life as one.

I stole a glance at André, kneeling before me, head bowed, boutonnière askew, handsome features serious.

"This is it, Lord. Here is the man You've given me. Help me to love him as You would have me to love. Thank You for the gift of a second chance. I treasure it. I treasure him."

From the way André kissed me at the end of the ceremony, I knew I was treasured, too!

"Woo hoo, God! Now that's what I'm talking about!"

"I now present to you Mr. and Mrs. André Van Heerden," announced Pastor Callahan as the recessional began. We smiled and waved our way down the aisle and out into the bright sunlight, where our photographer was waiting to capture more of our joy.

By the time we entered the reception, both the antipasto bar and the emcee's jokes were exhausted. A packed room cheered our arrival. As teenage volunteers delivering plates of fettuccine Alfredo squeezed between chairs, André and I floated from table to table, hugging and greeting our guests.

We barely ate anything. Instead, like butterflies we flitted around that room for an hour, sipping the nectar of friendship. We smiled so much our cheeks literally ached the next morning.

I longed to be able to sit for a while, basking in the love that flowed from each person who made an effort to share our special day. It was hard to move on to the next table, but we wanted to personally greet everyone before it was time to say good-bye.

When we reached André's parents, Trudi grasped my hands, looked into my eyes and said, "I am so, so happy. This is a wonderful day for us." In that moment, I knew she knew what transpired, and that she approved. Smiling past the lump in my throat, I kissed her soft cheek and thanked her for raising such a wonderful son.

Several songs, toasts, and slices of cake later, Mr. Wonderful and I prepared to make our exit. The crowd followed us outside. While André hugged his mother good-bye, I snuck a bunch of curious kids into the limo.

I noticed my students thronging at the open doors for a peek inside the limo. On a whim I'd said, "Go on in. Check it out!" Wide-eyed with wonder, they giggled and wiggled themselves inside, staying until their parents pulled them out.

I stepped up onto the limo's floor for a better view of everyone gathered to wish us farewell. Waving and blowing tearful kisses, I expressed my gratitude for their presence and love.

"Happy life!" Someone called as I ducked inside. André joined me, the heavy door closing behind him, leaving us cocooned in dark and quiet.

"Happy life." I whispered the words, as a prayer for each loved one on the other side of those tinted windows. We rolled out of the church parking lot in our ostentatious ride, feeling utterly overwhelmed with emotion.

"How's my wife?" André asked, taking my hand.

"I'm happy, with a twinge of sadness to say good-bye to people we may not see again for a long time. How's my husband?"

"I'm feeling good. I'm glad we had a church wedding. The show of support was phenomenal, wasn't it?"

"Yes. Can you believe this limo?"

"I feel a bit guilty, riding around in this thing. Eddie's a great guy. He's really spoiling us. This was a generous gift."

"Yes, it was. Did you know he even sent it to Jennifer's salon this morning to pick me up?"

"Are you serious? Wow! And the driver waited this whole time? I hope I have some cash to tip him."

André started patting his pockets and looking around for his wallet. Suddenly he stopped, apparently forgetting all about the tip. "You know, you are absolutely stunning today," he said, touching my hair. "Those little twirls are just killer. She hit it right on the money." He turned me by the shoulders saying, "And those sparkly hair clips at the back. Wow!"

"Thank you. Yes, Jennifer did a great job. Everyone did."

"Your dress is perfect!" I stiffened as he continued to gush compliments. "Where did you ever find it?"

"*Oh, God.*" I choked on his question. "*This is the moment of truth. I wasn't expecting it right here, right now. Please help him to understand. Don't let this ruin our honeymoon.*"

"Do you have a minute? I'll tell you," I half-joked as my cheeks began to flush. Thankful for the cool semi-darkness of the limo, I turned to face my new husband with the truth about my dress. "Well, the story goes something like this . . ." I began softly, unfolding the details of a long-ago trip to an Italian lace shop. After I finished explaining how I had tried to force myself into something new, but kept being drawn to the dress I loved, I sat back in silence.

I'd searched my husband's face as I shared the truth with him. It remained calm, yet his eyes brimmed with tears a time or two. He said nothing as a couple of Georgia miles rolled by. He just sat there, twirling his brand new wedding band 'round and 'round on his ring finger. Not knowing what to expect, I waited.

"You know," he leaned forward, his eyes forcing mine to engage, "we serve an incredible heavenly Father. He saw your heart as a twenty-four-year-old girl who grew up in broken homes. He knew your subsequent choices were bound to haunt you for life. Yet He allowed you the freedom to make them. He was with you the first time you wore this dress, and He is with you today."

I could feel warm pools welling in my own eyes as André continued.

"God longs to give us the desires of our hearts. When those desires are tainted, He allows time and experience to make them pure. When we mess up, Christ's white robe of righteousness covers our sin. I'm glad you wore this dress today."

He reached to take the fabric between his fingers. "It's a beautiful symbol of what God has done in your life. I believe it's His way of showing how He has redeemed the things you thought were lost. Every dream you had on your wedding day nearly sixteen years ago can be fulfilled."

As we embraced in the back of that long white limousine, André whispered into my ear, "I'm so happy and excited for you because I know how much I love you Juliet Louise. Nothing will ever change that."

The End Beginning

"For he has rescued us from the dominion of darkness and brought us into the kingdom of the Son he loves, in whom we have redemption, the forgiveness of sins." Colossians 1:13-14 NIV

Juliet Van Heerden is an educator, speaker, and writer. She holds a Master of Science in Literacy Education. Passionate about sharing hope with hearts wounded by addiction, Juliet initiated a 12 Step class at her church and encourages others to do the same. As an itinerant speaker for women, recovery groups and congregations, she joyfully shares her inspirational journey. In her down time, Juliet relishes healthy cooking, reading, foreign travel, photography and birding. Her favorite time of day is quiet early morning meditation, when she listens for God's voice. Juliet and her husband, André enjoy ministering together. They believe in God's power to restore broken people and are committed to sharing that message of hope with families and individuals wherever they are invited.

julietvanheerden.com

All *Same Dress, Different Day* book sales go to support Relevant Life Solutions, a nonprofit ministry for families affected by addiction.

relevantlifesolution.org

Thank You

To my husband, André Van Heerden, who gave me the courage to dig up my past and the ability to live joyfully in the present. Thank you for your selfless interest in this project and for praying me through the hard parts. You believe in me when I doubt myself. I adore being your wife. You love me well.

To Ami, my lifelong friend, for fearlessly resurrecting the details I'd buried beneath layers of pain. You make me laugh, even when it hurts. When I am fifty, you will be forty-six.

To The Ps, my inspiration that true love can be found later in life. Your compassion motivates me to live outside myself. Mother, thank you for being my late night companion as I revised this manuscript.

To the descendants of Mamaw, Grandma 'Dessa and Nannie, our family's matriarchs: Let us live our lives with integrity and hope, believing we will see them one day soon.

To Sandy Riddle and Sheri Wall, the friends who would discourage me from auditioning for American Idol, even if I thought I could sing. Your straightforward honesty is rare and valued. That's why I trusted you when you said, "Keep writing." I'm grateful for your unflinching opinions and our nearly twenty years of friendship.

To Barbara Foster, Lisa Lenda and Joy Sorensen, my initial editors: Your willingness to comb through first drafts of this manuscript and provide fearless feedback has been a gift I could not afford. I deeply appreciate the hours you spent and your heart for this work. You prepared me for Rachael.

To Stan Michael, the first man to read this work from cover to cover. Thank you for viewing it as "sacred ground." I appreciate your "manly" feedback and mediation. God sent you for such a time as this.

To Rachael Hartman, an amazing editor with deep compassion for the addicted. You turned my manuscript inside out. Thank you for thoroughly refining this work.

To my prayer sisters Carla Cantalupo, Heather Clark, Kathy Garske, Sharon Quevreaux, Sudie Slade Norman, and Tammy Shelby, for your unflinching intercession and interest in *Same Dress, Different Day.* Thank you for battling the spirits of discouragement in the name of Jesus, and for believing in the power of this work in His hands.

To Debbie Blount and Mervyn Shaw, who believed in this ministry enough to make the first financial donations. You started something.

To Emra Smith, who gently but relentlessly insisted I get off my duff and write my God story. Thank you for coaching and encouraging me to use my gifts for Him.

To Nancy Valencia and Rebecca Willhelm, who represent everyone with an unfinished story. Thank you for being part of mine. May this work bring you hope as you wait on Him to redeem your dreams.

To Celebrate Recovery and all providers of safe places for people with hurts, habits and hang-ups to heal and grow. Addicted Christians and their families desperately need godly recovery friends, sponsors and support. Thank you.

To my loved ones who have been given pseudonyms in this book: You have been the aroma of Christ to me. I will never forget.

Finally, to "Jon," who represents every father, mother, sister, brother, son, daughter and friend who struggles with chemical dependency. Thank you for your courage to live every day on the front lines of a battle the rest of us cannot fathom. Thank you for being the reason we learn to breathe God's grace and practice the miracle of forgiveness. Without you, there would be no story.

Resources

If you or someone you know needs help dealing with addiction or its aftermath, reach out to these powerful resources.

Al-Anon Family Groups | al-anon.alateen.org | (888) 4AL-ANON (888-425-2666)
Anonymous peer-led meetings and literature for friends and family members of problem drinkers.

Celebrate Recovery | www.celebraterecovery.com
Christ-centered recovery support and resources for children, youth and adults affected by addiction.

Co-Dependents Anonymous | www.coda.org
A fellowship of men and women whose common purpose is to develop healthy relationships.

Recommended Reading

The Bondage Breaker
  Neil T. Anderson

Necessary Endings
  Dr. Henry Cloud

Boundaries: When to Say YES, How to say NO to Take Control of Your Life
  Dr. Henry Cloud and Dr. John Townsend

I Should Forgive, But . . . 2nd Edition: Finding Release from the Bondage of Anger and Bitterness
  Chuck Lynch

Praying God's Word: Breaking Free From Spiritual Strongholds
  Beth Moore

A Woman's Guide to Breaking Bondages
  Quin Sherrer and Ruthanne Garlock

Our Written Lives
book publishing services
www.owlofhope.com

CPSIA information can be obtained
at www.ICGtesting.com
Printed in the USA
FSOW02n0729300615
8395FS